Swords & Circuitry

A Designer's Guide to Computer Role Playing Games

Neal Halford
Jana Halford

PRIMA TECH'S

GAME DEVELOPMENT

PRIMA TECH

A DIVISION OF PRIMA PUBLISHING

For my wife Jana,
who loves me even when I'm an idiot.

—Neal

 A Division of Prima Publishing

Prima Publishing and colophon are registered trademarks of Prima Communications, Inc. PRIMA TECH and the Game Development Series are trademarks of Prima Communications, Inc., Roseville, California 95661.

Publisher: Stacy L. Hiquet
Associate Marketing Manager: Jennifer Breece
Managing Editor: Sandy Doell
Acquisitions Editor: Emi Smith
Project Editor: Kelly Talbot
Technical Reviewer: Keith Davenport
Copy Editor: Laura R. Gabler
Interior Layout: Marian Hartsough
Cover Design: Prima Design Team
Indexer: Sharon Shock
Illustrators: Jon Gwyn, Jeff Perryman, Shawn Sharp, Jim Wible

Important: Prima Publishing cannot provide software support. Please contact the appropriate software manufacturer's technical support line or Web site for assistance.

Prima Publishing and the author have attempted throughout this book to distinguish proprietary trademarks from descriptive terms by following the capitalization style used by the manufacturer.

ISBN: 0-7615-3299-4
Library of Congress Catalog Card Number: 2001-111674
Printed in the United States of America

01 02 03 04 05 II 10 9 8 7 6 5 4 3 2 1

Acknowledgments

Jana and I would like to thank all the following people without whom this book would never have been possible. Our heartfelt appreciation goes out to:

Editors **Emi Smith**, **Kelly Talbot**, **Keith Davenport,** and **Laura Gabler** for thoughtfully handling all the billions of details that needed doing to get this book done and for giving us absolutely invaluable advice while sheparding us through our first joint collaboration; **Jon Gwyn**, **Jeff Perryman**, **Shawn Sharp**, and **Jim Wible** for their friendship, advice, and most of all, their absolutely wonderful illustrations**; Ellen Siders** for shooting some of the art on very short notice; **Gene Hallford** for digging up some interesting research on the computer gaming industry from an entirely different angle; **Chris Taylor** at Gas Powered Games for being extraordinarily patient about the lateness of the text for *Dungeon Siege* while Jana and I banged this out; **Ken & Anji Mayfield** for saving me from a career in radio and dragging me into the game design industry in the first place; **Jon Van Caneghem** and **Ron Spitzer** for giving me my first real job as a designer and showing me the ropes; **John Cutter** who took me under his wing and taught me what I wasn't too thick to understand and who asked me if I was "into dogs"; **Ron Bolinger** for riding in to the rescue more times than I really deserve; **Chris Medinger** for knowing when it was the right time to unplug the computer and indirectly saving my life; **Raymond E. Feist** for letting me play in Midkemia's sandbox and learning how the pro fantasy writers build their worlds; **Steve Cordon** of Dynamix Inc. for being *Betrayal at Krondor's* programming Radar O'Reilly and digging up a design document I thought long lost to the ages; **Mark & Valerie Tucker** for some very insightful questions early on in the life of this project; **David Michael** of Samu Games for miscellaneous advice, research, and being an all-round auxiliary brain; **Arnie Katz** of Katz & Worley, Inc. for providing several insights into the history of the computer gaming industry; **Mike Greene** for digging up a bit of *D&D*'s past; **Scorpia** of

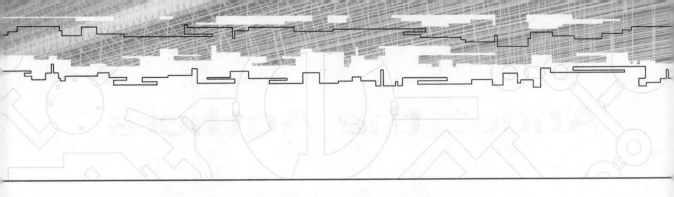

Scorpia.com for having been so very kind in reviewing my past games and for pulling a *Wizardry* factoid out of a hat when I needed it most. **Andy Caldwell** for telling me about Higinbotham.

Jana thanks **Mrs. June Mott** and **Dr. Margaret Doane** for encouraging her to make writing her profession, and **Drs. Ronald Johnson**, **Mike Shea**, **Anne Wallace**, and **Ervin Wheeler** for providing excellent, compassionate medical care.

And above all we thank our parents **Henry Hallford**, **Betty Hallford**, **Joseph Ondrechen Sr.**, and **Jacqueline French Ondrechen** for giving us all the wonderful gifts of time, love, patience, and understanding that helped us become the rather unique individuals we are today.

About the Authors

JANA ONDRECHEN HALLFORD

For me, games weren't *always* synonymous with fun. Growing up as one of the younger members of a big family, it was nigh impossible to win at board games like *Monopoly* that required basic strategic thinking. My smart big sister Mary Jo knew just what streets to buy and fill with lucrative hotels. She successfully built glittering financial empires, while I cried when my Scottie dog got sent to jail. After years and years of being soundly trounced by my family members, I was finally, in young adulthood, able to turn the tables and win game after game of *Trivial Pursuit*. (I cannot express the profound satisfaction that brought.) But all during those years of board game defeat, children from four streets regularly showed up at my house to ask "What shall we play today?" Coming up with a setting, characters, and stories never presented a problem for me. Long before I ever heard of role-playing games, I understood the allure of an evolving story and the special power of being the story teller.

A little less perfectly enculturated into the mainstream than most around me, I grew up looking at much of popular culture through the lens of an outside observer. To this day, I often prefer the view from behind the scenes. When I did see television, the commercials told me a lot about the intended audience. Although I hated being scared, I adored documentaries on horror movies, especially about the special effects. Biographies of famous people were fascinating, because they told not just what people did, but how and why.

I majored in art in college, but have always made a living as a writer. I started out as an art critic who also wrote general interest material. As a very young journalist in search of a story, I found myself at the San Diego Comic Book Convention years ago. I knew nothing about comics, but that was the payoff of reporting—I was always learning new things. At the convention, I met creative and dynamic artists, writers, and publishers. Comics were the main topic, but there were also tracks on other subjects. I didn't get addicted to comics, but I did get sold on speculative fiction and conventions, particularly of the science fiction and fantasy variety.

After getting my start with a newspaper, I moved on to public relations and marketing writing. During a long stint with a publishing company, I started moonlighting

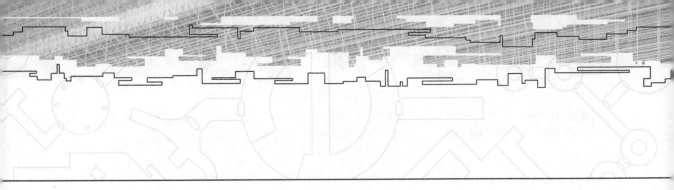

with more creative projects. My life long love of literature and my newer interest in fantasy merged in the creation of a guide book exploring the numerous references to books, classical music, and more in the CBS television series *Beauty and the Beast*. My agent sold it to the licensed publisher. Unfortunately, the publishing house folded while the typeset manuscript languished at the printer, but the experience still opened doors for me. I supplied background material to the Sci Fi Channel, and was invited to speak at science fiction and fantasy conventions in the U.S. and the U.K.

After I met Neal, I got to know something about the game industry. With my background, I immediately recognized the process of creating a game as publishing. I knew that selling a concept was just the first hurdle to clear. Some titles make it out the door, some, however promising, do not. A few sell well.

Like every other branch of the entertainment industry, the business of making computer role playing games is highly competitive and very demanding. At the same time, it is a flourishing industry with much room for creative expression. If you have a love for the genre, ideas to develop, and the will to make your dreams a reality, this can be a very rewarding line of work. Just as a good RPG offers many paths to success, your professional life offers a wide array of choices. There is no *one* way to create a successful game, but I hope this exploration of key concepts in the development process will help you find the direction that's right for you.

—Jana Hallford

Neal Hallford

Here There Be Dragons. The sign sits on my desk, reminding me daily of what my profession as a game designer is really all about. It's an invitation to wander off the beaten path, to go to the magical places no one has ever been and bring back the wonders and treasures that can be found there. But the sign is also a warning. Going where no one else has gone before can be dangerous. The natives may be inviting you to dinner, or they may be inviting you to *be* dinner. If you're already sitting in a boiling vat of carrots á la Bugs Bunny, you've learned the distinction too late. What you need is an experienced guide who's survived in this strange place for a while, and that's where I come in. Welcome to the edge of the map.

I began my own journey into the land of game design sometime in the mid 1970s. Cracking open my first *Dungeons & Dragons* kit in the back bedroom of my Uncle J.L.'s house in Stilwell, Oklahoma, I remember marveling at the strange multi-sided dice, the rulebook, the *Keep on the Borderlands* adventure module. I was perplexed at how it could *work* without pre-printed cards or little lead dogs to hop around a game board. It was unlike any game I'd ever played. It hooked me almost instantly.

In the years to come I moved on to the harder, more frightfully addictive stuff. *Advanced Dungeons & Dragons, Traveler, Runequest,* and *Call of Cthulhu* became regular fixtures in my life. I spent lost weekends playing strategy games like *Starfleet Battles* while inventing abberant variations of traditional titles like *Nuclear Risk, Zombies in Candyland,* and *Super Powers Poker.*

But it was my introduction to the arcade implementation of *Spacewar* that planted in me a permanent fascination with computer games. Within a few years I had my own Atari 400 computer, an understanding of BASIC programming, and a solid grounding in what seperates a good game from a great one. The only trouble was that there was nowhere in the world you could *go* in 1984 to formally study game design. Although the romance of the idea was certainly fanned by movies like *Wargames* and *Tron* which featured game-making heroes, I realized my chances of actually getting a job in the industry were vanishingly small. The handful of companies that existed at the time were primarily looking for code monkeys. While I could do some fundemental programming, it wasn't something I enjoyed much.

Like most people, I thought programming would be a pre-requisite to becoming a good game designer. Rather than waste my college credits on math-intensive studies which weren't my forte in the first place, I opted instead to pursue a journalism degree in radio, television, and film. Graduating from the University of Oklahoma in 1989, I was about to embark on a career in radio production when I got a critical phone call from an artist friend named Kenneth Mayfield. We'd been friends for years, and had belonged to the same science fiction fan club in high school. He was asking if I'd be interested in interviewing for an entry level writer/designer position just opening up at New World Computing—home to the *Might & Magic* series. It was an offer I could hardly refuse.

Right off the bat, my first job was to help prepare the text for *Crusaders of Khazan,* a computer rendition of the classic *Tunnels & Trolls* pen-and-paper game created by Flying Buffalo. I followed up with the manual and a hintbook, and quickly was asked by series director Jon Van Caneghem to help start generating ideas for two new games which eventually would become *Might & Magic III: Isles of Terra* and *Planet's Edge*. After months of intensive concept and design work on both, I eventually realized I would have to focus on one title or the other. Calling in my long time role-playing buddy Ron Bolinger to take over my duties on *Might & Magic III*, I finished up my work on *Planet's Edge* only weeks before another phone call would draw me off to a new opportunity.

Dynamix in Eugene, Oregon had recently acquired the rights to the Midkemian universe of best-selling fantasy author Raymond E. Feist. They were looking for a new designer who would be able to take the world of his popular novels and create an interactive experience. Project lead John Cutter thought I might be the ideal candidate, having remembered my work from *Planet's Edge*. After a series of long, intense phone calls about my ideas for the new project, I was packing my bags and saying goodbye to my good friends and mentors at New World Computing. On Halloween night of 1990, I headed north to start working on the bestselling, multiple award winning FRP, *Betrayal at Krondor*.

In the years since *Betrayal's* release, I've been a very busy bee. I've worked as a freelance design and story consultant on a broad spectrum of titles ranging from 7th Level/Sierra's *Return to Krondor*, Westwood Studio's *Nox*, Kinesoft's *Crimson Order*, and a new Playstation 2 title under wraps at Stormfront Studios. In 1997 I re-teamed with John Cutter to design the ground-breaking episodic RPG *Elysium*, sadly one of several promising titles which became vaporware with the collapse of the Seattle-based company Cavedog Entertainment. In August of 2000, I inked a deal with Cavedog alumnus and *Total Annihilation* creator Chris Taylor to write the story and dialog for Gas Powered Games & Microsoft's upcoming *Dungeon Siege*, a great FRP which should be hitting the store shelves about the same time as this book.

With nearly ten years under my belt in this business of making bestselling FRPs, I've *learned* where there be dragons. I should know. I've certainly been bitten by them a time or two. But more than just advising you on which dragons you can avoid, I'm also hoping to show you which ones you can tame to breathe *real* fire into your games! So grab your sword, or prep your spell, adventurer. We're about to go where the wild things are.

—Neal Hallford

To contact Neal or Jana, e-mail them at swordsncircuitry@aol.com, or visit http://members.aol.com/swordsncircuitry.

About the Illustrators

Shawn Sharp

After some years of providing the world with junk mail, corporate logos, catalogs and storyboards for commercials with thankfully the occasional illustration and comic book job, Shawn quit the world of advertising in 1990 to begin art directing computer games. In nine and a half years at Dynamix, he worked on titles ranging from adventure and role-playing to flight sims and educational games including *Heart of China*, *The Adventures of Willy Beamish*, *Space Quest 5*, *A10 2*, *Aviation Pioneers*, *Cyberstorm*, *Red Baron 2*, *Outpost 2*, *Tribes*, *Starsiege*, *Tribes 2* and at least eight others.

Since leaving Dynamix, Shawn has continued his freelance business doing fantasy and science fiction painting, illustration, production design, and Web site design and is currently art directing PS2 children's games for KalistoUSA in Austin. In his spare time, such as it is, he spends time with his family, rides (wrecks) motorcycles, hikes, plays games, and supports the economy of coffee producing nations with a severe espresso habit.

If you're interested in seeing more of Shawn's work, please check out his site at http://home.austin.rr.com/imaginaria/. Having an "art by the pound" approach to work he's posted perhaps a hundred of the originals that fill portfolios, boxes, sketch books and flat files in his studio. He can also be reached by email at: ssharp5@austin.rr.com.

Jon Gwyn

Jon Gwyn has cranked out some of the highest quality art in the computer gaming industry for the past ten years, and so far has six different titles to his credit. Starting at the infamous Cinemaware (a rallying point for many people in the industry,) he learned to his surprise that people actually wanted to *pay* him to create the images he used to doodle on the back of his school notebooks. In 1991 he met Neal Hallford while working at New World Computing on *Planet's Edge*. In the mid 1990s Jon partnered up with another New World Computing alumni, Andy Caldwell, to found Screaming Pink, a game development house which created both the Playstation and Saturn versions of Shiny Entertainment's *Earthworm Jim 2*, and handled jobs for Disney, Squaresoft, and Upper Deck. Eventually, Jon was able to parlay his experience into a fantastic job at Shiny Entertainment as the senior character artist on their critically acclaimed title *Sacrifice*. To find out more about what Jon's up to these days, follow his homepage link on the *Swords & Circuitry* page at http://members.aol.com/swordsncircuitry.

JIM WIBLE

With twenty-six years in the business of illustration and design, Jim has contributed materials to a wide range of extremely diverse projects. Early in his career he was a conceptual artist for NASA's Space Shuttle and Hubble Space Telescope programs, and later provided technical illustrations for various branches of the Armed Forces. Long a fan of comic books and illustrated novels, he's done linework and coloring for leading comic book houses including Black Thorne and Dark Horse. In recent years, Jim has guested at several large regional SF conventions as a featured artist, and has created a series of horror and fantasy sculptures for Podmaker, a San Diego-based business. Jim currently works for Mad Catz, Inc. in the design of video game packaging and promotion. Learn more about Jim through his homepage link on the Swords & Circuitry page at http://members.aol.com/swordsncircuitry.

JEFF PERRYMAN

Part of the super-secret cabal of game-designing "Tulsa Illuminati," Jeff Perryman has created art for several well-respected computer games including *Nuclear War, Arena: The Elder Scrolls, Terminator 2029, Aeon Flux, Aftermath, Ares Rising, Fading Suns: Gunboat Diplomacy,* and *Might & Magic Crusaders.* He is currently working his onscreen sorcery on *Warriors of Might & Magic,* a title in production by 3DO in Austin, Texas. You can find out more about Jeff and his work at jeffperryman.com.

Contents at a Glance

Contents

Part Two
The Designer's Domain 89

CHAPTER 4
WE FEW, WE HAPPY FEW—
DESIGNERS AND THE TEAM. 91

CHAPTER 5
THE LIFE CYCLE OF THE
ROLE-PLAYING TITLE 113

Part Three
Workshop of the Gods 141

CHAPTER 6
IT'S ALIVE!!! ALIVE!!!
ELECTRIFYING YOUR GAMEPLAY 143

CHAPTER 7
SOCKET WRENCHES OF THE GODS—
BUILDING LIVING WORLDS 215

CHAPTER 8
THE ARCHITECTURE OF FANTASY—
PUTTING THE ELEMENTS TOGETHER ... 247

LETTER FROM THE SERIES EDITOR

One of my goals as series editor for the Prima Game Series was to not only give the public books about game programming, 3D graphics, artificial intelligence, and so forth, but to relay some of the incredible personality, energy, and creativity that all game designers and developers have. I am pleased to say that *Swords & Circuitry* is one of those rare books that not only takes you on a journey through the exciting world of game design (with a focus on RPGs), but the book takes you into the heads of some of the world's most successful and brilliant game designers including the author himself Neal Hallford!

This book is for designers as well as developers that want to learn the thought process and fundamentals of real RPG design from the ground up. I think that we are seeing a revolution and acceleration of the RPG genre and there's a desire for information on this subject. The reason is that for the first time in history our computers have the technology to faithfully generate alternate realities on the screen that are both emmersive and photo-realistic. And since the sky is the limit (or at least the ionosphere), the RPG is the target since RPGs are the most complex types of games from a design standpoint one can make. *Swords & Circuitry* is written with this in mind to not only teach you the basics of the RPG process, but then to review real world examples of game designs, the thought process, and mundane realities such as design documents.

During the development of *Swords & Circuitry*, I found myself learning quite a bit in the first half of the book that covers RPG design itself. Neal has a wonderful way of taking the trillions of details relating to the design and development of RPGs and putting them all into a cohesive flow in the text. He successfully covered what an RPG is, the history of RPGs, the design of RPGs in detail, and then began to follow up on the real world human factors of building a game with large design teams. I think that this is one of the most important factors in game design, that is, building a team and making it work. Whether the team is 2 or 200 it doesn't matter. The design aspect of the text continues on drilling down on designing "fun" and "intriguing" RPGs and the mind set needed to do this along with the tools.

The remainder of the book focuses on your solid base on RPG design and the practical issues such as putting together teams, schedules, and design documents and moves from theory to reality by means of a number of real world interviews with desginers of some of the most successfull games on the market. I would have to say that this part of the book is one of the major reasons we wanted to do *Swords &* *Circuitry*, that is, to have a platform, so that you could listen to game design straight from the source without any translation. These people have the magic and they are feeling the "flow" :) They know that secret ellusive formula; if you can absorb just a little of their knowledge then you will have a jumpstart on the majority of game designers just getting into the genre.

In closing, this is one of the coolest books you'll ever read on game design. It's not only a technical book that covers RPG game design from the ground up, but it's a techno-novel about real people and real games and their amazing journeys during development. I recommend this book to anyone that wants an edge in RPG game design, and to anyone that just wants to learn about what a game designer goes through developing one of these massive pieces of interactive fiction.

Sincerely,

André LaMothe
Series Editor

Foreword

By and large, "computer role-playing" is an oxymoron. How can you "role-play" by yourself? Who is your audience? Whom do you impress? If we look back to paper role-playing games, the best-known example being *Dungeons & Dragons*, you have fun by playing an adult version of "let's pretend" with your friends. The characters you control are driven by their desire to acquire loot or advance in prowess, but you the human player are really just looking to have fun with your friends. The character's progress was important only insomuch as it gave you more status and fun in the game.

The early computer role-playing games (CRPGS) imitated the basic play style of the paper games, but they were unable to simulate the real, human involvement in these games. Most computer role-playing games (CRPGs) throughout the 1980s were really just puzzle-solving games, generally mixed with heavy combat. There was a plot somewhere in the background (usually something involving an evil wizard who wanted to take over the world), but the only real purpose of the plot was to explain why the world was full of monsters that it was okay for the characters to kill. Unlike the paper games, you had no game master or fellow players to impress with your wit or skill. It was just you vs. the CPU. The characters you controlled, as a result, were almost devoid of personality. Why would their opinions and feelings matter after all? They were just avatars which the player used to interact with the world.

This situation changed with the advent of Japanese CRPGs in the early 1990s. These games were heavily story-based, with intricately-related characters who had distinctive personalities and traits, and were often concerned with activities other than combat. The contrast with American games, which its drone-like warrior mentality, could not have been stronger. For a time American CRPGs were eclipsed. Many companies stopped making them. The Japanese games, such as *Final Fantasy* or *Lufia* seemed to offer more of the old-style role-playing, with people that cared about each other, fell in love or even had families.

For example, in most American RPGs up to 1995 or so, your main character had no background. He was just thrust into the world to go fight and win. But in most Japanese RPGs, your main character had parents, a house, often even kid brothers or sisters. Almost all the Japanese games featured romance; for instance, your character had a girlfriend! (A concept alien to the American games of the time.)

But once past the initial wonder, it turned out that even the Japanese games were still not role-playing in the classic sense[—]certainly your characters talked to one another, but you the player had no control over it. During the character interactions, you simply watched cinematics unfold, and made few or no choices. When actually playing the game, you still performed the same old activities featured in other CPRGs. The intricate personalities and relationships featured in these games was fundamentally just another structure to justify the character's monster-crunching and loot-acquiring progress. At least it was a more interesting structure than before.

American role-playing games eventually made a comeback, with games such as *Daggerfall* or *Diablo*, and are now quite respectable, though both Japanese & American games are still pretty distinctive. In general, Japanese games strive to be storytelling experiences, while American games strive to be interactive, choice-filled adventures. Both can be fun when well-designed.

In recent years, communications have progressed to the point that it has become easy to play games over a modem with other humans. Now, at last, true role-playing has become accessible. When you are playing *Baldur's Gate, Asheron's Call*, or one of the online CRPGs, the "other party members" in your adventuring group are each played by another human being. They may or may not choose to act out their part in character, but the players of these games are now driven by new goals, not seen before in CRPGs.

In a modern on-line game, the relationship of the players' goals and the game's activities has been reversed. Up to now, in a CRPG, the plot was a tool to drive the game activities. Now, once again, the game activities support the plot and human interactions.

Why do my friends enjoy playing *Everquest?* Not for the monster-bashing and dungeon-crawling, but because they like playing with other people. They try to increase their characters' levels in the game so that they (the player, not the character) can be more important, can act as a leader, can get more respect in his or her clan. The games have come full circle. You now play with other humans and get your reward for playing from other humans, just as we used to do back in the days of paper role-playing games.

Sandy Petersen
April 2001

Few figures in gaming can be said to have the stature or prestige of Sandy Petersen. One of the pre-eminent designers of role-playing games both on and off the computer, he co- designed pen and paper role-playing classics like RuneQuest and Call of Cthulhu for Chaosium Inc. In 1988 he jumped the digital divide to begin working in the computer gaming industry for Microprose, and later moved to ID Software where he was a designer on hit games like Doom, Doom 2, *and* Quake.

Introduction

Before you head on into the wilds, my first responsibility as tour guide is to let you know what lies ahead. I'd hate to take you on a white-water rafting tour of the darkest Forbidden Swamps of Zhul when all you were looking for was a cab ride into downtown Tulsa. Certainly both are dangerous modes of transportation. But it matters a lot about who you are[—]and where you're trying to go[—]when you choose your means of getting from point A to point Z.

By the fact that you picked up this book, it's a fairly safe bet that you're interested in role-playing games, also known as RPGs. You might play them, you might want to design them, or you may just want to know what Satanic devil potion we designers use to keep your spouse enthralled by the latest release of *Baldur's Gate*. Providing any or all those things are true about you, you're at least starting in the right place. Next you have to establish if there's a bus that's heading in the direction you want to go.

As you might have picked up from the word *Circuitry* in this book's title, this tome is primarily concerned with the creation of electronic games. This includes computer-based fare like *Planescape: Torment or Everquest,* but it can also include console titles like *Final Fantasy,* which you might play on your Sega Dreamcast or Sony Playstation. If you're interested in writing the next adventure module for *Dungeons & Dragons 3rd Edition,* you might find some of the chapters on world building helpful, but you aren't likely to discover any advice here on how to stop your players from rioting when it finally dawns on them that you're out of bean dip.

Another important thing you need to understand about this book is that it won't shed much light on the dark and evil art of programming. For some bizarre reason, strangers to the country of game development seem to think a game designer is someone who sits and writes programming code all day. While it is not unusual for a designer to sometimes *also* be a programmer, they are no more necessarily one and the same thing than my Aunt Marybelle is a platypus. Suffice to say that you won't find a single line of C++ code on our journey together, but you will get a very solid grounding in what the designer's craft is *really* all about.

To start this peculiar adventure, it's likely you already possess most of the skills you're going to need to make it out alive. You need to be someone who enjoys games, even if you aren't an expert player. It will probably be helpful to you to have some basic familiarity with computers or game consoles, though many of the principles we'll discuss will transcend issues of what a specific piece of hardware can or cannot do. Most importantly, you need to be someone who's curious about how and why people interact in a fictional reality, and how in turn that reality can provide the elusive quality called *entertainment*.

Here There Be RPGs . . .

Now I don't mean to terrify you too much at the start of this trip, but I think it's important that you understand something. You're about to delve into one of the most difficult to master genres in the computer gaming industry. There is no other form of game that is more demanding, more resource hungry, more complex, more expensive, or more fulfilling to create than the role-playing title. *None.* It truly is nothing short of creating an entirely new world from the ground up, and it's all going to be *your* responsibility. Sound intimidating? It should. Even game designers experienced in other genres have made the mistake of underestimating the RPG's enduring capacity to violate their every expectation. To make this point, I'd like to share with you a small moral lesson in why you need to study this genre before you throw yourself to the dragons.

Our story begins sometime in the waning years of the last millennium—okay, so it was 1995, but what fun is turning over the odometer if we can't at least play with the terminology? In the glittering kingdom of Hollywood, there was a start-up company dedicated to making games. The company had been founded by a multitalented legendary rock producer and was staffed by a collection of truly stellar talents from the movie industry. Having done very well with their first game—a puzzle title—they decided the best follow-up would be to do the sequel to a highly successful RPG whose license was now up for grabs. This company decided to lay down a rather astonishing amount of cash for the rights, and they called yours truly to provide advice on the design and the story.

After showing me some rather dazzling animations and proof-of-concept videos, they asked me what I thought about the project. I told them the game had great potential and might even be a blockbuster someday. The only stumbling block I saw was that they were in no way *ready* to tackle an RPG.

From the beginning, they insisted with all the manpower they had to throw at the game, they could easily complete the project in 10 months. I told them they'd be lucky to have it done in 24 since they didn't even have a game engine ready yet. They indicated the numerous successes they'd had in Hollywood. I pointed out they still needed to learn the ropes of true interactivity. They touted the success of their puzzle game. I said that a game with a fixed relationship with the player was nowhere near as difficult to create as a world where the player can go almost anywhere or do almost anything they want—often things the designer never even thought they'd try to do.

At virtually every point, the ruling powers of this company failed to recognize that the basic complexities of putting together a role-playing title were not going to vanish in the face of money. They weren't going to dissolve away because the lead producer had experience on Broadway. They weren't even going to fall away for the team of very skilled programmers who had made a very fun puzzle game. If someone at the top had understood from the beginning what putting together an exceptional role-playing experience necessarily entailed, they might have been spared the many painful lessons they were forced to learn on their own.

In the end, the "Hollywood" attempt to create an RPG took nearly 48 months and went through a succession of producers, and two companies collapsed before the game was ever brought to market. Had a book been available then that could have taught them all things that I'm about to share with you, they might have known to be more cautious in that turbulent, yet wondrous region of game development marked "Here there be *RPGs!*"

Uh, Anybody Bring a Map?

If you haven't run screaming for your lives by now, you're either half-mad or amazingly courageous. I applaud both qualities. Game designers *need* to be the kind of people who go where angels fear to tread. But even the most adventurous souls understand the value of knowing *something* about the environments they're about to enter. With my old Boy Scout motto of "Be Prepared" echoing in my head, I think it might be a good idea to lay out a general map of the territory we're going to cover.

Swords & Circuitry is divided up into four different parts, each providing information on an important stage in the development of a role-playing title.

The first stop on the tour is called "Shadows of the Past." In this part, I'll dissect this patchwork Frankenstein called the RPG genre and try and determine what features are critical to give a game *life* as a role-playing title. You'll also get a chance to look at how the genre has evolved, tracing it from a Saturday afternoon pen-and-paper hobby created by Gary Gygax to a modern multimillion-dollar industry with more facets now than a hydra has heads.

Next up is a brief stop in "The Designer's Domain," where you'll take a close look at the actual job of the game designer and meet the people without whom the job would be a billion times more difficult. In the Domain, I'll also lead you through the process of how a game idea moves from just being an idea on a napkin at Denny's to becoming a full-fledged, fire-breathing, can't-keep-'em-on-the-shelves RPG.

Once I've safely walked you through all the basics, you'll be escorted into part three, also known as the "Workshop of the Gods." Here I'll let you lay your hands on some of the most jealously guarded tools of my profession, ranging from the theories of gameplay that underlie *all* games to the secrets of building stories and worlds that will suck your players in and never let them go. I'll also show you the basics of presenting a professional design document and explain how RPGs can be affected by their presentation on different machines or in different markets.

Lastly, you'll take a scenic stroll through part four, a little place I like to call "The Games." Five of some of my most respected colleagues have come down from the mountaintops to share the lessons they've learned while creating RPGs and will give you insights into how they approach both the art and the science of making great games. You'll also have the opportunity to examine some of the technologies that are currently emerging and to try to predict which ones may hold great things for the future of the role-playing genre.

Can't You Read the Sign, Buddy?

If you look off the main path during your journey, you'll occasionally see a few peculiar road markers that might be difficult to interpret without a little assistance. Here's a quick rundown on the signs and symbols of *Swords & Circuitry*.

Background

Unless you've been playing computer games for a long time, it's likely you're occasionally going to see names of people and products you've never heard of before. Background boxes indicate information that will help give you a better understanding of where someone or something in the gaming industry came from.

Terminology. There's a lot of jargon, both official and unofficial, that is used in the gaming industry. The Terminology scrolls will spell out exactly what specific technical terms mean.

On Target

Although everything in this book is geared to help you understand role-playing games, there are some points that are absolutely critical for you to understand or consider. You'll find this information pointed out by the On Target signs.

Ouch!

Game designers are just as prone to make dumb mistakes as anybody else. Ouch! markers indicate things to beware of and sometimes highlight stories of lessons learned the hard way.

Wagons, Ho!

So now that you've caught a glimpse of what you're going to find inside this book, you've got two choices. You can go back to playing games and paying your local Software Etc. $50 a shot for whatever role-playing adventure designers choose to kick out of the door, or you can come through the looking glass with me and learn the real craft of making your *own* interactive worlds of imagination that you can share with thousands of people all over the world. The gate between worlds is down, artisan. Cross the threshold and come with me . . . *if you dare!*

Part One

Shadow
of the Past

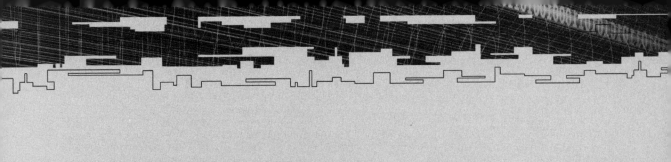

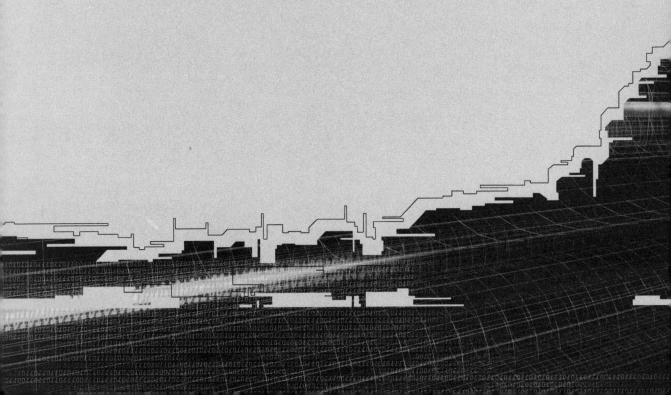

CHAPTER 1

KING FOR A DAY—THE ROLE-PLAYING APPEAL

SHARP

"We roll the dice, we cut the cards—don't think it's all we're doing
This is the oldest magic; drums around the tribal fire
We bleed for stories and we make them come alive and breathing
We're weaving tapestries of danger and desire

You can call us children, you can call us fools
But you choose to live in a world with one set of rules
You can say we're devils, throw our books on the fire
If your heart's too small to handle danger and desire

You see us moving little men across the kitchen table
Laugh if you must but we know every one of them by name
Forged in the heart of childhood, wakened with a living language
They're ready to die for dreams of honor or of fame

You can call us children, you can call us fools
But you choose to live in a world with one set of rules
You can say we're devils, throw our books on the fire
If your heart's too small to handle danger and desire

Out in the wood between the worlds we spread our picnic blanket
We cross the gates of wonder dancing on a burning wire
And in the living room our circle opens up the gateway
To shining cities built on danger and desire

You can call us children, you can call us fools
But you choose to live in a world with one set of rules
You can say we're devils, throw our books on the fire
If your heart's too small to handle danger and desire"

— "Danger and Desire" © Allison Lonsdale 1998

Ask any eight-year-old child to show you the fastest way to navigate through a maze, and they'll quickly draw a line backward from the maze's *end* to its *start*. As much as we adults tend to punish this bit of Merlin-like thinking, it's honestly the most *intelligent* way to solve the problem. By thoroughly understanding where you're going before you leave, you can you avoid the dead ends, the false starts, and the aggravatingly self-recursive paths that can only take you back to the point at which you began. If you ever hope to get anywhere, the first thing you have to do is figure out where your finish line is.

When asked, most developers say their ultimate objective is to *make a great game.* That seems like common sense. We all want to create titles so insanely fun and addictive to play that it's darn near impossible for people to walk away from them. We'd all like to have game systems that will allow players to do almost anything they could ever imagine. But the problem that arises with this stated goal is that it falls just a hair short of what the professional game designer is *actually* after.

Games aren't made for their own sake any more than sports cars are made only to be great-looking machines. Certainly there's tremendous craftsmanship invested in the way that the heads of a '65 Mustang are bored or in the astonishing capability of the Lithtec game engine to assemble texture-mapped polygons into the brooding facade of Fortress Gloom. Both are unquestionably works of art. But both Porsches and RPGs exist to be tools of human passion, instruments that have the power to evoke the excitement, the wonder, and the engagement of the *people* who use them. The finish line lies not within the machine, but in the emotional response of the gamer. At all times, your goal as a designer is to *make your players happy.*

Now I know there will be a few of you at this point rolling around on the floor and foaming at the mouth about such a Pollyanna-ish sounding objective, but let me assure you this is the single most important factor in making a best-selling game of *any* kind. Your career as a designer is going to depend on the favor or disfavor of the game-buying public. Make them happy and they'll buy your games. Let them win and they'll be back for the sequels. Give them the opportunities to be heroes and gamers will let you play god on a mountaintop for years to come. Never forget that no matter how great a game *you* think you've made, your success or failure in this business is ultimately going to be determined by the people slogging their way through your world. (Think about that while you create your oh-so-cleverly engineered Trap of Unavoidable Doom.)

For the record, I should state that not every designer agrees with me. Some believe players should get their happiness from the makers of Prozac and leave computer games to the players who thrive on the cycle of "die and restart." I've witnessed meetings where designers actually even *gloated* over the fact that only a tiny percentage of players had finished the games they've designed. These self-deluded individuals have mistaken frustration for challenge, and what's worse, they've utterly abandoned the gamer in a mad rush to erect electronic monuments to their egos. Fortunately for the rest of us, designers of this ilk are eventually weeded out of the industry *Survivor*-style by the one law of the global player council: *Cater to our fantasies, or flip burgers for a living.*

As intimidating as this law may sound at first, by focusing on the wants of your players from the get-go, you're actually doing *yourself* a tremendous favor. Instead of firing blindly in the dark in hopes that you'll hit something, you'll have a very clear picture of the targets you need to hit to please your audience. You can use this information as the criteria by which you weigh the strengths and weaknesses of your game. If players really seem to *hate* things that resemble feature X on your original wish list, you may be able to find ways to modify it so that it's not only palatable to your audience, but it's even something that really excites them.

Of course the difficulty is that you're not going to have every single person who will ever play your game sitting at your elbow—nor would you want them to be. If the secret to putting together a best-selling game was merely to implement every pet idea of every player in cyberspace, it wouldn't matter *who* was sitting in the designer's seat. It could be you, it could be your next-door neighbor, it could be Bobo the trained ficus. All games would very quickly devolve into one reeking, homogeneous, uninspired pile of dog poop.

To be a designer, you have to have the discretion to know when to do what the audience expects and when you need to wander off the beaten path into Never Never Land. It's going to be your job to give the games you develop a style, a flavor, and a direction that will make them stand out from everything else that's ever been done before. It will never be enough to simply say, "I want to make another *Might & Magic*, but this time we'll do it with aardvarks!" The players want you to give them an all-new experience, but presented in a format that's not so alien that it will require a Ph.D. to understand how to play. In essence, you're going to be forced to walk a tightrope between your own natural intuition as a player and the evident wishes of the marketplace as a whole.

For the majority of you, this balancing act shouldn't be all that hard to manage. The typical designer's instincts are usually in line with public sentiment most of the time—unsurprising if you consider that most all of us started off as dedicated players to begin with. But like the best-laid plans of mice and men, the developer can often go astray. Occasionally we let our attachment to certain features or content cloud our judgment about how the public may receive a new element. Sometimes we innocently make a catastrophically bad design call because we aren't thinking about things from the player's perspective. Whenever possible, you need to back up from your project and run it through the wringer, asking yourself three questions at every critical juncture in the design:

- What does the player want to happen here?
- What can I do to make the player feel great?
- What am I doing right now that will keep the player glued to their seat?

Try and keep these questions uppermost in your mind as we move forward. All three are important evaluation tools you'll use as you begin to look at other games critically and as you develop game concepts of your own. If it helps you, try writing them down. Tape a copy of them over your computer monitor. Carve them into the surface of your computer desk if you like. Have them tattooed on some body surface you're likely to see on a daily basis. Whatever you do from this day forward, always try and look at your game projects through the lens of your prospective players.

Who *Was* that Masked Man?

So who *are* these people you're trying to entertain? What do they like? What do they hate? Where do they come from? How can you ever hope to know what they really *want*?

The answer to all these questions is *there is no single right answer*. Players will be many things. They're going to bring a host of likes, dislikes, biases, preferences, and expectations to the table that you never even considered. You're going to get hate mail because you inaccurately calculated the tidal effects of your world's twin moons on the seas of your fictional kingdom. Players will praise you for that secret subquest you put into *Dungeons of Despair IV*, which in *reality* was just a random fluke of the game engine. If there is anything at all that you can know for certain about your audience, it's that it's ruled by the Heisenberg Uncertainty Principle. You might know where it is today, but you can never be sure what direction it's going to head.

Back in the dark ages of the 1980s, it didn't take a genius to figure out who was playing computer games. You could spot them in a crowded room as easily as you'd notice a purple hippopotamus at a church social. They would never be the person who got picked king of the school prom, but they were often heavily recruited for help with science homework. Gamers were able to quote faithfully from every episode of *Monty Python's Flying Circus* and understood why dividing by zero was a bad idea. In 1983, Matthew Broderick faithfully brought one of these "joystick jockeys" to life with his big-screen portrayal of David Lightman, the geeky, computer-hacking hero of the teenage techno-thriller *WarGames*.

But as clear-cut as the gaming audience had been to the developers of the 1980s, it turned on its head in the decade that followed. The increasingly widespread distribution of CD-ROM technology not only changed the numbers of American households equipped with a family computer but led to a very big shift in the *kinds* of games that began to move off the store shelves. The record-breaking sales of the stylish, vastly simplified adventure game *Myst* in 1993 sent shockwaves through the game development community. Rabid debates erupted everywhere about what *Myst*'s anomalous sales figures said about the evolving

> **Game Engine.** In its simplest terms, the *game engine* is a collection of highly reusable programming code that assembles and arbitrates the reality of the game world based on data provided by a designer. Modern engines are extraordinarily powerful and often are given tasks ranging from the simple placement of a graphic on the screen to the calculation of how torch light should look when reflected off armor. Ideally, by simply changing the *assets* upon which the core game engine relies—say, for example, the data files that determine how a certain monster looks, what the monster sounds like, what kind of damage he can do, what kind of objects he carries—a designer can use one game engine to generate literally thousands of different games, each with its own look, style, and feel.

market. The arrival of the Sony PlayStation in 1994 further muddied the playing field, bringing a more diverse group of players to the gaming consoles than had ever been seen before.

Today, the task of defining the "typical gamer" is more difficult than ever. Many long-standing stereotypes about the likes and dislikes of players have begun to break down as new gamers move into the market. Todd Pratt, a 38-year-old fan of the RPG *Ultima Online,* typifies just one of the ways in which the industry has already expanded—the inclusion of "graying" players. The owner of Ianstorm.com, Todd provides a forum for his fellow players of online role-playing games. And when he's not slaying dragons, Todd plays another kind of game in a much more public arena. He's a catcher for the New York Mets. "I started playing *Dungeons & Dragons* young, and now the computer age has only multiplied my interest," Pratt says. "I spend between five and six hours a day playing games like *UO, EverQuest,* and *Asheron's Call.*"

While the participation of people like Pratt in the hobby seems to indicate a mild shift in the playing demographic, there's mounting evidence to suggest an even more drastic change may be on the horizon. Despite the fact that most game companies are focusing the majority of their time and money on males between the ages of 14 and 25, a controversial report released by the Interactive Digital Software Association in September of 2000 indicates that 43 percent of game players are now *women* and that the average age of these female players is 29 years old. The report also goes on to say that 32 percent of *all* American players are over the age of 35, and a startling 13 percent are over the age of 50.

As fun as it is to lob these statistical hand grenades back and forth with colleagues, modern developers have to look at these numbers with a practical eye and ask, "Okay, so how do I use this information to make a fun game that everybody wants to play?"

Even at the best of times, there's rarely a true consensus on what makes a traditional game attractive. When we begin to venture into the uncertain territories of "girl-friendly" or "gray-friendly" games, there simply isn't a magical feature set that we can slam into a game that will automatically make it a "must have" for these emerging audiences. Most of the factors that seem to prevent these new players from joining the role-playing ranks are more closely tied to social misrepresentations of age, race, and gender than to the inclusion of any specific game features. In few arenas has this conflict been more evident than in the quest to capture the attention of the female gamer.

For years, the relationship between women and games has been rocky at best. Roberta Williams broke critical ground at Sierra On-Line by introducing the first playable female protagonist, Princess Rosella, in the fourth installment of the long-running role-playing series *King's Quest*. Others following in Williams's footsteps often missed her point, portraying their heroines as weak or ineffectual ornaments who stood aside while male heroes inevitably rushed in to save the day. It is still sadly common to find female characters allotted lower hit points to make them "more realistic" or objectified as the iconic difficulty selector for an "easy" game. By equating femininity with simplicity, it seems some designers are determined to reinforce the old stereotype that "playing like a girl" is necessarily a bad thing.

Other factors that may figure significantly in the lack of interest of some female players may have to do with the types of content currently available. Some girl gaming advocates have indicated the level of violence in today's titles drive off female players. Opposing groups of feminists point out the inherent sexism in the assumption that "girls don't frag."

> **Frag.** Although popularized with the rise of games like *Doom* and its numerous offspring, this term meaning to kill or destroy something actually dates to the Vietnam War era. Individuals unfortunate enough to have met the business end of a fragmentation grenade were often said to have been "fragged."

Unfortunately, some women never even have to open the box to be turned off by some of today's hottest-selling games. Lara Croft of the wildly successful *Tomb Raider* action series is arguably the most recognizable video game character on the planet. Although presented as a very capable character, Lara's biggest success has not been with women, but with adolescent males drawn to the marketing of her supernaturally overemphasized sexual characteristics. "I have never played *Tomb Raider*. It might be a great game. I have been told outside of Lara's back-breaking hooters, she is quite a role model for young girls. She is smart, adventurous, and independent," says Chella Kline of Grrlgamer.com. "This may be so, but I never see these qualities promoted. The impression I get from the ads is this game is marketed towards the pizza-faced nerds with sticky palms and hairy knuckles."

And so the debate rages on.

If there's anything to be learned at all in this quagmire of passionately conflicting attitudes about girls and games, it's that sometimes the key to making a better game isn't about what you put into it, but *what you leave out of it.* It would take a full-bore, insensitive moron today to make a commercial game whose hero was a slave-trading magnate. The public would be fully justified in burning a development house to the ground if that company made a role-playing game glorifying the oven operators at Auschwitz. As a developer, if you want to open the doors to new players, you need to be aware of what you're really putting on the table to attract these new audiences. Whenever possible you should do everything you can to eliminate any reason a player might be inclined to walk away from your experience. Broaden the appeal of your game and you'll not only make it more fun for more people to play, but you're very likely to do better at the cash registers as well.

Hunting the Great American Gamer

Okay, so we've talked a bit about a few possible suspects, but you don't have enough information to issue an APB on this "player" fellow just yet. He might be 16, or he might be 60. He could be tossing pizzas at your local pizzeria, or he could be tossing pitches for your hometown baseball team. There's even an excellent chance that the *guy* that you thought you were looking for is really a *gal.* Clearly there's more to tracking down the elusive Great American Gamer than just looking at a basic demographic chart. What you need to know goes much deeper. You've got to crawl inside the heads of your audience, shake out the gray matter, and find out exactly what players want from their game-playing experience.

If I could, I'd give you a definitive list that says, "Put features X, Y, and Zed into your design, and you'll automatically have a smashingly terrific game that absolutely everyone will love." Unfortunately, it isn't that easy. Human beings have a persistently irritating tendency to form their own preferences. That makes the job you and I want to do all the more difficult. No one will ever create a game that will appeal equally to all players everywhere. It's certainly possible to create a title that includes a broader audience than most games enjoy today. It's even reasonable to assume someone might make an RPG more phenomenally successful than a best-seller like *Diablo.* But for every choice you make about what features will or will not be included in your game, you'll also be defining the kind of gamer who will want to play it once you are done.

Consider a few of the general reasons why some people like to play games. Some may want to temporarily escape the boredom of their everyday lives by becoming bold adventurers on a heroic quest. Some might want to explore mysterious new worlds. Some want to feel stronger, smarter, or more attractive than they may be in real life. Regardless of their individual motivations, all gamers are drawn to the titles they play because those games are catering to the essential fantasies of that player.

In the broadest sense, we can classify these player fantasies in terms of *genre*, much in the same way that books are shelved in a particular section in a book-store. If someone dreams of being a general, they might choose something from the *real-time strategy* genre, which allows them to direct armies of loyal soldiers. Another type of gamer might want to be a martial arts master, so they'll probably gravitate toward games in the *fighter* genre, which lets them out kung-fu opponents. These broad categories can be useful when trying to describe the general experience a player will have while playing a specific title, but they aren't detailed enough to serve as a blueprint for creating a game. *Nox* and *Baldur's Gate* are both classified within the RPG genre, but each focuses on the needs of very different kinds of players.

Let's take a quick example from the sci-fi RPG *Deus Ex*. A description of the game features appears on the back of the box:

> "Character interaction that matters. How you choose to deal with scores of NPCs affects the outcome of the game, minute-to-minute, mission to mission, start to finish."

Even before cracking open the box, the player knows a big part of the experience of *Deus Ex* is going to involve interacting with characters in the game. Immediately, there's going to be one type of gamer who is going to put the box down because they hate having to talk to characters, while other players will be very excited to know that *Deus Ex* features a strong story line. By explicitly pointing out this feature to the prospective buyer, the designers are letting people know the game has been *ideally* engineered for players who tend to enjoy artificial social interactions. More fundamentally, buyers are being told the game has been created with a specific player profile in mind.

The Hallford Player Pyramid

In the late 1960s, a psychologist named Abraham Maslow transformed the world of psychoanalytic thought by introducing what he called the Hierarchy of Needs. The basic principle behind Maslow's hierarchy was that every human being has an ascending series of needs that must be met in a specific order before a person can achieve their full potential. So before people can feel truly loved, they must feel safe from harm. Before they can feel safe from harm, they must be able to meet physical needs like having food to eat or oxygen to breathe.

On the surface, it may seem that Maslow's theories are a long, long way from computer game design, but the model is actually very useful for thinking about everything from how you later structure your design team dependencies to how you fashion the artificial intelligence of the monsters roaming your game world. With just a small amount of modification, it becomes quite a handy tool to evaluate the needs of players, regardless of what platform or genre you're dealing with. I like to call my own little spin on Maslow's theories The Hallford Player Pyramid:

- ◆ **Investiture**. Players need to feel their interaction counts. They want to be important to the gaming experience and have their interaction at some level create a discernable effect on the world, the story, or some other element of the game.

They *Hunger*

Imagine for the moment you're a starship cook who's been charged with keeping some wildly uncommunicative alien ambassador alive and pacified. If the alien dies, the thousand-year peace of the Galactic Consortium will collapse, and you'll probably be back to scrubbing the exterior of the ship's hull with a sonic toothbrush. You *could* try feeding him randomly selected items off the ship's standard menu in hopes you'll find something he likes, but it's equally possible human food might turn him even greener than normal or make him explode like that last unfortunate chap from Creosote IV. A better approach might be to study the alien directly. Scan it. Watch its behaviors. Learn its

- **Reward**. Players need to be rewarded when they do things well. Throwing them a bone for the things they've accomplished keeps them motivated, and the promise of worthwhile rewards will keep most players moving forward through a game, even if they're worried about what's around the next corner.

- **Endowment**. Players need to know the game will provide whatever is required to win. No matter what challenge they are faced with, they must always be certain that there is a tool, skill, or bit of information available within the game that will let them overcome whatever stands in their way.

- **Validation**. Players need to believe the game reality operates in a fair, consistent, and comprehensible manner. If they can see there are universal laws that are uniformly applied regardless of situation, they will not only buy in to the pseudoreality of the game, but they will also be more confident in their ability to make informed, reasonable decisions.

- **Mastery**. Players need to be able to achieve mastery over the experience. There's ultimately little point in playing if the player can't win, or at least master some element of the gameplay. Goals and opportunities need to be clearly demonstrated so that the player understands what they are working toward. This is the pot of gold at the end of the rainbow, which they must always know can be reached through attention and perseverance.

metabolic needs, then synthesize something it not only can digest, but maybe even something that it actually *likes* to eat. While the latter method might take a little more effort, in the end it will be more productive for the peace talks, and it will probably save you the trouble of cleaning up the messy aftereffects of yet another culinary disaster.

Players can be very much like the hungry alien ambassador. Their needs define an essential "hunger" that the game designer must find a way to feed. You can try to shake together an arbitrary collection of game features in hopes that you might *accidentally* find someone who will like what you've made, but there's significant financial risk in taking such a blind shot in the dark. Computer games now typically cost millions of dollars to produce and advertise and can sometimes take two years or longer to make. In the same way that you don't shove bananas into the gas tank of your car when it's running low on fuel, it's important you understand the appetites of your players before you start making the games you mean for them to play.

Ask any designer to categorize the people who typically play games, and it's likely they'll already have a list they can rattle off for you. Compare the answers of several developers, and you'll find most everyone seems to be working from the same basic list of profiles. It isn't that we were all issued *Zhul's Basic Handbook of Player Taxonomy* when we enlisted, but the people designers regularly come into contact with *do* seem to divide into generalized profiles defined by the experiences they want to get from playing games.

Two Camps, One Goal

There's an ideological war raging within the computer gaming industry right now, though you might not have noticed it. Its outcome may very well shape the kinds of titles we see in the years ahead. At stake are nothing less than very complex issues touching on how difficult games should be to play and master, how detailed the environments should be, whether a story line should be presented for the gamer, how much control a player should have over the total experience—in essence, virtually every aspect of game design is being challenged as *hard-core* and *casual* gamers battle for control of the future of the industry. But unlike real wars, which leave only a trail of poverty and devastation in their wake, this conflict of ideas is actually leading to a fruitful reevaluation of the reasons why games are made and for whom we are making them.

The Hard-Core Gamer

The label we apply to this group should tell you most of their story. This kind of player eats, drinks, and dreams about the gaming experience. They will spend most of their waking hours either playing, talking about, or reading documentation on games. While they should be concentrating in real life on the forklift they're driving or the handsome blond who's trying to buy them a drink, they're probably thinking instead about how they can get past the Vibrating Blue Squirrels that are guarding the Sacred Crypt of Vandersmirch. To the *hard-core* player, *the game is the life.*

Since the earliest days when games began to pop out of disk duplicators, the hard-core gamer has been the primary foundation upon which the industry was originally built. Without them, there would never have been a *Zork,* a *Wizardry,* or a *Bard's Tale.* It's largely thanks to hard-core gamers' willingness to shell out significant portions of their income that computer users now get to enjoy SoundBlaster sound cards, Voodoo 3D graphics accelerators, high bandwidth Internet connections, and generally higher clock speeds as standard features of home computers and gaming consoles. Today the hard-cores are still leading the charge into new arenas, pumping significant time and energy into massively multiplayer games like *EverQuest,* a still-evolving game format whose strong social components may eventually attract a far less hard-core-oriented audience. It is also from this camp, not so coincidentally, that most new game designers have traditionally sprung.

Central to the hard-core player's worldview is that a game must present a Herculean challenge that must be overcome through a combination of tenacious attention to detail, serious commitment of time by the player, and a willingness to do whatever is necessary to gain the bragging rights for having mastered a particular game.

Titles that require hundreds of hours to complete are often highly regarded by hard-core players, and they may even replay games numerous times in order to achieve the best possible outcome. Hard cores tend to be interested in statistical issues and will be extremely vexed with designers who aren't rigorous in their universal application of world-logical laws. (If, for instance, the player is given a fireball spell, the hard-core gamer expects to be able to set fire to anything that seems like it ought to be flammable. Otherwise, they believe they've been given a bogus deal.) Of particular importance to these players is that they have a high degree of control over the ultimate direction of the game and even over some aspects of the interface. Leading the hard cores through a game with anything more than a very subtle set of nonintrusive clues is considered a sin of paramount evil.

Developers have long considered it nearly holy writ that no game can be successful which does not capture the interest of the typical hard-core player. This attitude is hardly surprising. For over three decades now, the hard-cores have been the one audience upon which the industry could consistently rely, rain or shine. Reviewers for game magazines and Web sites typically belong to this audience, as do most of the people working in the software outlets where games are

O N   T A R G E T

The Hard-Core Player Wants

- ◆ An extremely high level of challenge
- ◆ Games that deliver extended hours of gameplay
- ◆ A structure that lends itself to a degree of replayability
- ◆ A highly detailed and internally logical environment
- ◆ Access to numerical information on characters, objects, spells, and any other statistically driven aspects of the game design

sold. Most designers clearly identify themselves as hard cores either through direct admissions or through the kinds of games they usually offer the playing public. It's hard to argue with the logic of the situation. So long as the games they make remain profitable, they have few reasons to switch the kinds of people with whom they're used to doing business.

But as the explosive growth of the industry has vastly intensified competition for increasingly precious shelf space, the pressure to make only best-selling titles has also sharply driven up production and advertising costs. Profit margins and market share are not what they used to be. With more game companies than ever all competing for a piece of the pie, some executives have begun to reassess the value of putting all their eggs into the hard-core players' baskets. More and more they are turning their attention to the eye-opening success of RPGs like *Diablo* and the casual gamers who played a significant part in helping turn it into an overnight success.

The Casual Gamer

If we think of interactive entertainment as a kind of benign drug, it's clear the hard-core players are incurable addicts. The games they play are as inextricably wound up inside them as they are inside the games. To them, at some level, the game truly matters. Turning the looking glass to the other extreme of the player spectrum, however, will uncover an utterly different type of gamer who occasionally gets a buzz by fragging his buddies on Saturday afternoon but can walk away from the experience without a second thought once he turns off his PlayStation. To this kind of gamer—the *casual* gamer—games are just a fun diversion from life, *not* the main event.

Despite the fact they've received an increasing amount of attention over the last few years, casual gamers have actually been around for a very long time. The first generation of them were bred with *Pong* on the old Atari 2600 game consoles, then nourished through their teen years with terrific arcade fare like *Defender, Rampage,* and *Gauntlet.* As home computers gained the ability to pre- sent photorealistic images and digital stereo sound, casuals slowly began to migrate into the market just in time to discover *Myst* and its decidedly more violent and arcade-like cousin, *Doom.* With a one-two punch of an easy-to- understand first-person perspective and a significantly simplified interface, both these games began to lay the foundations for what amounted to a casual gamer's revolution starting in the late 1990s.

This new audience has yet to provide a conveniently written manifesto, but it's fairly clear there's one quality they seem to respond to above and beyond all others: simplicity. Give them a game that requires a manual to be read before they can start playing, and you've already lost them. At all levels, a game cater- ing to this audience must be easy to install, easy to play, and easy to return to after a prolonged period of absence. Sliders or buttons that allow the player to scale a game's difficulty have proven very popular with casual players. Story lines and game objectives need to be strongly stated in the most straightforward way possible and engineered in such a way that if the player accidentally misses something, they'll still be able to complete the game and have a good time.

Casuals also differ from hard cores in the level of time they're willing to spend in your fictional universe. Instead of engaging in six-hour marathons of dragon slaying, the typical casual may only play between 30 minutes and an hour before being pulled back to real life by other responsibilities. As a result, a game catering to this audience must provide extremely rapid opportunities for advancement and very frequent rewards in order to hold the interest of the player. In the long term, this affects the way the game is balanced and how much total play time can be reasonably sustained. While this might initially seem like a negative, it is actually a factor that plays into another strongly indi- cated appetite of this class of gamer—the need for short-term resolutions.

The Casual Player Wants

- Simplicity, simplicity, simplicity

- A shallow *learning curve*—the game's interface and the basic mechanics of gameplay must be learnable in a very short period of time

- Extremely rapid advancements and frequent rewards

- Production values centered on look and feel

- Clearly provided game goals and objectives

- A short-term time frame for game completion

Casuals don't want to play for three months to reach the end of a game. If it takes much over a month for them to finish, they'll simply lose interest. They have to win soon, and they have to win big.

Another significant factor is that casuals are essentially gaming outsiders. They are much more heavily influenced by the look and feel of television and movies than they are by computer games. You should never assume they've even *heard* of *Final Fantasy*, let alone played it. Even if your title looks a million times better than game brand X, the casual gamer is going to see your title in reference to the *X-Files* or *Star Wars* or other more traditional forms of entertainment with which they are more likely to be familiar. They will also be very unsympathetic to seemingly arbitrarily imposed rules rooted in long-standing gaming traditions. The reasons why a wizard can't equip himself with a chain-mail shirt and hack at monsters with a broadsword aren't very clear unless you've been playing *D&D* for a long period of time. To someone who's never played a role-playing game, this simply seems silly and counterintuitive. You can try and explain this sort of thing to them, but remember for every explanation you have to provide, you're adding a layer of the very sort of complexity that tends to drive this audience away.

You should understand that the relationship between the hard-core and casual audiences is not exclusive. You will very definitely find casuals who like exploring one game for months on end. And there are absolutely some hard-core gamers out there who guiltily play *Myst* and don't tell their friends. The point in discussing these two camps is to get you thinking generally about the broad spectrum of player attitudes and what audience is likely to be most receptive to your ideas.

The (Un)usual Suspects

We've covered quite a bit of ground so far, but have no fear. Our player hunt is nearly at an end. You know their neighborhood, and you have a few clues about their general appetites. The trick now is to narrow your target list. For your convenience, I've taken the liberty of yanking in a few of the people seen in the precinct again and again and again. It's time to introduce you to the folks we call the *usual suspects*.

The Fragmaster

The *fragmaster* lives by sword, bullet, and brawn. If it moves, it must die. If it doesn't move, it still needs to be shot, stabbed, and thoroughly annihilated so it won't cause any trouble later. Potted plants are highly suspect. Stained-glass windows are positively asking for it.

Games that cater to the fragmaster must put the combat system at the very center of reality. The world design must proceed with the notion that every room should have either a monster that will attack or an environmental element that can be broken open or crashed through. In other words, all the major resolutions in the game can in some way be solved by violent confrontation. Story lines need to be flexible enough in these environments to allow minor characters to die without impacting the ability of the player to do what needs doing.

ON TARGET

The Fragmaster Wants

◆ Game objectives that are primarily resolved by combat

◆ Primary focus on the combat capabilities of the characters

With this focus, emphasis on unique combat moves, varied spell effects, and numerous monster types tend to pay off very well for the designer. What becomes troublesome is making sure there are enough expendable resources available at all times (like magical mana or bullets, etc.). Even if the player has been recklessly wasteful, they should still be provided with enough resources to finish the game. Because monsters are necessarily more plentiful in this kind of title, the designer must also take great care that each presents a unique threat and has an identifiable fight personality and that all monsters have a flaw or weakness that can be exploited by the player.

The Problem Solver

Where the fragmaster tends to model himself after Conan the Barbarian, the *problem solver* sees himself more like Sherlock Holmes. He wants to find a way through a problem using the prevailing rules of the game reality. If a problem solver finds a chasm in a dungeon, he's going to go looking for rope so he can swing over it. If he sees a titanic ogre standing in a pass, he wants to climb up to the nearby ledge and shove that precariously balanced boulder onto the monster's unsuspecting head. Whenever possible, problem solvers want to be able to outthink the game.

To center your project on the problem solver, you need to be able to present the player with creative options to combine objects, actions, or strategies in different ways to solve the same fundamental problems. A flexible combat system that allows superior strategy to overcome sheer firepower will play very well with this audience. Puzzles, riddles, and mazes will also be welcomed if they seem to be internally logical in the ways in which they are introduced. Instead of giving problem solvers explicit orders about what they need to do, give them enough information about whatever problems you've dreamed up and let them take their own initiative. If they find the mystery intriguing enough, they'll explore it in their own time, especially if it seems like an intellectual challenge.

The biggest danger of designing for the problem solver is that it's a very difficult approach to tackle. Complex systems can grow unwieldy very fast. At some point you have to test your project, and if there are thousands of ways to solve every problem, you can't possibly test them all before you'll have to ship your game. Even if you're producing an online title that you can update quickly, you can still end up making players very angry if you remove malfunctioning elements because you haven't had the chance to explore all the implications of your designs. The important thing to remember is that you don't have to make complex rules to get complex results. Chess has only 16 playing pieces per side

ON TARGET

The Problem Solver Wants

♦ Flexible game objectives with multiple possible resolutions

♦ The ability to combine objects, actions, and strategies to arrive at creative solutions to game problems

but is capable of generating astonishing complexity through only a handful of very simple principles. On the first move, there are 20 possible choices. By the second move, there are over a thousand possible options!

The Treasure Hound

For the *treasure hound,* game worlds are really nothing more than a particularly twisted shopping mall. Every last barrel, box, chest, bag, tree trunk, and snuff case in the world exists only for their plunder. Zombies differ from store clerks only inasmuch as the fact that zombies take more shots to keep down and usually have more stuff on their ex-persons that will actually be useful further on down the road.

Critical to the treasure hound is the presence of a comprehensible game economy that allows a wide variety of things to be bought, sold, or bartered. Shops and merchants should be omnipresent, each offering their own deals based on location and disposition to the protagonist's plight. A powerful inventory is also mandatory, allowing players to easily identify, organize, and study all the booty they've scooped up during their adventure. The option to zoom in on objects, rotate them, or learn more about their histories also provides increased interest to treasure hounds who want to better understand the value of the things they have in their possession.

Of course, the value of any particular inventory item is a relative matter. It really depends on why players are gathering objects in the first place. Some people want to have lots of gold for its own sake and strive to finish with as much of it on hand as possible. Others want it only for its ability to buy the critical goods and services that will be needed through the course of the game.

The Treasure Hound Wants

- Frequently distributed and valuable booty

- Flexible game economy with many opportunities to find bargains and make shrewd sales decisions

- Inventory system with strong organizational properties and mechanisms to learn more about objects

Treasure items can be worth a great deal in the artificial economy, but some players collect them for their intrinsic artistic merits. Arcane magical artifacts are not only valuable but have special powers that can actually help the gamer defeat enemies or perform other acts critical to the completion of their quests.

The only trouble with presenting lots of stuff to the player is that you've got to *do* something with it all. Magical artifacts need to have some power that can be put to use, which, if you have lots of artifacts, can begin to overwhelm the combat system. Too much gold or too many treasure items can begin to cause ridiculous inflation in the game economy. Most practically, dealing with large numbers of objects of any stripe can seriously impact the usefulness of an inventory system. If during combat a treasure hound has to scroll through long lists of items to find a critical object, the Slorg that's been charging toward them will probably be munching on their skull by the time the needed object is found. The trick with dealing with this audience is learning exactly where, when, and how much to give the player without overwhelming the system as a whole.

The Story Chaser

A *story chaser* is someone who wants a semiguaranteed experience. They want to be assured that after they put in all their time, blood, sweat, and tears to support the heroic side, the big stuff will go the way that it should. The Death Star must always blow up at the end, even if they've made a few mistakes. The Lifestone beneath Sethanon must still be prevented from falling into Tsurani hands, even if they never figured out whom that weird telescope belonged to in the Eastern Kingdom. In the end, the story chaser must always arrive at a satisfying, well-crafted resolution.

Titles that have been geared toward story chasers tend to require only very minor tweaks to a game's inner workings. Some additional maintenance may be required behind the scenes to track who has spoken to whom, what objects have been delivered to their rightful places, and what quests have or have not been completed. Interfaces that govern character interactions tend to be slightly more robust when crafted for this audience, though not by any excessive degree. If anything, the most seriously affected technical issue in a chaser game involves how any prescripted turning points in the story are handled. Whether the game plays a pre-prepared movie, puppets the game characters to react to their current situation, or uses some other mechanism to deliver highly dramatic content, any switching between interactive and noninteractive modes must be carefully accounted for from the beginning of the project. If they can't be meshed together effectively, the designer has lost half the appeal of the game.

One reality that today's chaser-favorable developers must face is that heavily story-driven titles are expensive, no matter which way you cut them. If you decide to insert a pre-prepared movie—sometimes known as an FMV—you're going to spend a serious portion of your budget on graphics and animation. If you go for a more *Resident Evil* kind of approach, where the characters are puppeted around the screen and recorded dialog is used, you're still talking about quite a bit of time in a professional recording studio and on a motion-capture stage. Neither is a cheap prospect. Remember that for every line of dialog you

ON TARGET

The Story Chaser Wants

- A story line that rewards their efforts

- Well-written dialog and a solid story line

- Ability to talk with game characters and follow one or more story threads record, you're limiting all the possible reactions your characters can make to the world around them. On-screen text used to work very nicely to provide broader choices to the player, but on all fronts there appears to be growing hostility toward any kind of gameplay that requires the player to read *anything*. It's a hard sell. Players coming from a modern television audience expect to hear the voices of the characters they see on-screen.

The bottom line for aiming at the chaser audience is that you're going to have to make it worth their time. Nobody is going to sit and listen to dialog that sounds like it was written by your company's janitor. Players are going to get annoyed if the story line is so bumbling and awkward that it would get thrown out of even the worst comic books. You need a professional writer who's been trained to work in an interactive medium and knows how to mesh interactivity and noninteractivity in a fun and dramatically compelling way.

The Navel Gazer

The *navel gazer* is a true child of Narcissus. Everything must ultimately be all about *them* . . . or at least all about the character they play. Kingdoms can rise or they can fall, but navel gazers really care about is that their guy ends up as the toughest, coolest, smartest, best-dressed, or richest bravo in all the world. No one and nothing else is even remotely important.

In order to make the typical navel gazer happy, you need to provide them with a system of skills or attributes that can be steadily built up and whose growth can be clearly monitored. If you provide them with combat skills, you need to throw lots of monsters at them so they can see how tough they're getting. If you put in a computer hacking ability, they should be able to see how they're breaking higher and higher level security codes to access increasingly better information. Whatever abilities you grant the gazer, you must provide ongoing opportunities as frequently as possible for those abilities to be tried, tested, and improved.

Without a doubt, most RPGs do a fairly good job of catering to the gazer, at least in respect to their combat skills. It's exceedingly difficult to finish almost any game today without having maxed out a character's ability to swing a sword or hurl a fireball. Unfortunately, there are whole classes of other skills that typically are overlooked or underused. The challenge of providing meaningful ongoing tests and outcomes for abilities like wood carving, forgery, or nuclear physics rarely justifies the effort of their implementations. Skills that have no consistently useful function are likely to become nothing more than a heap of meaningless numbers largely unexplored by the player. It behooves a designer seeking a navel-gazing audience therefore to make sure early on in the gameplay that there is a clearly demonstrable benefit to all the skills that are being offered.

The Tourist

Had they time or money, game *tourists* would rather be shopping in Prague or exploring the mountaintops of Tibet than chatting up hobgoblins in Kyrandia. For them, games are a surrogate reality, a place to explore ideas or landscapes they could never encounter in day-to-day life. They're hoping beyond hope you can show them something wild, something special, something *magical*. Failing that, they want you to distract them for a half hour before *Ally McBeal* comes on.

Of all the various types explored so far, the tourist is probably *least* interested in having some profound effect on the world or the story. At most, the character they're piloting around is just a person-shaped car, not anyone whose ultimate fate and statistics mean anything other than its capacity to get from point A to point B. Their primary desire is to explore an exotic or whimsical place that invites them ever deeper into mystery, beauty, and terror.

To seize the interest of the tourist, you must put them fully in the moment, drawing heavily on tools like 3-D and surround sound to present a highly detailed and interactive environment that immerses as many senses as possible.

If a tourist discovers a ballista in a courtyard, they want to be able to see it fire, even if twiddling around with it accomplishes nothing in terms of game objectives. The tourist wants to climb to the top of the highest towers of the spaceport, just to see the sweep and scope of starships taking off and landing. It's the small details that make the world real, that make it worth exploring. Whether it's the perception that there's a more beautiful vista around the corner, an even weirder alien performing some strange ritual, or a more peculiar landmark just begging for examination, there must be cues that will keep the tourist wondering what will be discovered next. Games like *Unreal* often exploit their powerful 3-D engines to bait the tourist, giving them fleeting glimpses of bizarre towers or hidden temples that promise even further opportunities for exploration. When well handled, a map can be as much of a reward as a tool, showing where the player's been and what they have yet to explore.

Constant forward momentum creates the prime energy of the tourist title, requiring that there always be a fairly low challenge threshold for the player to overcome in order to continue exploring. Unfortunately, herein also lies the biggest trap for the designer targeting this brand of player. As those thresholds are lowered in an effort to streamline the experience, the designer runs the risk of creating what amounts to a 3-D museum rather than a game. It's not to say that creating virtual realities is an invalid pursuit—they can be very fun and fascinating places to explore—but if there aren't any significant challenges put before the player, there is simply no *game* involved. What's potentially worse is that the player may perceive that nothing is "going on" in the title and will simply lose interest. This is the potential catch-22. You must keep the player moving forward, but you must also throw up the occasional roadblock to make the journey seem worth taking.

So there you have my six prime suspects: the fragmaster, the

O N   T A R G E T

The Tourist Wants

- A large explorable world

- Detailed environments that invite player interaction

- Game maps that indicate where a player has and has not been problem solver, the treasure hound, the story chaser, the navel gazer, and the tourist. I could probably dig up a few more for you, but these are the people you're likely to see again and again in the coming years of your career. These are the basic types who are going to be driving your biggest decisions about where your titles go and what you decide to put in them. Each has a long history and a specific motive that drives them. More importantly, each represents an intensely polarized ideal about what a specific kind of player may want from the games they play.

This is not to say that someone can't have reasons for playing games that span several categories—most people looking at this list would be able to identify *something* from each type that speaks to their particular player appetites. Nobody is all one and nothing of the other. In point of fact, what all these player types have in common is that each represents a critical audience that every role-playing title currently on the market tries in some way to reach. If you make a game that appeals more to a fragmaster than a Puzzle Solver type, you're going to arrive at a title that feels like *Diablo*. Give primacy to the story chaser player, and you're going to arrive at something similar to *Planescape: Torment*. In the end, it is going to be how you mix and mesh the preferences of all these different kinds of players that will determine the final feel and style of the games you wish to make.

The Player's the Thing

If I leave you with nothing else, I hope this chapter is the one that sticks with you for the rest of your game-designing days. If you become someone who is willing to pay attention to the needs of your players, you're going to be one step ahead of most of the newbie designers who will have to learn this lesson the hard way. Remember that players really want to enjoy the games they buy, and they're going to try to clue you in on what you might be able to do to make them happy. If you can find common ground between your own ideas and those of the game-buying public, you'll not only find you're putting out the kinds of great games that people can't stop playing, but you'll also discover that people won't stop talking about them for years to come.

Exercises

1. Unless you're a telepath, you're going to need to do some good old-fashioned footwork if you want to find out what your fellow mortals are thinking. Set aside some Saturday afternoon when you don't have anything else you have to do and commit yourself to surfing through player postings on the major gaming Web sites. If you aren't already doing this on your own, this is as good a time as any to develop the professional designer's habits.

2. The next time you're playing a game, try to identify what different kinds of people might be portrayed by the characters you encounter, especially if any of them seem to be loosely modeled on existing people or cultures. Now imagine that you've been invited to speak at a convention entirely composed of the individuals that have been portrayed. What positive things can you say about them? Don't have anything you can say? If so, consider how you might be able to improve those standings when you start thinking about your own titles.

3. Play through some of your favorite games and try to think about the content in the light of the list of player types I've listed. Do you think the games are hardcore or casual? Which of my six listed player types do you think each of these experiences was primarily created for? What elements would you change to make them appeal more to a different kind of audience?

CHAPTER 2

THE OFT EXPECTED PARTY— A BRIEF HISTORY OF THE GENRE

"Welcome to the land of imagination. You are about to begin a journey into worlds where magic and monsters are the order of the day, where law and chaos are forever at odds, where adventure and heroism are the meat and drink of all who would seek their fortunes in uncommon pursuits. This is the realm of the DUNGEONS & DRAGONS® Adventure Game. . . . "

    — Gary Gygax, *The Keep on the Borderlands* introductory scenario for *Dungeons & Dragons*, original copyright TSR 1981 (used with permission of Wizards of the Coast)

"A few minutes before ten, Marion, back in her Mrs. Peel jumpsuit, appeared carrying a stack of weapon charts and other data necessary for conducting the adventure. 'God could use a computer for this,' grumbled the Dungeon Master."

    — Sharyn McCrumb, from *Bimbos of the Death Sun* (1988)

"You are standing at the end of a road before a small brick building. Around you is a forest. A small stream flows out of the building and down a gully.

?"

    — Willie Crowther and Don Woods, first prompt from the original *Colossal Cave Adventure*

Growing up, whenever I felt hopelessly stuck over a project or a plot line for a story, my father would take me aside, sit me down, and reassure me that "absolutely nothing comes from nowhere." At the time I never found this advice the least bit helpful. But now that I'm starting to gray a bit at the temples and I have the chance to look back over my 11 years of working in this crazy business, I'm beginning to realize just how much sense my country-bred father really had.

Sometime not too long after I put this book to bed, Microsoft and Gas Powered Games will release *Dungeon Siege*, a fantasy RPG I've been helping to create in between my fevered sessions assembling the text before you. The brainchild of Chris Taylor of *Total Annihilation* fame, *Siege* combines a unique blend of RPG, real-time strategy, and action game elements into one very exciting little package. In many ways, it feels like an utterly unique title, something not exactly like anything ever seen before. In another sense, however, virtually every component that has gone into its creation has a history stretching back almost to the start of the 20th century. Many would argue the line goes back even farther, to the birth of games like chess in northeast India sometime in the seventh century A.D.

Every significant development in this industry draws upon the innovations of the past and lays the foundations upon which tomorrow's titles will be built. As Sir Isaac Newton once said, "If I have seen farther, it is by standing upon the shoulders of giants." This chapter will look at some of those giants that have helped bring the modern RPG to fruition and try to set some of them into the broader cultural contexts that made their innovations possible.

As you will see, the history of this business is no more strictly linear than any other kind of history. Lots of strange things had to collide in just a particular way to bring about a specific result. Alliances had to be forged. Ideas had to be tested. The stars had to be just *right*.

By way of disclaimer, let me preface this chapter by saying that you're about to take a rocket ride through five decades of game evolution. If your favorite title doesn't get mentioned here, don't take it as a personal slight. When games reached beyond the mainframe and the arcade, the number of titles began a near exponential rate of growth. Over the past 20 years alone, a mind-numbingly huge number of RPGs have been released, and it's frankly beyond the scope of this book—let alone this chapter—to catalog and fully describe every game that's had a lasting impact on the industry.

When reading this, therefore, understand that this is my own personal assessment of what the important milestones in this industry have been, and it's very possible you could come up with your own chronology of important events, which might look very different from my own. Although in mythology Minerva sprang as a full adult from the head of Jupiter, the RPG was not born from one person with an idea that came from nowhere. Whatever games you decide to put on your own list, you should be able to see that the RPGs of today have come from the confluence of many turbulent rivers of technology and imagination.

Of Little Wars and Returning Kings

In 1901 Europe had not yet seen the horrors of its first "world war." For decades Queen Victoria of England had managed to keep affairs on the Continent relatively civil. Her authority as the grandmother of half the crowned heads of Europe may have been far more terrifying to her grandchildren than all the armaments and unexpressed malice of neighboring countries. But following Victoria's death, decades of pent-up stress and war-wishing were percolating to the surface throughout the Western world. A sense of inevitable conflict was in the air, but there were many who hoped mankind would find a less violent way of resolving its problems, expressing their frustrations through a dignified Victorian tabletop battle of wits rather than on the larger, more appalling canvas of war.

One such individual was one of the most renowned pacifists of his time and the author of several highly imaginative articles and stories dealing with subjects ranging from women's rights, to sexuality, to the fate of humanity. Although history would later best remember H. G. Wells for his science-fiction tales like *The Time Machine, The Invisible Man,* and *The War of the Worlds,* he is also credited for his creation of *Little Wars,* the first collection of English rules for amateur war gamers.

"How much better is this amiable miniature than the Real Thing! . . . no smashed nor sanguinary bodies, no shattered fine buildings nor devastated country sides," Wells says in his book, expressing sentiments shared by many of the peace-loving gamers who still follow variations on his rules to this day.

The rules of *Little Wars* were very simple, based on a 19th-century Prussian game called *Kriegspiel* (war game), which used dice to determine the outcome of various aspects of battle. Brought to England following the Franco-Prussian War of 1870–71, the *Kriegspiel* concept was used primarily as a military training tool, but Wells saw possibilities in it for an enjoyable hobby. Stripping out details he found overcomplicated or too tiresome, he was able to create a set of rules that he felt children could follow and fathers would appreciate and released his interesting diversion to a new game playing public in 1913.

Only four short years later, however, the world had become a very different place. Many of the romantic, bloodless battles that Victorian literature had held up as shining examples of English virtue were forever tarnished, obscured by a world war in which men fought and died in muddy trenches over inches of unimportant ground. Tanks and planes and other machineries of war had made it possible to kill at a distance, to die without seeing the face of the enemy. The world was not as it was. The old ways were fading away in favor of a new reality that held both great dread and great promise.

Stricken with shell shock, another English writer returned home in 1917 to begin the creation of a tale of fantasy that would impact popular culture to a degree unparalleled by any other 20th-century work of fiction. John Ronald Reuel Tolkien's hesitant start on the poems and tales that would make up *The Silmarillion* was only the first step in a brilliant career. His works would set the stage for an entirely new genre of literature and later serve as the primary source of inspiration for a tabletop gaming revolution.

Tolkien became a distinguished Oxford professor of English language and literature, interested primarily in the linguistic aspects of early English works like *Beowulf* and *Sir Gawain and the Green Knight*. He published several scholarly philological and critical studies of these classics but also authored a series of novels based on the universe and mythology he'd begun in *The Silmarillion*.

The Hobbit and the three-volume set of books making up *The Lord of the Rings* brought to life the magical and terrifying world of Middle Earth with an astonishing degree of realism. Unlike the haphazard and illogical way that most writers had treated the fairy stories of English tradition, Tolkien imbued his world with a depth of history, culture, and tradition unlike anything ever published before. Of all the amazingly diverse races of elves, dwarves, orcs, and trolls, each spoke their own carefully constructed language, wrought through years of tireless work as Tolkien developed their lives piece by intricate piece. Even the magic that flowed through his tale radiated a certain solidity, a factualness that made it impossible to dismiss. As Tolkien himself said in his essay "On Fairy-Stories," "If there is any satire present in the tale, one thing must not be made fun of, the magic itself. That must in that story be taken seriously, neither laughed at nor explained away."

The greatness of *The Lord of the Rings* extended far beyond the individual details of the lives of its mythical inhabitants, however. At its center rested a highly moral tale that told of the ultimate battle between good and evil, a story of heroism, sacrifice, and high adventure. For his readers Tolkien had fashioned a world more beautiful, terrifying, and exciting than anything that could be provided by mere reality. He created a fantasy world that readers wanted to *experience for themselves.*

Despite moderate initial success in the United Kingdom, the first American paperback edition of *The Lord of the Rings,* published in 1965, was met by a largely perplexed audience. Retailers had no existing category to place it in, its content being so utterly unlike anything else in publication that it was supremely hard to shelve. The infamous Ballantine edition was also plagued by a particularly hideous cover to which Tolkien objected vociferously in letters to his U.S. editors. Despite these hurdles, his work began to circulate through the college campuses of America, and professors started to share their discovery of this amazing new English classic with their students. Word spread, and it wouldn't be long before many of those students would begin to have ideas of their own about how to bring Tolkien's world into a new, interactive dimension.

Dungeons & Dragons: Where Worlds Collide

Before Tolkien came along, most war gamers were obsessed with history. Using the rules that had been set down by Wells in *Little Wars* and extensively modified in the intervening 55 years, teenagers would pit hordes of little metal men against one another on a tabletop, trying to reshape the outcome of infamous battles with names like Marathon, Constantinople, Waterloo, and Gettysburg. Beginning in the mid-1960s, however, players who'd read *The Lord of the Rings* were beginning to re-create the fictional battle of Helm's Deep, to plot the overthrow of Mordor, to launch campaigns to smash the tower of the evil wizard Saruman. Fans were clamoring for a system that would give them a rustic fantasy universe where magic worked and dragons flew. Clearly, a new set of rules would have to be dreamed up to facilitate the use of such fantastic new elements, but a small group of gamers were already laying the groundwork for something that would go far beyond the bounds of traditional war gaming.

In 1967 Dave Wesely was running a straightforward tabletop strategy game when he decided it might be fun to give players individual goals to accomplish during the course of battle. When more people showed up than he had anticipated, he scrambled to make up new parts for players and struggled to keep the game in balance as unexpected circumstances continually unfolded before his very eyes. Players were huddling in corners, making secret alliances, performing activities that the war-gaming system was scarcely equipped to accommodate. Following a long and complicated night of creative game moderation, he apologized to his players for the abysmal failure of the experiment only to learn that almost everyone had loved the experience and begged him to try it again in the future.

Later, when Wesely was called away by the Army, fellow gamer Dave Arneson took over Wesely's duties as game master and began to add his own rules and modifications. He continued to expand on the idea of individual goals and pushed his scenarios further and further into the realm of fantasy. "This was in 1968," Arneson says. "Although crude, it was the very first step towards role-playing."

In the meantime, Gary Gygax and Jeff Perren had been diligently working on the rules for a medieval war game called *Chainmail* and had begun to exchange ideas with Arneson about various details of gameplay. By the early 1970s Arneson was running campaigns in which participants were playing recurring characters across multiple scenarios, and he had adapted some of Gygax's rules for subterranean exploration.

For the next few years Arneson and Gygax would collaborate heavily on ideas, and Gygax would found a company called Tactical Studies Rules (TSR) to publish *Chainmail*. A later, more widely distributed edition would be the first war game to include guidelines for the use of magic spells and fantasy creatures. From there it was only a matter of a small hop, skip, and jump to the creation of the first official role-playing system, *Dungeons & Dragons*.

Word got around quickly about Arneson and Gygax's innovative gaming system, and soon they began to be flooded with requests for the rules to *D&D*. In 1974 TSR published the first edition, and although it took nearly a year for them to sell the first thousand copies, the second set of a thousand sold out in half that time. By 1979 *D&D* was selling seven thousand copies a month and was rapidly on the rise as an emerging form of popular entertainment.

Unfortunately for Arneson and Gygax, the heady era of their energetic collaboration was about to come to a painful end. Troubles loomed on the horizon. While *D&D*'s players were delighted to see hobbits running about in their favorite RPG, Tolkien's attorneys were not amused. Shining a cold light of intellectual property law on TSR, they forced the game company to change the name of the diminutive race, and thus "halflings" made their appearance in later editions. Creative differences between Gygax and Arneson proved irresolvable, and eventually Arneson left TSR, later taking Gygax's company to court over unpaid royalties. In time the real-world battle was resolved, but the *D&D* phenomenon remained above the fray. Legal wranglings mattered little or nothing to players. As long as the rule books and supplements continued to appear on store shelves, gamers would continue to buy them, regardless of whose names were on the inside cover. The public was hungry for interactive fantasy, and TSR was there to feed them.

About the time Arneson and Gygax were beginning to experience their creative rift at TSR, I was frequently exposing myself to a mind-altering experience in a back room of my uncle J. L.'s house in Stilwell, Oklahoma. For hours on end I would watch little balls of light bouncing hypnotically back and forth, muttering to myself as they did things I didn't expect. While there might have been some who thought I was under the influence of Stilwell's allegedly second-most-famous crop after strawberries, what I'd discovered instead was the Atari 2600 rendition of *Pong*, the first breakthrough, wildly successful home video game.

It was during one of many such sessions of near-oblivious transelectronic bliss that I recall a friend of mine named Steve Garrett coming in and dropping a copy of a strange-looking box on the edge of the bed. It was red and blue, and it had a picture of a dragon, a wizard, and a warrior on the cover. I had absolutely no clue what *Dungeons & Dragons* was supposed to be, though I very much liked the art. My older brother had recently coerced me into reading J. R. R. Tolkien's *The Hobbit* and I'd enjoyed it, so the idea of a game in which I might get to fight a dragon like Smaug sounded very appealing.

At the time I couldn't have appreciated the significance of the moment. I was sitting with the forefather of role-playing games in one hand and the first commercially successful home video game in the other. In just a few short years the two gaming paradigms would fuse together into a major new gaming genre, and I would somehow be lucky enough to participate in a later phase of its evolution.

Tennis for Everyone: The Technology Is Born

In 1958 all William Higinbotham was trying to do was make his laboratory seem a little friendlier to a nonscientific crowd. As a renowned physicist working on a computer project at Brookhaven National Laboratory in Long Island, he hoped to showcase some of the more interesting research going on at his facility. Unfortunately at the time, people typically came in, took a quick look around, then left without comment. For the traditional Visitor's Day, Higinbotham had it in his head that he wanted to do something more interactive, something that would hold people's attention for more than just a few seconds. But while he was interested in creating a captivating experience, it didn't occur to him that

Higinbotham's Unregistered Patent

Higinbotham registered a number of patents throughout his life, but it never even occurred to him to protect the rights to the invention of the computer game *Tennis for Two*. Ironically enough, had he patented the game, the royalties owed by today's computer gaming industry would have flowed into the pockets of none other than the United States government.

he'd be creating anything more than just a curious one-time demonstration. He certainly hadn't thought that he would be leading the way to an entirely new form of leisure entertainment.

Enlisting the help of colleague David Potter, Higinbotham used a small analog computer wired to an oscilloscope to fashion *Tennis for Two,* a game that took them only two weeks to complete. A simple graphic of a net and a ball appeared on a small black-and-white screen. Wind speed, gravity, and bounce were factored into the movements. Using two control boxes, visitors hit the ball back and forth.

The game was a huge hit, eclipsing all other exhibits. The next year, Higinbotham gave the public a larger screen and more sophisticated settings. (Players could even simulate a tennis game played on Jupiter or the moon.) Then, figuring that was enough, he dismantled his invention and forgot about the amusement as he immersed himself in more serious work. Many of his visitors were more impressed, however, and would later trace the origins of an industry to Higinbotham's unambitious *Tennis for Two.*

Spacewar!

With *Tennis for Two,* William Higinbotham had successfully taken a traditional sport and given it two-dimensional life as a computer game. But at the Massachusetts Institute of Technology in the 1960s, programmers and engineers exploring the graphic capabilities of new computers pushed not only the look but the content of gaming into unexplored territory.

In 1960 Digital Engineering Corporation's relatively user-friendly PDP-1 computer was in development. Priced at $120,000, it generated quite a stir. It featured a cathode-ray tube graphic display, was less cumbersome than its forerunners, could be operated by only one person, and didn't have to have air conditioning—all revolutionary features at the time.

In a 1981 article in *Creative Computing* magazine, J. Martin Graetz recalls how in 1961, he, mathematician Wayne Witanen, and Stephen R. Russell, a specialist in artificial intelligence, were all young fellows at the Hingham Institute. Excited by the potential of the PDP-1, the three began discussing what they'd like to do with it. Fans of the *Lensmen* and *Skylark* science-fiction stories of Edward E. Smith, the three began developing the concept for *Spacewar!* Part action and part strategy, it would be the forerunner of countless future computer games.

Spacewar! featured simple needle and wedge ship outlines that started in opposite quadrants of the screen, and players could use a pair of primitive control boxes to steer the ships around. The controllers were something innovative, built by two young colleagues who were also model railroad enthusiasts. Graetz notes, "With the control boxes, two players could sit comfortably apart, each with a clear view of the screen. That, plus the carefully designed layout of the controls, improved one's playing skills considerably, making the game even more fun."

Later, Graetz added other features to the game, including the ubiquitous dimension of hyperspace, which no modern space opera can do without. "The idea was that when everything else failed you could jump into the fourth dimension and disappear."

Completed in April of 1962, *Spacewar!* delighted attendees of MIT's annual Open House in May. Then that summer the original *Spacewar!* team drifted off to pursue their careers. But the seeds had been sown. A standard demonstration piece on all 50 PDP-1 units, *Spacewar!* made an impression on a highly influential group of technocrats. "Others took up the maintenance and development of *Spacewar!*" Graetz continues. "Program tapes were already showing up all over the country, not only on the PDP-1, but also on just about any research computer that had a programmable CRT."

Spacewar! never became a household word, but its influence on programmers, engineers, and future game developers was profound. The simple rules governing the way that objects moved, collided, and interacted with their environment became the model for every graphics-driven computer game to follow in later years.

Cartridges and Consoles: Gaming Finds Its First Home

Right around the time William Higinbotham was pulling the plug on *Tennis for Two,* Ralph H. Baer joined Sanders Associates, a New Hampshire company that produced sophisticated electronics for the military. Encouraged by the proliferation of television sets in American homes, he began to see alternative possibilities for the still-emerging technology. Forming a special team in 1967, he began to design and develop a prototype for an appliance unlike anything anyone had ever thought of before, a game machine that could be hooked up to an ordinary household TV.

Buddy, Can You Paradigm?

As innovative as Baer's cartridge-driven game machines were, they weren't the only trick up Baer's sleeves. In the late 1960s he actually tried to interest cable operators in the idea of electronically distributing game content, but the concept was so innovative no one else was ready for it. Working around the technological limits of the day, his plan would have allowed subscribers to download video game graphics over standard cable lines. It would take decades of game development and the creation of the Internet before the cable business eventually caught up to his groundbreaking ideas.

In this era before the microchip, Baer not only had to figure out what the basic elements of gameplay should be, but he also had to invent much of the technology that would make such electronic gameplay *possible* in the first place. Devising a removable circuit board that could be hardwired with all the special electronic instructions or rules understandable by his game machine, Baer created one of the first cartridge-driven game consoles in existence. Although each cartridge could only hold the instructions for one kind of game, it offered a way for him to sell one machine that would be capable of presenting hundreds of different titles, depending on how each cartridge was wired.

With his cartridge machine ready for demonstration, Baer turned his efforts to the makers of televisions, and at last he was able to attract the attention of a visionary vice president at Magnavox. Showing off a very simple prototype of a Ping-Pong-type game, he eventually convinced the subsidiary of North American Phillips to give the okay to have a few of Baer's strange devices built in 1971. Pleased with the results, Magnavox gave the final go-ahead for the development of the Odyssey and released it to widespread success in 1978.

King Pong

For years MIT alumnus Nolan Bushnell had been working fruitlessly on a *Spacewar!*-like experience he hoped to bring to the coin-op market, but arcade companies repeatedly told him his games were just too complicated. People in bars simply weren't ready for games of great complexity. If he wanted to make something for the arcades, he would have to make something simple.

Inspired by a demonstration of a Ping-Pong-type game created by Ralph Baer's group at Sanders Associates, Bushnell returned to the drawing board and at long last came up with the idea that arcade companies had been looking for. *Pong* was an instant success, and soon lines were forming in front of Bushnell's machines all across the United States. Some became so stuffed full of quarters that they ceased functioning. Bushnell had struck arcade gold.

Quietly, Bushnell's new company paid royalties to Sanders Associates while building a name brand that would soon become a household word: Atari. In 1978 the Atari 2600 game machine would invade living rooms and dens everywhere. *Pong* would become a significant part of computer gaming history and a surefire piece of modern Americana.

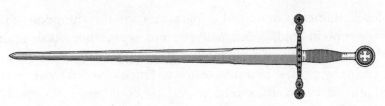

By the time I was finally able to figure out all the complex rules of the pen-and-paper edition of *Dungeons & Dragons,* I could see that its largest obvious flaw lay in the fact that mere human beings were responsible for running the game. Player politics that had nothing at all to do with the game itself often caused major disruptions and sometimes led to disastrous results for exploration parties as a whole.

During a particularly lengthy campaign in the summer following my graduation from high school, I can recall my group's principal Dungeon Master (DM) being fairly put out with many of us. He was determined to run the campaign during as many weekends as possible throughout the summer vacation, but several of us had other plans. While we all enjoyed our time to kick down doors, swing over chasms, and generally fight all manner of evil, we needed to have time away from it to carry on with the business of our real lives. James would grow quite irate if we didn't all show up at a session, however, and he had a tendency to use the game as a way to vent his supreme displeasure with us.

> **DM.** Short for Dungeon Master. In the pen-and-paper version of *Dungeons & Dragons,* the person who creates and controls scenarios for the benefit of other players.

On one occasion when we were all gathered at Nick Luedtke's house for our traditional dungeon crawl, we had a notable number of truancies from the session. James was in a particularly foul mood over the absences, but we carried on with the expedition as valiantly as we could with the people we had on hand.

The dungeon du jour was loaded with dragons, and none of them were even remotely in a forgiving mood that particular day. Despite their best efforts to do us in at every turn, our party of predominantly high-level characters managed to barely escape this dungeon of doom with a fortune in gold, gems, artifacts, and experience. At this point all that remained was the simple matter of dragging our casualties to get patched up by a priest in a nearby town. Once our dead were resurrected and all our wounds were healed, we could enjoy the spoils of our victory.

On the way back to town, however, James insisted on rolling up a wandering monster.

Now given the fact that we'd worked very, very hard to survive in this dungeon and we'd done nothing profoundly stupid to bring on such an arbitrary roll, this was an act of pure DM vindictiveness. After the rigors of that dragon-infested hole, our party was no match for the menace he summoned up. As a result, every single character in our party was slain irretrievably and forever, thanks to the most humiliating monster James could dish up for us.

Squirrels.

Our recent, far more heroic battles had left us so temporarily weakened and disarrayed that our vulnerable ankles could not withstand even a few wicked jabs of tiny rodent teeth. While in the context of the game the outcome was entirely by the book, it was a clear manifestation of the fact that when human beings run the rules of the reality, there are going to be judgment calls that sometimes are clearly uncalled for.

Of course, there were other, more obvious aspects of role-playing that could be relieved by taking the game out of human control. Adding up dice rolls and calculating percentage to-hit probabilities in my head were unquestionably good exercises for improving my notoriously bad math skills, but they were impeding my ability to enjoy the sense of immersive adventure. At times it could take an hour to determine the outcome of a short sequence of combat. Although I loved the evolving story content, I didn't enjoy having to repeatedly consult long and complicated tables. Arguments over the interpretations of rules sometimes turned friendly gaming sessions into no-holds-barred shouting matches, rivaling any enemy encounter in the game. Without question, there were many things about pen-and-paper RPGs that sucked the fun right out of the gameplay, and even then I was thinking that there had to be a better way. . . .

Adventure at the Crossroads

Well into the 1970s, while the first cartridge games were being developed, the popularity of the pen-and-paper version of *Dungeons & Dragons* continued to grow. Technology and RPGs were fast approaching a crossroads, largely thanks to exciting cross-disciplinary pollinations between Tolkien, *D&D,* and high technology. In some educated circles word was also spreading through a new tool: electronic mail. Those PDP-1 computers that had once spread *Spacewars!* from engineer to engineer had given way to PDP-10 machines hooked up to a powerful network of interconnected computers known as the *ARPAnet*—the forerunner of the modern Internet.

Much of the new technology was coming out of Bolt, Beranek and Newman in Boston. Like many innovative companies, BBN attracted a lot of smart people with wide-ranging interests. Will and Pat Crowther, a husband and wife team working for BBN, spent many of their off-hours exploring caves. In fact, Pat had helped discover the link between Kentucky's Mammoth and Flint Ridge caves, a major find that revealed a combined 144-mile system. Will used his free time and a BBN computer to create underground maps for the Cave Research Foundation. But spelunking and cartography weren't his only leisure-time pursuits. When BBN personnel formed a *D&D* group, Will became an enthusiastic regular player.

When the Crowthers eventually divorced in 1976, Will did everything he could to stay as involved with his children as possible. Putting his computer programming skills to work, he struck upon the idea of creating something that would combine his knowledge of subterranean exploration with his interest in roleplaying. He called his simple game *Colossal Cave Adventure,* and unlike *Spacewars!* which had given players very rudimentary graphics but a very small playing arena, *Adventure* was relying solely on descriptive bits of text to create the illusion of its vast, labyrinthine world.

Although Will's children liked the *Adventure* game he'd made for them, he didn't develop it further than its first steps. When he took a new job with the Xerox Corporation in California, he left the program behind on a BBN computer file, never realizing that the game would soon take on new life of its own.

Don Woods Seeks the Carbon Unit

At Stanford University graduate student Don Woods had heard about *Adventure* from a friend and managed to download a copy from the Stanford Medical School computer. The game, designed for young children and put together over a few weekends, was a bug-infested mess and very difficult to run, but Woods was impressed with the promise of its interactivity. Curious to learn more about it, he engaged in a rather desperate measure in order to contact its creator. Shotgun e-mailing Crowther at every host on the fledgling network, Woods managed to locate him at Xerox's Palo Alto Research Center and got the original code.

Woods cleaned up the bugs and glitches, added some Tolkien-esque elements, and ramped up the complexity of the game by a notch. Mazes got trickier, and some treasures could only be obtained through puzzle solving. Within a few months the Woods-modified version of *Adventure* was up and running, and he quickly invited the world in to share.

Following Woods's posting of *Adventure* on a Stanford computer, players were getting seriously hooked on the experience. According to some accounts, everyone who played it put their real work on hold for two weeks until the alluring maze was mastered. Written in FORTRAN, it was workable on a wide variety of computer systems, and like *Spacewar!* before it, it spread across networks like wildfire.

With the blessing of both Crowther and Woods, users were encouraged to copy the game and even to e-mail the creators for help. The atmosphere of cooperation was astonishingly open by today's standards, a positive reflection on a pursuit that would later be marked by clear distinctions between the creators and players of games. It was also the real-world embodiment of the cooperative play that *D&D* groups knew well, and the openness of its development eerily prefigured the architectures that would later make mod-friendly games such as *Doom* so popular.

mod-friendly. A game whose content can easily be modified by users in order to create new scenarios by changing art, sounds, and other game-specific elements.

Adventure went on an adventure of its own and was translated numerous times across multiple platforms. It reached the first personal computers by 1981 and was sold commercially for the first time. The Digital Engineering Corporation user group, DECUS, took up distribution of the game, and the product was endorsed by Crowther and Woods as the "official" version. Players who successfully completed the game received a secret code at the end, redeemable for a Certificate of Wizardness.

Zorking in the Underground Empire

By early 1977 *Adventure* had swept the ARPAnet. Countless individuals had their first lesson in how a simplistic computer-driven role-playing game could put work, sleep, and human relationships on hold until the game was solved.

At MIT Marc Blank, Tim Anderson, and Bruce Daniels feverishly worked through *Adventure,* then turned their attentions to creating their own game. They drew maps and hashed out the details of what would become *Zork.* (According to Anderson, back then "zork" was a common working title for programs in development.)

Following the Tolkien-inspired conventions of *D&D* and *Adventure, Zork* featured a maze, a troll, a forest, and other rustic fantasy elements. Presented with short written scenarios, a player typed in brief commands to propel the action along. Like *Adventure* before it, *Zork* had no visuals. If you wanted a map, you plotted one out on graph paper as you blazed your trail.

The real beauty of this deceptively simple game lay beneath the surface. The creators had carefully and cleverly set up interactions between objects, verbs, and locations, making it easy to add new elements whenever they were wanted or needed. The creators added elements and quests to the game, releasing new versions as they went along.

After the last puzzle was incorporated in 1979, the creators joined forces with some other MIT colleagues and formed Infocom, one of the first computer game companies in existence. Infocom then partnered with Personal Software in 1980 to publish *Zork* for the first wave of personal computers, including the Apple I.

Adventure had been best known among hard-core computer enthusiasts and was marketed late in life, almost as an afterthought. *Zork,* on the other hand, had

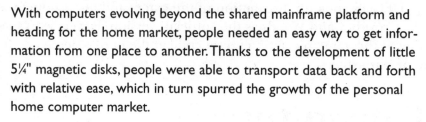

Size Matters

With computers evolving beyond the shared mainframe platform and heading for the home market, people needed an easy way to get information from one place to another. Thanks to the development of little 5¼" magnetic disks, people were able to transport data back and forth with relative ease, which in turn spurred the growth of the personal home computer market.

The 5¼" diskettes were designed with the personal computer in mind, replacing the 8" floppies used previously. By 1978 at least 10 manufacturers were producing 5¼" floppy drives. Hard drives hit the home computer market in 1980, although many regarded them as a luxury item for years to come.

The first 3½" floppy drives and diskettes, introduced by Sony, hit the market in 1981. Adopted by Hewlett-Packard in 1982, it became the industry standard, prevailing over its 3¼", 3", and 3.9" competitors. (Clearly, this was an industry that needed a microfloppy standard.)

The next wave, compact disc read-only memory, or CD-ROM technology, was on the market by 1985 but would not see widespread usage until the 1990s.

the advantage of coming of age at the dawn of personal computer usage. Promoted through advertising and given other advantages of a commercially supported product, it was a huge popular success.

Mystery House: A Game with a View

By the late 1980s Roberta Williams was regarded with a near rock-star like reverence by many would-be game designers. She and her husband, Ken, had established Sierra On-Line in the small mountain community of Oakhurst, California, creating one of the first true powerhouses in computer game publishing. But unlike the generations of computer hacker heroes that had preceded her, Roberta was definitely something new under the sun, the first of a new breed of non-code-savvy game designers. Not only had she known absolutely nothing about programming when she got started on the development of her first title, until Ken had exposed her to Crowther and Woods's *Adventure,* but she had expressed no interest in dealing with computers at all. Engaged by the power of the story-driven game and lacking any new titles to play after she completed *Adventure,* she decided it would be up to her to make her own.

At the time, Ken was a programmer working for Informatics. As Roberta began to sketch out the maps and puzzles and characters that would populate her new text-driven world, Ken encouraged her to continue, but advised her she would need to come up with something new to sell the game. Roberta replied that what she'd really like to do was be able to draw pictures on the screen of what people were supposed to be seeing instead of simply describing everything. Ken thought maybe it would be possible and got to work on his expensive new Apple II to tackle Roberta's problem, while she concentrated on creating the gameplay. In just over a month, Roberta's *Mystery House* became a computer gaming landmark.

Although the graphics for *Mystery House* were little better than stick figures on a screen, it offered a blend of text and graphics unlike anything that had ever been seen before. The Williams marketed the game themselves on a shoestring budget and received a flood of orders. Taking hint calls in their home while Roberta worked on a second, longer game called *Wizard and the Princess,* they quickly found they had the money to finance a move into the mountains. Soon their fledgling company would change its name from On-Line Systems to Sierra On-Line and would hire its first employee to field the nerve-shattering hint calls that were sometimes coming in at six o'clock in the morning.

For three or four years the Williams experienced an American success story—a home-based business that grew into an interactive entertainment company with more than 130 employees. They hit major success with arcade games such as *Frogger* and *Jawbreaker.*

The home computer and game console market was promising in the early 1980s, but the battle for operating system dominance was up in the air. A dizzying number of systems went on the shelves, all of them completely incompatible with each other. It wasn't just a question of which machines, but which operating systems would last. There was really only room for a limited number of platforms. Inevitably, many of the earliest players would not survive.

For consumers, the risk was buying a machine destined for quick obsolescence, but the stakes ran far higher for software developers. Deciding which technologies to support was a make-or-break crapshoot. By the end of 1984 Sierra On-Line had sunk large amounts of venture capital into developing games for cartridge-based systems that lost the race for the home market: The Vic-20, the Atari VCS, and the Coleco Adam. Sierra On-Line would have faced complete disaster if it hadn't been for a knight in shining armor. Specifically, Sir Graham of Daventry.

The previous year, Roberta Williams had designed a game for the new IBM home computer, the IBM PCjr. Asked to showcase the model's then impressive 16-color palette, three-channel sound, and 128K of memory, Sierra broke new ground and came up with the first animated, interactive "cartoon" game, complete with sound effects and music. Called *King's Quest I: Quest for the Crown,* it featured the story of the young knight Sir Graham (so named because Roberta loved graham crackers) on a quest for lost treasure that could make him king.

On this first quest Sir Graham was nearly foiled. Even a business giant like IBM couldn't guarantee success in the uncertain home computer market. The PCjr had a non-user-friendly keyboard with keys so tiny that users frequently called them "chiclets." Worse yet, it couldn't run regular IBM PC software. The PCjr flopped, big time. This might well have done Sierra in if the Tandy 1000 hadn't hit the market in 1984.

Over several decades, Radio Shack had become the best-known distributor of electronic parts and supplies to the general public. Owned by the Tandy Corporation, the company was able to do what most other computer manufacturers could only dream of. It could put a consumer-friendly computer in nearly every shopping mall in America. The MS-DOS compatible Tandy 1000 became the leading home computer, and mercifully for Sierra, it also ran PCjr software. *King's Quest* became an instant best-seller, and Sierra On-Line was able to solidify its leadership for the adventure/role-playing market for years to come.

Throughout its history, *Sierra* proved to be a growth company, blazing trails on numerous fronts. A storyteller rather than a programmer was shaping the development of its games, opening opportunities in the industry to a new kind of designer. Its technological innovations had lent a visual impact to the previously blind adventure/RPG market. And last but not least, it had survived a tough market to become one of the most successful computer game development houses in the country.

Ultima: Rule Brittania

The origins of one of the most successful computer RPG series of the 20th century began not with a corporate proposal but with several lines of handwritten code inscribed into a project notebook bearing only the cryptic label *D&D28*.

Within were 19-year-old Richard Garriott's code for his 28th text-based fantasy role-playing game, based loosely on the principles of pen-and-paper RPGs like *Dungeons & Dragons* and *Tunnels & Trolls.* He'd begun programming simple fight-the-monster-grab-the-treasure games on computers as early as 1974, and then in 1977 he and a few of his friends had begun their own computer programming course at their high school.

But it wouldn't be until the release of the Apple II that Garriott saw the light . . . or more accurately, the *pixel* light. Intrigued by the graphic capabilities of the new computer, he began converting D&D28 into a graphical RPG, which he would name *Akalabeth.* Making a deal with California Pacific Computer to distribute zip-lock bagged copies of the title, Richard's first foray into game publishing sold an astonishing 30,000 copies in 1979.

For his next title he adopted a more professional approach, hammering together a solid user interface and an intricate plot, a task that apparently daunted Garriott somewhat. (By his own admission at the time, he said that he'd never read more than 25 books in his life.) By 1980 he had the sequel to *Akalabeth* ready for mass consumption, marketing it under the more manageable title by which the rest of the series would become known: *Ultima.*

Convinced that California Pacific Computer wasn't paying all the royalties due him for the sales of *Akalabeth* and *Ultima I,* Garriott announced he was going to leave his current publisher for the production of the sequel. Almost immediately he was surrounded by interested parties willing to grant him the unprecedented 30 percent royalty he was demanding, but Ken and Roberta Williams's well-established On-Line Systems clinched the highly coveted deal, adding *Ultima* to their already impressive roster of software.

Following up *Ultima I* with a second adventure in the land of Brittania in 1982, Garriott continued to teach himself game design and programming as he went along. Once *Ultima II* had been completed and released, he gave up his full-time studies at the University of Texas to devote himself wholly to the creation of *Ultima III.* Along with his brother Robert, his father Owen (who incidentally had been a Skylab-3 astronaut), and On-Line Systems' resident Atari wizard

Role-Playing under Siege

While Garriott was founding ORIGIN Systems and preparing the virtues-based concept behind *Ultima IV*, role-playing was under attack by conservative extremists who saw it as demonic and amoral. *D&D* in particular became the target of an all-out smear campaign.

It got started when a gifted but troubled youth disappeared in 1979, leaving a rambling note that purportedly mentioned *D&D*. The boy was found but committed suicide the next year at the age of 16. He had a sad history of emotional instability (there was also evidence of abuse), but through some irresponsible reporting, his tragic death was publicized as a "*D&D* suicide."

When a second young man, one with known delusional behavior, killed himself in 1982, his mother wrote a book blaming her son's death on his interest in *D&D*. Right-wing radicals took up the cause with all the fervor of an old-time witch hunt, insisting children were being lured into all manner of madness and depravity because of role-playing. The make-believe magic of the game was condemned as a dangerous portal to the occult. A miniature comic book tract entitled *Dark Dungeons* and Rona Jaffe's novel *Mazes and Monsters* helped further fan the fire.

Role-players responded to the ill-founded attacks and banded together for antidefamation efforts. The gaming industry stepped in and commissioned studies of claims made by the anti-*D&D* crowd, and the resulting facts helped discredit the emotion-laden propaganda. No links to suicidal, antisocial, or criminal behavior were ever substantiated. Ultimately, good sense and the industry triumphed. But sadly, vestiges of the misinformation campaign linger to this day.

Chuck Bueche, Garriott founded ORIGIN Systems in 1983. At last the highly successful series would be developed in a real office space instead of out of his parents' bedroom closet in Houston, Texas.

Fittingly enough, after growing up on fantasy role-playing and computing, Garriott helped the computer RPG genre reach another level of maturity with the development of *Ultima IV*. Distressed over the fervor of a strong anti-role-playing movement at the time, he wanted to disprove accusations that games like his were amoral or worse. Even more, he wanted to grow past the limiting thrust-and-parry-grab-and-carry mentality of past efforts. He wanted to offer *new* gaming objectives.

After a great deal of research and thought, he gave his mythical world a moral dimension, a kind of karmic cause-and-effect element that would govern everything that occurred in his world. Players used to plundering and killing their way to glory could pursue loftier quests based on honesty, compassion, valor, justice, spirituality, sacrifice, honor, and humility. Sure, you could still raise hell if you wanted to, but from this point on in Brittania, you'd have to live with the consequences.

Although Garriott had some concern over how his new concept would be received, fans felt there was indeed room for such high-mindedness. The concept of the virtuous Avatar, introduced in *Ultima IV,* would become a centerpiece of the series and reappeared in all the subsequent titles from *Ultima V* to the last single-player installment, *Ultima IX: Ascension.*

Wizardry and the Party Line

Before 1981 gamers playing on a computer had only two possible representations of their in-game selves to choose from. They could either roam the vast and dangerous dungeons of the world alone, or they could rumble across a sodden battlefield in the guise of 2,000 screaming sword-swinging barbarians. Between these two extremes there was nothing available for players who longed to replicate the basic tactics of even the rudest pen-and-paper RPGs. Into this vacuum of player choices stepped Andy Greenberg and Robert Woodhead with the first true party-oriented computer RPG, *Wizardry: Proving Grounds of the Mad Overlord.* Being fair-minded souls, they also let the forces of evil get in on the tag-team concept, transforming the standard monster encounter into the lively exchange of combat orders that became *Wizardry*'s unofficial motto: "Fight, fight, fight, parry, parry, parry."

Modeled heavily on tried-and-true role-playing standards, *Wizardry* strove to re-create the sense of traveling with a diverse band of talents, each contributing their own skills and experience to the adventure. Influenced by a variety of pen-and-paper RPGs, including *D&D*, and early computer games like *Adventure,* Greenberg traces the direct beginning of *Wizardry* to "a rather ludicrous challenge from my dorm buddy, Paul Murphy. He was frustrated by my petulance during one exam study-week, and challenged me to 'go put *D&D* on my computer or something.' Well, never one to pass up a challenge, and particularly when the challenge was an excuse not to study for exams . . . I built this game for buds." The next 8 to 12 months of the creation of *Wizardry* were "the most wondrous of my life," Greenberg admits, though it got hard to get much sleep with his friends constantly play-testing the game at ungodly hours.

In addition to providing a party-based concept for *Wizardry,* Greenberg also slipped in a number of other elements that were familiar to veteran RPGers. Each character in the party belonged to a particular race (Human, Elf, Dwarf, etc.), possessed a certain level of strength and agility, and was a member of a specific character class (Thief, Fighter, Mage, or Priest). With experience, a character could advance to a higher level within that class. Gone were some of the more charming aspects of playing live with friends, but so were the frequently arbitrary dice rolls and the ensuing arguments over obscure rules.

Wizardry I's graphics were minimalist, featuring wire-frame-walled corridors and motionless monsters that materialized seemingly from nowhere. Attacks were heralded by a tinny sound on the Apple's primitive speaker, and a small color picture of the offending creature was displayed in the upper-left corner of the screen. But for all the danger posed by these mobile menaces, there were other challenges just as vexing with which players had to contend. Green slime was an ever-present threat. Everywhere there seemed to be a dizzying array of traps, pits, spinners, and concentration-shattering teleporters. Puzzles tested players' wits, and always there was the search for the sacred object, sword of power, or gem of great value. Almost anywhere the player cared to go in the world, there was always something that could be done.

Looking back at their achievements, Greenberg says he's proudest that they managed to get a game the size of *Wizardry* on a 48K Apple II. "It was an awesome feat for its time. There were no great development tools. The solution was continual space-for-time trading, building layers upon layers of interpreters, and having the top-level interpreter driven off by a database defining the game scenario. This provided not only a solid product on a tiny platform but also a great scenario and scripting platform for new game development."

From the very start of its design, Greenberg's goal was to constantly present an experience that provided the right mix of incentives and rewards. The challenge

Number 9, Number 9, Number 9 . . .

While *Wizardry I* is perhaps best known for its introduction of multi-character parties to the computer-driven RPG, it is also famous for having one of the greatest "undocumented features"—or to be honest, *bugs*—of all time. As a result of one small slip in the programming code, suddenly players everywhere were intentionally creating whole dungeon parties comprising *exclusively* Bishops. Why was this? It was all due to a teensy slip in the game coding that looked something like this:

```
if (ch >= "1") or (ch <="8") then...
```

Now Bishops were a class of characters like any others *except* that they had an added special ability. When the party picked up new items, they could be given to the Bishop character so that he could *identify* whether or not the objects were cursed. (Pretty handy, especially if you want to make sure that scroll isn't cursed before you try to use it against a ravingly irritated orc.)

The way that inventories were set up, only eight items could be carried per character. The player indicated which item the Bishop would identify by hitting the number on the keyboard that corresponded to the item's slot number. So if you wanted to identify the object sitting in the seventh object slot, you hit the 7 on your keyboard. Easy enough. Fortunately for the players, thanks to the use of an "or" in the programming code when an "and" should have been used, if the player accidentally hit the 9 key, then something truly bizarre happened. Suddenly a member of the party would instantly gain an unbelievable number of experience points!

Of course, once players discovered this amusing flaw, they immediately pounced on the opportunity and set out on their adventures armed not with the typical swords and helms, but more often with staffs and miters.

"When we released the PC version, we left the bug in for reasons of fairness," Woodhead says, happily taking the flak for the error. "It might be the first case of a designer saying, 'It's not a bug, it's a *feature!*'"

was making sure that the game's balance didn't get out of hand in the process. "It was an adjunct of the separation of concerns in the database, and the capacity to have the game constantly play-tested. I began with an algorithmic model to balance experience, monsters, treasure, and the like, and then tweaked and fine-tuned it by collecting data from the game players."

Although *Wizardry* was originally created to entertain his friends, Greenberg later teamed up with Robert Woodhead to take it further. "Woodhead and I built the commercial prototype with a makeshift scenario, and we launched it at a Boston computer convention in 1980."

In 1979 Robert Sirotek and Fred Norman founded Sir-Tech Software to distribute *Wizardry I* to the public, turning the humble game that Greenberg had only whipped up for his "buds" into a much larger and very influential title. More than two decades later, *Wizardry* is still cited by many designers as the prime inspirational force that convinced them to create RPGs of their own.

Sitting on the floor of my friend Ron Bolinger's first apartment in Tulsa, I remember squinting up at my DM while I tried to decide what my magic-user was going to do next. The outcome of my decision had the potential to resolve the fate of the entire party. Life and death hinged on whether or not Fandercast would attempt to defend himself or risk wasting the last spell he had available. Things in Skara Brae were very bad indeed.

After hastily conferring with my coadventurers, I drew a deep breath and informed James of my final decision. Nodding in agreement, he turned to the glowing face of the Commodore 64, which was bathing us all in green glow, and very quickly he hit all the appropriate keys to issue my command to my electronic alter ego. Fandercast parried successfully, and we all survived for yet another round of battle.

As usual it was a weekend, and the members of my role-playing group were camped in an entranced semicircle around the computer, each prepared to issue new orders to our on-screen counterparts. James was sitting at the helm, skillfully piloting our party through the hazards of Interplay's *Bard's Tale*. Although I didn't realize it at the time, it was one of the first computer RPG spin-offs that had been heavily influenced by *Wizardry I*. In only a few years I'd be working on the *Might & Magic* series, yet another spiritual grandchild of the *Wizardry* legacy.

Despite the dire predictions of naysayers that electronic games would destroy the weekend role-playing session, there I was, sitting shoulder to shoulder with my long-time comrades in arms, perfectly content to let the computer handle all the tedious table checking, which had been the bane of our previous pen-and-paper campaigns. The technology still had a long way to go to create the kind of really immersive gaming we all wanted to see, and true 3-D environments were still down the road by several years.

But as limited as that first computer role-playing experience was, it was clear that the fundamental features of the RPG could be successfully translated into an electronic medium. From here on out it would only be a matter of pushing the technology harder and faster, expanding the degree to which we could freely interact with the environment. We speculated wildly about how long it would take for computers to catch up with our imaginations, but we had no way of knowing what was developing behind the scenes. The industry was preparing to explode in a multitude of unexpected directions, and the face of gaming would be forever changed.

DraQue: RPGs in the Land of the Rising Sun

By 1982 role-playing games had become so much a part of everyday American life that they had begun to be reflected in other forms of popular culture. In the opening minutes of Steven Spielberg's seminal science-fiction flick *E.T.*, the young hero Elliott is shown doing what many children might be doing on a typical Saturday night—sitting down to a healthy session of *Dungeons & Dragons*.

But while the role-playing phenomenon was relatively old hat in the United States, in other countries RPGs weren't even a blip on the radar yet, let alone an industry that annually was drawing in dedicated fans and steady revenue. It would take a potent trio of console games introduced to the Japanese market between 1986 and 1987 to get them used to the idea, but they would seize hold of this new genre with a passionate fervor and give it a unique flavor all their own. In the years to come Japanese-produced RPGs would not only become the primary staples of the Nintendo, Sega, and Sony Playstation platforms, but they would play critical roles in the long-range survival of the consoles on which they appeared. Time and time again, machines that failed to attract a strong RPG developer soon found themselves in the technological graveyard.

Though there's some debate over what qualifies as the first console-based RPG, most would agree the May 5, 1996, Enix release of *Dragon Quest* for the MSX personal computer and Nintendo Famicon probably triggered the Japanese RPG revolution. Heavily inspired by the PC title *Ultima, Dragon Quest* stripped down the statistics-heavy American role-playing experience, opting for a faster, more streamlined game based on exploration and battle. The product of a fruitful collaboration between writer and scenario designer Yuji Morii, a famous cartoonist named Akira Toriyama, and composer Koichi Sugiyama, *Dragon Quest* was a spectacular success in Japan. In 1989 it would debut in the United States with a slight name change, appearing as the first of the *Dragon Warrior* series for the Nintendo Entertainment System.

In time *Dragon Quest* became to the Japanese what *D&D* is to most Americans: the progenitor of its genre. Players began to use the term "DraQue" to generically refer to *any* form of role-playing system, either on or off the computer. *Dragon Quest II* further established it as the benchmark by which future console RPGs would be judged, but it was the release of the third installment in the series that would forever cement its reputation in the minds of the Japanese people.

When *Dragon Quest III* hit the market on February 10, 1988, it made national headlines. There was a rash of school truancy as children skipped school to buy the new game. Long lines formed, sometimes stretching several city blocks, as retailers struggled to meet the rabid demand for the RPG. There were even multiple reports of customers so desperate to get their own copy that they mugged others when supplies in the stores evaporated. In the interest of preserving social order, the Japanese Diet, Japan's main legislative body, decreed that future *Dragon Quest* games could only be released on Sundays or holidays to reduce any further interference with the regular conduct of education and business. *Dragon Quest* proved not only to be a highly successful product but one of the biggest cultural phenomena to hit Japan since Godzilla had risen out of the waters of Tokyo Bay.

Ultima Underworld: RPGs Enter a New Dimension

From the moment Roberta Williams lifted the veil on her graphics-adorned *Mystery House* in 1980, designers committed increasing time, money, and effort to bring their imaginary worlds visually to life. Creative and unusual environments became hallmarks of the genre as each title tried to one-up the "eye candy" of the competition. Artists gleefully churned out endless worlds based on the four Greek elements of air, earth, fire, and water (and all believed they were the only ones who had ever thought of it). Programmers dipped into their fractal toolkits to whip up atmospheric fogs and flowing waters, which lent an illusion of life to otherwise static scenery. But until ORIGIN Systems introduced a technologically sophisticated spin-off of the *Ultima* line in 1992, the worlds in which gamers had been playing had really never been more than pretty-looking backdrops. *Ultima Underworld: The Stygian Abyss* would not only give people the world's first fully 3-D RPG, but it would also begin to challenge many of the core assumptions designers brought to their role-playing projects.

Following his work on a pre-*Wing Commander* ORIGIN Systems game called *Space Rogue*, Paul Neurath wanted to make a first-person perspective, real-time, 3-D fantasy game. He'd already learned several lessons from *Rogue*'s combined space-flight tactics and ground-based role-playing system, and he thought he could knit the genres together into a compelling experience. Contracting an ex-ORIGIN artist named Doug Wike to do the concept work and pulling in several members of the infamous "House of the 10 Dumb Guys," Neurath set up shop in Salem, New Hampshire, and named his new company Blue Sky Productions.

One of the first big technical hurdles of the project was tackling the texture-mapping process, which would play such a major role in the production of *Underworld*. Contacting a talented IBM PC programmer named Chris Green he'd gotten to know through past collaborations, Neurath tasked him to create the project's texture-mapping algorithm.

"For some unfathomable reason his [Chris Green's] test texture was a black-and-white photo of Abe Lincoln," Neurath says. "So at first we got to see lots of twisted and distorted Abes staring back at you in 3-D."

Within a few months, the first prototype for *Underworld* came together. Although the demo featured nothing more complex than a character walking through a 3-D texture-mapped dungeon, it left many developers gaping. Nothing like it had ever been seen before.

Doug Church was an MIT grad and one of the "Dumb Guys" whom Neurath had wisely brought on as part of his decidedly un-dumb team. "He went to the May 1990 CES [Consumer Electronic Show] with a demo three of us coded that month," Church says. "Paul's initial design doc was a little aggressive, featuring goblins on the prows of rowboats tossed in the waves, shooting arrows at the player above on a rope bridge swinging in the wind." Lead artist Wike helped pare down the busy, ambitious scenario and created a 30-second sequence in Deluxe Paint Animator. "The animation showed the main user-interface screen and a hand-drawn 3-D view. A goblin came out, moved towards the camera, and swung its club."

After shopping it around to several potential publishers, Neurath interested ORIGIN Systems in *Underworld,* signing a deal with them in the summer of 1990. ORIGIN believed the project would benefit by leveraging it against their already successful *Ultima* line, so the project was renamed *Ultima Underworld* with Neurath's hearty blessing.

But the licensing deal signed with ORIGIN was only the beginning of a very complex process. "In reality, like all projects, it was very iterative. We tried out many things, watched them break, and then tried something new," Church says. "We wrote four movement systems before we were done, several combat systems, and so forth. The programming team was mostly just out of school and new to game writing, so we were improvising almost the whole time."

While the 3-D aspect was only the most obvious of the "improvisations" that Church and his fellow team members brought to *Underworld,* there were a number of other approaches to the game that set it apart from the RPGs of old. Gone was the traditional turn-based style of combat, replaced by a controversially dynamic form of melee that had players and monsters trading blows in real time. Instead of switching back and forth between different windows to handle different game tasks, almost everything could be handled in the main view window with the click of the mouse. Even the fundamental linearity of most RPGs was challenged by a design that replaced often illogical puzzle solving with environment-based problem solving.

Despite its very promising start and its hearty support by ORIGIN's founder Richard Garriott, the early days of Blue Sky's relationship with its publisher could sometimes be vexing. Two separate ORIGIN producers assigned to the project left the *Underworld* team in contact limbo. One was gone from ORIGIN a month before Neurath was even told about the departure. If not for the project's eventual championing by Warren Spector, the innovative title might never have come out at all.

"The VP of Product Development, Dallas Snell, had assigned Jeff Johannigman to produce the game—much to my chagrin—and I sort of watched jealously from the sidelines," Spector says of the project. "When Jeff left the company, I begged and pleaded and whined until I was given the assignment of producing the game."

Spector's passion for the project paid off. He understood very clearly what Neurath was trying to accomplish and did everything he could to give *Underworld* all the attention and resources it deserved. "My first real impact on the project came when Paul and Doug Church, a programmer on the team who eventually moved into the project director role, came down to ORIGIN to pitch me and Richard Garriott on the story and the core gameplay concepts. I played an active role in the project from that point on, flying up to Boston on a regular basis to work with the team and talking with Doug pretty much on a daily basis."

Roughly two years after starting the project, Neurath and his team eventually finished *Underworld* and released it to the public. After selling roughly half a million copies and winning numerous awards, it became one of the biggest games ORIGIN had produced to date. Later Neurath and Spector would separately go on to produce other well-known RPGs like *System Shock, Thief: The Dark Project,* and *Deus Ex,* but *Ultima Underworld* would be *the* game that introduced the role-playing genre to the third dimension, and developers to a whole new way of looking at the world of game design.

The Final Symbiosis

Studying *Dungeon Siege* with the same careful consideration that a father gives to the face of his child, I see familiar family features. That rustic medieval flavor that permeates it from start to finish can only have come from great-granddaddy Tolkien, with maybe a dash of cousin Arneson thrown in. Its freewheeling, do-what-you-like level editor that invites players to make their own worlds is *pure*

Table 2.1 Influential Releases

Title	Year	Publisher
Adventure	1976/1981	-/DECUS
Zork	1980	Infocom
Mystery House	1980	On-Line Systems (Sierra On-Line)
Ultima	1980	California Pacific Computer
Wizardry	1981	Sir-Tech
King's Quest	1983	Sierra On-Line
Temple of Apshai	1983	Epyx
Bard's Tale	1985	Interplay
Gauntlet	1985	Atari
Starflight	1986	Electronic Arts
Might & Magic	1987	New World Computing
Pool of Radiance	1988	SSI
Dungeon Master	1989	FTL
Faery Tale Adventure	1989	MicroIllusions
Drakken	1990	Infogrames
Darklands	1991	Microprose
Eye of the Beholder	1991	SSI
Planet's Edge	1992	New World Computing
Ultima Underworld	1992	ORIGIN Systems
Lands of Lore	1993	Westwood Studios
Betrayal at Krondor	1993	Dynamix
Stonekeep	1995	Interplay
Dragon Quest	1996	Enix
Diablo	1996	Blizzard
The Legend of Zelda	1997	Nintendo
Final Fantasy	1997	Square
Fallout	1997	Interplay
Ultima Online	1997	ORIGIN Systems
Baldur's Gate	1998	Bioware
Thief: The Dark Project	1998	Looking Glass Studios
Planescape: Torment	1999	Black Isle
Deus Ex	2000	Aspyr

uncles Crowther and Woods, an antiestablishment hacker ethic only recently revived by crazy cousin John Carmack (of *Doom* fame). *Dungeon Siege* also inherits the basic physics of object interactions from great-uncle Graetz and gets its classically good looks and charm from godfather Neurath. In every feature, there's a member of the family I can see, but at the same time, this child has its own personality, its own style. There's nothing wrong with having come down this particular electronic family tree. It belongs to a long and heroic lineage that would do *any* designer proud. It certainly could have done worse.

I could write up a hundred different RPGs in this history, and I'd still never touch on all the fantastic games and terrific ideas that made this industry what it is today. Off the top of my head I can think of several notable omissions deserving further explorations, which you should conduct on your own. There isn't a console RPG in existence that hasn't been in some way influenced by Nintendo's *Legend of Zelda* or Square's *Final Fantasy* series. Heavily action-oriented RPGs like *Diablo* and *Nox* owe as much to the 1985 Atari coin-op game *Gauntlet* as they do to ORIGIN's PC implementation of *Ultima*. In *Betrayal at Krondor,* John Cutter and I pushed the limits of storytelling and innovated a number of features that other games have since adopted. More recent RPGs like *Fallout, Baldur's Gate, Planescape: Torment,* and *Everquest* have been left out simply because you can still look at those games for yourselves; the long-term ways in which they will change the field are as yet to be determined.

What I hope most that you'll see in this history is how all of these titles are connected and how one often led to another. As you're struggling to put together your own ideas, be aware of the fact that it isn't going to be up to you to create something out of nothing. *You don't have to reinvent the wheel every day.* Many of the games I've mentioned took a preexisting idea and built upon it, sometimes only by changing the content and adding a couple of new features.

This isn't to say you should just blindly rip off everything that's in circulation—I heartily charge you *not* to do that. But being aware of what other people have done, and what they are *still doing,* will only help you make better decisions about what's a good idea and what's a bad one. Best-selling games don't happen by accident. People don't buy gazillions of copies of a game or give them lots of awards if there isn't a good reason that explains that behavior (even mass insanity will have a cause). You might think a game just utterly *bites,* but if it's flying off the store shelves faster than the store clerks can keep copies around, you owe it to yourself to at least look into *why* people enjoy that game. You don't always have to agree with a lunatic to learn something from his madness.

Exercises

1. Look at the current games that you enjoy. Find out when they were released, then see what other games were released about the same time that have similar or identical features. Create a checklist comparing what they have in common and what they don't, then try to find out how each of those games sold. Are there any unique features that might explain why certain games sold better or worse than others? What other factors do you think might have had an impact on sales that have nothing to do with the gameplay itself (bad advertising, a great-looking box, stories about it on television, etc., etc.)?

2. Read industry magazines and watch for designers talking about the games they love. Is a certain title mentioned again and again by designers? If so, locate a copy by whatever legal means you have. If you can't find it for sale in the usual places, try bargain bins and online auction houses, or check with your friends. (Also, look at the publisher's Web site—some companies have copies of their older titles available for download.) Play the game and take notes, concentrating primarily on the gameplay. What do you think it was about the title that drew in people's interest?

3. Borrow or rent a copy of a popular game you think you'll probably hate and play it for as long as you can stand. If it feels different than your preconception about it, what feels better or worse than you expected? Is there anything at all in the title that you enjoy? If so, how do you think you might be able to modify that idea to use in a game of your own?

CHAPTER 3

DEFINING THE PERFECT BEAST—THE FUNDAMENTALS OF THE RPG

"*Gel214th*: By that statement I can anticipate that you perhaps don't consider these Computer RPG's too highly?

"*Gary Gygax*: Not now. They are really action-adventure games with a few RPG elements added. With AI improving, though, that will change. And I enjoy playing such games even as they are—so much so in fact that I stay away from them so as to get my work done."

> — Angel "Gel214th" Stewart & Gary Gygax, *Interview with Gary Gygax: RPG Legend,* www.carigamer.com (October 20, 2000)

"To define is to exclude and negate."

> — Jose Ortega y Gasset, *The Modern Theme*

"Then He asked him, 'What is your name?' And he answered, saying, 'My name is Legion; for we are many.'"

> — Mark 5:9, *The New King James Bible*

Not many years ago at the annual Game Developers Conference held in San Jose, California, a group of designers gathered for a friendly chat about their favorite genre. The hope was that if several of the best-known luminaries of the industry were brought together to discuss the art and science of how role-playing games were made, everyone would walk away with a better understanding of the ground rules for creating top-notch RPGs. In theory it was an excellent idea, but there was one small problem that the panel organizers hadn't fully anticipated when they'd put the session on the schedule. Although the marketing label had been bandied about for nearly two decades, no two people in attendance could agree on what an RPG actually *was*.

The roundtable moderator kicked off the discussion with a vehement rail against *Diablo*. It had recently been selected as the RPG of the year, and he didn't feel it deserved the award, or even the *right* to be included in the RPG category. Spirited dissenters argued that while Blizzard had not officially touted its game as a role-playing title on the box or in its advertising, *Diablo* had many of the hallmarks of an RPG. Another faction pointed out that almost universally, pen-and-paper developers say there's no such thing as a computer role-playing game, and it's patently silly to waste time arguing over a label for something that doesn't really exist in the first place. Fingers were pointed, names were called, and the sacred name of role-playing was defended on all sides from the godless heathens who were obviously bent on soiling the sanctity of the one true genre.

While semantic debates of this sort can be highly entertaining to witness, you shouldn't take them too seriously. Squabbling over which products do or don't qualify as role-playing games is as pointless an activity as two differing sects of one religion arguing over the color of priestly vestments. There's no regulatory commission determining what an RPG should be. When players fire up their favorite adventure, most of them won't care if the gameplay elements match up with some abstract definition. All they care about is having a game that's fun to play.

If you look under the hood of games like *Nox*, *Asheron's Call*, and *Final Fantasy*, you'll find they have more similarities than differences. Certainly each has an individual look, feel, and underlying game mechanic, but they are all unquestionably variations on the same RPG theme. The key is to evaluate what good and bad qualities each brings to the role-playing table, and to use what you learn from each to make better and better games.

Now at the risk of losing my rank as a role-playing guru, let me give you a piece of advice that may offend some RPG purists. Saying that you want to make the best role-playing game that ever existed is a lot like saying you want to make the best cable-access show in downtown Minneapolis. Thinking of your game only in terms of its relationship to a narrowly defined category is to strap on a set of blinders that may prevent you from exploring new ideas. There's absolutely nothing wrong with using the paradigm of the role-playing game as the basic foundation upon which you'll build, but it's only by leaving yourself open to extra-genre concepts that you may find ways to make your title stronger and more entertaining. The point is, don't aim to make the best RPG that ever existed, but set out to create the best game in *any* genre, and use the RPG elements that will best reinforce your goal.

Regardless of what genre you're working in, slavish adherence to preestablished conventions has never been the path to making a memorable game. While *Diablo* offended the sensibilities of some old guard designers, it was also the first computer-driven RPG ever to sell over a million copies. By introducing thousands of new players into the genre, it disproved a long-standing belief held by industry naysayers that role-playing games occupied a niche market incapable of reaching a broader audience. Thanks to the reputation built by its predecessor, *Diablo II* was able not only to retain many of the new players that had been drawn into the genre but also to successfully introduce riskier traditional RPG elements into its second incarnation. The net effect has been to benefit everyone. Not only are players anxious to see

> **Niche Market.** A marketing subcategory referring to a specific group of consumers sharing a specialized interest, demographic, or buying habit.

the third incarnation of the *Diablo* series, but now a much larger audience regularly plays and enjoys titles bearing the RPG marketing label.

For all the flexibility the role-playing genre offers, however, there *are* limits to how far you can mutate a title and still have something that will be recognizable as an RPG. If I were to whip up a pinball game that featured a wizard frantically running through the playfield while avoiding a huge silver ball, it would be nothing short of fraudulent to advertise it as a role-playing title simply because there's a character *somewhere* in the game.

If the RPG label is too broadly applied so that the player can't tell the difference between an RPG, a real-time strategy (RTS) game, and an adventure game, then none of those genre identifications will continue to be useful to game buyers seeking a specific experience. When you intend to label your game as an RPG, therefore, you should attempt to reflect at least *some* of the traditional traits associated with role-playing games in order to earn and sustain the trust of the player. Be assured that ignoring any or all of the basics of the standard RPG will do absolutely no harm to the genre as a whole, but it may damage your company's reputation if it isn't selling what it's advertising.

My Guy: The Roots of Role-Playing

Although role-playing games have only *officially* been around since *Dungeons & Dragons* made its appearance in 1974, a form of them has been with mankind as long as there have been children. If you strip away all the tables, the classes, the world building, the treasures, the play balancing—if you take away all the window dressing but leave the very *heart* of what the role-playing experience is really about—what you're left with is nothing more complex than a good old-fashioned game of make-believe. Depending on who you ask, the game might be called *Let's Pretend,* or *Dress Up,* or *Heroes,* but my personal favorite is *My Guy,* simply because that name describes exactly what children are most concerned with throughout the game—the progression and ultimate success of their "guy."

A typical game of *My Guy* has a rather predictable structure. Before the players do anything, they first sit down to decide what role everyone is going to play during the game. If a bank robbery is the scenario du jour, then everyone involved will decide whether they are going to be the cops, the robbers, or the innocent screaming tellers. (In my childhood games, the tellers usually had short life spans of 20 seconds or so before they got waxed, usually due to the fact that players were too stubborn to hand over the cash to the bad guys.) Sometimes the settings of *My Guy* can turn more surreal, leading to highly imaginative role-playing sessions as children portray cowgirls, spacemen, airline stewardesses, and tyrannosaurs all joining forces to defeat the evil Nazi storm troopers who are bent on an invasion of the planet Mars.

If we compare the opening moments of a role-playing game to the start of a new game of *My Guy,* the differences lie only in the degree of detail that the player first establishes about their *avatar* (i.e., the character they want to play in the game). Depending on the RPG, the gamer might either create a new avatar from scratch using some form of *character generation system,* or they might just pick from a gallery of preexisting avatars who represent different kinds of characters that the gamer might want to play. Just as in *My Guy* a child might choose to play a cowboy or an Indian, a role-player might choose to be a wizard or a princess, a private eye or an alien bounty hunter. What both experiences allow is for the gamer to step temporarily into the skin of a fictional character and assume the role of a hero—or in some cases an antihero—and pretend for a

The terminology for role-playing games can often become quite muddy, with several terms often being used interchangeably to refer to what might seem like essentially the same thing. Here's a quick rundown of several identity-related terms that are frequently used in RPGs:

- ◆ **Avatar.** The on-screen representation of the character that is being controlled by the player. The avatar is the entity that takes damage, swings swords, opens doors, and otherwise does everything that the player bids them to do.

- ◆ **DM, or Dungeon Master.** A term dating back to the pen-and-paper days of role-playing. A DM is an individual who creates a role-playing milieu and is generally in charge of guiding players through the experience. Although in recent years it has had little applicability in the computer gaming arena because the DM's traditional duties have been handled by the computer, a whole new generation of computer-driven RPGs are enabling DMs to create new gaming experiences and share them with others via the Internet. (*Vampire: The Masquerade—Redemption* and Bioware's upcoming release of *Neverwinter Nights* are both examples of this new hybrid form of RPG.)

- ◆ **Monster.** Any creature or individual in the game who is bent on killing the player. A bear, a dragon, or an angry castle guard are all regarded as monsters if they're trying to actively slay the player's avatar.

- ◆ **NPC, or Nonplayer Character.** This refers to any characters that can be met in the game whose actions are not controlled by the player.

- ◆ **Player.** The real-world person who is sitting at the computer and playing the game.

- ◆ **PC, or Player Character.** This term is sometimes used interchangeably with the word *avatar.* For all intents and purposes, it means exactly the same thing.

short while what it might be like to *be* that kind of person. For a brief period of time the player is given permission to pretend to be all the things they could never be in real life, to do all the things that might be dangerous, illegal, or impossible in the world of day-to-day reality.

For all the possibilities for imaginative play posed by *My Guy*, the biggest problem confronted by the players is that the game very rarely has a set of consistently applicable rules. While all children understand that if another player catches them in the open and announces that they have been shot, stabbed, gassed, lasered, clubbed, or generally fragged, there is still always the tendency to want to manufacture a Johnny-on-the-spot rule that somehow "fixes" the undesirable end result. Go to any park where kids are playing and you'll ultimately hear a conversation that goes a little something like this:

> *Player 1:* Bang! I shot you, you're DEAD!
>
> *Player 2:* Unh uhh, you're out of bullets!
>
> *Player 1:* Am not! I only fired four times!
>
> *Player 2:* Yeah, but My Guy stole two bullets from you, so you're OUT!
>
> *Player 1:* Oh yeah, well My Guy knew you were stealin' 'em, and he had another clip hidden and he reloaded!
>
> *Player 2:* Don't matter, 'cause I've got a bulletproof vest!
>
> *Player 1:* My Guy knew where you keep your vest, so he went back in time and he took out all the plates and put in explosive wadding, so not only are you dead, you're blown to bits! Ha HA. . . .

Children can be remarkably creative in their efforts to save their make-believe characters. In the hands of the right kinds of players, these exchanges can develop into an entertaining game of one-upmanship that usually ends with both players achieving the status of omnipotent gods capable of warping all laws of time and space. More commonly, however, the game usually devolves into an all-too-real fistfight and shouting match, coming to a close only after a concerned parent drags both the screaming upstart deities off the playing field for a stern lecture on how to play nice.

Where RPGs depart from these poorly thought-out childhood games of imagination is in the way that they structure the experience. By creating a universal system of reasonable, unbreakable rules, role-playing games allow players to interact in fun but fair situations in which all the players have a reasonable chance of success—providing, of course, the players don't try and do something that's obviously stupid, such as an inexperienced peasant whacking a dragon in the knees with a garden hoe.

In the online game of *Everquest* when two players are engaged in a battle to the death, the matter of who wins or loses is not going to be determined by one player simply announcing to another player that they've been seen, so therefore they're dead. What will happen instead is that both players will guide their PCs through the motions of the combat, using all the native skills with which they have gifted their avatars. If the players are duking it out with swords, the game engine will take into account how strong both the avatars are, how skilled each is with their weapons, and what kind of armor each might be wearing to protect themselves. Equally important to the outcome is the matter of *random chance,* taking into account the fact even the most skilled individuals in the world aren't going to be successful at what they attempt 100 percent of the time. Instead of delivering a highly subjective judgment about who wins based only on the capabilities of the players to out-scream new rules at one another, the game will allow only the luckiest, most experienced, best armored, and most clever-thinking warrior to win the day.

The real beauty of the RPG is in the way it allows the player to attempt things they can otherwise only dream of. While playing *My Guy* in the front yard with my buddies, I always liked to *imagine* that I was the speedy superhero The Flash, but the reality was that I was a fat, stubby little asthmatic kid who was never going to catch the other players unless they tripped, ran into dead ends, or simply took pity on me. While I could *think* of myself as The Flash, the experience didn't match up with what I was able to do in the game.

By contrast, whenever I play a role-playing game, the rules allow my avatar to do everything that I imagine him able to do. If I'm playing a character that's a wizard, he can cast arcane spells to walk through walls or freeze enemy characters in place. If I'm out to save the galaxy from an alien menace, my character is able to crack even the toughest alien computer codes and hit a Xarrglebeast at 80 yards with a standard issue pocket blaster. For every unusual thing a player tries to do, a good role-playing game should have mechanisms in place that allow the player to attempt to do the seemingly impossible.

Randomness & RPGs

The interjection of an element of random chance into any gaming situation is really what makes gameplay both challenging and exciting. The biblical story of David and Goliath is an entertaining story because all the odds are against David, but he gets lucky and drops the giant. If it were 100 percent sure bet that Luke Skywalker would get the torpedo down the ventilation shaft in *Star Wars*, the ending of the movie would lack the dramatic tension that kept audience members glued to the edges of their seats. Keep in mind that randomness = risk = danger = emotional involvement. Always make sure there is always at least a remote possibility for the player to win or lose at every step of your game. *Nothing* should be absolutely certain.

Although computers don't use real dice in order to generate random content, it's not unusual to hear designers using phrases that are throwbacks to the dice-driven days of the pen-and-paper RPGs. When players are allowed to create characters, some designers speak of "rolling up PCs." When referring to how tough a monster is, you may hear someone say that a monster has "10d6+7 hit dice"—an indication that the creature in question has somewhere between 17 and 67 *hit points*. How did I decode this mystical range? 10d6+7 is old role-player's shorthand for "Roll 10 six-sided dice, and then add seven to the result." Using that formula, 17 is the lowest number I can roll, and 67 is the highest, thus yielding a 17–67 point spread.

The Defining Ingredient: Developing the Role of the Player Character

No matter what other features or qualities are lumped into the mix, role-playing games are at their root about the player's identification with one or more avatars. Through these alter egos the player will be able to explore the game world and perform all the tasks required to save the planet, rescue the prince, or uncover whatever dark conspiracy may be lurking in the shadows. But the characters over whom the player exercises control need to be more than just human-shaped vehicles with an attitude. The player should always perceive them as though they are living, breathing individuals with needs, feelings, and problems all their own. It should be a cause for grief if an avatar is somehow lost to the schemes of the opposition, or a moment of pride when the PC is awarded a new level or honor for a quest well done. Developing ways to foster the player's intimacy of feeling for their avatar should remain a priority throughout the development of any RPG title. As one player reported in Sherry Turkle's scientific journal article *Parallel Lives: Working on Identity in Virtual Space*, "You are who you pretend to be. . . . You are who you play."

As in the real world, first impressions count. The way in which the player is first introduced to their character will likely shape their long-term feelings about that individual. If the introduction is bland and generic, you can expect no strong feelings on the part of the player toward the plight of the viewpoint character. If, however, the on-screen alter ego is first presented in such a way that the player can see that they are a lifesaving hero, or a wrongly accused star pilot, the player will have much greater interest in forming a close emotional bond to both their person and their cause.

The ways in which players have been introduced to their avatars over the years have run the gamut from the straightforward to the peculiar. In *Ultima IV*, players used a very unorthodox character generation system which required that they answer some basic moral questions which would form the basis for the on-screen protagonist's abilities. Other systems have stuck with a more traditional means of rolling up characters at the beginning of the game or simply handing over a pregenerated character for the player to control. For all the different variations on the theme, there are really only three basic methods that seem to be commonly used, each of which cedes a different level of control over the avatar's initial traits, abilities, and appearance.

- **Character Generation.** This approach is typified by games like *Baldur's Gate*. At the start of the game, the player is presented with a series of screens from which they must make several choices about the avatar's name, what sex they will be, what they will look like, what race they belong to, and what profession and specialization they're involved with, and the player may even be required to repeatedly click on buttons to "roll up" a new character, or the player may have to decide how to divvy up points between the avatar's many initial attributes.

Advantages: Games that utilize a character generation system cede a significant amount of control to the player over the initial qualities of the avatar and often are very popular with people who are familiar with role-playing games in general.

Disadvantages: Character generation screens tend to look overly complex to novice players. For those who are unfamiliar with the genre, a screen full of buttons asking for input on things they don't yet understand the significance of is an unnecessary turnoff and something that bars quick entry into the game.

- **Class Selection.** *Diablo II* is an excellent example of a game that provides a class selector. At the beginning of the game, the player is allowed to choose their avatar from a selection of different professional classes (e.g., warrior, mage, thief, etc., etc.) and is asked to give a name to their avatar.

    Advantages: Class selectors allow players to very quickly identify the basic kind of character they want to play and turn them loose into the gameplay very rapidly.

    Disadvantages: Games that feature class selectors have historically been bound to a class and level system, meaning players will be necessarily stuck with whatever skills and restrictions are associated with the class that they choose at the start of the game.

- **The Foundling Approach.** *Final Fantasy VII* is an example of the foundling method of avatar introduction. In a situation that doesn't seem much different than discovering a baby left on the doorstep, the player is given no control over the initial attributes of the avatar, but they are often given a limited degree of freedom to control the ways in which the character develops through the title, thus allowing them to "grow" the character of their choice.

    Advantages: Players aren't required to understand any of the complexities of classes, skills, or attributes and can immediately jump into the gameplay.

    Disadvantages: Although games of this variety generally provide a means by which hirelings can be brought into the group, the player is usually stuck with a main character they haven't chosen and who may not reflect the kind of character that the player really wants to play.

Once the avatar has been either generated or otherwise introduced to the player, the next thing most people want to do is get into the thick of everything and take a look around. While an unimaginative designer will treat this as nothing more than an exploration of the outer world, a savvy game developer will use this initial experience as a means to educate the player about the *inner* world of their character. By providing a rich environment in which the abilities of the avatar can be showcased, you'll be giving the player the chance to get to know more about their on-screen alter ego. A rough-and-tumble PC might be able to kick down a door that would be impervious to others. If there's a computer console glowing in a corner somewhere, a hacker-oriented character should be able to do something at the console that might be denied to a less computer-literate kind of character. In terms of an interactive experience, always remember Neal's First Law of Character Development: *Game characters are what they can do.*

Attributes and Skills

Adventuring around in any kind of role-playing universe will inevitably lead the player's characters into dangerous or challenging circumstances. As each experience is encountered, the avatar should learn from their successes and failures, honing their skills and wits as they gain mastery over the roles to which they have been assigned. If the player's avatar is only a humble hedge mage at the beginning of the game, she may develop through multiple stages of competence until at the end of the story, she is the most powerful sorceress in all the land. Continuously providing opportunities for the player's characters to grow and develop throughout the role-playing experience is absolutely critical. If a game cannot offer meaningful character advancement perceptible either through the story or through the character's statistics, a title cannot rightfully be considered a role-playing game.

The easiest way to represent character advancement in an RPG is to break down everything about the avatar into some form of a numerical statistic and then increment those factors upward as the player grows stronger, smarter, and more efficient at their jobs. These *statistics* can then in turn be used as a yardstick by which the player can measure their progress.

The statistics that reflect the innate physical capabilities of an avatar are frequently referred to by the umbrella term of *attributes*. Things like a character's strength, speed, dexterity, health, intelligence, and general appearance are all usually covered by the attribute tag and collectively represent all those capabilities that an avatar natively possesses without any training. (To these standard attributes, *Call of Cthulhu* also adds the delightful *Sanity* quotient, measuring how much psychic shock a player can take before losing their mind.) The one attribute with which the player will be concerned more than any other is the health or *hit points* attribute, which measures how much physical damage the avatar can take before dying (or in some cases only falling unconscious). Depending on the game system, attributes may grow very slowly or not at all. Because they are usually tied to the character's physical body, making significant changes to an avatar's attributes can sometimes have unbalancing effects on other aspects of the gameplay.

Were the player's characters nothing more than the sum of their inborn talents and deficiencies, there would be little reason for them to travel far from home. Unable to learn or to adapt to the challenges of the outside world, they would find a multitude of unpleasant deaths awaiting them in even the most unheroic of situations. It is only thanks to the avatar's ability to develop *skills* that they will be able to triumph over the challenges they will face. A thieflike character might acquire talents for picking pockets, breaking locks, and moving about stealthily. A starship engineer is likely to be more concerned with picking up abilities that would allow her to evaluate broken ion drives, repair weaponry, or hack into failing computer systems. The set of skills the player chooses to develop in each avatar becomes an integral reflection of who those characters are and what their primary function will be within the game.

Like attributes, skills are usually expressed numerically, though they often take a slightly different form. In a *percentile skills system,* an avatar's skill level might be represented as a number between 0 and 100, reflecting their basic chance to succeed at a given task. (Thus, if Zorg the Monk has an Arrow Snatching skill of 20 percent, that means he has a 20 percent chance of grabbing the flaming arrow that's zipping its fiery way toward him. If when the player directs Zorg to snatch down the arrow and the computer makes a random roll of 34—rolling a percentage *greater than* 20 percent and thus too high to succeed—Zorg will miss the arrow and possibly even take damage in the attempt.) In a *threshold skills system,* the avatar is assigned a basic skill level that is then pitted against a difficulty rating for a given task. If the difficulty threshold is higher than the player's ability, then the attempt simply fails, and no element of chance has any influence on the attempt one way or the other.

Both the percentile and threshold systems have their supporters as well as their critics. Some modern developers insist the old percentile system is archaic and inappropriate in a computer gaming situation, failing to take into account that the player can *save* before trying certain skills, thus rendering the whole issue of randomness moot. (For example, in many of the *D&D*-based games, a memorization "skill roll" is made by the computer every time a mage attempts to learn a new spell from a scroll. If the mage succeeds, then the spell is memorized and added to their spell book. If it fails, then the scroll dissolves and the mage can't make any further attempts. If, however, the player saves immediately before trying to memorize the spell, they can continue to reload from the save point until the computer finally makes a successful memorization roll on behalf of the mage.)

While the threshold system successfully eliminates the save and reload cycle unfavorably associated with the percentile system, it also eliminates any chance of a lucky shot. The underskilled slinger David could *never* hit Goliath, and the novice safecracker could never accidentally stumble on the right combination. A threshold system enforces a certain unrealistic rigidity to the gaming universe, making it less friendly to players who may be a hair underprepared for certain tasks.

Regardless of which you use, the value of such systems is that they provide a means by which the character can grow and develop throughout the title. As characters survive and overcome the obstacles in their path, they'll accumulate *experience points*. These experience points can then be distributed by the player among the skills of their choice in a skill-based system. In a class and level system, the player is automatically granted a new level of skill proficiency once a certain threshold has been reached.

Classes, Levels, and Character Differentiation

Skill systems of various stripes can play an important role in helping a player define who their characters are. One problem that can crop up without proper design consideration involves the tendency for all the avatars in a player's party—or all the characters in a multiplayer online environment—to develop an overly homogeneous set of skills. If all characters in a game are unrestricted in the number of skills they can learn and are equally capable of learning all skills, the tendency on the player's part is to act like a concerned parent. They want to see their alter egos optimally prepared for all possible scenarios and as a result will try and max out all of the skills possessed by their avatars. While in the real world such relentless attempts at self-improvement are to be commended, in a gaming world this results in an environment full of generic characters who skill-wise have nothing to distinguish themselves from any *other* characters. This problem is known as the *character differentiation dilemma,* and over the years designers have struggled with various schema to balance the freedom of player choice with the maintenance of a diversely talented gaming populous.

The oldest solution to this problem involves the inclusion of a *class and level system.* Under this arrangement, when a player either selects or creates a new avatar, the new character is bound to a rigidly defined class or profession that dictates exactly which skills they can develop, and in some cases what kinds of objects they can or cannot use. In exchange for binding themselves into these narrowly defined *class* categories, characters usually receive some kind of gameplay bonus. They may gain more experience and learn faster from certain kinds of experiences than they do from others or receive special new abilities for each new *level* of mastery that they achieve in their class. Thus, if a space marine and a laboratory tech were both to get into fisticuffs with an alien pugilist, the space marine might gain more experience for his fighting skills simply because that's related to his particular profession. If the space marine learns enough from the fight that he gains a new level of expertise, he may have figured out a new attack to use against opponents, which will become part of his permanent skill set.

Another somewhat less elaborate solution to the character differentiation dilemma involves the employment of a *skills limiting system,* whereby each character is given a limited number of skill slots that can be filled with any collection of skills that the player so chooses. In a way this can function much like a less restrictive class system, but unless the player is required to take at least a few skills from several different categories, a system like this may accidentally end up hamstringing the player. If for instance the player decides that they really like the sound of the Animal Sense, Track Beast, Food Preparation, and Aardvark Conversation skills, they may find themselves utterly unable to get from point A to point B safely if they haven't picked any combat skills with which to defend themselves. The flip side of this coin, however, is that if a character in this particular predicament is in an online world, they can find other characters in the environment who can offset their limitations, and each individual should have valuable skills and services to offer the others.

If you aren't too keen on the Malthusian idea of limiting the total number of skills a player can use, there are still a few other options that are open to you. One is to employ a *skills capping* methodology, so that the more skills the avatar possesses, the maximum competency that an avatar can achieve in any one of them is limited. This leaves the player with the option of self-limiting their character's skills in order to achieve higher levels of competency. Another variation is the old "use it or lose it" principle. In *Ultima Online,* if a player doesn't use certain skills for a while, their level of competency in those skills degrades, forcing the player to make a decision about what skills they wish to keep current in the game, and which ones they'll let lapse into obscurity.

A last solution is to essentially eliminate the use of a skills system altogether, investing the avatar's special abilities in unique objects that can be found in the world. Instead of Spider Bob the superhero having a special innate ability to climb a wall, he's able to find a one-of-a-kind pair of boots that allow him to sticky foot it up any vertical incline. For as long as Bob has the boots, there's only one person playing on that particular server that has the ability to walk up a wall. To further limit Bob's actions, objects that endow him with unusual abilities might be made very large so that they take up several spaces in a limited size inventory or made heavy so that the player can't carry more than one or two of them at a time. In effect, this means Bob would be able to use his special ability only by surrendering his capability of carrying other large or special objects. The advantage of course is that each character is forced to behave in different ways, and thus is vaguely *characterized* in different ways, based on the items they are carrying in their pockets.

The Lesser Seven Ingredients of the Classic RPG

Aside from the genre-definitive quality of strong character development, RPGs tend to be strongly associated with seven other characteristics. These qualities are sometimes also found in other computer gaming genres, but they each play a critical part in creating the overall ethos of the classic role-playing title. There are other designers who would add even more qualities to this list, but these are the seven irreducible factors that, in my opinion, a great RPG simply cannot do without.

Immersive Exploration

The opening lines of the *Star Trek* television program embody the very heart and soul of what the best role-playing games should be all about: to boldly go where no one has gone before. In no other gaming genre is it so wholly important that the player have the feeling they have been transported to an entirely new world, whether it be a land of dragons or a far-flung future ruled by killer robots. Second in importance only to the growth of the character, role-playing fans demand that the worlds into which their characters are introduced are immersive, compelling, intricate, and internally consistent. Every character the player meets and every bit of world mythology the player is exposed to should feel as though they are drawn from a real, living history, not just fluff that fills in the gaps between quests.

Epic Story

Being dumped into an exotic alien locale may be diverting for a while, but unless there's something going on in the environment that will involve the player and pique their interest, there's really no reason for them being there. In a single-player game, there should be significant reason for the player to take action, a threat that demands a heroic response. This doesn't mean that the entire world must hang in the balance, but the events that draw the player into the action must be in some way important to the avatar. A friend may have been kidnapped or the PC's home or reputation may be on the line. Whatever the larger situation into which the character is thrown, the player must be made to empathize with their plight and therefore care about solving their problem.

Virtually every review of a role-playing title has something to say about story, quests, threads, and linearity. What gamers seem most concerned with is that they have some choice in where they go, when they go, and how much influence they have over events in the game. Players don't wish to feel as though they are being led on a rope or forced to do something in some predetermined way that the designer has in mind. The story of an RPG needs to invite, intrigue, and inspire, but leave the actual action up to the player.

Combat

If the characters in an RPG are well developed, and they are given enough of a life that they seem believable and alive to the player, the greatest emotional involvement you can incite is to threaten the life of the avatar. If life and death are the stakes, the player cannot help but respond in defense.

An exciting, intuitive, and fast-paced combat interface will do as much for the success of your RPG as almost any other factor. In many cases it will be the prime draw for certain kinds of players, especially if action is the primary thrust of your RPG.

Interim Quests

Saving the world can take a lot of time. Gamers will spend somewhere between 100 and 200 hours playing the average RPG, so it behooves a designer to give players small interim goals, or *quests,* to complete, which may or may not be in support of the larger problem the player is out to solve. (In most massively multiplayer games, these may well be the *only* problems the designer hands out for the player to deal with, which makes them all the more important to the game.) A quest can be as simple as an old man sending a player to go and find an artifact that's been mislaid or as complex as the Federation president ordering the player to destroy a starbase that is holding up a stellar war convoy.

Whatever the scale of the task, there should always be a good reason for why the player should go out of their way to accomplish the stated goal. They should be rewarded with money, items, resources, or maybe just a favor that will help them elsewhere in the game. Subquests also provide a way of patting the character on the back and making them feel good for having accomplished something. Even when the big goal may lie far ahead of the player, these smaller milestones will keep the egos of the players pumped up and make them feel good about continuing forward through the game.

By providing multiple solution paths to single problems, you'll give players a sense that there's more than one way to get through the game—an especially important concept to convey if the game's overall experience has a strongly linear structure. If your aim is to create a game with a high degree of replayability, quests that vary based on the actions of your hero can also be a very powerful way to entice players to go back and try different paths.

Grabbing Treasure

Exploring the world of an RPG should feel a little bit like a shopping spree crossed with a treasure hunt. Players are always curious about what they will find in boxes, and barrels, and crates, and bookcases. Anything that looks like it might be some kind of *inventory* container is going to attract the attention of players, and it's going to be up to you to decide what they're going to find when they go looking. You might provide them with weapons, with ammo, with magic items, with treasure, or even with new kinds of clothing. Whatever you do, you should strive to give players things that they can actually use in the course of the game. Avoid creating *dead squirrels* at all costs. It's fine to employ an object as the goal of a quest, but let the player be able to do *something* with it while it's in their possession.

One of the major joys of playing an RPG comes from finding cool new stuff and then putting it into the hands of the avatar. With these new discoveries, the player's character should become faster, smarter, tougher, or more skillful at all the things they need to accomplish. Never underestimate how much fun players can have just playing "dress up the avatar" with all the goodies they've picked up.

Dead Squirrel. An object that has no usable function for the avatar but which must be ferried around in order to complete some task or quest. This is in opposition to a *vibrating blue squirrel*, which is any random common object that can be found in an inventory container or on the body of a slain opponent.

Resource Management

Historically, the management of resources has always been a major part of role-playing games. Players have often been required to manage a variety of mundane tasks on behalf of their avatars, including making sure that the characters have enough to eat, that they're getting enough sleep, and even that all their weaponry has been oiled and sharpened. In recent years, RPGs seem to be trending away from such mundanity in an effort to streamline the overall play experience.

Even with this trend toward simplicity, most RPGs still require that the player employ a degree of strategic thinking about the management of their expendable resources. Because certain items are rare or hard to find in the world, players need to think about when the right time will be to use battery packs, arrows, bullets, health kits, magic potions, or mana (the power required to cast spells). Role-playing games also usually force players to think about how they'll use whatever money they have on hand, and whether it is better spent on buying better weapons or on bribing the troublesome castle guards.

Problem Solving

The last hallmark of the RPG is its presentation of a wide spectrum of challenges that the player will have to solve during the gameplay. In combat the player must continuously develop new and different strategies as they encounter increasingly deadly monsters. The gamer occasionally will confront mind-bending puzzles and aggravating traps that have been set for them in dark dungeons and madmen's mansions. At a more abstract level, players will have to decide which NPCs are to be believed and which are pointing the way to destruction. Judging what the best course of action will be with the resources and information they have on hand is a big part of the RPG, as is dealing with the minutia of how best to arrange the marching order of the party in an attempt to ensure their survival in the case of a surprise attack.

Keep in mind that a merely good RPG can be highly exciting over a short period of time. An outstanding title that lasts in the long run is the one which is always presenting a new and different kind of challenge to the player so that they're always having to use their head. Never, ever, ever, ever give the player a chance to develop a "same old stuff, different level" mentality about your game.

The Big Picture

When thinking about any of the principles that I have listed above, I urge you *not* to think of them as a grocery list of features or qualities that you *have* to put into your game. They are neither ingredients in a unchangeable recipe, nor are they sacred dictates that were carved into golden tablets on some stormy, eldritch mountaintop. Feel free to leave parts out that you don't like, move things around, or substitute new ideas for old concepts that won't work with your basic gaming premise. The purpose of looking at these role-playing basics is not to throw a leash around your neck and tell you what you have to do, but instead to give you a grounding on what's been done before, and give you a starting point from which you can start developing your own exciting game concepts.

The enduring power of the RPG lies in its ability to transcend the mundane, to take players to exciting and interesting new worlds and give them the opportunity to make a difference in the fate of families, towns, kingdoms, or galaxies. If there is one message that seems to be implicit in all role-playing games, it's that *individual people have the capacity to make a difference.* Don't forget this lesson. It is a primary reason why many people choose to play role-playing games, and it is something you need to reinforce at every level of your game.

Exercises

1. Think about the Character Differentiation Dilemma and see if you can come up with your own solution to encouraging individuality among avatars/players.

2. Study a non-RPG game and try and see if you can identify any RPG-like elements that may be in it. If you were asked to include RPG elements into it that weren't present, what would you interject? How do you think it would change the gameplay?

Part Two

The Designer's Domain

CHAPTER 4

We Few, We Happy Few— Designers and the Team

"The history of the world is but the biography of great men."

> —Thomas Carlyle, *Heroes and Hero Worship: The Hero as Divinity*

"Search the parks in all your cities

You'll find no statues of committees."

> —David Ogilvy, *Ogilvy on Advertising*

"We few, we happy few, we band of brothers;

For he today that sheds his blood with me

Shall be my brother; be he ne'er so vile,

This day shall gentle his condition;

And gentlemen in England now a-bed

Shall think themselves accurs'd they were not here,

And hold their manhoods cheap while any speaks

That fought with us upon Saint Crispin's day!"

> —William Shakespeare, *Henry V,* Act IV, Scene III

Becoming a professional game designer is a lot like joining a UFO cult. Oh sure, you won't be issued a spiffy black sweatsuit and a white pair of Nikes whenever you sign up, but as far as how people outside the industry will view you, you might as well be someone waiting for the mothership to come down and take you away.

Try as you might to explain what it is that you do for a living, unless you're talking to someone moderately initiated into the mysteries of computer entertainment, you've got virtually no chance of having anybody understand what you're saying to them. When I meet strangers on trains and they ask me what I do for a living, I usually just tell people I write technical manuals and leave it at that. A few times I've actually 'fessed up to the truth about my game designing occupation, only to be treated to the glassy-eyed, tight-lipped, somewhat resentful what-kind-of-no-account-underachieving-computer-hacking-freakazoid-are-you stare, which is usually accompanied by the socially permitted utterance, "It must be so *nice* to get paid to play games all day." I frequently have to chew off the end of my tongue to keep from firing back, "Yeah, that *would* be nice. I sure as hell wish that's how I earned my paycheck every month."

The plain fact of the matter is, *playing* a game is nothing even remotely like *making* one. People don't assume that watching a movie is a process equivalent to directing one, and yet surprisingly enough, that's the gist of most people's misunderstanding of the game design process. It's as if we game designers just sat around in our offices all day blithely playing and playing and playing while a magical game design machine spat out new titles whenever we hit the mega-bonus round in our super-secret unreleased advance copies of *Diablo XVII*. Trust me, if such a terrific device were really available, I'd have 10 of them cranking away in my office so I *could* sit around playing games all the time. Unfortunately, no one has invented the Santa Claus game machine yet. Like every other poor schlub on the planet, I've got to spend my workweek trying to get all the millions of things done that need doing so that at some point, some entertainment-starved soul can sit down, switch on their computer, and enjoy playing an all-new role-playing adventure.

Admittedly, most of the time, a designer's job can be a lot of fun to do. Most days, I love what I do. There are few things more rewarding than working your tailbone off for two years and then having people from all over the globe raving about how much fun they're having in a world of your creation. Just short of sex, chocolate, and standing in the actual shadow of Westminster Abbey while eating a fistful of Jelly Babies, there are few things you can experience that will be more energizing than tossing ideas back and forth with your team members and watching your idea grow from a few sketchy ideas on paper into a fully realized virtual world.

But for all the rewards you'll reap both personally and professionally in the computer gaming industry, you have to realize a game designer's job requires long hours, intense dedication, and lots and lots of very hard work. I don't know many designers who have the luxury of a 9 to 5 schedule; 10 to 10 seems to be a much more common day for most people. It isn't at all uncommon for me to be up and out of bed at three o'clock in the morning, hammering away at something that has to be done for a specific milestone or the company loses millions of dollars for a schedule slippage. There are very few other jobs I can think of that regularly send otherwise healthy 20-something-year-old workers to the hospital with stress- and fatigue-related illnesses. Before you go charging off to become a designer, you need to ask yourself if you're really up to a job that will frequently push you past your breaking point. If you aren't capable or willing to put in 110 percent *all the time,* this isn't going to be a career for you. If, however, you're willing to occasionally sleep underneath your desk, give up any pretext of a social life, spend most of your time with your coworkers, and commit every drop of your creativity to the amusement of other people . . . you may just have the right stuff to be one of the few, the proud, the desperately in need of caffeine.

The 10 (or 15) Virtues of a Good Game Designer

Assuming you aren't wholly averse to the Vampirella-like complexion you'll develop while chained to your computer, there are a few other qualities that all good game designers have in common, and which I highly recommend you cultivate if you really think you're cut out for the game designing lifestyle:

- **You're an Avid Game Player.** I've stated this point before, and I'll continue to hammer this point home throughout this book, but I really can't stress this enough. In order to be someone who makes good games, you

Passing Milestones
(or, Maybe You'd Better Sit Down for This)

When you're working on a game, you'll usually be called on by the powers-that-be to take all the tasks that need to be done and divide them into smaller chunks of work known as *milestones*. Each represents a stage in a project's development, so milestones are important in helping producers or project managers keep track of your game's progress.

Hitting milestones on time is frequently a cause for celebration—it's a sad-but-true fact that historically very few game projects ever come out on time or on budget. This is largely due to overambitious goals set by team members coupled with the fact that creative people tend to be notoriously bad at making good estimates. Whenever a team member tells you how long something will take, multiply their answer by two or three and you'll probably be in about the right neighborhood. (This is sometimes referred to as Scotty's Rule #1.)

While missing milestones is all too common, it isn't something you can take lightly as a designer. Missing one or two milestones *might* not bring about the end of the world, but depending on the severity of your slip-pages or the number of milestones you miss, you could still end up losing your whole project if you don't get a handle on things. Do everything possible to avoid slipping if you can, and always have a plan for how you may be able to trim fat off each milestone if things start to look undoable. It will always be better to ship a product that might not be *all* that you originally dreamed of than to have the whole kit and kaboodle go down the tubes just because you couldn't let go of one or two details that were really unimportant in the larger scheme of things.

need to be someone who both *enjoys* playing games and has both a depth and a breadth of game playing experience. You'll get *depth* from playing a handful of games very intensely, learning very intimately how the rules are structured and what kinds of strategies of gameplay emerge from the experience. *Breadth* of experience comes from playing many, many different kinds of games in many different genres. Don't just limit yourself to RPGs. Play real-time strategy titles, adventure games, puzzle games, flight simulators. If you've got children, play *Where in the World Is Carmen Sandiego?* with them. Leap off your computer for a while and try your hand at traditional board games like *Risk*, *Diplomacy*, or *Talisman*. Challenge the next-door neighborhood kid to a round of *Starfleet Battles* or *Magic: The Gathering*. No matter whether the game is good, bad, or somewhere in between, you'll often find there's a game design lesson to be learned.

- **You're a Creative Person.** Players want to see something new and different when they fire up a computer game. If they didn't, they'd keep playing the same thing over and over and over again and there'd never be a multimillion dollar industry cranking out hundreds of new titles every year. You've got to be innovative, but there are a multitude of different ways to be a "creative" person. You might do it by creating an entirely new style of gameplay or a milieu into which role-playing has never been taken before. Another way of using your creativity is to fuse together existing ideas into a new form, like taking the style of one game and meshing it with the gameplay elements of another. The important thing is that you have the capability to take players down a path unlike anything they've ever experienced before.

- **You're a Curious Person.** All role-playing designers are really dabblers in about a dozen different subjects. Knowing a little bit about *real* medieval history will help you create more convincing fantasy role-playing games as you deal with siege engines, and castles, and knights, and crossbows, and similar trappings. Studying psychology and sociology can give you a better understanding of how people think during gaming situations and will help you create better ways for players to interact with the game or with each other. A high-tech RPG might shine a little brighter if the designer has spent some time studying astronomy, genetics, or nanotechnology. No matter what subgenre of RPG you're out to make, it will never hurt to crack open the textbooks or get out in the world and *do* some of the things you're trying to represent on the small screen. (For the benefit of all the nervous mothers of hyperactive teens out there, let me qualify this by saying that I do *not* endorse that you try to rob the bank, chop your neighbor's python to bits with a broadsword, or hack into the federal government's missile defense system. Wait to do all these things until aliens are invading or your Aunt Matilda morphs into a blood-sucking mind flayer out to rig the local PTA elections.) Be curious about the world you're in, and *use* everything you learn to more effectively twist, warp, and change all the rules as you know them. If you've got the opportunity, get thee to a university and take some classes. A higher education will *never* hurt your game designs or your long-range career goals.

- **You're a Critical Thinker.** If the old saying holds that "god is in the details," game designers need to be as "godlike" as possible. They need to be comfortable with studying problems and finding the simplest, most logical solutions. It's good to be the kind of person who takes things apart to find out how they work or who tries to guess who the murderer is before the movie detective does. A designer needs to be able to look at the rules of the game and understand where conflicts in game logic may arise and have solutions that will be fair and will make sense to the player. Having a strong objective sense about the trade-offs that various features of the game will present is a true bonus, and being fully prepared to cut or modify things that interfere with smooth or entertaining gameplay is an absolute necessity.

- **You Must Be Ambitious.** No successful company has ever put a sticker on the outside of a box that says that product X is "the second-best role-playing game of the year!!" or is "nearly as good as somebody else's game!" No gamer is interested in buying the second-best game any more than a development house is interested in making one. When you walk in the door and hand off your resume to a prospective employer, they've got to believe you've got the ambition not to make an "okay" seller, not to create a "not-bad" seller, but to create a no-holds-barred, runaway, can't-keep-it-on-the-store-shelves best-seller. Anything else will be a waste of the company's time and resources. Obviously, your ambition has to be tempered by a realistic estimation of your own abilities and a critical understanding of the resources you have on hand. But if you wish to make a long-term career in this business, you must always be aiming high.

- **You're an Organized Person.** Role-playing games require the generation of an enormous pile of stuff. Getting your game conceptualized efficiently and effectively, and then getting that concept developed on time and on budget, will require organizational skills that will sometimes rival the 10 Feats of Hercules. You'll need the ability to track whether or not all the art, programming, and sound effects for a new monster are being implemented on time, and you'll need to be able to keep straight which list of things are being *added* to the project and which list of things are being *cut*. You'll need a talent for understanding how something like a lag in the development of the game script may impact the recording schedule you've slated for late March, which in turn may force you to rethink whether you're sending your sound person off to Game Developers Conference. In many ways you'll need to be something like a project Rosetta Stone, wherein all things are analyzed, stored, and cataloged. The ability to think in terms of both the needs of the game and the needs of the team will be crucial, and at a moment's notice you'll need to be able to find and convey critical information to whoever needs it.

- **You're a Good Leader.** A game project needs someone at the helm who not only has the capacity to come up with great ideas but who also is the kind of person that people naturally want to rally behind. Lead by example. Be the kind of heroic boss that people respect rather than fear, and never ask the team members to do things you wouldn't be willing to do yourself. Keep in mind the people around you may not have as much vested in the project as you do, and they may not be receiving the same level of compensation for what they're contributing. It's one thing for you to stay all weekend long and do whatever needs doing when you're pulling down in excess of 50K a year. It's quite a different matter if you're asking for a second-string artist to do the same thing when he's making half your salary and doesn't have nearly the same level of benefits. If you're going to demand performance above and beyond the call of duty, give people a real incentive to do the extra work.

- **You Care About the Player Experience.** Few things will be more valuable to you than the ability to voluntarily step back from your project and develop a degree of amnesia about it. Forget all the good things you intended or everything the players were meant to see or understand. You need to be able to *see* how someone who isn't a game designer and who isn't even necessarily an experienced game player will view what you've put in front of them. The best designers in the industry are the ones who are the most capable of regressing to this level of player naiveté.

- **You're a "Down Board" Player.** In chess, thinking "down board" means that you're thinking several moves ahead, staying focused on the big strategy that will mean winning or losing the game. This is one exceptional way in which designing a game *is* like playing one. You're going to spend 18 to 24 months of your life concentrating on one game idea at a time, and there will be stretches of the development cycle when you're going to want to do something, *anything* but what you're doing at the moment. At times like this you must remember what it is you're working toward and be able to keep focused and motivated. Give yourself a few things to do on the side that will be fun but not so overwhelming they'll suck all your energy away from what you need to be concentrating on. Always keep your eyes on the big prize.

- **A Designer Is Trustworthy, Loyal, Helpful, Friendly, Courteous, & Kind.** Okay, okay, okay, so I'm ripping off the Boy Scouts' Law here, but there is a kernel of value in this rather pedantic-sounding list of virtues. (Holy Shades of *Ultima IV,* Batman!) The upshot here is that it's never a bad idea to employ any of these traits when you're dealing with your teammates, with the media, or with the people who will play your games. As a designer you want to be trustworthy in the way that you produce consistently great titles, the kind gamers will want to come back to again and again and again. You want to be loyal to the fanbase who make your games a success and honor the fact that they've played a major part in keeping you employed by slapping down their hard-earned cash, erecting fan Web sites praising your hard work, and flooding chat rooms all across the Internet telling others to go out and buy their own copies of your role-playing epics. Be helpful by feeding reporters that extra exclusive about your upcoming epic so they'll be positively predisposed to you and everything you're doing. As for friendly, courteous, and kind, I think you can see commonsense applications for those qualities that go without further explanation. The rock-bottom point here is to be a good scout, a good boss, a good neighbor in the computer gaming community. If all else fails, you must at the very *least* adhere to the Boy Scouts Motto: Be Prepared!

If you're especially fond of generating long lists of virtues and qualities, you could also add to this list the exhortation for a designer to be "obsequious, purple, and clairvoyant," as Steve Martin so wisely advises in the "Grandmother

Song," but those are all qualities that will only be used in very obscure circumstances and are better discussed elsewhere with your personal physician.

In all seriousness, if you're going to be a game designer, it helps to have most, if not all, of the qualities I've listed above. Depending on what companies you sign on with, some of things I've listed may end up being less important to you than others. If you work with a producer or a project manager, your abilities to lead the vision of the product and to think critically may end up being the skills most critical to your job performance. If you don't end up being the lead designer, you may only need to be a highly creative individual who's comfortable with implementing someone else's idea. Whatever the mix of qualities that nature and education have doled out to you, it's good to know your areas of strength and to make sure you work with team members who will excel in areas where you're weakest.

Working with a Team

Say the word "teamwork" to your average wannabe game designer and most of them will break into a hysterical rant. You'll hear a stream of invectives that will cover everything from George Orwell's "groupthink," to starving Communist farmers in China, to the Borg Collective featured on *Star Trek: Voyager*.

In the West, we've been brought up on such a steady diet of philosophical rugged individualism that we're all culturally leery of *anything* that smacks of creative collaboration. We point to well-known solo creators like Thomas Alva Edison, who despite his reputation in popular history books did *not* come up with all his inventions himself but rather ran a sweatshop for underpaid, uncredited scientists including, for a short while, one Nikola Tesla, inventor of alternating current. People often praise Walt Disney for his creation of the world's foremost entertainment empire, but he didn't single-handedly create all of the classic cartoons his company is known for any more than he built all the rides for Disneyland with a screwdriver and band saw in his own backyard.

Like it or not, if you want to put out a commercially viable title that has the potential to reach the broadest possible audience, you are going to have to sacrifice a small bit of your ego and learn to work with other people. Without further ado, let me welcome you into the wonderful and terrifying world that is *teamwork*.

As a designer, there are few relationships you'll ever experience that will be more schizophrenic than the one you'll experience with your fellow team members. On the one hand, these people you'll be working with will be your collaborators, your cocreators, your partners in crime. You'll sit around sketching interface layouts on napkins, or blue-skying ideas you'd all like to see brought to life. You'll bounce into each other's offices with a sketch, a quest idea, a bit of programming code that will take the concept you've all developed in an exciting new direction. I have fond memories of sitting around at three o'clock in the morning with Eric Hyman during the making of *Planet's Edge,* both of us wolfing down cheap Del Taco hamburgers while playing *Battleship* and talking shop about the game we were making. The atmosphere of a good game company is free-form, collegiate, and fun, a place where you feel free to throw ideas back and forth and feel like you're making a real contribution to the project, no matter what kind of title you're holding.

On the flip side of the teamwork coin, however, you'll have days when a jaunt through *Soldier of Fortune* will seem only mildly violent in comparison to what you'd like to do to your coworkers. You'll occasionally get someone on the team who just hates the direction in which you're taking the project, and they'll daily offer up their oh-so-helpful suggestions about why their unimplementable ideas would be so much better than your too mundane mass-marketable concept. Sometimes people will refuse to pay attention to the design document and will insist on coming into your office every five minutes to ask you about something they could just as easily have found out by skimming a table of contents. You will learn to loathe the phrase "artistic/poetic license," and your blood will run cold whenever someone sniffs about the way things are done in "a *real* RPG." Everyone on your team is going to have an opinion, and sometimes those opinions are going to run contrary to what you've got in mind.

The misconception that many designers have about teamwork, however, is that by working with others they'll be forced to give up creative control of a project. There's always the fear the designer will be thrust into a room with 20 people, everyone will throw around all the ideas they have, and the designer will be forced to commit to paper whatever a quorum of people in the room have decided will be "a fun game." This is known as the "Design by Committee" concept. Although to my shame I have witnessed this abomination of a design process at least once, I have to say there is almost no danger of this happening

The Capra Touch

Although it didn't happen in the computer gaming industry, there's one story from the history of film that demonstrates rather well what can happen when a lead designer loses touch with his or her own importance in the creative process. As the story goes, the famous film director Frank Capra was often highly praised in the media for his ability to put his own storytelling "mark" on his films. This was often called rather ostentatiously "the Capra Touch." Outraged at his work being credited for the dozenth time to Capra's lone genius, Robert Riskin, one of Capra's regular screenwriters, turned in a draft for his next film in a rather unorthodox format. Inside the traditional cardboard cover were 120 pages of completely blank paper. When Capra seemed confused by Riskin's submission, Riskin is reported to have told Capra, "Hey, you're such a fabulous director, why don't you try putting the Capra Touch on *THAT!*"

Moral: It's fine to be the guiding vision of a project, but never let yourself be deluded into believing that you've done it alone. Always give credit where credit is due, or you may end up getting far worse than a blank script from the people working with you.

on most projects in reputable, well-established companies. The products of these sessions are frankly often bland and execrable, and most game companies know this process to be an unviable way to design a solid title. As a book needs an author, and a movie needs a director, a game will always need a lead designer who directs the creative vision of the product and who makes the final decisions about what will and won't go in. Even the producers of heavily player-influenced titles like *Ultima Online* make it clear that the design process *is not and should not be* a democracy (see Carly Staehlin's comments on this in Chapter 14).

Rather than viewing teams like a collective mind of equals where a janitor's opinion is given the same weight as a programmer's analysis of the game code, you need to view your team members' ideas in the light of the skills they've brought to the table. Creative teams flourish when each member clearly understands his or her role, and when and where their opinions will be appropriate. When you give an individual control over some aspect of a project, they need to feel as though they are the king of their own domain. If you appoint someone to be art director, but you're constantly coming in and overriding their art decisions, you've undermined their authority with the people working underneath them, and they'll stop offering up their best ideas for the project. Presumably when you hire someone, you do so not to have a malleable puppet that will do whatever you want but to have someone whose opinions and talent you value and respect. Try to find a way to negotiate with them. Be willing and able to compromise when people come up with viable ideas that might not be what you originally intended but still fit in with the needs of the overall project.

If some aspect of the game *has* to be a certain way because the powers-that-be who are controlling the money or the license have decreed it, or the appropriate team leader has made a critical judgment call, don't ask opinions or take an obligatory vote and then disregard what people have to say. Some well-meaning designers simply wish to provide an illusion of greater team participation than actually exists, but in the long run this ends up being a huge leadership mistake and a real morale killer. If you have to give a directive but want to get a feel for how it will go over, devise some other method of getting this information without giving team members a false impression of choice. You will never be more respected than when people feel like you're playing straight with them and not running some kind of secret agenda behind their backs.

> **Feeping Creaturism. Also** sometimes more simply referred to as *creeping featurism.* This derogatory phrase refers to the tendency for features to continue to be added to a program, even past the point when the addition of such features is practical or feasible. This mentality is especially prevalent among new designers who feel as though they need to cram every single feature they can think of into a title.

Of course speaking out of place can oftentimes be as much a case of badly timed feeping creaturism as it's a matter of someone overstepping the bounds of their job description. During the making of *Betrayal at Krondor,* when we were well into the "death march" phase of the project, we recruited a handful of the members of the testing pool to come in and help finish out some of the level design duties that neither John Cutter nor I had the time to deal with. One fellow in particular—we'll call him Jochi—was very anxious to leave his own permanent imprint on the game and began a rather persistent campaign of assaulting the rest of the design team with some of his 11th-hour "improvements." Now Jochi was a very intelligent fellow, and he had a number of very interesting ideas about things that could be added, but the fact of the matter was that it was far too late in the development cycle for the team to be considering *any* new features to be added to the game. When it became obvious to him that we weren't going to implement any of his new ideas, he became increasingly persistent and irate, pushing ever harder to get his viewpoint heard, despite the fact we'd already heard him loud and clear. Finally, after numerous talks with both John and me, he finally began to understand how the production cycle worked and how with the project so behind schedule as it was, it simply wasn't practical for us to change our course. Luckily we were able to complete the project successfully, but only because we knew when it was time to trim the sails, batten down the hatches, and ram our way through the final raging waters at the end of the project. The siren call for "just one more feature" will always beckon to some member of your team, but you must always know how to keep everyone focused on the needs of the game.

Meet the Team

If you're lucky, you'll get to spend somewhere between a year and a half to two years with the people on your design team. You'll learn more than you'll probably ever *want* to know about these people as you live, breathe, eat, and sometimes *sleep* alongside them during the long and treacherous process that is game development. You'll discover what food allergies they have as you order late-night pizzas for each other. You'll know whether they like to listen to Rage Against the Machine, Jon Michel Jarre, Garth Brooks, or Beethoven's "Ode to Joy" when they're coding, rendering, or writing. At some point, someone on the team will probably get married, and you'll be invited to a bachelor/bachelorette party and be witness to events for which you'll be sworn to a secrecy more binding than what you'll find in your average nondisclosure agreement. In some ways these people will be closer to you than family, so it's a good idea for you to get to know them as well as you possibly can. While my crystal ball can't give you the specifics about the individuals you'll be serving alongside, I can tell you very briefly about what each of these individuals will be doing to help bring your project idea to its fruition.

Producer/Project Manager

If the company you work for uses producers or project managers, you'll find that these individuals' jobs are often mainly administrative. They handle all the big picture stuff related to the project, like funding, scheduling, staffing, and acquisitions of resources. If you need to get a new computer monitor, it's going to be the producer who's going to be the person who will handle your problem. You'll also turn to them if you need a new assistant, have a conflict with one of the team members, or need to discuss a scheduling extension that may have a large-scale impact on the team as a whole.

Another important aspect of the producer and project manager is to be the spokesperson for the project, both internally and externally. When the team needs an increase in the budget, the producer is going to be the point person who goes to bat with the CEO, development house, or project backers to get what your game needs. They'll also be the primary point of contact after the marketing department when it comes down to the project's representation to the outside world. They'll do interviews with media outlets, travel to trade shows, contact contractors, help arrange advertising, and take care of the hiring of actors or the rental of studio time. The point of the producer or program manager's job is to make it possible for the design team to be able to concentrate on the design and not have to worry about any of the distractions that can come from also having to run the business side of the project.

Design Staff

Throughout this book I've spoken rather generically of designers as if they were all really one position, but there are typically a number of different people who serve on the design staff who will have the title of designer in some way attached to their titles. Here's the lowdown on the titles and what the essential differences are in their jobs.

Lead Designer

The lead designer is the creative heart of the project. Often they will be the person who generates the original proposal and the design document upon which a title will be based. They may also adapt a preexisting property like a television show, movie, or book into a playable format. No matter where the idea originates, the lead designer's role will be to define the basic look, feel, and interface of a project and lay out the underlying rules that will govern the gameplay.

First and foremost, the lead designer will be responsible for the creation and maintenance of the design document. It is through this most important technical specification that everyone on the team should be able to see and understand what the basic idea is behind the project. From the design doc they should also have enough guidance from the lead designer to be able to take the next steps and turn the outline into all the programming, art, sound, and story assets that will be needed in order to complete the game.

The lead designer must also be the design team's primary cheerleader and manager. They must keep everyone inspired, motivated, and feeling great about the project they're all working on. They operate by one very important rule at all times, that excited developers will make exciting games, and it must be their goal to keep the home fires burning.

Immediately after successfully pitching a proposal, it will be up to the game designer to either directly appoint or work with a producer to hire the core members of the team that will be needed to create a project. Typically these core team members will include the lead programmer, lead artist, and lead writer. With a smaller company, the game designer might also be the lead writer. The lead programmer or artist might also serve as the project manager.

As the project grows and develops, the lead designer may then become responsible for directing the work of several secondary designers who will handle specialized aspects like story or event design and level design.

Story and Event Designer

A story and event designer is a really game-savvy professional writer focused on creating the large overall story content of a gaming title. They'll create a world bible that details the history of the world and the back history of the immediate conflict of the game, and they'll develop the ideas for some of the cultures and traditions that the gamer may encounter while playing. If NPCs are being presented, the story and event designer will be responsible for writing all the dialogue for all the characters, as well as the majority of the text that will be presented both on the screen and sometimes in the manual. Story and event designers also design the main quest and subquests that the player will need to complete during the course of the game and will have significant influence over the contents and basic looks of rooms, dungeons, and other locations in the game. In some teams, level designers report directly to the story and event designer instead of to the lead designer.

Level Designer

A level designer is responsible for building all the areas of the game that have been specified by the lead designer and the story and event designers. Using either an in-house world editor or a 3-D modeling package like 3D Studio Max, the level designer assembles all of the art and programming assets like monsters, spells, and artificial intelligence into exciting arenas in which the gameplay will be presented and the story line played out.

Programming Staff

Like the design staff, programmers on a project can wear a number of different possible programming hats. A lead programmer may be concerned with assembling all the logic needed for the core game engine. Assistant programmers may be focused on individual programming tasks specific to a project like dealing with texture mapping, handling video input, dealing with tiles, or handling networking routines for use in multiplayer modes. For nearly every feature you can put into the game, there may be just one or two programmers assigned specifically to handling the problems associated with just that particular aspect of the game. If you want to know more about the kinds of tasks programmers usually deal with, there are several good books in the Prima Tech line dealing with the black art of programming. I suggest you go check out *Beginning*

Direct3D Game Programming by Wolfgang F. Engel and Amir Geva or *OpenGL Game Programming* by Kevin Hawkins and Dave Astle.

Art Staff

Artists are no exception to the many hats rule, and like designers and programmers, they are often segregated by the kinds of art being handled.

Lead Artist

A lead artist guides the primary look of the interface, the monsters, the objects, and all the different areas that will be presented in the game. Depending on their art specialization, a lead artist might take any of these aspects as their primary contribution to the game art and delegate the rest to their secondary staff members.

When not involved in the process of actually creating art themselves, the lead artist's job is to oversee and manage the art staff.

3-D Modeler

A 3-D modeler is someone who spends their entire day just building the basic structures of three-dimensional computer models using a 3-D package like Maya or 3D Studio Max. This might involve creating dinosaurs, rocketships, or architectural features like towers or castles. Sometimes there's a subdivision of the modelers known as a character modeler, who specializes in creating realistic people with very individual artistic "personalities." Depending on the project, there could be literally a whole team just of modelers working under a lead who reports to the lead artist.

Texture Artist

A texture artist spends most of their time coming up with interesting textures that can be mapped onto a 3-D computer model. Typical textures could include dinosaur skin, blasted metal for starship hulls, realistic rock textures to be used in castle walls, or fake portraits that can be hung in an imaginary throne room. If there's a 3-D model out there, the texture artist has to find ways to make them seem real and alive.

Motion Capture Animator

This is a highly specialized artist who can use motion capture equipment to digitally record the motions of actors and then apply that information to the 3-D models that have been developed by the 3-D team. These artists sometimes have to "clean up" motion capture files to smooth out jerkiness or join motions together that have been performed separately.

Animator

If a project isn't using motion capture to create the animation, then there will usually be a team of artists whose job it will be to create all the animations for all the characters, monsters, and equipment that can be found in the game.

Background Painter

In some games, particularly adventure-like titles, there may be artists whose job it is to create beautiful backgrounds against which the characters will do their thing. Although this variety of artist isn't being used as frequently in this era of the rise of 3-D, you'll still find a few hanging out in game companies all through the industry.

Music and Sound Effects

In most cases, the music and sound effects departments of most game companies are still notoriously small, and in some cases these jobs are often farmed out to outside companies. Nonetheless, music and sound can be very powerfully used in computer gaming titles, and with the advent of things like 3-D surround sound becoming more common in most games, the way in which sound effects and music can be used in the gaming environment are growing in importance.

Sound Effects/Foley

The sound effects and foley artists on a project are responsible for giving all of the things that happen in the game their distinctive snaps, crackles, and pops. Footsteps, explosions, and creaking dungeon doors are all the domain of the lords of sfx and foley.

Music Lead

The music lead is usually one or two people who have the very difficult task of creating exciting music that can loop nearly endlessly and yet remain entertaining and unannoying. Very few people have yet mastered the art, but up-and-comers like Jeremy Soule may very well take game music to an entirely new level of excellence.

Testing Staff

I will end my discussion of the different leads of the design team with a very special thanks to the oft unsung heroes who take an enormous amount of abuse and rarely get the credit they deserve.

One way to get into the computer gaming industry is to start out as tester—the guinea pigs who get to "road test" the game in its initial form to see how it works. Like many lower-echelon employees in countless other fields, testers perform an essential function that is low on prestige and pay.

The sad fact of the matter is, not even the play testers who *do* get paid to play games for a living are really having as much fun as most ordinary people might think. Instead of getting the well balanced, crash-free, beautifully presented Wonderlands that consumers get to see, play testers are often forced to slog through half-baked, bug-riddled, haphazardly documented game playing hells that are *not* much of a joy to mess with. On the first two or three passes, they can enjoy getting to see how things are coming together, but by the 40th time they've wandered through the Swamp of Despair trying to see if that same crash bug comes up when they try to unseal the Tomb of Really Bad Things while wearing the Helm of Zhul, most of the romance of the product is gone. By the time testers finally are starting to see a nice, polished product that isn't constantly crashing, erasing their hard drive, or doing some other equally unspeakable thing, the game is taken out of their hands, boxed up, and shipped to the public. In its place the testers are given a new game and a new batch of problems, and the cycle starts all over again. Not surprisingly, most testing departments tend to have a high rate of turnover.

Exercises

1. Go through my list of the critical qualities of game designers and ask yourself how well you measure up to them. If you don't feel like you meet some of the criteria, ask yourself if you're comfortable moving in some of the directions I've suggested.

2. Look at some of the RPGs in the market right now and try to find out how well they've done their research on the factual things they've presented. Pay close attention to where they've veered off from fact and created their own spin on reality. Why do you think they went the directions that they did?

3. Start up your favorite game and watch the credits . . . all of them. Try looking at an older title and see if you recognize people who were grunts in older games who are now better known.

4. See if you can get enrolled as a beta tester on an RPG project and ask to play the buggiest version they've got available. Keep playing it over and over, especially the parts that seem to crash *a lot*. Do everything to figure out why you think it may be crashing. Think about the poor guys who have to mess with the game in this state and never forget that lesson.

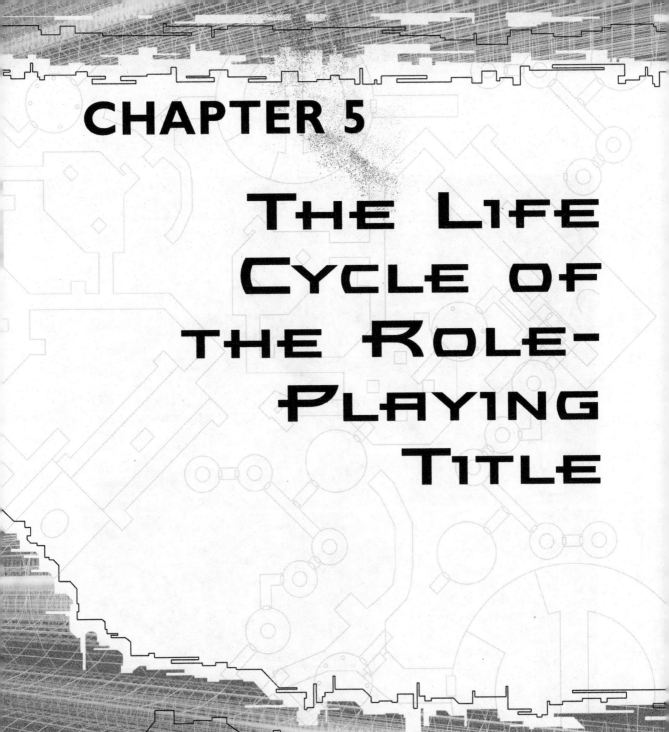

CHAPTER 5

THE LIFE CYCLE OF THE ROLE-PLAYING TITLE

"Nothing contributes so much to tranquilize the mind as a steady purpose—a point on which the soul may fix its intellectual eye."

—Mary Wollstonecraft Shelley, *Frankenstein* (1818)

If you've ever sat with a medically oriented friend while watching an episode of *ER* or you've gone out to see the latest *Star Trek* movie with someone who's an astrophysicist by profession, you're probably well acquainted with the post-show analysis: all the microminutial, verging-on-Asperger's-Syndrome dissections of everything the writers and cast fundamentally got *wrong*. (You may even be the sort who likes to *do* the grousing.) If, however, you go to a film that's supposed to be portraying the life of a game designer in some fashion, you'll be exposed to nearly as many myths and inaccuracies about the game design process as you'll find science flubs in your average sci-fi flick. If you haven't seen the way the process is often portrayed on the silver screen, here's the stereotypical set-up:

*   *   *

FADE IN

ENTER TEENAGER, a BATTERED SKATEBOARD under one arm. He's an intelligent, good-looking kid overall, but he could use a little help in the Clearasil department. The pizza boxes scattered around the room tell us where he gets his complexion, but we're still perplexed about how he can eat that way and stay so thin.

The boy moves to his computer terminal and hits a key. Immediately the computer comes to life, a dazzling array of wire-framed 3-D figures endlessly spinning on invisible carousels. The boy CRACKS HIS KNUCKLES, wiggles his fingers, then begins typing on the keyboard as the figures suddenly start MORPHING BEFORE OUR EYES!

Hacker Kid:

Heh heh. Watch out, world. Here comes
ULTIMATE BLOODY DEATH, part IV!

After a few more keystrokes, a character appears
on-screen, sheathed now in skin and clothing. A GUN
big enough to mount on a panzer tank appears in
the character's hands, and the synthetic soldier
grimaces at the hacker kid.

Hacker Kid:

That . . . about . . . does it. Six months'
work finished! We're ready to roll, Baron
Blastem! That'll be another hundred mill in
the bank!

The kid finishes typing, reaches down and pops a
diskette out of the computer's drive. He slaps it
into a manila envelope, grabs his skateboard, and
heads out for fame and fortune. . . .

*   *   *

I understand, of course, the needs of an entertainment medium. Veracity must
sometimes be sacrificed to convey the essence of an experience *without* boring
laypeople with all the details. It's much easier to identify with one individual
pushing a lone vision than a team of 20 people all trying to agree on what they
want to do. Following the development of a game through its many mutations
and its long development cycle would frankly put most people to sleep before the
end of the first reel. It's a fun and rewarding way to make a living, but it would
make a rotten and confusing spectator sport, and I'm mostly glad the screenwriters of the world have spared us an accurate depiction. For those of you who
aren't sure *why* the above scene is an inaccurate portrayal, however, here's a very
quick checklist of the reasons I hope *The Making of Ultimate Bloody Death, Part IV,*
would never get made into a rather misleading major motion picture:

- **The Kid Is Working Alone**. Once upon a time, back when I was first getting interested in making computer games of my own, this was still an industry where one or two people could sit around in a garage and do all the programming, the art, the writing, the music—essentially everything that needed to be done. Before founding Sierra On-Line, Ken and Roberta Williams hammered out their ideas on a kitchen table. Jon Van Caneghem sold his enormously successful first installment of the *Might & Magic* series out of his living room. There are numerous examples of the "one-man show" that date back to the beginnings of the industry, but you should be aware that things have changed a great deal since the golden era of the 1980s.

  Gamers today expect the titles they buy to be technologically advanced and to feature top-quality music, writing, and art. Some developers might have an above-average aptitude at several of these skills, but realistically, very few individuals have eclectically enough of the right stuff to crank out a saleable modern project entirely by themselves. This isn't to say that it's absolutely impossible, but it's such a rare occurrence today that you should have no delusions about your prospects if you choose to work alone. If you succeed in creating tomorrow's best-selling RPG all by yourself, you will do so against all the odds, and you'll have to work 20 times as hard get the job done right. This doesn't mean you have to join Monstrously Huge Games Incorporated to succeed, but you *are* likely to need help.

- **Nobody Creates 3-D Art by Typing**. Okay, so it's a really anal and picayune point, but it's a pet peeve of mine to see someone frantically typing away on the keyboard and things just magically happening on the computer monitor. Not since I was 17 and trying to draw a picture of a TARDIS on my old Atari 400 by programming DRAWTO commands in BASIC have I done any kind of image manipulation that involved *typing*. Designers today use mice, drawing tablets, graphics accelerator cards, joysticks, music synthesizers, digital audio tape decks, and a vast host of other specialized equipment that helps create the stuff out of which games are made. Understanding how to use all this external hardware will play as much a role in the game development process as knowing how to use the computer keyboard.

It's also important you know you aren't going to be using any *one* computer program with which to create your role-playing extravaganza. You might use a program like Adobe Photoshop or Illustrator to create sketches of the interface, Lightwave 3D to model your vicious-looking troll, 3D Studio Max to create levels, and a suite of programs like Microsoft's Word, Excel, Access, and Project to create all the design docs, databases, budgets, and presentations that will be necessary to keep your project rolling along. Your ability to understand and use all these resources will very definitely impact how employable you are as a designer. The more you understand about multiple forms of software and technology, the greater your clout will be in landing that position you most desire.

- **Professional Games Are Not Made in Six Months**. After six months, most games are barely off the drawing boards. The idea you could ship product after such a psychotically short development cycle is, to put it bluntly, insane. (You may quote me on that.) Certainly in that time frame it might be possible to do "plug-in" work, like creating an expansion pack where only a handful of new levels or new monsters are added into a preexisting engine, but you are not likely to ship an entirely new title in anything under a year and a half.

ON TARGET

The Any 2 Rule

Occasionally an otherwise bright-seeming CEO comes along from outside the gaming industry and thinks they know a way to speed up this process, but they very quickly discover what all of us who have been down in the trenches for years learned long ago: You cannot speed up the process without it adversely affecting the budget or the quality. It's an irritating fact of game management, but that's the reality of development. You can have it *fast,* you can have it *cheap,* or you can have it *right*. You can even choose any two options, but you aren't going to get all three.

Typically development will take somewhere between 18 and 24 months, depending on the needs and scope of the project in question. Although this wasn't carved in stone on any mountaintop that I'm aware of, there's actually a pretty good reason why projects take about this length of time. Most practically, that's how long a team needs to build a new piece of technology, create all the content that needs to be poured inside, and then finally test the results for several months before releasing a (hopefully) bug-free product to the masses. A little more abstract reason has to do with technology lag. If a project is in production for *longer* than 24 months, it runs a severe risk of being technologically obsolescent by the time it is released. When you get started designing the game, your concepts will probably be very cutting edge, but if it's going to be longer than two years before anybody actually sees anything you're doing, the technology and tastes of your audience may have moved in the direction of other games that beat yours to the marketplace.

But while the game production cycles themselves have remained relatively stable since about 1993, the budgets required to support them have ballooned substantially over the intervening years. SSI/Westwood Studio's *Eye of the Beholder* cost around 1.2 million dollars to produce in 1991. Today that might be considered an extremely conservative budget estimate for a major release, and it's not unheard of today for projects to cost over four or five million dollars to produce.

- **Game Designers Do Not Typically Become Millionaires.** There's a strange public misperception that people who make computer games can light their fireplaces with $20 bills and sleep in beds cushioned with all their excess cash. Unless you get very, very, very, very lucky, you aren't going to get rich in this business. You may be able to make a decent living for yourself, but you aren't going to be retiring any sooner than most of the people you grew up with. If you become a game designer, you should do so because you love to make games, not because you have the notion that you're going to become fabulously wealthy.

- **No Fully Featured RPG Will Fit on a Floppy Disk.** Today's role-playing games are big. Not just *large* mind you, but whopping gigantic epics that can be difficult to squeeze onto multiple CD-ROMs. The free space players are required to have on their hard drives in order to install their favorite RPGs averages around 515 megabytes (MB), and the arrival of the larger

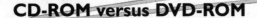

CD-ROM versus DVD-ROM

What's the difference in capacity and performance between CD-ROM and DVD-ROM? The first big contrast has to do with the rate at which your computer can siphon data off the disc. A 1x DVD-ROM drive spins at about the same *physical* speed as a 3x CD-ROM but transfers information at about the same *data* speed as a 9x CD-ROM drive. This means DVD-ROMs can cook through a great deal more data than a CD-ROM in an equivalent amount of time. The second, most dramatic difference between the two has to do with the amount of data you can squeeze onto the two formats. CD-ROMs can hold in the neighborhood of around 650MB of data. DVD-ROMs can hold anywhere between 4.5 and 17 *gigabytes* (GB) of data, depending on whether they are single- or double-sided and whether they've been burned in single or multiple layers. Even if you're only using a single-sided, single-layered DVD-ROM disc, you're going to have about 7.23 times more room for your data than you would if you used a CD-ROM based format.

capacity, higher performance DVD-ROM will only serve to further grow the size of the average computer game. A single, standard floppy diskette capable of holding a mere 1.4MB is simply out of the question.

If there is any trend that has been more apparent in recent years, it is that RPGs are continuing to grow in size, scale, and depth. The ramifications to the industry are profound. The ability for games to increase in complexity while maintaining the 18–24 month production schedules and keeping their budgets low enough so that the consumer can afford to buy the games is going to become one of the biggest challenges that the industry will face over the coming decade.

The preceding laundry list is only a brief example of some of the things people commonly misunderstand or are generally unaware of in regard to the computer gaming industry. I'm sure some of my designer colleagues have a few other things they'd contribute to this list based on conversations with friends, family, and reporters in the media. In the next chapter I'll go into greater detail about the specifics of what the game designer actually *does,* but first I want to walk you through all the stages a game is likely to go through on the way to becoming a player-beloved, chart-topping sensation. Without further ado, let's roll tape on the fascinating life cycle of the Great American role-playing game. . . .

The Idea Asylum: Letting Out Those Crazy Concepts

Usually when I'm sitting on a panel at a science-fiction and fantasy convention playing industry ambassador to the world, there's one question I can always count on some twerp in the audience to throw out at me: "Where do you get your ideas for your games?"

There are many writers and designers who have utter contempt for this question and will either dismiss it, give an unthoughtful answer, or perpetrate some ungodly hoax of a methodology just to see if the audience will actually swallow what they're being told. For my own part, I try to be sympathetic to the asker simply because at one point in my life *I* was the twerp asking the question. Unfortunately, it isn't something that has an easy answer. It's not all that different than asking, "Why did I choose to wear the color green this morning?" or "What just made me think about the only time I got swats in Mr. Gray's office at Twin Cities elementary?" I'm sure my neuroscientist of a brother who teaches Communications for the University of Oklahoma has some elaborate theory about where this stuff comes from, but it's a process that I'm still trying to get a handle on myself. I've tried to boil it down into a concise, clever answer of the one- or two-sentence cocktail party variety, but no matter how I word it, the essential gist of what I end up saying is, "I get my ideas from everywhere."

When I go back and think about the design of various titles I've worked on, I find a very strange soup of inspirations for things I've done. In *Might & Magic III: Isles of Terra,* a lot of the stories and characters that I discussed with Ron Bolinger to put into the game were actually rather elaborate puns on classic rock. *Planet's Edge* was very obviously inspired not only by the *Starfleet Battles* license that New World Computing held at the time, but it also drew some of its spirit from a set of inspirations as diverse as the sci-fi themed pen-and-paper

RPG *Traveler*, the stage version of Andrew Lloyd Webber's *Phantom of the Opera*, and the semiotic writings of Umberto Eco. *Elysium* was possibly one of the most peculiarly influenced titles I've ever worked on, its original foundation heavily based on the theories of the collective unconscious of Carl Jung and the universality of myths discussed by Joseph Campbell.

If you survey a wide range of other designers, you'll find they have similar responses about where they get their concepts. Will Crowther created *Adventure* based on his background in exploring and mapping caves. *Deus Ex* creator Warren Spector says reading a newspaper and just getting out and "doing some living" is as important to coming up with game design ideas as lifting material from the most recent crop of science-fiction or fantasy novels. There is one source of inspiration, however, upon which all game designers rely but which is so blindly obvious that most people don't even think to talk about it. If you're out to design games, the first thing you should do is have a lot of experience *playing* them.

The point at which many people realize they want to become a game designer is usually the moment they find themselves frustrated, limited, or simply bored by an existing title. Rather than simply stop playing, the future game designer says, "Hey, I could do better than this!" and then they promptly begin to think about how they'll improve the experience. Sometimes this might mean changing a troublesome core rule by which a game operates. At other times it may mean slamming together two ideas that have never been combined before. The creators of *Dungeons & Dragons* combined the war game concept with fantasy elements inspired by Tolkien's *Lord of the Rings*. The result was a wonderful groundbreaking title and gave us a whole new genre of gaming. Richard Garriott's *Ultima* series really took off when he replaced the standard "fight-the-monsters-grab-the-treasure" game objective with quests for noble character traits. In some respects it was comparable to gaining experience points or reaching a higher level of expertise in previous systems, but the philosophical or spiritual roots of the new system also called for some different gaming scenarios. It not only provided a new feel for fantasy role-players, but it also helped define the unique way in which *Ultima* would be distinguished from its competitors.

In the end, whatever source you use for your gaming ideas, all that you need concern yourself with is that you be able to move past simple inspiration. Thinking of concepts is easy. Seeing what other people have done wrong is even

A Shopping List for Your Mental Mall

If you're desperate for a place to look for new game ideas, here are a few suggestions of places where you can start looking, or ideas you might use as a point-of-departure for your gaming concept.

- ◆ Hobbies and interests
- ◆ Cultural roots or explorations
- ◆ Philosophical or spiritual realms
- ◆ Actual historical events
- ◆ "What if" twists
- ◆ Paradigm shifts
- ◆ Altered social conventions or structures
- ◆ Different physical laws
- ◆ Unusual approaches to almost any element of life
- ◆ Military training manuals
- ◆ Catalogs of hi-tech gear or medieval weaponry and garb

less difficult. For many people the idea phase is where their concept both begins and ends, but working to take those proposals somewhere is what separates the wannabes from the pros.

Dreams for Sale

If you're really not all that interested in developing your own rules system, or if you don't feel like worldbuilding your game universe from scratch, you may not be as out of luck in the game development industry as you might imagine. The fact of the matter is, it's common for companies to have to turn to outside sources to provide technologies and content that might be otherwise difficult to develop in-house. This practice of paying an external source for the one-time use of programming code, artwork, stories, or other preexisting intellectual properties is known as *licensing*.

The advantages of dealing with a preexisting property are numerous. If you're dealing with an already well-established set of rules or a universe that has already been popularized in another form of media, your ability to sell your game idea will pack more punch, starting with your first pitch to a publisher or your in-house superiors.

The money people are often more open to licensed material on the assumption that the name recognition will give your product a built-in market. Presumably the acquisition of externally generated materials also means that team members may not need to work as long on certain aspects of the project, which theoretically in turn means a reduced duration for the production cycle and lower overhead costs. Going the licensing route isn't an absolute no-brainer, however. There are many examples of licensed products based on highly successful technologies, rules, or universes that failed to become best-sellers. In many ways it's comparable to casting a lead role in a film: A promising unknown might be the next superstar, but those holding the purse strings might insist on using a big-name performer. It will be up to you to determine what will best serve the interests of the kind of game you want to make.

Licensing a Universe

Of the two common kinds of licensing, the use of a preexisting fictional universe is probably the most employed by developers. We've been given an interactive peek at the science-fiction and fantasy universes of prominent authors like Arthur C. Clarke and Gentry Lee (*Rama*), Robert Jordan (*Wheel of Time*), and H. P. Lovecraft (*Alone in the Dark*). *Star Trek* has been a perennial favorite for computer game adaptation, and currently a massively multiplayer version of the *Star Wars* universe is under development at Verant Interactive (the same folks who brought you *Everquest*).

In 1991 I had the privilege to take a crack at a licensed property based on the popular fantasy novels of Raymond E. Feist. In exchange for a check from Dynamix, Feist and Midkemia Press generously handed over stacks of development materials upon which his Midkemian books had been based. Armed with this material and all eight of the books that Feist had written at the time, John Cutter and I began the laborious process of turning all that raw material into a new story and a game design that we could mate with our preexisting 3-Space engine. The result was the 1993 release *Betrayal at Krondor*.

On the one hand, using the licensed material was a true advantage. It saved me about three or four months' worth of work that I otherwise would have spent just dreaming up the cultures, the maps, the histories, the religions, and the other background material that is necessary as the backdrop of any well-developed RPG. Feist's name and stature in the fantasy literature genre was also beneficial in helping attract some of his readers to our humble little computer game. But as detailed as many of the documents he provided us with were, there were many small details that had never been committed to paper. From time to time I'd have some elegant solution worked out about the way something was going to function in a particular part of the world, only to discover later that I couldn't do it because 15 years ago he and his role-playing buddies had decided at three o'clock in the morning that thing X could never occur in Midkemia. He was certainly entitled to make those kinds of decisions about his universe, of course, but there would be nothing in any of the documentation that explained this fact.

Dealing with a licensed universe can have other disadvantages as well. You can find yourself hemmed in on several fronts from a gameplay standpoint by the necessities of remaining true to the spirit of your borrowed world. Significant characters from the stories cannot be killed or given experiences that might conflict with any planned future adventures. If two characters have never met in the book or the television show and there's an important reason why they should never meet, you may have to resort to some drastically stupid measure in order to ensure they stay separated in your game. In a book series there may be an all-powerful wizard capable of smashing cities into dust, but if you allow players to *play* that character, you have to ensure that having the most powerful magician in the known universe in your party won't utterly unbalance all of the combat events in your game. To be true to the role-playing experience, characters who otherwise might be presented as experts in the books will have to be presented as moderate- to low-level characters so that they have room for their skills and powers to grow throughout the course of the game.

Despite the numerous difficulties of meshing all these conflicting needs of the gameplay and license together, I was extraordinarily lucky. *Betrayal* became a best-seller at a time when other licensed properties were not faring very well.

Thanks to the time that the license bought John and me to concentrate on the actual details of the game itself, we had the opportunity to put a true polish on a role-playing title that would otherwise have taken much more time and much more effort to successfully produce.

Licensing the Rules

If you feel fairly confident about dealing with the story and the universe in which gamers will be playing, but you aren't so sure about your abilities to construct a set of rules that will govern the ways in which characters interact, you might look into the possibility of licensing a preexisting rules system. If you've been keeping up with most of the major new RPG releases over the past few years, you'll notice that many of them are linked with a traditional pen-and-paper counterpart. *Baldur's Gate, Planescape: Torment,* and the upcoming *Pool of Radiance 2* are all titles that use a slightly modified version of the basic *Dungeons & Dragons* rule set. *Fallout* and *Fallout 2* both featured a GURPs-driven heart, and *Vampire: The Masquerade—Redemption* is based on the highly successful Storyteller rules that were created by White Wolf Publishing.

As with the licensing of a fictional universe, there are many advantages and disadvantages to using an extant rule set. There are many things that will make your life both easier and harder as a developer when dealing with someone else's vision of reality. But there is one distinct advantage that I think bears consideration above all others. *A preexisting rule set is already designed to be used as part of a gaming experience.* This means you aren't going to be spending lots of time trying to figure out how to adapt it to work within your gaming framework. Once you have the rules, you have the skeleton on which your gameplay will be constructed.

This isn't to say you'll be absolutely scot-free of difficulty once you've got the game system of your choice in your hot little hands. You will still have to deal with the fact that most pen-and-paper RPGs deal with combat in a turn-based system while most computer-driven RPGs offer real-time combat. There are many skills and abilities typically given to players in traditional role-playing games that fail to adapt well to a multimedia environment. Most critically of all, you're going to have to develop methodologies to resolve or avoid the kinds of problems that in a sit-down gaming session would usually be solved or arbitrated by the Dungeon Master, Keeper, Storyteller, or what have you. In a table-intensive system like *D&D*, which is well adapted to the number-crunching capabilities of your average home computer, this adaptation will likely go fairly smoothly. When dealing with a system more heavily slanted toward storytelling, like *Werewolf: The Apocalypse,* you may end up having to specially tailor a more statistics-driven engine than you had in mind in the first place.

If you're prepared to put a licensed role-playing system on the table, you'll have the immediate advantage that many players will already understand much of the mechanics that make the game work. Players tooling around in a *Call of Cthulhu* based title will understand how important it is to hold on to their sanity points, and they'll instinctively realize that they need to nab all those little star-shaped symbols in order to ward themselves from the evils of Nyarlathotep and his minions. If, however, a spellcaster wandering around in an authorized *D&D* product casts a fireball and it does 1d4 points of damage per level of the caster instead of the 1d6 points that the 3rd edition rule book specifies, they are going to begin to distrust how well the game they love has been adapted. If you end up having to modify too many specifics of the original rules system, you'll have as many players mad at you about your shoddy modifications as you would

Ladies & Gentlemen, License Your Engines!

Another form of licensing that is still coming into its own is the process of licensing the *game engine,* the body of programming code that controls all of the major functions of the game. This is a particularly useful practice for small development houses that don't have the time, money, or resources to adequately create a full-featured, technologically sophisticated engine that can compete successfully against those developed by larger companies. Although licensing fees for some game engines can be rather exorbitant, they can still be cheaper than trying to develop the technology in-house. Probably the best-known licensers available today are the Lithtec, Infinity, Halo, and Unreal engines, just to name a few of the most prominent players in the field. If you'd like to learn more about them, you can check out the 3D Engines List on the Web at http://cg.cs.tu-berlin.de/~ki/engines.html.

if you accidentally killed off a character in a licensed fictional universe. Never underestimate that people can be as loyal to a specific set of rules and procedures as they can be to a fictional character. Whatever you license, if it's something with which the public will have an intimate knowledge, be respectful of the material.

Appeals to the Higher Powers: Crafting the Proposal

Once you've had a chance to kick around some of the basic ideas about the kind of game you want to make, the next thing you're going to have to do is start worrying about money. Unless you're independently wealthy and can afford to hire those legions of programmers, writers, artists, and voice-over actors you'll need to turn your assemblage of ideas into an actual game, you're going to have to come up with a compelling pitch document that explains why your idea is the best thing in which a development house can possibly invest. This brief but highly important sales document, known as the *proposal,* will have the power to either get your project off the ground or send it crashing down *Hindenburg*-style in dejected failure.

Every designer handles the writing of the proposal in a different way. Some consider it the beginning of the game design process, but to me it's only the phase of the project in which I finalize my choices about what it is I really want to do. Before I even put the first word to paper, I've done an enormous amount of preparatory work. I've thought about what kind of game it is that I want to make, how it should look, what kind of world I'd like to put in front of the player. As I'm firing up my word processor I'm calling up several files with story notes behind the proposal window, flipping through a yellow tablet full of interface sketches drawn in the middle of the night or during family get-togethers. For me, the secret to a successful proposal has always been to describe a world and an experience that already fully exists in my imagination.

Not everybody is so introspective. Some use the process of writing the proposal to call the ideas down out of the ether, content to let the ideas for the game coalesce as they go along. Others might prefer to first build animations, do test coding, or even try prebuilding some of their basic gameplay ideas in a game engine similar to the one they hope to use in the final product. All of these approaches are equally valid so long as the designer comes away from their pre-proposal work with a clear idea that they will be able to communicate in writing to the people holding the purse strings. (For more information about how to structure your own proposal, see Chapter 8, or read the sample proposal for Betrayal at Krondor, which appears in Appendix B.)

After you've committed your grand plan to paper, you'll need to locate the people who will fund your expedition into the dark and dangerous lands of game design. If you're fortunate enough to be working inside a development studio, this will usually only be a matter of getting the document passed up the chain of command to the creative director or the vice president of development. If you're an unsigned talent exploring the wilds of freelancing, you can try shopping your idea to any companies you might have working relationships with, or you might consider showing your idea to a game agent who can identify what companies might best be suited to helping you realize your creative vision. In either case, once you've got the attention of the resident powers-that-be, you will engage in the time-honored tradition that has defined the proposal review process for over three decades: *You wait.*

In the ulcerating period of time while you're wondering whether or not they're going to give your idea the green light, there will be a team of different people who will be crawling through the guts of your proposal with an endoscope. Producers and designers will be looking at the specifics of the game itself, seeing if there are any technical red flags that might make the project hard to implement either technologically or logistically. An accountant will be tabulating what they expect will be the likely cost of getting the project off the ground. Marketing executives will be looking at how saleable it will be in the projected market and if there are any current consumer buying trends that might help or hurt the sales of a project like the one you're proposing. Last, but not least, virtually everyone is going to be chiming in on whether or not they think your idea sounds like it will be fun for people to play. Even if you clear all the other hurdles, this is the one thing your proposal must absolutely get right, otherwise there's little reason for the development house to throw all their resources behind you.

No matter how great an idea you think you're throwing out, don't be surprised if you get rejected on the first pass. This isn't always a bad thing. If the developers don't immediately sign on to your idea, unless they think your proposal just absolutely bites, they'll usually have the courtesy to tell you why they're turning the idea down. It may be they think your description of the interface was unclear or that you hadn't defined where your game would stand in the overall marketplace. Whatever they tell you, listen to what they have to say and try to be objective about your concept. Remember that many of these people are gamers as well as developers, and they've developed good instincts about what will and won't fly with players. If there are changes you can make to the idea that might bring it more in line with what they're looking for, ask yourself whether you think those changes will help or harm your project. Providing you're comfortable making a few adjustments, try tweaking out your idea in the direction they suggest and resubmit it. Otherwise, hit the road again and see if you can find someone else who may be more receptive to your original concept.

Assuming you've dotted all your "i"s and crossed all your "t"s, and you've at last addressed all the concerns of the higher powers about your game design, you may be lucky enough to finally get the funding and approval you'll need to move on to the next stage of your project's development: the writing of the design document.

Plans for World Domination: The Design Document

Procedurally speaking, you will find there are going to be a few differences between preparing the proposal and creating the design document. Most proposals are usually created by one or two designers, often with very little input coming from outside during the creation process. Before the proposal gets approved, your idea doesn't have the constraints of a budget, a team, or a timeline that must be rigorously adhered to. All of these things will have changed by the time you start construction on an official design spec. Everything you promised to do in the proposal will now need to be turned into a very specific blueprint that your teammates will be able to understand and follow. By this time you'll likely have already brought all your departmental leads on board, and you'll have begun to discuss with them what the best way will be to get from where you are to a finished game that people won't be able to stop playing. As you tap into the intelligence and the creativity and the imagination of the people around you, you'll begin to pour all of this into a very powerful document that will represent the vision of what the finished product will be like. (For more information about how a design document is structured, see Chapter 8.)

At this point it will also be very important to begin to establish team priorities so that a firm schedule can begin to be drawn up and so that people will begin to see how they may be interdependent on one another. It's a good idea to break down critical jobs and classify them in such a way that people will understand which tasks need to be done and in what order. Typically you might have a breakdown that looks something like the following:

- **Primary Tasks.** These are all the things that must be done in order for the game to even function. These are sometimes also known as *critical path elements.* This most critically is going to deal with the development of the game engine, the level editor, and the basic rules system under which the game will operate.

- **Secondary Tasks.** Most secondary tasks are still very important but are primarily concerned with the game's content. This includes elements like the major story line, the central characters, the major villains or monsters, and other main parts of the story. These are components than help support the basic gameplay.

- **Tertiary Tasks.** This is also known as the "wish list." This is a collection of features or ideas that are not essential to your main objectives but are nice to add if you have the luxury of time and budget to enhance your game. This could include side quests, secret levels available only to players who reach a certain level, treasure items, auxiliary game functions, etc., etc.

The assembly and maintenance of a good design document will be an ongoing process. Until the day you ship your game out the door, you'll likely be amending the design document on a weekly, even daily basis. It is admittedly one of the most tedious aspects of the game designer's job, but it is a critical task that needs to be done so that everyone on the team can stay on top of what is going on with a project.

Admittedly, there are some individuals in the industry who feel there's no need to put together a design document, that it's a futile time-eating waste of energy that only serves to give the project writer something extra to do. While I respect the rights of other designers to say this, let me categorically say that this is a load of dingoes' kidneys. If you look very carefully at the loudest proponents of this position, you will find one or more of the following facts to be true about them:

1. They never have held any position lower than lead designer.
2. They work entirely alone.
3. They don't like having their ideas reviewed by others.
4. They lose team members faster than a sinking ship loses rats.
5. They no longer work in the industry.
6. They have *never* worked in the industry.

Tunnels, Trolls, & Troubles

In 1990, just six months out of college, I couldn't believe my incredible luck when I landed my first job in the computer gaming industry as a writer. I had been brought in quickly for my first assignment, the U.S. DOS-based port of *Tunnels & Trolls: Crusaders of Khazan*. On my first day of work, I was presented with a phone book-sized stack of all the game text and informed that they needed it rewritten so it could be usable in the U.S. edition. The text had been rather badly translated from a Japanese version of the game created by a company called Starcraft (no relation to Blizzard) and was laced with wonderful little gems of incomprehensibility like "sudden boat turns turtle!"

Unfortunately, there was absolutely no design documentation available. There was nothing that explained under what circumstances any of the text would be delivered. No maps, no outlines, no design notes. Just when I was beginning to despair I would never learn what the heck was supposed to be going on, I was graciously given a computer with *Tunnels & Trolls* already installed. In Japanese. For the next two months of my life, that provided the sole source of "documentation" upon which my translation of the text was based. Although I learned a great number of lessons about designing games while translating *T&T*, probably none was more important than the need for team members to always have some form of detailed design documentation available.

For a designer to refuse to maintain a design document is essentially the same as refusing to tell their team members what is going on. It's nothing more than a sheer egotistical laziness.

Walking Frankenstein: Building the Prototype

As the design team begins to plug away at their objectives and your project begins to take shape, there's one priority you need to concentrate on which no CEO will ever tell you about, but it's as critically important to the long-term survival of your project as hiring the right people. If you want to keep people on your team motivated, if you want to make sure the investors are happy, if you want to get magazine reviewers excited about what you're doing so that you'll get continuously good coverage about your product, you must, must, must think very early on about building a solid prototype of your game.

The prototype is a very important tool. You'll use it internally as a way to reassure investors that all the money and resources they've sunk into your project are being put to fruitful use. Externally you'll use it at trade shows to show off your game to magazines and future players, giving them some sort of visual hook on which they can fix their imaginations. Just throwing out an imaginative name for your product is rarely going to be enough to get people excited. You may be thinking you've got a year or so before the product is going to ship, but unless you get editors excited now, you may not be able to get the magazine covers you need next year, which are planned *months* in advance of actual publication.

As for the specifics about what you typically need to pour into your prototype, there are many different ways you can go. If it's very early in your production cycle, you may only be able to create noninteractive demos that just give a basic idea what it will be like to walk around in the world. If you've got a little more of the game engine functioning, you might want to show off combat in action or some other aspect of your game that makes it truly revolutionary. The most important thing is that you show, in a nutshell, the basics of the interface. Essentially, you are providing a visual version of the proposal. A *proof of concept demo* should be short but effectively convey some sense of the following:

- **The Look.** Buttons, menus, perspective, etc.
- **The Rules.** What's behind the decisions being made (procedural algorithms, flow charts, etc.).

- **The Content.** The story, script, art, music, etc. Much like a good movie trailer, the demo should present a sense of the aesthetics of the entertainment experience.

Although there are several specialty events held around the country every year that cater to some segment of the gaming population, most of the computer game business calendar revolves around one industry conference and trade show: E3. Every May, game professionals from around the globe gather to network, tout their latest releases, and hype their upcoming titles. It's a gigantic show and quite arguably the loudest one on earth. Some vendors even give out earplugs as promotional items.

With an average product development cycle of at least 18 months, chances are your title will be prepromoted at E3 more than once. How much of a demo you take to the expo will depend on how close you are to your anticipated launch date. If your game just got under way, you have a short, basic demo, perhaps shown only to representatives of the trade publications. If your game is close to release, you may have stations set up in your company's booth where attendees at large can sample the gameplay. The closer your title is to completion, the more everyone will expect to see.

The biggest impact E3 will likely have on your project, however, will be the way in which it can negatively affect your production schedule if you haven't already slated in at least three to four weeks before the event to create a demo. It is a recurrent problem that happens all through the industry, and it is astonishing how many designers always forget to account for it in their development schedules. If you don't know when E3 is this year, go find out and pencil it in on your calendar. Never forget. It is the one milestone of your project over which you will have absolutely no control.

Death March of the Sugar Plum Fairies: Getting Through to the End

Once your game engine is built and the prototype is impressing the media, most of the job in front of you is just going to be surviving the day-to-day necessities of creating the content, pouring it in, fixing any of the bugs that will inevitably crop up, and doing whatever you can to keep from going mad in the process. While I can't give you an absolute set of rules that will work with all development teams, I can at least give you a few choice pieces of advice that may help you survive the process.

It never fails to amaze me what designers will do in the name of this profession. All over the globe there's a small army of people who daily sacrifice their time, money, best ideas, and sometimes health on the altar of the great god Game Design, all in the name of making a steady paycheck and giving players what is hoped will be a fun way to waste people's weekends. And while the benefits of the gaming corporate culture are well known—pizzas, Nerf bat fights, company days off for the release of the latest *Trek* film—what is less talked about is the time-hallowed ritual of initiation through which we all bond, the end-of-project insanity that we affectionately call the "March of Death."

Regardless of what industry you've worked in before, you've probably experienced your own version of The March. As the headaches and nosebleeds mount, and your project careens with horrifying speed toward the iceberg that is your ship date, the laws of reason begin to crumble. Team meetings begin to take on a Donner Party quality, with all your department heads bravely providing the answers they think the project lead wants to hear, while secretly wondering how long they can keep it quiet that they can't complete the hundred critical tasks they've been assigned. In the end, all your team members are sitting in their cubicles at three o'clock in the morning blearily browsing the Internet for downloadable copies of Derek Humphry's *Final Exit*, wondering if it's possible to overdose on Diet Coke. Unfortunately, many of the keys to survival can only be learned in the trenches, but there are four choice Gems of Wisdom I've learned as a team leader that might ease your own passages through The March.

- **Manage Your Tow Trucks.** If a member of your team falls behind schedule, it's rather like having an accident on a busy freeway. Everyone who was depending on that individual is suddenly stuck behind them, and until that person's problem gets cleared up, nobody can move. When panic sets in, management tends to pull out all the stops and starts sending in all the tow trucks they can, magically believing somehow that 10 tow trucks can get the car out of the way faster than just the one that's required. The reality is all the tow trucks just get in each other's way and unnecessarily burn up precious company fuel, and the problem takes even longer to get cleared up. The time to add people to your project is at the beginning, not at the end. If you absolutely must bring on new help, make sure you only bring in as much as you really need.

- **Send the Zombies Home.** Chances are, that fiery-eyed look you're getting from the staff isn't a reflection of their passion for the project, but the idiot-light indicator that your troops are exhausted. The occasional all-nighter isn't necessarily a bad thing, but if you're regularly pulling 18-hour days, you aren't making as much progress as you'd like to believe. Zombie employees make dumb mistakes. They spend valuable company time repeatedly having to go back and fix things that shouldn't be broken in the first place, and they tend to turn in material that's subpar. Sleep is the most valuable weapon that your team will need to help slay the dragons that stand in their way.

- **Burn Your Map.** Don't give up all the good ground you've gained by robotically adhering to a battle plan written a year ago. Lobbing shells at where you *thought* the enemy should be, as opposed to where he really *is*, only serves to waste good explosives and irritates the natives. Adapt to reality. Get your bearings on where you are, and draw out a map of what you realistically can accomplish between where you are and where you need to be. Establish priorities that emphasize the spirit, if not the letter, of your original plan.

- **Keep Making Noise.** If you're in the jungle and everything suddenly falls quiet, there's a good chance you're about to be eaten by something unpleasant. Silence during The March means team members are being stalked by confusion, worry, or anger. Do whatever you can to encourage people to maintain regular radio contact with home base so that you can address any questions or concerns they have. This isn't to say that there has to be a constant drone of conversation going on—posted "quiet hours" can do miraculous things for team productivity and morale—but just make sure that everyone is at least getting the information they need before they most critically require it. Remember that every empire in history was built on a foundation of good communication.

The most important thing to remember about The March is that it will end either when you ship your product or when the bodies of your team members are being identified by loved ones. Keep in mind that during this phase no one else is enjoying themselves any more than you are, and people desperate to hit deadlines are bound to make mistakes. Be forgiving. If you stick together with your comrades in arms, you've got the best chance of getting through The March sane, prosperous, and ulcer-free.

Epilogue: To Market, to Market

What you've looked at so far is the *development* cycle of the game. After you are finished and have slept in for the first time since The Death March got under way, you may feel that you've thrown your game over a wall and out into the stores. At this point, what happens will be largely out of your hands, but it is helpful to know a few basics about what you can expect once your title hits the market.

There are no guarantees in business, and once a product hits the market, it may not go anywhere. However, if your game makes it past the introduction phase, it may go through the following stages. Just remember, it could go from introduction to decline, or from growth to decline, without experiencing the full cycle.

- **Introduction.** Your product is introduced and initially reaches the public. With development costs to recoup and advertising to pay for, in most cases even the most promising title is still a big cash sinkhole. Likely your backers will not be making money just yet. Traditionally, the price point is higher than later in the product's life.

  With RPGs, there is often an initial splash of sales when a new game appears, then things quiet down until word gets around. However, if your product is a sequel to a hugely successful game or is anticipated with a high degree of excitement in the industry, the introduction phase could be brief.

- **Growth.** This is a phase marketers love. Your competitors watch jealously as your title takes off and gains acceptance. If it was an innovation, start watching for the "me too" products bound to follow, as others try to cash in on your market share. Promotion continues but starts moving beyond the die-hard gaming market to a broader audience. Efficient and widespread distribution is a key factor in success. At some point in this phase, the price point may be adjusted down, to help penetrate a larger market.

- **Maturity.** Your title isn't the new kid on the block anymore, but sales are steady overall. Distribution channels may be expanded further. If all goes well, this can be where the real profits come in. In fact, a prolonged stay in the maturity phase is often what makes a product a best-seller.

  However, the steady sales of the maturity phase don't always happen without some intervention. After all, by this point competition from newer titles is causing sales to level off. This is often where marketers attempt *brand revitalization*. Examples of revitalization include releasing the game on a newer platform or releasing a "director's cut" or "platinum" edition. Other gimmicks are to announce a "hidden" level of the game or release an expansion pack to spark more sales of the original game.

- **Decline.** Usually, it isn't a big surprise when a product reaches this point. Sales drop off, distribution channels narrow, and it's time to make room for newer games. If your title successfully goes through all the previous phases, then finally begins to fade from the scene, don't feel bad. This is a natural and normal development after your product has lived a rich and full life.

Is That All There Is?

Introduction, growth, maturity, and decline. Is that all there is, you ask? Not necessarily. Sooner or later, a successful game may experience some additional marketing phases:

Brand revival might bring a product back on the strength of its name. The nostalgia factor can be a very strong force in the market. For example, adults who fondly remember a childhood arcade game might buy an updated version for home use. A good game from the past with a dated look might get a makeover. Classic games may also reappear on newer platforms.

International markets could open up and generate sales abroad after the product matures or declines in its home market. This might be due to a lag in technology; for example, in developing countries where slower computers are common, an older game might be more playable than the latest wonder.

Localization is the biggest factor in the international market. All the dialogue has to be translated and rerecorded. The more dialogue involved, the longer it will take to bring the title out. Text, including any writing on buttons, must also be translated.

International markets can also open up new markets, with separate product life cycles, simply because a title gains a following beyond its original borders. For example, many Japanese console games have been translated and successfully sold in the export market—in fact, with console fare, this is the norm. Virtually all major console RPGs originate in Japan. Cross-cultural exchange is a two-way street and doesn't always originate in North America or Europe.

Exercises

1. Go to the Internet and look up all the information you can find about a recently released title. Try and find press releases, interviews, or other promotional bits of information that talk about features of the game. How did the title deliver or fail to deliver on its early promises? How did some things seem to change through the coverage of the product?

2. Try to find some computer game titles that are utilizing popular licenses like *Star Wars* or *Dungeons & Dragons*. Look very carefully at the title and try to establish what real benefits or deficits you can see that the license is bringing to the game. Try to identify places where you see restrictions or problems that were probably brought up by use of the license.

Part Three

Workshop of the Gods

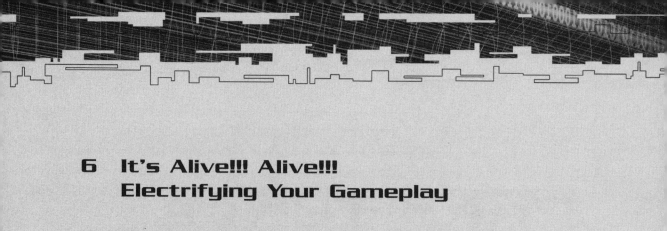

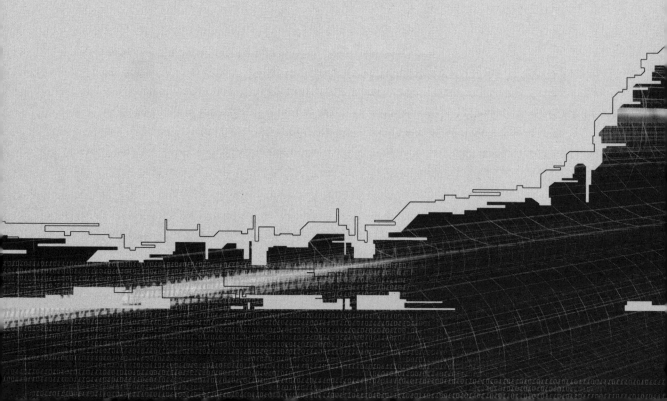

CHAPTER 6

1t's Alive!!! Alive!!! Electrifying Your Gameplay

SHARP

"Daring ideas are like chessmen moved forward; they may be defeated, but they start a winning game."

—Goethe

Mankind has been *engineered* to be a game-playing machine. Millions of years of evolution have rooted the instinct as deeply into our genes as our need to eat, breathe, and sleep. When our ancestors were prowling the grassy savannas of Africa with the aim of bringing down a mammoth, they were calculating strategies that would allow them to subdue their dinners while at the same time avoiding their leonine competitors. Early urban planners pitted themselves against the gods of chance, devising games of contingency to plan against wars, floods, and famines. Today we use games and simulations to explore ideas and worlds we may never know in reality, but *always* there has been a primal reminder of the origins from which our hobbies have sprung. To win is superb, but more important is the need for us *not to lose*. Games are powerful because we know that losing isn't just the end of interaction, it's the metaphor for the end of everything. To lose is to *die*. To play games is to learn how to avoid death and master the unmasterable.

In this game-playing world in which we live, we toy with virtually everything that surrounds us. As children we engage in wordplay to learn what is and is not allowable in the languages we're taught to speak. Early socialization games allow us to step into the shoes of our parents as we play doctor, soldier, chef, or spy. Once we get older our games become more serious, and whether or not we're conscious of our behavior, we daily engage in games to compete for money, power, sex, or prestige. We risk jobs, and fortunes, and lives on things that may be as important as ideologies or as irrelevant as who manages to get a leather ball across a muddy field.

It may seem ruthlessly reductionistic to suggest that serious issues like war, world hunger, and sexual harassment are all some form of *game,* but the harsh reality is that they can be very accurately described by a set of gamelike rules that affect the decision-making process of the "players." While these rules are essentially worthless when it comes to predicting the exact outcome of a specific situation, they can at least describe the general *way* in which the "game" will be played. The study of all these seemingly inborn rules is known as *game theory,* and its applications today are used to analyze everything from a game of chess, to the fluctuations of the stock market, to whether or not there's a best

Game Theory

Game theory has been with us a long, long time. In the Talmud—an ancient body of law and tradition of the Jewish people—a scribe attempted to resolve the "marriage contract" problem and formulated what is generally considered to be an early forerunner of the modern theory of cooperative games. In 1912 the French mathematician Émile Borel issued *La Theorie Du Jeu,* an important paper on games of chance and theories of play.

Probably the best-known games theorist, however, was the Hungarian-born mathematical prodigy John Von Neumann. Publishing both *Zur Theorie der Gesellschaftspiele (The Theory of Parlour Games)* and *The Theory of Games and Economic Behavior* (a collaborative work with Austrian economist Oskar Morgenstern), he established himself as one of the most influential figures in modern game theory. But Neumann's value to us goes far beyond just establishing an elaborate model of how games work. In the 1940s Neumann was an instrumental part in the development of computers, and many of his concepts about using "stored" computer programs laid the foundations for the computer software in use today.

military strategy to be employed against psychopathic third-world dictators armed with biogenic weaponry.

But the games with which *we* are most interested are a little different than those which weigh on the brows of the formal games theorist. While we may be concerned with heroes, and swords, and quests, and dragons, the theorist is only thinking about the nature of the relationships *between* those things. You and I would definitely see a difference in whether or not the combat we engage in happens on a computer screen or on a real-world battlefield. To the games theorist the reality or the unreality of the situation is irrelevant. The only important consideration is whether or not the possible actions and the outcomes of those actions are clearly defined to the players and whether or not the participants in the game have distinct preferences for one outcome over another. Fun to them may only be a by-product—not a reason—to play a game, and that's certainly a long way off from where you and I both want to be.

As different as the ways are in which game developers and games theorists look at games, there *are* valuable things to be learned from the theorist's studies. You won't find anywhere in their canon a convenient blueprint for building a blockbuster game, but they have done an excellent job of identifying the essential features that all games seem to share.

The Anatomy of Games

It seems schizophrenic that *Monopoly, You Don't Know Jack, 7th Guest, Pictionary,* and *Asheron's Call* can all be called games, but everyone recognizes them as such almost immediately. If I switch on my television set and see Regis Philbin on *Who Wants to Be a Millionaire,* I know pretty quickly that I'm watching a game show. Even were I to eliminate the stereotypical game show set and drop the host and the guest into the living room of *Friends* or *Buffy the Vampire Slayer,* I'd still be clued in very quickly to the fact that I was watching a game show just by listening to the back-and-forth questions and answers that define the trivia genre.

Usually we know a game when we see one, but sometimes it takes a little more work to look beneath the surface and find all the things that make games alike. The things I do while playing *Risk* may seem very different on the surface than the way I play *Dino Crisis,* but many of the same principles underlie all gaming experiences. If we break games down into their component parts, we will find that all of them have the following characteristics:

A Game Has at Least Two Players

If you're going to play a game, it stands to reason there's someone you're going to play *against*—or at least this is the essential assumption of game theory. Common sense would seem to agree with this idea, but there are numerous examples of games that get played every day that only seem to serve one player at a time. If we were to rigidly apply this concept in the context of any computer-driven experience, we would be invalidating virtually every computer game that predates the use of a local area network (LAN) or the Internet. By this definition, *Might & Magic, Ultima, Wizardry, Legend of Zelda,* and all the rest might be entertaining experiences, but they wouldn't qualify as games. This would in effect invalidate the entire concept of the single-player role-playing game.

The problem here is actually not in the supposition that there must be two players, but in our assumptions about what a player *is*. (You didn't realize becoming a game designer was going to require becoming an Existentialist, did you?) If we take a closer look at what the classical definition of a player is, we begin to see that we were right about thinking of CRPGs as games all along.

- A Player Makes Choices
- A Player Gets Payoffs

Obviously, the person who sits down to play a computer role-playing game does both of the above. They make choices about what things are going to happen in the game, and they get payoffs for the decisions they make while playing. But even if there is no other person in the room with them, and there's no other player connected to their computer via a network, there is still always a second player at work in the game. I usually refer to this phantom entity as the *metaplayer*, and it exists in all games in which some form of artificial intelligence is being pitted against the strategies of the player.

Granted, the metaplayer isn't always very bright, but the question of whether or not it is capable of making *excellent* choices is irrelevant in this context; living, breathing players make dumb game decisions all the time What *is* relevant is that the metaplayer does make choices about the moves it's going to make (like attacking the player, moving NPCs around, etc., etc.), and it can receive a payoff by defeating the human player. In some games this is extended even further by allowing monsters to steal items from the human player or use items that have otherwise been discarded.

The important concept to take away from this is that a role-playing game always requires some *force* of opposition that actively works against the goals of the rest of the players. Without opposition there is no conflict, and without conflict you don't have a game.

A Game Has Rules

People don't usually equate the word *rules* with fun. The word conjures up memories of having to eat all our Brussels sprouts before being allowed to go outside to play or being told we can't stay up past 10 o'clock to watch the *Late Nite Plenty Scary Movie.* But rules—or at least *good* rules—are never created with the intention of making people's lives miserable. Instead, in both our real lives and in games, we use them to give people an expectation of how things work and what the consequences may be for taking certain actions. Rules are the basic fabric out of which realities are woven, upon which cultures are based, and without which games wouldn't exist. If you want to give people the freedom to play, you first have to define what the rules and boundaries of the gameplaying experience will be.

Imagine what it would be like trying to talk to other people if there weren't any commonly understood rules for the English language. I might be trying to communicate that your dog is on fire, but unless we are both working from a somewhat shared vocabulary, syntax, and grammar, *zarabneech cohant snarf brak bogga bogga* is likely to leave you scratching your head in puzzlement instead of running for the firehose to extinguish ol' Sparky. Only by choosing to limit ourselves to a common language—or more specifically to a set of very specific linguistic *rules*—will we be free to communicate with other people and make ourselves understood. The same principles hold true during the construction of a game. It is only through the perception and understanding of a game's core rules that players can recognize how it can be played, mastered, and potentially won.

Think for a moment about chess. At the beginning of a standard game, why can't the first player simply take a pawn, reach across the game board, and instantly capture the opponent's king? *Physically* there's absolutely nothing that should prevent this from happening, short of the second player trying to knock the pawn out of the first player's hand. Both players, by initiating a game of chess, have agreed to a certain *reality* that chess represents. The rules have defined the size of the world, the arrangement of the pieces at the start of the game, the ways in which those pieces can legally move, the ultimate objective of the game, and even the behavior of the players. Even though there's no dictum that expressly says "a pawn cannot immediately kill the enemy king," the rules have defined a world in which that move is impossible to make based on the pawn's *movement characteristic* (i.e., the ways in which it can move) combined with its *starting position* and the positions of other game pieces. It is precisely because of the way in which the pawn and other pieces have been limited that makes chess a game and not just an exercise in rearranging little figurines on a tabletop. The gameplay challenge entails working within these rules and limitations to achieve the goal of capturing an opponent's king.

In an RPG you will be tasked with creating a set of interlocking rules that go far beyond those laid down in a game like chess. You will have to define all the ways in which players will be able to interact with their avatar, with the environment, with objects, and with other players and monsters. Some of these rules will take the forms of *algorithms* that dictate the way in which certain situations will be resolved, like determining what happens when a player tries to kick down a door. Other rules will just be general principles universally applied to the design that will help the player understand how your gaming universe works. Collectively all these ideas must work smoothly together to create a seamless, internally consistent body of procedures known as a *rules system*.

A Game Requires Players to Make Choices

If creating games were only a matter of setting down rules and dictating empty realities, there would be little point in the exercise. It would be boring to visit a world where you'd have to do everything you were told. Players want options, selections, *choices*. It is this freedom to be a part of what happens that sets a game apart from older, more traditional forms of entertainment. The ways in which games are different from their predecessors are akin to differences between lectures and conversations. While both are oral forms of communication, what people *get* from both experiences are very, very different.

In a formal lecture, the audience is *passive*. They have no control over what topics are going to be covered by the lecturer or in what order. They sit, they listen, they watch, and after it's over everybody goes out for coffee and donuts. Nothing that is presented has *anything* at all to do with the will of the attendees. Even if delivered to an auditorium full of empty chairs, the speech would be exactly identical to one delivered to a coliseum full of cheering fans simply because in both cases the audience has no *choice* in the flow or emphasis of the material presented. Books, and movies, and plays all follow the lecture format, but games are meant to be an interaction between the player and the situations created by the designer. For this reason, games tend to be more like a conversation.

In a conversation, the participants are all *active*. If someone mentions a topic that interests a listener, the listener is then *somewhat* free to control the direction in which the conversation will flow by making choices about what questions will be asked or what new topics will be interjected. A good RPG needs to flow in the same way. Players want some degree of control over where they go, what they do, and when they do it. People want to know what kinds of choices they have and how those choices will impact the ways in which the game can be played.

The Button of Death
Design Dilemma

Choices are only interesting when the people who are making them have some idea of what benefits or penalties are likely to be incurred by making them. The necessity to provide players with an adequate amount of information so that they can make informed choices can sometimes lead into troublesome design problems. One conundrum that raises its nasty little head from time to time is a little number that I call The Button of Death Design Paradox.

Imagine that while exploring the world a player comes across a button set into an otherwise featureless wall. Being that the purpose of a game world is that it should be explored and that everything in that world is presumably made to be used, most players are going to push the button to see what happens. Let's say on this occasion that pushing the button opens a secret door that was hidden before, and the player can now access a new area that would have been otherwise unavailable.

By providing precisely this scenario, you've just instructed the player with a "rule" about how your world works: Buttons open doors. Armed with this knowledge the player should be able to apply what they've learned throughout the rest of the computer game in order to make an informed decision about whether or not they should push buttons.

Now let's assume the player is stuck in another location somewhere later on in the game, and they lay eyes on a well tucked-away button hidden in a corner. Informed by past experiences, they hit it expecting a secret door to open up, but this time they get hit with a fireball that does a massive—even potentially lethal—amount of damage.

If the designer hasn't provided some kind of clue about what sets this button apart from the door-opening variety, they've just violated a rule that's already been established by the game. The value of choice has been taken away from the player because they have no way of knowing whether pushing the button opens a door or whether it will do some catastrophic amount of damage. While this would certainly add a heightened degree of tension to the pushing of any buttons in the game, it really is nothing more than a way of arbitrarily punishing the player for being curious. Even worse, the value of the things that the player has learned are now worthless, making the winning of the game more a matter of chance than of acquired skill.

Being the good and conscientious designers that we are, let's try and take care of this situation. Let's add a small visual detail that will give the player some idea what the consequences will be for pushing a particular *type* of button. If players push blue buttons, they will consistently open a locked secret door. If they push red buttons, they will always get hit with the fireball of doom.

Under the new "rules" that we have established, there are several interesting effects on the gameplay. Players will be able to determine which buttons are good to push and which ones are bad, and therefore be able to make informed choices. It will also have the added bonus that players will pay a little closer attention to their environment to see if there's anything new around them that may lead to new kinds of experiences.

But Houston, we *still* have a problem.

Provided that players manage to catch on to our clever little color-coding scheme and they begin to apply what they know, there's going to be an almost immediate effect on how they proceed through the game. After they've pushed two or three of the red buttons and gotten the idea that hitting them is a bad thing, why on Earth would they ever hit any others, excepting for the occasional decision made in haste? Peppering these little jewels of destruction through the rest of the levels of your game will be pointless because players will know better than to fool with them. At first it might seem like removing red buttons from the later levels is a good idea, but this actually just makes the whole situation worse. If the player is wandering around in the world and they've learned that red buttons are bad things, but if there aren't any red buttons around for them to choose to push or not push, the rules that you've taught them are now utterly *worthless* from a gameplaying standpoint. Never offer people a choice that doesn't really exist. If you've designed some element that would always run contrary to a player's wishes (a generally bad idea overall), don't irritate players by pointing out the fact that you're tying their hands.

So how do we get out of this little dilemma? The first and most utilitarian way is to simply not have little buttons around that will do damage to players. From a worldbuilding standpoint these kinds of traps are exceedingly silly conventions to begin with. What kind of idiot attaches a flamethrower to a light switch in their office? Under what possible circumstances would a trap like that be necessary or even all that useful? If the point is to make something a trap, does it really make sense from the builder's standpoint to give the potential target a clue that they're about to be *toast*?

Ignoring these more pragmatic issues, there's still a way that we can slightly retool our color-coded buttons to ensure what the player learns remains useful throughout the entire game. The trick is to pair the red button's negative effect with a positive one. What if pushing the red button has an additional function similar to that of the blue button? Instead of just getting hit by a big ball of fire, let's assume that red buttons will now also open up secret doors or caches where treasure might be found. Under these circumstances the player now has a truly meaningful choice they can make. They can decide to take the damage that red buttons dish out in exchange for finding out what's behind door number three. This principle can be used throughout the entire game, and it provides a good rule upon which a designer can build—and upon which the player can rely.

The decisions that will be open to the player can range from the simple to the complex. At the very start of a game when players know relatively little about how a game works, the best choices offered to players should be simple, like deciding on whether they're going to wear the tight leather cuirass or the looser silk blouse. As they begin to progress through the game and can see what's important, they should be offered increasingly more meaningful choices, like deciding if they're going to join a guild or how their accumulated experience points will be distributed among their various skills.

Complexity and simplicity aren't the only factors that will differentiate one kind of choice from another. Of very great importance to players will be whether their decisions will have *transitory* or *permanent* effects on the gameplay.

A transitory choice is one that a player makes which can be undone *within* the context of the game. For instance, if you allow your avatar to walk into a shop and sell her magneto boots, she ordinarily should have the option to later return and buy them back from the shop. Depending on how you engineer your economic system, you might sell them back to the player for the same amount they got for selling them, assuming she comes back the same day. If the player's been gone a month, however, she may discover her boots have been marked up in order for the proprietor of the shop to make a reasonable profit on their sale. The value of the transitory choice is that it doesn't punish the player for making dumb mistakes. If they've accidentally sold something they didn't mean to sell, they can get it back almost immediately without being penalized. Even if they are eventually forced to pay a higher fine, they still have the opportunity to undo something they might not have wished to do.

A permanent choice in a game is a much more serious matter. The nature of these decisions is that once they are made, the player is going to be forced to deal with the long-term effects of that decision *for the rest of the game*. If the player doesn't like what happens, they may be forced to retreat to a previously saved game or in some cases start an entirely new game from scratch. A very prominent example of a permanent choice is the selection of a character's class. That means that through the entire title, the player is going to be stuck with whatever bonuses and restrictions come along with being a member of that class. It is a decision that, once made, cannot be undone.

If you intend to offer a player a choice that is going to have a permanent effect, they need to be made aware at the time they are making the decision that it's something that will have a profound impact on their game experiences. It may be a bit artificial to have a character start yakking about the probable effects of something the player might choose to do, but never forget that an uninformed choice is really no choice at all.

Um, Sure . . . Make Me a Whatchamacallit . . .

A common complaint I've heard from new players is that they dislike having to make choices about their classes or attributes before they have a firm grasp about what all those things *mean*. If you simply throw a wad of numbers at them at the beginning of the game, you're forcing players who are unfamiliar with your rule system into making a *value-less* choice. Give people the chance to bum around in your gameworld for a while and see how things work. Let them run into different classes of individuals or characters who are very proficient at a certain skill set. Once they can directly experience what benefits are to be gained from a certain set of attributes or a certain class, they'll be informed enough to be able to make a good decision. Allow the player to make choices about who their characters are *after* they've had a chance to learn the ground rules of your reality.

While it's true that you can put information about complex issues in the player manual, never rely on materials external to the game to be the primary source of the player's understanding of your game! When most individuals buy a title, they expect to be able to pull the disk out of the box, slam the CD or DVD into the drive, and in a few moments be up and able to play the game. Design for that instinct. Let the players learn about the gameworld *in* the gameworld, not from elsewhere. You *never* want to focus the player's attention on anything but the things that are going on onscreen. This is an important part of keeping the player immersed in the fantasy of your world.

This doesn't mean players expect to be able to decide everything that can happen in a game. The reason they have come to play in your universe and not just build one of their own is because they want the *unexpected*. Players want certain things to be out of their control, to be just beyond their reach. If winning a game were merely a matter of pulling down a drop-down menu and clicking on the "Instantly Win the Game" option, there would be little challenge in playing in the first place. Challenge is a function of risk, and risk can only exist when the circumstances are at least partially out of the player's hands. Sure, if you choose to offer up the tools that you built your game with so players can construct their own scenarios, they need to have the ability to do whatever they want when they are supposed to be in charge. But when it comes to a single-player experience that you've crafted for them, all players really want is a say in what happens, not total dominance.

A Game Provides Payoffs to the Players

People aren't generally interested in making choices just for the sake of making them. It's highly unlikely you'll find someone who dislikes ice cream hanging around Baskin-Robbins perversely choosing between flavors just because they *can.* In games and in life we all have preferences of outcome. We will engage in choice making so long as we believe one choice provides more benefits to us than another. It is this belief in potential future benefits that drives people to vote for one candidate instead of another, to buy product X rather than product Y, to fight the transgenic evil gerbil king instead of retreating to the starting point of the game. If your goal is to design something that other people will want to play, you must provide them with frequent *payoffs* that make the journey personally worthwhile. From start to finish you should always be asking yourself: *What is the player going to get out of this?*

Going back to the earliest days of the 20th century, psychologists began to stack up evidence for a theory of learning that's become one of the greatest, but least frequently discussed, cornerstones of modern game development. While the bulk of their studies primarily dealt with rats, levers, food pellets, and electric shocks, they verified a very *human* principle that governs the behavior of game players everywhere. The upshot of this study was simply this: If you reward a living creature for a behavior, they will continue to engage in that behavior until such a time you stop rewarding them. If, however, you punish a creature for a certain behavior, they will eventually stop engaging in that activity altogether.

Called *operant conditioning,* this idea of modifying behaviors through frequent rewards or punishments can seem a little Machiavellian, but it does underline a very important concept. So long as you continue to appropriately reward the player for making an effort, they will continue through floods, fires, and famines in order to finish your game. It seems like common sense, but it's surprising how many developers forget that it's the victories and the treasures—not the obstacles—that make people interested in playing in the first place. If you stop giving out the carrots that will keep players excited, or even worse, if you start *punishing* them for their curiosity, you're only going to drive away the very people who *want* to enjoy your game.

Payoffs to the player can take many different forms. If I find a password that lets my avatar board a starship, it's a very different award than the one I get for finishing the game, even though both of them are technically given to me as a payoff for my efforts. These types of rewards, when broken down for analysis, constitute the following four distinct categories:

- **Rewards of Glory.** Glory rewards are all the things you're going to give to the player that have absolutely no impact on the gameplay itself but will be things they end up taking away from the experience. This includes winning the game by getting all the way to the end, completing a particularly difficult side quest, or defeating the plots of evil monsters.

  Glory rewards can be some of the easiest to distribute to the player and will cost you very little time or effort to create. You can provide screens that congratulate achievement as in the Quest completion panel featured in *Diablo II*. You can also have word "spread" among the nonplayer characters so that when the player goes into the next town they can be hailed for their heroic deeds. If you succeed in making the player feel good about themselves, and you give them things they can brag about to other players, they will by extension also feel very good about your game and will recommend it to others. This will also make them much more likely to come back and buy a sequel.

- **Rewards of Sustenance.** Rewards of this nature are given so the player can maintain their avatar's status quo and keep all the things they've gained in the game so far. These might include health packs that heal injuries, mana potions that increase a player's magical abilities, high-tech armor that shields a player from e-mag radiation, robots that remove curses or diseases, or even storage boxes or beasts of burden that allow a player's avatar to carry more resources along with them.

  It's never a bad idea to be generous with handing out sustenance rewards. These are things that make it *possible* for the player to keep playing. Without plentiful supplies of these rewards, players are repeatedly forced to go through the very un-fun process of obsessively saving and reloading, and this can discourage exploration and make players reluctant to try new things.

- **Rewards of Access.** Rewards of access have three critical features: they allow a player access to new locations or resources that were previously inaccessible, they are generally used only once, and they have no other value to the player once they've been used. Keys, picklocks, and passwords are typical examples of this kind of reward. (By using a key, a player gains access to a new area, and often the key is then simply discarded because it's no longer usable.) Blueprints and treasures are useless to a player except as a one-time medium of exchange to acquire other objects, services, or technologies. Favors granted by NPCs also tend to fall into this category since they are usually only a temporary avenue to an alliance, a service, or the opening of an area previously barred to the player.

  The implication of rewards of access is that there must be bottlenecks in the design through which the player must pass in order to get to the next level, area, world, etc. In order to pass through those bottlenecks, the player will need to pass a certain minimum threshold, like possessing the right code card to get through a specific door or having enough cash on hand to buy the weapon needed to kill the guard.

  From a design standpoint, access payoffs can be very desirable since their long-range effects can be relatively easy to predict. With the exception of currencies, the circumstances under which each will be used and the resulting long-range effects are known *binary quantities*—the player either has access or they don't.

  The downside of these kinds of rewards is that if overused by the designer, they can begin to choke the player into overly specific courses of action and thus make the game feel more like a cattle chute than a gaming world.

- **Rewards of Facility.** Rewards of facility enable a player's avatar to do things they couldn't do before or enhance abilities they already possess. When well handled, they should increase the number of strategies and options the player will have for playing the game. A good example of a facility reward might be a magic orb that lets an avatar walk through a stone wall or a cybernetic software upgrade that lets them shut down enemy gun turrets at a distance. Both of these examples would provide the player with new ways to play (but both will also complicate the designer's work immeasurably if not well considered).

Facility rewards can be used anywhere and at any time and will have one of three duration characteristics. For instance, a magic potion might give an imbiber only a *temporary* boost in health, while a magic ring that grants an extra level of capability to the wearer would have a *transitory* duration, meaning the reward is granted to one individual only for the length of time they are wearing or using it. *Permanent* duration facility rewards would include spells that have been learned by the avatar or skills that they have acquired through experience and hard work.

Although players are often happiest with receiving facility rewards, these are the most difficult kinds of things to steadily introduce into a game. Facility rewards are notorious for upsetting the balance of a title and require significant thought and testing before they can be safely introduced into a game.

So, overall, what are the best kinds of rewards to introduce? That depends entirely on what kind of audience you're looking to attract to your title. If you look at the six player types I defined in Chapter 1 as representing six fundamental player needs, you already have half of a successful equation for motivating your players. If you want to appeal to a navel-gazing audience, you might want to structure your game in such a way that there are frequent opportunities for character advancement. To appeal as strongly as possible to this audience, you'll have to hand out experience points and levels more frequently in order to hold the player's continued interest. If, however, you hand out treasure items more frequently than you increase player levels, you'll attract Treasure Hounds as your primary audience, which in turn will end up affecting how you structure your inventory management. Every choice you make about the kind of rewards and payoffs you're going to give to the player will affect the flow, feel, and mechanics of your overall project.

A Game Has an Objective

What is the objective of role-playing games? You climb the mountaintop and pose the question to the wise and ancient guru of games, She Who Knows the Truth. Looking deeply into your eyes, she hands you something, *The Book of All*

Answers. You open the tome expectantly . . . but find only your own face staring back at you, reflected in a mirror sandwiched between the tattered covers. You descend from the heights laughing at your own foolishness, realizing that role-playing games are really about *you,* and your trek to find the answers in the external world has been nothing but a journey of folly. . . .

It's possible my little Zen-tale answer is a joke, but I'd be lying if I said there wasn't at least a kernel of truth to it. In other kinds of games, it's easier to nail down what players are playing *toward.* In blackjack whoever gets closest to the magic number of 21 without going over it wins the game. In football the winner is whatever team can score the most points before the buzzer sounds at the end of the fourth quarter. Pick almost any title in any other genre and you'll find the main reason why people are playing is to *win* the game. But winning always requires goals toward which the player must strive, else the experiences are not technically *games.* If there's no preestablished victory condition that all the players understand and can agree upon, then no one can ever be declared the winner.

Most single-player RPGs that are produced and sold in the United States still adhere to this classical definition of a game. *Baldur's Gate, Diablo, Planescape: Torment, Deus Ex,* and *Final Fantasy* all drive toward a confrontation in which the player will pit their avatar against all the forces that have been aligned to destroy them. In some cases there are *multiple* endings available, allowing the ultimate conclusion to depend more directly on the player's actions. But whether these experiences are *linear* or *multilinear* in structure, there is still a point at which the player may win the game.

Unlike other genres, however, role-playing games don't exist purely for the purpose of reaching an ending. Players invest a great deal of themselves into the building up of their characters, teaching them skills, and buying them better materials. Gamers speak of their avatars in the same tone that most people reserve for conversations about their children or good friends. They have pride about what their on-screen personas have achieved, but they are mostly proud about what their characters have *grown into.* The final challenge at the end of the game is not solely a victory, but a defining test of a player character's hard-earned mettle. The ending is the answer to a dramatic question that has been posed throughout the entire game: *Is my hero up to taking on the bad guys?*

The answer to this ultimate question of whether or not the player's character is really up to the challenge is really a deflection. No one plays an RPG to benefit a small bundle of pixels living somewhere on the hard drive. Even when

Multimadness—Rise of the Neverending Game

Even though a single-player game's end exists to challenge the hero, and the hero spends the majority of their time developing skills so they will be prepared to meet whatever awaits them at game's end, there is a cruel irony built into this system of problems and problem solvers. At the cathartic moment that the avatar has finally proven themselves truly worthy, the player must then bid them farewell. The ending brings about the resolution of the great menace, but it also means that the player can't do anything further with this marvelous creation they've spent so much time building up.

To address this problem, game developers in the 1990s began to try new ways to enable players to *keep* playing with their avatars. Some developers made their games replayable by introducing *multilinear* story lines, plots that would end in different ways depending on the choices the player made during the game. Around this same time *expansion packs* began to appear. These products were not whole games in and of themselves, but only add-on levels that could be "plugged in" to an existing game engine, which would allow the player to pick up new items, encounter new monsters, and overall explore new territories.

Following the introduction of *multiplayer* action games like *Doom,* role-playing developers saw opportunities to introduce RPG elements into a hybrid genre focusing more intensely on combat. In games like *Nox,* players can still play through a single-player experience to defeat a nemesis set up by the designers, or they can choose to play cooperatively or competitively against other human players in short objective-driven minigames like capture-the-flag or king-of-the-hill.

gamers play a character fundamentally different from themselves, that character still represents the *players'* interests in the game. If an avatar's arm is broken, then the player has lost that ability in the world. If that avatar is killed and can't move forward, it is the gamer who suffers the consequences. Avatars are a direct extension of the player's ego, and everything that benefits or thwarts that character is something that is done directly to the psyche of the player.

Other developers saw the possibilities of creating large environments in which the player's avatar could theoretically play forever—or at least so long as they pay a monthly access fee. *Ultima Online* hit the market in 1997 with the first commercially successful massively multiplayer persistent universe and broke critical ground by giving players a way to build and play characters over long periods of time while also interacting with thousands of other players who were doing the same thing.

Today all of these different solutions to extending the synthetic life of the avatar remain valid, but each also comes with its own consequences to the experience. Multilinear titles can be interesting ways to reexplore worlds or stories, but the overwhelmingly epic scope of many of today's games is preventing most players from finishing even one story thread, let alone three. Expansion packs can be a quick way to extend the life of a product, but the resources used in development can sometimes eat up funds and time needed to create true product sequels. Multiplayer games often suffer shortcomings by capping the capabilities of individual avatars in order to provide a balanced experience for everyone.

When and if you think about extending the life of your game so that players can continue to play, go back to the most important question in regard to the game's objectives. What is the player getting out of the experience? Are you giving the player lots of really fun new things to do, or are you just providing busy work both for players and for your team?

So we come full circle back to my little Zen joke at the beginning of this section. Role-playing games are ultimately about the player and what the player wants. If you're a smart designer, you'll try to create a game that will make the player feel good about the game and themselves. You want them to feel like they're the heroes they're pretending to be. They want to feel smart, beautiful, and courageous, like they have the world by the nose and can do anything they ever want to do. Is this realistic? Who cares? Realism isn't the point in an RPG any more than realism is the point in an *Indiana Jones* movie. Life in the universes you create for players is supposed to be escapist and oversimplified. That's what makes them amusing and not a bundle of accounting homework. The objective is to provide the player with *fun*.

The Dance of Shiva: Rules, Structures, and Balance

In the mythology of India, the dance of the many-armed god Shiva defines the nature of the universe. Out of it come the conflicting forces of creation, preservation, destruction, revelation, and concealment. It is the interplay of those forces that gives form and meaning to the reality we know, and it is through Shiva's efforts that those energies are kept in a carefully maintained balance for the good of all the universe.

Absent a few critical facts, I might swear the description applied to the inner workings of a computer game rather than the actions of a Hindu deity. In a microcosm all the same purposes must be served by both the software and the god. They exist to give their universes direction, to provide them with structure, and to hold in check the forces that seek to unbalance the Creation. Without them their respective universes cannot exist. The dance brings reality to both.

Within every computer role-playing game there are four fundamental forces out of which the "personality" of the game will be created. Although these are not necessarily forces that are in opposition to one another, they represent different polar functions that you as a designer will have to address in order to create a cohesive experience.

Rules provide a definition for how everything will work within the fictional universe and the ways in which the player will be able to exert their will. *Structures* provide a framework for the events and causes that the player may choose to follow or reject. Out of *Balance* flow general principles that ensure that the player's experiences are always tilted in their favor and that the game is fun to play from the beginning to the very ending.

In this chapter you will take a closer look at the first three principles of Rules, Structures, and Balance, all of which are generally organizational in nature. A fourth and last principle, *Worldbuilding*, will be covered in Chapter 7.

The Rules System Can't Dance, But It Sure Got Algorithm . . .

It may or may not be true that Isaac Newton got himself bonked on the head by an apple and thus discovered gravity. Factually true or not, we all know that it's at least *plausible* because it illustrates a law that anybody can test at any point on Earth at any time. Barring a major rupture of the space-time continuum, I can be reasonably assured that if I toss an apple into the air, it's going to fall back to Earth within a certain amount of time, at a location dependent on how hard it was thrown and in what direction it was originally propelled. I also know by extrapolation that if someone heaves a tennis ball, a kitten, a VW Bug, or the Empire State Building into the heavens, *all* of them will come crashing back down again (though with admittedly varying consequences to the thrower).

The reason I can predict the behavior of all these oddly airborne objects is that they all exist within a reality that follows rules of gravity that I understand. Because I can predict these actions, I can also make plans for the future. To put it explicitly into gaming terms, I can *strategize* appropriate measures that will prevent me from being crushed under falling Volkswagens even *before* I lob them skyward. If, however, the rates at which cars fell were inconstant, or if the locations in which they hit were truly unpredictable, no amount of strategizing of mine would ever do me any good. Random moves would be just as valid as predetermined ones in choosing a course of action that might shield me from vehicular precipitation. Either I would be saved or I wouldn't. Reason would be useless.

In the same way that comprehensible rules let me live out my life in a reasonable fashion in *this* reality, well-crafted rules help players understand how your universe works and give them the tools to develop strategies they can apply throughout the gameplay. Players will trust that you're playing fair with them if they feel as though you're being consistent in the way that you apply your rules. If there's anything you can do to anger gamers most, it's to yank the rug out from underneath them by changing the way things work whenever it strikes your fancy. Don't get into an unfair competition with your audience. Nobody will want to play by your rules unless you're willing to play by them too.

As useful as a rules system can be in aiding the understanding of the player, that understanding is only a by-product of its *primary* function. A rules system exists to provide the computer with the basic algorithms it needs to determine how things work or how to solve certain problems. From beginning to end your

Messin' with the Magic

Over the years, I've repeatedly witnessed enthusiastic green designers getting themselves into a froth over an old, bad design idea. Although it has taken various forms depending on the game in question, it usually goes a little something like this:

> "Hey, let's set up the magic system so that whenever the avatar moves from one area of the world to another, the *ways* in which all their spells work will change!"

Whenever I hear this said, I sigh nostalgically. I sympathize because at one point *I* was that idiot green designer. Those very words have come out of my own mouth at points in my career when I just didn't know better.

All in all the *idea* is interesting in an academic sort of way, but it does two very bad things in terms of gameplay.

First, it simply causes confusion, and confusion detracts from strategy. Players can't reliably plan a course of action unless they're fairly certain how the resources they have can be used. They could, whenever they enter a new area, simply test all the effects of everything they have, but in the long run this would become a maintenance chore rather than an act of exploration—just one more thing that the player is *forced* to do in order to figure out the gaming universe.

job as game designer is really going to involve being the High Priest or Priestess in service to the great god Algorithm. It's probably time you met your new Lord. He is a very, very unforgiving master. Mwaaahahahahahaaaa . . . *(Cue: sheets of lightning, ominous music soundtrack, visions of screaming game designers running for their lives. . . .)*

You might not be conscious of it, but algorithms play a critical role in your day-to-day life. You use an algorithm every morning when you get out of bed and search for where you left your wallet or your shoes the previous night. When your friend calls to ask you directions from their workplace to the evening party you're throwing, you use an algorithm to explain all the turns and stops they'll

The second and more insidious effect is that it invalidates the value of the player's experience. If they've learned that this is the way that spell X works, that knowledge is utterly worthless to them later in the game. True, by constantly forcing the player to relearn everything they know, they are less likely to have elements of their knowledge just lying around inert because it's of no use to them in later levels. But rather than changing the rules by which the magic operates, it's a much more interesting solution if you let them use what they *do* know in new ways as they journey through your title.

Let's say that early on in your game you give players a spell that makes things cold. In the early levels of the game, the player can use it to freeze an opponent to the ground for a few rounds. Not necessarily an earthshakingly powerful spell, but useful. In later levels of the game, the player might be able to snuff out a burning bush by freezing it with the same spell. Even later still, the player might realize that by using their freezing spell they can cross what appears to be an otherwise seemingly uncrossable river by freezing a series of stepping stone-like patches across it to reach the other side.

In all three of the above instances, you have applied one consistent spell rule—that it freezes things—but achieved three very different benefits for the player. It was by presenting different ways in which they could reuse old knowledge to solve new problems that you kept the value of the cold spell alive throughout the life of the game while also letting the player experience new gameplay.

have to make to get to where you live. Even when you're cooking up a vat of your family's famous spaghetti sauce, you're probably working from your dear old great-great-grandmother's award-winning Secret Algorithm that's been passed down from one generation to the next. As imposing as the word sounds, an *algorithm* is just a fancy word for a systematic procedure broken down into a series of discrete but finite steps used to answer a question, solve a problem, or complete a task.

While you are developing a game, one of your biggest responsibilities is going to be determining how and why things work. In order for the computer to know what it should do when faced with certain situations—say, like when a monster attacks an avatar with a sword—the designer and/or programmer must supply it with an algorithm that precisely details what "an attack" *means*. It seems like it should be a simple task, so let's take a crack at developing a quick 'n' dirty attack algorithm.

```
1) Select a Target.
2) Walk to Target.
3) Swing Sword at Target.
4) If Target Is Hit with Sword, Do Damage...
```

Seems pretty straightforward, right? There are only four basic commands in this algorithm that the computer needs to worry about, so it seems like it should be very easy for the computer to do. Unfortunately, unless you've done some other work beforehand, the computer is going to get hung up on step 1 and never even *get* to part when the monster whacks the avatar. Why is that? Let's take a second, more critical look at the command list:

```
1) Select a Target.
```

How exactly is the computer supposed to *select a target?* To you or me that's a commonsense phrase. We've ostensibly got free will, and making selections is pretty much a breeze to us. But until such a time that we define this phrase to the computer, it's just a collection of three words, 13 letters, and two spaces.

Before it can make its selection, the computer must be told *how* to evaluate its potential targets and upon what basis it should make its final "decision." This means that you will have to develop a *second* algorithm that will give the computer the logic it should use when selecting its targets. In a simplistic game this might only entail telling the computer-controlled monster to go after a random character or whoever is closest. A slightly more sophisticated artificial intelligence algorithm might drive a monster to prey on the weakest members of the player's party. No matter how simple or complex the process is going to be, the computer still will have to be instructed how it should make its selections before it can move on to the next step in the attack algorithm.

If you go back to the list of four steps now, you may begin to see the inherent complexities that remain in the simple-seeming list of instructions. Before you can get through step 2, you're going to have to think about algorithms that determine exactly what *walking* is. What if there's a stand of trees between the monster and the character that's been selected to be attacked? You'll have to write a *pathing* algorithm that tells the monster how he'll be able to get around the trees, rather than simply stopping when he runs into them. In step 3, the computer will have to know what a sword is before the monster swings it and which one the monster is currently holding. Step 4 grows even more complex as the computer must use an algorithm to resolve the effects of the attacker's attacking capabilities versus the defender's defensive capabilities. As you break it down, you may end up using something that looks vaguely like what you might find in a high school algebra textbook:

A)   If (TDS + TAC + TWDB + E + ST) > (AAS + AWB + E) then HIT = FALSE ELSE C
[The computer checks to see if the target's combined defense skill, armor class, weapon defense bonus, enchantments, and saving throws is greater than the attacker's combined attack skill, weapon bonus, and enchantments. If true, then the target has been hit, and the actions specified in step C should be undertaken. If false, then the computer simply proceeds on to step B.]

B)   RETURN TO EVALUATE   [The computer returns to an evaluation algorithm that will determine what the monster does next; e.g., run away, attack, defend, etc.]

C)   THP = THP - (AWD + ASTR)   [If a hit has been determined to have occurred in step A, then in step C the computer deducts an amount of damage from the target's hit points equal to the target's hit points minus the attacker's combined weapon damage and strength.]

At every step in this process, the computer will make dozens of evaluations and decisions, but the reasoning the computer will use to make those decisions are all going to originate in the processes defined by the design team.

If your head is starting to boggle thinking about all those algorithmic steps that will be necessary just to get one monster to cross one patch of ground to attack one opponent, you're beginning to see how complex a web of interactions that putting together the rules system for a game is going to be. You will be doing nothing less than constructing the rules and rationale for reality. But as daunting as this can seem at first, don't be too overawed by the deceptive enormity of this task. If you work *smartly,* you can develop a system of rules that will be usable in every corner of your game and not only in special circumstances.

The exact number and types of rules you'll need to develop for your game are variable. The largest determining factors will depend on how rich an experience you want to deliver to the player. For everything they can experience while traversing your game world, you're going to have to come up with the ways in which things are going to work. If the player's avatar can climb up walls, under

Instance and Class Relationships

Let's say you want the player to be able to blow up a certain wooden door in a game with a hand grenade found nearby. To make this possible in the game you could create a rule that says, "If Hand Grenade A hits Wooden Door B, Wooden Door B will be destroyed." That's a straightforward, functional rule that's known as an *instance relationship*. That means that in the one particular instance specified by the terms of the rule, that rule will always apply.

Although the rule as stated above will work, it is limited by its specificity—you won't be able to use it anywhere else in the game. If you want to be able to blow down *other* doors, you're going to have to create a separate algorithm for every other instance. In time it's going to get a little tiresome to have to create a whole new algorithm every time you create a new door. But if you take a step back and think about how all doors are destroyed, you might realize that your rule can be generalized and made more "portable."

Instead of limiting the rule to deal with the instance of one specific hand grenade destroying one specific door, think about *any* object A destroying *any* object B. By saying that all hand grenades belong to a master category of objects that have the quality of doing *damage* and that all doors belong to a master category of objects that have the quality of being *breakable,* you've established a *class relationship* between those objects. Based on this idea, you can then develop an algorithm that says that whenever any object that has the damage quality comes into contact with any object that has the breakable quality, the breakable object will then be broken.

The advantage in using this system is that *any* object that has the damage quality, *not* just the hand grenade, can now be used to break down the door. That also means that you could make a whole class of objects that are breakable and could use anything from hacksaws, to handguns, to hamsters to break them open so long as those objects have the ability to do damage.

what circumstances is that possible? Do they need any special equipment or skills before they can do it? Can they fall off the wall once they start climbing? If they *can* lose their grip, what consequences are they going to suffer for smacking into the pavement? Will falling damage be fixed or variable depend-

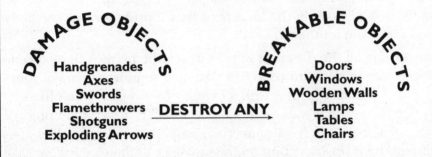

INSTANCE RELATIONSHIP

Handgrenade A ——————DESTROYS——————→ Wooden Door B

CLASS RELATIONSHIP

DAMAGE OBJECTS

Handgrenades
Axes
Swords
Flamethrowers
Shotguns
Exploding Arrows

DESTROY ANY ——————→

BREAKABLE OBJECTS

Doors
Windows
Wooden Walls
Lamps
Tables
Chairs

Figure 6.1   *Instance & Class Relationships*

By thinking in the broadest possible terms, you'll expand the ways in which players will be able to interact with the gaming universe. Instead of wasting effort trying to specify what happens in every instance when object A interacts with each of objects B, C, D, E, F, G, H, I, J, K, L, M, N, O, P, Q, R, S, T, U, V, W, X, Y, and Z, all you'll have to do is create one rule that specifies how all objects of type A interact with all objects of type B and so on. Upfront it's going to seem like a lot of work, but in the long term it will give your rules system greater flexibility and will save you an enormous amount of work further on down the road.

ing on the height from which they fall? For every complexity of gameplay you add, there will be a corresponding host of rules you'll need to develop in order to deal with how those elements function within the game and what the good or bad consequences may be to the player's character.

Just by way of suggestion, I'm going to throw out a few different categories of rules you may want to address in your own role-playing systems. As I've said elsewhere in the book, these aren't all requirements of things that you should feel obligated to put into your title, but they may give you a good place to start thinking about your own rules system.

- **The World.** Once you set them loose in your virtual playground, players are going to begin fiddling with nearly everything they can see. When they find doors, they're going to try and kick, beat, or burn them down. If there's a tree standing in the open, they'll try to shimmy up the trunk so they can take a broader look around. If there's a headstone in the graveyard and you give them a shovel, they'll try to dig up bodies just to see if you buried anybody in the hole (and they'll probably loot the body in the process, if you let them).

  Rules concerning all the different ways in which the player will be able to interact with your gaming universe will take up a significant part of your rules system. You'll have to deal with all kinds of mundane issues like what happens if an avatar walks into a barrel—will it move? If an object moves when bumped, will it have inertia? Can players shove boulders downhill onto their unsuspecting opponents? The commonsense approach to dealing with world rules is simply to think about all the things that players might want to do and how you can give them things they can use to improve the gaming experience.

  Another factor in the development of a game world's rules will have to do with how the environment affects the player. Can it rain in your universe, and if so, how will this affect the avatar? Will this make the ground muddy, and therefore harder to traverse or too slippery to move across? Can the player's character drown or be poisoned by environmental factors? Are there other forces in your world that may threaten the player or that may provide them with critical resources they need?

- **Character Rules.** Another set of rules you'll definitely spend some time on are the rules that govern how your characters live out their artificial lives. Do they need to eat or sleep? How fast can they regain lost points of health or magic/technology points that they'll need to perform special tasks? Can characters die, and if so, can they be resurrected?

  Of very high importance in the development of an RPG is the determination of what kind of advancement system you're going to use. Will players be bound to a skills-based or a class-and-level system to advance the abilities of their avatar? How fast will experience points be accumulated, and how will they be distributed if the player is controlling more than one character? Are there any items that characters will or will not be able to use based on the class they've chosen? How many objects can they carry at one time?

For a very good example of how character rules are developed, see Appendix C, the design sample from the fantasy-action RPG *Nox*.

- **Economic System.** Players are going to want to be able to purchase items they can't otherwise find in the world, and this will necessitate that you set up an artificial economy and set the values of various items. This will also require that you set up rules about how those values may vary from one situation to another. Can different shops charge different prices for the same item? Does the supply of an item affect its price? (In *Ultima Online*, for instance, the amount that a shopkeeper is willing to pay players for items depends on how *many* of that particular item the shopkeeper has in stock.) Does the reputation of the avatar have any bearing on prices, as it does in *Baldur's Gate*? Can currencies themselves devaluate, and how will this affect trading and supplies in your world at large?

- **Magic/Technology System.** Systems like magic and technology, which can radically change the circumstances of gameplay, will have to have well thought-out rules governing how they work. You'll have to address issues of dependencies and the permanence of certain effects. Do the systems require external energy sources, and if so, where will those resources be found? How common are they? Are certain resources self-regenerating? What kinds of effects can be rendered, and will those effects be limited by times, distances, or effective regions of control? Are there any limitations on who can use these special forces? What is required to gain access to those skills or powers?

- **Artificial Intelligence.** Part of what makes a role-playing world seem alive are the artificial people who inhabit that universe. Artificial intelligence routines are used to give nonplayer characters "lives." These routines can govern things as simple as how they move around the room to determining what their motivations are for performing certain activities. I'll discuss artificial intelligence and its relation to the nonplayer character a bit more in Chapter 7.

Deus Ex-cerpt

The following excerpt from the design document of Ion Storm's successful RPG Deus
Ex *demonstrates the kind of behaviors the design team wanted for various types of
nonplayer characters to employ and exhibit in the game world. (Used with permission
of Ion Storm. Special thanks to Warren Spector.)*

NPC Base Behaviors

Unlike shooters, roleplaying games don't consist of waves of mindless goons
trying to kill the player. *Deus Ex* should have believable, recognizable *characters* that talk and act differently from each other. The A.I. will be tailored to
reflect this.

Many of our characters will use the same base classes (guards will guard,
pedestrians will, uh, pedest), so we will need to distinguish many of these
NPC's in the conversation system rather than the A.I. We will subclass some
of these classes, however, to tweak the A.I. for special cases. (Guards in Area
51 will act differently than guards at a party. . . .)

On the other hand, all the major characters (Tracer Tong, Jojo Fine, Walton
Simons, etc.) will have A.I. scripted specifically for those characters (and, of
course, different conversation options). Most of the differences between
these characters will be handled in *Unreal* Script, rather than by tweaking
parameters; this will mean more work, but it will also make our most important NPC's unique.

Civilian

   Does not harm civilians

   Ignores unidentified sounds

   Aware of alarms

   Issues warning before attacking

   Flees when wounded below X% (where X is high)

   Tends to protect self

   Ground-based movement, normal

Thug

- No concern for safety of civilians
- Investigates unidentified sounds
- Aware of alarms
- Attacks without warning
- Flees when wounded below X% (where X is low)
- Tends to protect self
- Ground-based movement, normal

Military

- Does not harm civilians
- Investigates unidentified sounds (if possible without abandoning post)
- Aware of alarms
- Issues warning before attacking
- Never flees when wounded
- Ground-based movement, fast

Animal

- No concern for safety of civilians
- Flees unidentified sounds, or makes noise (e.g. barking) (special cases)
- No awareness of alarms
- Attacks without warning
- Flees when wounded below X% (where X varies based on animal type)
- Tends to protect self
- Special-case behavior code must be written on a per-animal basis (dogs, cats, rats, roaches, pigeons, etc.)

Robot

- Does not harm civilians
- Ignores unidentified sounds (?)

O
N

T
A
R
G
E
T

Unaware of alarms (or sends alarms from self?)

Issues warning before attacking ("you have fifteen seconds to comply")

Never flees when wounded

Tends to protect self

Ground-based movement, slow

Actor States

NPC's will have a number of different states. States are special *Unreal* Script features that allow actors to behave in different ways. Our NPC's will go to different states based on things they see and hear, and what their A.I. tells them to do. Here are the most important states for the NPC's in *Deus Ex*.

Standing. Just kinda standing there.

Wandering. Moving from place to place in aimless fashion.

Patrolling. Moving through a predetermined set of waypoints.

Attacking. Attacking the PC or another character.

Fleeing. Running away from the PC or another character, or running to a "home base."

Following. Following the PC or another character.

Leading. Leading the player.

Shadowing. Inconspicuously following the player.

Sitting. Sitting.

Seeking. Looking for enemy NPC's without knowing where they are.

Waiting. Causes the NPC to wait until he sees a specific person or thing. Once the person or thing is spotted, the NPC moves toward it and tries to touch it (usually, though not always, to initiate conversation).

GoingTo. Causes the NPC to walk towards a specific actor.

RunningTo. Same as GoingTo, but causes the NPC to run to the actor.

Combat A.I.

Here are some general guidelines for how NPC's will act during combat. These are not hard and fast rules. We will almost certainly change them to balance gameplay, and on an individual basis depending on the NPC stats....

How the NPC Fights

When in combat with the player, the NPC will change his fighting strategy depending on how both he and the PC are armed:

If the NPC is unarmed, but the PC is armed, the NPC will run away like a scared rabbit. (Unless he's *completely* berserk or very, very desperate....)

If both the NPC and the PC are unarmed, the NPC will either run away or close in to slug it out with the player, depending on his nature.

If the NPC is armed but the PC is not, the NPC will maintain a distance from the player, stand in the open, and take potshots with impunity. This will be a deeply satisfying experience for the NPC.

If both the NPC and the PC are armed, the NPC will generally maintain a distance, hide behind objects for cover, and periodically move into the open to shoot.

If the NPC is seriously overmatched, or badly wounded, he may opt to run away.

If the player has an explosive weapon, like a GEP gun, the NPC might try to close in on the player in hopes that the PC won't fire a rocket at point-blank range. Also, if the NPC and the player are close, the NPC may put away his own weapon and engage in hand-to-hand combat, depending on what he's armed with.

If the NPC is close to the player, he may also try using the tried-and-true *Quake* circle-strafing technique to prevent the player from getting a bead on him.

We will create a special PathNode class where actors will go for cover. Again, these can be added from the *Unreal* editor. When an actor wants to hide, he will seek out the nearest of these pathnodes that doesn't have a direct line-of-sight to the player and move there. The disadvantage to this method is that the designers will have to place more actors to make the NPC's hide, and it will be less obvious (from a programming standpoint) where the actor should come out to shoot at the player. On the other hand, the NPC will be able to hide behind *any* terrain....

O N   T A R G E T

In situations where the NPC has no cover, he might crouch in order to present a smaller target to the player. Also, while running, the really smart NPC will zig-zag so it's difficult for the player to hit him.

If the NPC is running from the player, and has no weapons, he might try throwing any sharp and/or heavy objects in his possession at the player while he makes a break for it. (Okay, it's silly, but it's realistic . . . I know *I'd* do this. . . .)

Hiding behind Objects

Unreal has no built-in way to make enemies take cover behind objects during a firefight . . . so we'll need to handle this capability ourselves. This is one of the trickiest A.I. strategies to program.

We will create a special PathNode class where actors will go for cover. Again, these can be added from the *Unreal* editor. When an actor wants to hide, he will seek out the nearest of these pathnodes that doesn't have a direct line-of-sight to the player and move there. The disadvantage to this method is that the designers will have to place more actors to make the NPC's hide, and it will be less obvious (from a programming stand-point) where the actor should come out to shoot at the player. On the other hand, the NPC will be able to hide behind *any* terrain. . . .

- **Combat System.** In Ye Olden Days the combat system was an entirely independent entity, but anymore most combat systems are merging into the world rules and the artificial intelligence routines of monsters and NPCs. A fireball tossed at a wall does the same amount of damage as a fireball tossed at an ogre, though the circumstances are somewhat different. Combat is still special because it involves the group dynamics of monsters and how certain problems of damage resolution are solved. How will NPCs react in situations in which the avatars have killed other characters?

What strategies will be employed by monsters in order to overwhelm the player? How are the various offensive and defensive skills of players resolved, and how do things like armor, blessings, and other banes and boons affect combat performance?

Hopefully you've begun to see why a rules system is important and can understand how algorithms are used to develop a game's underlying logic. In my example dealing with a monster's "attack" routine, you may have noticed how intimately algorithms must mesh together to create a cohesive system. Each rule relies critically on the proper functioning of all the other rules upon which they depend. If something breaks down in the chain—say, the pathing routine doesn't work—then every other algorithm that requires information on how to navigate through the world breaks down. Monsters won't know how to move. Tanks will freeze in their tracks. The universe of a computer game is a massive web of interdependence with virtually every element of a game eventually touching virtually everything else. Like life, a well thought-out RPG is complicated beneath the surface, but it's the nature of those complications that make the experience *interesting*.

Structuring the Experience

As a child, I grew up adoring Sherlock Holmes movies. I liked that Basil Rathbone could prowl the streets of London armed with nothing but his trademark pipe and a formidable maxim of Victorian rationality with which to catch the villains. "Once you've eliminated the impossible," he frequently told his sidekick, Dr. Watson, "whatever remains, however improbable, must be the truth."

While truth isn't really the game designers' primary stock in trade, the process of deductive reasoning they employ while building their games is *very* Holmesian. Starting not with a dead body but a list of the things they'd like the player to be able to do, they move step by step *backward* up a chain of causality, arriving at last at a set of rules that *must* exist before the player can experience the desired activities. The end doesn't just justify the means, it imposes order on the entire reality of the gaming universe. The rules serve only to make possible the gaming scenarios that the creators had in mind in the first place.

If you peek into a game designer's notebook in the early stages of a project, you're likely to see lots of very basic scenarios like "a big dwarven mine with functioning mine cars," or "a haunted derelict alien starship," or "a graveyard in New Orleans," or "a GOP convention overrun by right-wing militia zombies." Story-oriented RPG developers take things even a step further and create a series of interlocking scenarios or circumstances through which the player will have to pass in order to reach the game's end. In both cases the designers have imposed a *structure* that will create certain moods or themes, while also providing a framework that will *balance* the experience for the player.

Imagine for a moment you've been gifted with an entirely *un*structured game. The designer hasn't imposed any of their evil deterministic will on the makeup of the world, so the game engine is free to randomly distribute jewels, castles, security turrets, and carnivorous bunnies wherever there's adequate space to put them. Into this brave new world of freedom you send your avatar, armed only with everything that a beginning adventurer needs: a rusty dagger, ambition, and a head full of dreams. Seeing an evil-looking creature doing harm to a helpless little old lady, you march your avatar in to save the day . . . and promptly your PC gets their head lopped off by a Level 40 balrog who took out your player character without so much as blinking an eye.

Without a designer to craft an experience that's meant to be player-friendly, that's precisely the unfair sort of gameplay a totally unstructured environment is going to dish up. In order to be *balanced,* the challenges that the player faces should be defeatable with the resources they've had reasonable opportunity to obtain. Monsters who are too tough for a beginning player to take on are going to be cloistered in a top-secret military lab, isolated in a spot the player's avatar won't be able to reach until they've appropriately built up their stats or acquired the right kinds of equipment.

Good structure also places opportunities in front of the player to test and improve their skills so that they can *grow* their characters in the direction of their choice. While a locked door can technically be an obstacle, a thinking designer will come up with ways to let the player creatively solve the problem, like picking the lock, kicking it down, burning through it with a flamethrower, using a spell to phase through the surface, or one of dozens of other possible solutions. The beauty of approaching the structure of a game this way is that players retain a high degree of freedom over how they play the game, while still enjoying the benefits of a structured environment designed to serve their interests.

Quests: The Fundamental Unit

If you were to take any RPG on the market, and you began to chop it into smaller and smaller game structures, you'd eventually arrive at its most irreducible element, the *quest*. Like the atoms that make up molecules and the bricks that make up buildings, quests provide the fundamental unit out of which all game structure is built. Quests can come in all possible sizes, shapes, and configurations. One might be so large and complex that it takes an entire game or level to complete, while another may be so small and simple that the player can polish it off with only a few minutes of effort. But what are quests, and how does a designer properly use them in a game?

In the most simplistic of terms, a quest is simply a task the player may or may not have to complete before finishing the game. Usually this involves the avatar engaging in some dangerous or difficult activity in exchange for a benefit to themselves or their general cause. Every James Bond movie ever made follows a quest-driven format: retrieve the diamonds, find the spy, steal the nuke, destroy the weapons depot. The same holds true of most RPGs. When you break it down from a structure standpoint, a quest has *traditionally* had three stages:

- **Notification.** The player learns what the situation is or what needs to be done. At this point they are usually also informed what potential benefit may be reaped for completing the task.

- **Process.** The player engages in whatever activities are necessary to complete the task.

- **Reward.** The player goes to a predetermined place or person in order to receive a reward for their efforts.

Just like the algorithms that you explored in the rules section, you'll see that the quest is really just a series of steps the player can choose to go through in exchange for a certain benefit. The player is notified, they go do the job, then they come back and get their reward.

The problem with adhering too rigidly to the quest structure I outlined above is that players have free will. They're going to go places and do things all out of the order that you so carefully have accounted for. You may *want* them to first meet the Federation Commander, go wipe out the alien invaders in Sector 9, then go to the Chief Legate for the Valnarian uplink node. What is more *likely* to happen is that about half the time the players will never have met the

Federation Commander, they'll wipe out the aliens they find in Sector 9 anyway, and they'll never realize there was a Valnarian uplink node to be had for killing the alien invaders.

In a second circumstance the players may have gotten the idea from *other* players that they could go to the Chief Legate to get the uplink node after they've killed the aliens. Unfortunately, if the players go straight to the Legate, he won't give them their reward yet because he's never been informed by the Federation Commander that the assignment has been made in the first place. On a technicality, the players will then have to go *all* the way back to the Federation Commander to have him give them an assignment that they've already completed, just so the Chief Legate on the other side of the galaxy will finally know to give the players the node that they've already rightfully earned!!! Phew!

As tiring as both the examples I've discussed above can be, I've seen manifestations of both in too many otherwise good RPGs. In the first instance, the problem of the player never learning about the reward is an *information flow problem,* and it's typically a very easy thing to fix. By providing players with multiple sources of information about quests, you'll give them greater freedom to roam through your universe and they'll have greater opportunities to experience all the things you've provided for them.

The second scenario presents a slightly more serious *sequence problem.* By requiring that the player be told about the reward before they can receive it from the Legate, the designer has unintentionally lost the quest's focus. It's the elimination of the aliens and not the speaking to the Federation Commander that presumably is the point of the experience in the first place.

The best quests that you can build into your game are going to be the ones that provide the following:

- **Real Benefit to the Avatar.** Never send players off on a quest that doesn't directly benefit them in some way. There are few quests more irritating than to meet some random character, but before they'll condescend to speak to you, you first have to go out and gather 20 different colored petunias. If you choose to make a quest somewhat diversionary in nature, make sure that what you send the player off to do would be fun and beneficial to the player even if it weren't something they needed to do in order to complete the quest.

Thinking about NPCs

As early as possible in the design process, you'll need to consider how critical a role you want NPCs to play in the overall experience. You might be thinking there are critical bits of information or specific objects the player will need that can *only* be obtained by talking to characters in the game. Be aware, however, that a decision like this will sometimes tie your hands as a designer. If a specific character must be spoken to before the game can be finished, then you'll be obligated to make sure *that none of your important NPCs can ever die*. Otherwise, you'll be sticking the player in a situation where they may unintentionally wipe out their only means of completing the game. They may not even realize what they've done until much later, and forcing the player to go back by several saved games will not make you or your title very popular with your players. Certainly you aren't responsible for every little dumb thing the player may do while they're in your world, but you *are* obligated to make sure that the player has an exceptionally good chance that they can continue to move forward through your game no matter *what* they do.

To follow this chain of problems further, depending on how you handle the immortality of your important NPCs, you can end up with several undesirable side effects. If you choose to simply prevent the player from targeting important NPCs, this will send up a red flag to the player. By sweeping their cursor across the area, they'll quickly realize that the only characters in the world worth talking to are the ones they can't target. True, it will have the effect of letting players zero in on important people, but it will also result in players never talking to the second-string NPCs. Ultimately, this will mean you'll be wasting time and money on developing characters the player will never speak to.

A second, equally awkward solution to the immortal NPC problem is to simply give these individuals an infinite number of hit points. While this is a reasonable kludge that will achieve the desired result, it is an inelegant solution at best. The all-powerful sorcerer and his many legions who have taken over half the globe can all be laid waste by you and your four best friends, and yet the tailor in the local shop can take multiple hits from your Staff of Ultimate Doom and still remain cheerfully willing to give you the best prices in the Middle Kingdom.

O N   T A R G E T

- **Proportional Rewards.** In every case the reward for completing the quest needs to be proportional to the risk posed by taking it on. Sending players off to kill dragons, then giving them six gold pieces is simply mean-spirited and bad design practice. Make the reward fit the effort.

- **Forward Momentum.** If possible, try to structure your quests so that they always propel the player *forward* through the game. Making players go back to someplace they've already been simply to report that they've done what they've been assigned is just plain old boring. RPGs are supposed to feature a strong element of exploration, but you'll defeat the player's sense of discovery if they keep having to recross old ground. If it's critical that the player meet with someone they've already spoken to, either move the quest assigner so they'll be somewhere in front of the player at quest's end or provide new routes or shortcut ways for players to get back to places they've been to before.

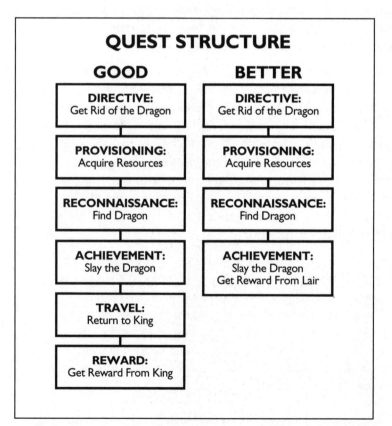

Figure 6.2

Good and Better quest structures

- **Support for the Story Line.** If there's a large story line at work in your game, use quests that support that larger theme so the player always feels as though their actions are relevant to the title's primary drive. In *Dungeon Siege* I generated subquest ideas based on the larger idea of the battles raging across the Kingdom and tried to show through quests how this conflict was affecting the lives of both soldiers and commoners.

Always remember the central point of quests is to provide entertainment. They should never take on the characteristic of chores or things the player is forced to do just because the designer has tied a rope around their neck and ordered them into action. Put interesting things out into your world for the player to do, and let them decide if and when they're ready to take the next step. When creating quests of your own, ask yourself what the important idea is in it and what real benefit the player is going to get out of having performed it. Most of all, how can you use the quest to advance the overall structure of your game?

Storytelling in an Interactive World

If you've read books on game design by my colleagues, you no doubt have noticed that storytelling in games is a *very* hotly debated issue today. A small but very vocal minority of misguided souls have even gone so far as to charge that designers who put stories into their games have "frustrated author syndrome" and that stories have no place in gaming whatsoever. Having cowritten the story for a *New York Times* best-selling novel in addition to a string of best-selling computer games, let me categorically state that I am in no way a "frustrated" author, and I have *never* received one critical letter from players about the story lines that I've introduced to the role-playing public. Story remains one of the most powerful and frequently cited reasons why many RPG players say they enjoy this genre, and it should not be something that is taken lightly.

Most people are coming to the table with the expectation that *you* are going to entertain them. If they come in believing you've prepared an interactive version of *Aliens,* but all you've got to offer them is some bizarre form of improvisational theater set in deep space, you're going to lose your audience. People playing role-playing games *expect* to be given a goal and to find themselves immersed in an involving story line. Once they've got a larger purpose on which they can fix their gaze, they should then be allowed to do—or not to do—whatever you've suggested.

THE NEALOMATIC LAZY QUESTMAKER

It's three o'clock in the morning, and you've got to come up with something to help fill in a part of the world that feels a little too empty. The bad news is that you've been up for four days straight and you've run out of legal stimulants—your brain is dead, and you can't think of a darn thing to put in there. The good news is that you've got a few characters, objects, and locations that haven't been used to their full potential yet, so you've got room to create an interesting quest for them. What do you do? You use the Nealomatic Lazy Questmaker, that's what! Just get yourself a good old fashioned six sided die, grab the following chart, and roll up a quest idea. Make two rolls, and apply the reuslts as below:

Table 6.1 First Roll

If Roll is	the *action* of the quest is to
1	Liberate/Recover/Intercept
2	Destroy/Kill
3	Guard/Defend
4	Transport/Escort/Journey to
5	Create/Build/Summon
6	Gather information about

Table 6.2 Second Roll

If Roll is	the *object* of the quest is
1	Item
2	NPC
3	Message/Data
4	Secret or dangerous location
5	Magical Equipment/Scientific Technology
6	Monster

ON TARGET

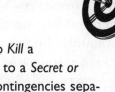

So, for instance, if you rolled a 2 and a 6, you'd have a quest to *Kill* a *Monster*. If you rolled a 4 and 4, the quest would be to *Journey* to a *Secret or dangerous location*. Note that for all of the actions there are contingencies separated by slashes. It doesn't make sense that the player would *transport* or *escort* a location (unless you've got a *really* weird and flexible game engine).

The beauty of the Nealomatic is that you aren't of course restricted to using my lists. You can plug in your own selection of actions or objects and generate content that will be much more specific to your project. If you use 10, 20, or 100 sided dice, you could create an extremely diverse selection of things out of which to create your quests.

Keep in mind that I view the Nealomatic as purely something to get a quest idea *started* in circumstances when you're just too tired or lazy to come up with something new on your own. Don't let this take over the design process. Overly randomized games tend to create silly, stupid, or just plain awful gameplay. Your games will always be all the better if they employ quests that are tied in to the problems and circumstances of your world.

The value of story in the context of your game's structure is that it helps organize all those quests you've laid out into a comprehensible whole, giving players a sense of direction and purpose for their actions. Story also goes a long way toward orienting the player into a world that will otherwise be strange and alien to them, even if the game is set into a 20th-century milieu. Legends about founding figures and war heroes of old will give a sense of historical reality to the game and give players a yardstick with which to judge their own accomplishments. At every point, story needs to serve the purpose of helping the player understand the situation into which they've appeared and give them a map they can follow if they don't enjoy trying to invent things on their own.

So how is the experience of telling a story in a game different than telling it in a book or in a movie? Aside from the very obvious fact that the player is being active rather than passive, there are several important concepts that you're going to have to rethink:

- **The Player Ain't from Around Here.** Despite the fact that the player is hopefully going to identify with the avatar, they're not going to have the benefit of knowing all the things that a person from that world should reasonably know. Even if the game is set in a contemporary Earth setting, they still won't know that the creepy looking guy standing behind the counter is really a "friend" of theirs. Interactive storytelling requires a great deal of work to get players the information they need about the world and their avatars in a timely and concise manner.

- **Players Are Going to Perceive Negative Plot Turns As Gameplay Related.** If you arbitrarily take over the game and arbitrarily kill off a member of the player's party, they are going to go nuts trying to find at what point they could have done something differently in the course of gameplay to change that outcome. If you're just absolutely bent on doing something like this to the players, it's best to still let the player make a choice in who will sacrifice themselves for the good of everyone else.

- **Bad Endings Are Just Bad.** Players who have spent hours and hours playing through your game are not going to appreciate being hit with a bad ending. It works in literary fiction because the reader has spent limited time with the story and because the reader at no point was making choices that led to the story's end. Computer games are different. Players work very hard to get through them, and they deserve to have a good ending. Multiple endings are just fine, but they all need to make the player feel glad they participated.

■ **Players Want to Decide, Not Follow.** You should never shove the experience down the player's throat nor abdicate the responsibility to be an entertaining host. The point is not to act as a prison guard that whips players down a particular path, but instead to act as a kind of tour guide, suggesting interesting things for the player to check out whenever they've got the time. What I said about good quest design holds just as true here: You want to give players things that they can choose to do, not things they are being ordered to do. Let the story advance when the players choose for that advance to happen.

If there's one overriding concept about interactive fiction writing that's more useful than any other, it is that you need to *pull,* not *push.* Think about the stories that you present in computer games in the same way you would about the chapters in a page-turning novel. The reason why people keep reading "just one more chapter" is exactly the same as when players want to play "just one more level." Players and readers have to keep going because they're just dying to know what's around the next corner.

I can always tell when I'm playing a game that's been written by someone who's inexperienced or simply not used to dealing with fiction. The tendency is to have nonplayer characters rush up to the avatar and tell them *everything.* That tends to leave the player with little to do but go and confirm everything they've been told. What *you* want to do is make your plot mysterious. Make the player ask questions: Why did she do that? Where are those monsters coming from? What's that sound? Why would the orcs murder their king and then leave the body in the middle of our town square? What about Naomi?

Whatever tricks you employ to suck players in and keep them interested, always be mindful of the fact that your job is to help the players out and to keep them entertained. If the player wants to wander off and do something silly for a while, let 'em. This can sometimes be very beneficial to you, especially if the player is feeling stuck. If they just want to sit by your artificial river with a fishing pole and catch virtual fish for a while, there's absolutely nothing wrong with that. Small details can sometimes gain you surprising support from players, and anything that keeps your audience playing your game and *not* shutting it off is never going to be a bad thing. When possible, offer them enticements to come back and see what's going on with the story's main spine, but let the choice remain in the player's hands.

Mything Links

Many people who study the stories of computer games have noted the classically mythic structures that are reflected in many of today's computer gaming titles. Writer and literary consultant Christopher Vogler is an expert on mythic structure, and he's served as a consultant on myth to several modern-day filmmakers including Steven Spielberg and George Lucas. At the Game Developers Conference in San Jose, California, in March 2000, Vogler spoke on applying the mythic structure to stories for computer games. Comparing the basic components of Campbell's classic "hero's journey" to a collection of essential tools, Vogler said: "It is, among other things, a matrix of design principles that great artists use, consciously or unconsciously, to structure their works and make them meaningful and entertaining . . . But above all it is a key to the audience, opening a door into their minds and spirits, into their dreams, wishes, fantasies and desires. It's an ancient system for connecting the audience with the story, for making that powerful bond between the user and the experience we call 'drama.'"

Vogler bases many of his ideas on those first evinced by the great American editor and translator Joseph Campbell, author of *The Hero with a Thousand Faces*. Campbell's works on comparative mythology became very well known, and his identification of several patterns that are frequently repeated in all mythic stories are highly useful in analyzing some of the elements that sometimes appear in RPGs. Here are the basic "stages" that Campbell gives for the typical "Hero's Journey."

1. **The Ordinary World.** We meet the avatar in his or her Ordinary World, surrounded by the things that are familiar to them. This is home.

2. **Call to Adventure.** At some point the avatar is confronted by a change: a coming war, a summons from the king, a friend showing up and mysteriously dying while carrying an ominous message. It is a call to do something, to find out what's going wrong, to deal with a new problem.

3. **Refusal of the Call.** The hero feels uncertain about their abilities, about the wisdom of chasing after whatever is going on. Hesitation occurs for any number of reasons, from selfish motives to honest self-

doubt. (In literature and movies this step happens fairly frequently, but in games this step virtually vanishes. Games require the player to act, to immediately accept the Call to Adventure.)

4. **Meeting of the Mentor.** The mentor provides guidance and perhaps even magical gifts to assist the hero. This could be an agent of the supernatural, a wizard, or a seasoned veteran ready to coach the hero. This is a *staple* of the genre.

5. **Crossing of the Threshold.** The avatar goes out into the big, dangerous world beyond. This is the departure from Candlekeep in *Baldur's Gate,* the moment at which Luke decides to leave Tatooine in *Star Wars.* The world the hero or heroine discovers is unlike anything they've ever known before: big, weird, and dangerous.

6. **Allies, Enemies, and Tests.** Along the path to deal with the big problem, the avatar finds themselves surrounded by people who may help or hurt them. They are challenged everywhere, and always their life or cause is in danger.

7. **Approach to the Final Cave.** After pinpointing the heart of the problem, the avatar heads toward their nemesis to confront them.

8. **The Ordeal.** Once inside the stronghold of the enemy, the avatar must struggle for their life, sanity, and soul as they confront their ultimate enemy.

9. **The Reward.** With the enemy defeated, the avatar achieves their goal. This may be simply the removal of the threat to their lands or people, or it might be the acquisition of something, as when Indiana Jones retrieves the Ark of the Covenant at the end of *Raiders of the Lost Ark.*

10. **The Road Back.** With the enemy vanquished, the avatar begins the journey back to their Ordinary World as a victor and is reunited with friends or family.

11. **Resurrection.** After coming up against various obstacles, the avatar faces yet another severe test, often with a symbolic death and rebirth.

This may be the confrontation of something left unfinished from the start of the experience or some other event that demonstrates how the hero has changed.

12. **Return with the "Elixir."** The hero at last returns to the Ordinary World, bearing something special or magical. This could be literal (a cure for a disease, money to save the farm) or figurative (greater wisdom and insight, strength to stand up to the local bully) or anything else to make living in the Ordinary World easier.

Before moving on to the discussion on balancing, let's look at the three primary storytelling structures that are used in computer games.

The Linear Game

During a panel at Northwest Bookfest back in November of 1999, my copanelist Jane Jensen of *Gabriel Knight* fame passed along her definition of a linear game, which describes the storytelling structure fairly well. "The trick is to design it like a string of pearls," Jensen says. "Inside each pearl the player can do things in a nonlinear fashion. They can do whatever they want, whenever they want, in whatever order they want."

The driving idea behind a linear game is that there is only one ending possible to the experience, but the player will still have a great deal of freedom inside each of the "pearls" that make up the *main spine* of the story.

For instance, the big story in the game may be that there's a war raging in the next kingdom over. There's some worry that it may spill into the avatar's home country, and already there are several castles along the border that have been threatened. That plotline constitutes the game's *main spine.* But let's say while the player's journeying down the road to see what's going on with the war, they might meet a goatherd off to the side of the road. The goatherd tells the player's avatar that the dwarves are busy fighting some kind of weird creature that popped through a portal in the dwarven mines not long after the war started, and it seems to be intent on getting something that was lost by the dwarves there a long time ago.

The 12 steps above more or less represent the "ideal" mythic structure, but obviously this is not sacred doctrine set in stone. For example, I can think of any number of good, powerful stories that skip the Refusal of the Call. In some cases, including lots of real-life dramas, the challenge is taken on willingly, without hesitation—indeed, to refuse could be tantamount to suicide or to consigning someone else to a gruesome fate. And in a gaming context, you aren't going to see too many calls to adventure refused. After all, if someone didn't want to be a hero, why were they embarking on an RPG?

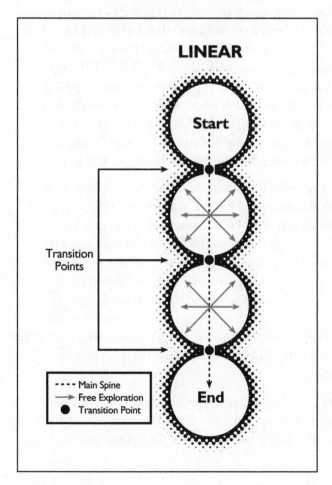

Figure 6.3

Linear game structure.

At this point the player has a choice. They can either keep going and find out more about what they've heard about the war, or they can follow up on this new thing that's going down in the mine and maybe even find out something that will be useful to them later. The dwarves may even be offering a reward for taking out the weird beastie.

After thinking over the problem for a minute you decide that going on to the border castles is more important, so you bid farewell to the goatherd and continue on your dangerous journey until at last you reach Stormcliff. Upon arriving at Stormcliff, you witness a bizarre vision outside the castle walls as good King Adenulph confronts Baron Helno. Soldiers are charging around everywhere as civil war is declared between the two, and thus you slide into part two of the main spine story. . . .

If you look at the illustration of the linear story structure (Figure 6.3), you can begin to plug in the various different elements that I've talked about. The main spine about the war is represented by the dotted line passing through all the rest of the pearls. This is the primary story that will "thread" all the different pearls together. The gray arrows inside each pearl represent nonlinear paths the player can take whose outcomes are *completely up to the player*. The trip to the dwarven mine represents just such a nonlinear path. It is entirely up to the player to choose whether they want to investigate it or not, but the "completion" of that subplot isn't required in order for the player to finish the game.

The last element—Baron Helno's rebellion against the king—is represented by the black dot in the neck between the pearls. This is a transition. This is the point during the player's travels at which they come to a major turning point in the main spine's story line. Until the player gets to the border castle, the kingdom remains at peace, though threatened by the distant war. If the player wanted, they could spend forever just knocking around without going to the border castle, and the main story would never advance. It *waits* on the player. But at the point at which the player arrives, the main story is advanced a notch, and the world changes. From this point on, the home kingdom will increasingly be torn apart by a civil war, and this will affect everything as the player enters a second "pearl" of possible activities.

Now to make the game even more interactive, you should make the transition points more connected to the player's actions. In the first one, the player just had to show up. To transition into the third pearl, maybe they have to rescue an imprisoned prince or destroy an important bridge. This transforms each pearl in the story line into an individual quest that the player must complete in order to finally drive all the way to the end.

The Multilinear Game

In most respects, creating the multilinear game is not going to be technically much different from crafting its less-complicated progenitor. The team will still have to perform the same kinds of tasks, but there *will* be small differences in the planning and testing phases. Because a multilinear game is slightly more complex than a strictly linear title, the need for clear communication is going to be all the greater, and continuity details will require a slightly higher degree of attention.

The biggest problem for game developers will be deciding exactly *how* thematically divergent each thread is from the others and how the project is going to share resources between the multiple threads without creating items that can be used only once. If each of five paths through the game has an entirely independent set of locations, monsters, spells, characters, subquests, and game objectives, the designer is essentially faced with creating five wholly different *games*. While gamers might love getting this package of minigames all for the price of one, the development house is likely to be less thrilled. The resources needed to create all those different paths are apt to be expensive and hard to come by. If on the other hand the paths are allowed to share significant numbers of resources, the question that then arises is "What's the point of having different paths if what the player sees along the way in all of them is only different by a few degrees?"

Arguments can be made on both sides. The one certainty is that multilinear developers are going to find themselves constantly engaged in a balancing act trying to maximize the relative uniqueness of each path's experience while at the same time struggling with the fiscal necessity of building reusable resources. Even when developers are working on linear titles, there's extraordinary pressure to find ways to reuse monsters and objects. Sometimes this is accomplished with quick palette tricks, changing monster AIs, and using other tricks to suck the maximum mileage out of each individual resource. The development of a multilinear title can push these creative uses to their limits, and the designer on such a title needs to be prepared for this very special challenge.

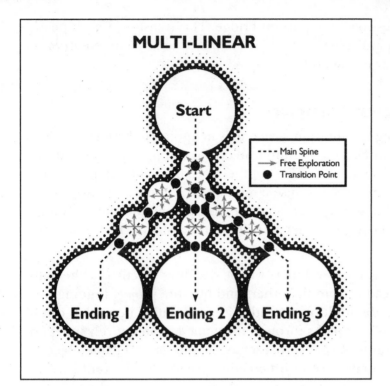

Figure 6.4

Multilinear game structure.

The biggest difference between the multilinear and linear title is obviously that the multilinear game has multiple story paths with multiple endings. If you're planning on using a lot of prerendered computer graphics for the big finale, you may have another reason to be hesitant to proceed. With five different endings to support, you're also less likely to have enough money to pay for eye-popping finales for each one. This may mean ending up with five "adequate" endings rather than one really spectacular one. While this may be acceptable to you, your audience may be less sympathetic to your financial constraints and is likely to look very critically at your game in comparison to your competitors' show-stopping "renderfests."

The challenges of dealing with multilinear titles can be very expensive, but this shouldn't necessarily deter you from giving this form of RPG a shot. If you're clever, you'll figure out how to branch your title in such a way that the turning points come relatively late in the title, meaning that significant portions of your resources will be shared by the plotlines until they split off from one another

Consoling Thoughts

One very major example of the different ways in which role-playing games are received across different cultures can be seen in the differences between American PC-driven RPGs and Japanese console titles. Japanese audiences tend to be much more receptive to multiple-linear titles and don't seem to be as outraged by games that end on a "down" note. American audiences tend to be much less forgiving in this regard and will spend hours trying to save "doomed" characters.

near the end. In contrast to the possible multilinear structure found in Figure 6.4, you could also create a game that had "side pockets." Rather than diverging from a main spine and remaining that way for the entire length of the title, you could have alternate story lines that weave in and out of the main spine, only splitting off for short periods of time.

The Nonterminal Game

Exclusively a feature of massively multiplayer online games (MMOGs) that feature persistent universes like *Ultima Online, Everquest,* and *Asheron's Call,* the nonterminal game has no beginning and no end, only an ever-present *now* in which thousands of players romp, communicate, and take combative swings at monsters or each other.

From the moment they enter the nonterminal story, the primary goal of players is not to solve some world-threatening problem, but to relentlessly build up their avatars. Players can wander the wilds slaying monsters in order to become the world's greatest warrior, or they can choose to become a baker and sell goods to other players. Virtually any possible role that a player might want to assume is possible in most MMOGs, allowing them to become the "hero of their own story."

Early on in the development of these massively multiplayer online games, developers realized that standard approaches to storytelling weren't going to work. If designers cooked up a devious little subplot involving a thieving con man, the

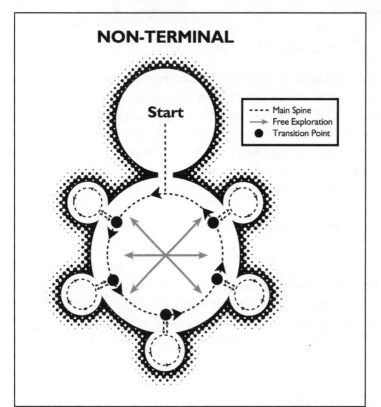

NON-TERMINAL

Start

- - - - Main Spine
———▶ Free Exploration
● Transition Point

Figure 6.5

Nonterminal game structure

gag would be over after he'd duped half a dozen players into helping him save his "poor, ailing ol' Gran." Players who had previously fallen victim to the robber would warn away new players via Web site postings, instant messages, and a wide variety of other communications tactics. Clearly there was something very different about the playing dynamic of MMOGs, and this required designers to take a very different tack with creating online content.

Throwing out the idea that the design team would create everything players became involved with, many MMOG developers have opened the door so that the majority of "story" content is created by the interactions of the players. Rather than preparing elaborate story lines that can be overthrown by player communication in mere moments, designers have focused on creating *global* situations so that the players feel compelled to create their own intrigues. By providing players with hierarchies into which they can interject themselves and by making certain that some items and resources are rare, designers have backed away from creating story lines and focused instead on creating interesting environments in which the players can interact. Occasionally they also can introduce "pocket story lines" (these are the small lobes that branch off the main "story" in Figure 6.5), which players can explore if and when they want, but the outcome of the player's experience is going to be largely unchanged. The world remains the same, and the player comes back to a situation that will be relatively familiar to them.

By and large, these brave new experiments have been successful. Multiplayer environments have attracted very loyal followings of people who are willing to pay monthly access charges. At times there have been in excess of 40,000 players all playing at the same time in each of these virtual universes, and with every passing month, that number continues to balloon upward. There are many developers who are betting all their money on the idea that massively multiplayer environments are the wave of the future and that the single-player RPG is doomed to extinction.

But before you go scrapping all your single-player console ideas and start running to join the bleeding edge of progress, there are a few things you need to consider before leaping into the chaos that is MMOG development. For all the wonderful promise that these titles hold for future generations of gamers, there are still some kinks that need to be worked out of the system. While players can be heroes of their own stories, they're never really allowed to be *the* hero. In *Dungeon Siege*'s single-player game, an avatar can *save the world* because they're allowed to be more important than anybody else. Today's MMOGs can't provide that kind of personally transcendent experience simply because you can't have a thousand people who are all simultaneously allowed to be the *best*. Players can have avatars that are very, very good at what they do, but in the end they're just one of thousands of very, very good avatars. It's eminently possible to save the flower girl from marauding goats, but saving the world is never going to be option in MMOGs—at least as they're currently structured.

A Parting Word about Story and Games

If you're debating about whether you need to go linear, multilinear, or nonterminal with your story, keep in mind that the best-selling RPG of all time has actually been a *hybrid* of all these concepts. *Diablo II* features a strongly linear single-player story line, but it delivers a slightly different experience when you play with each of the different character/class types. If you choose to play the multiplayer game, there's no story that you have to follow, and it can be played thousands and thousands of times with other players, and you'll never experience exactly the same thing twice.

Emerging technologies that are coming down the pike by the end of 2001 stand to make these lines even blurrier. *Neverwinter Nights* and *Dungeon Siege* will both ship single-player experiences while also providing players with editing tools to create their own dungeons, worlds, and stories. The inevitable effect will be to bring players back into the role-playing experience as they have never been before, and the structures they demonstrate in the coming years will be highly instructive about what kinds of experiences they want us to provide to them.

Balancing Acts

Once you've created the rules and come up with a structure for what the player can do, the last thing on your design agenda is going to be balancing the experience. No matter how clever, brilliant, or well meaning a designer you are, you're going to be blind to certain problems in your design until such a time as you can park your behind in a chair and actually wade through the experience itself. Unfortunately for all of us, achieving a good symmetry between challenge and reward is more of an Art than a Science. Balancing tricks that sometimes work in one game will be utterly useless in another. Each game has its own center, and you're going to have to spend a great deal of time searching for where it's located. In the meantime, there are just a handful of general principles you may want to apply that may save you some work near the end.

Balancing Character and Monster Attributes

Have you ever wondered when you were playing *Dungeons & Dragons* why the wizard always starts out weak or why choosing an elven character gives you higher dexterity but lower resistance to poisons and illness? Contrary to what you might think, those decisions weren't made arbitrarily for the purpose of ticking you off. Tradeoffs of this nature are meant to provide ways for players to differentiate their characters from one another while also helping maintain a certain degree of balance in the gameplay. The class-and-level system evolved specifically for this purpose, allowing players access to certain powers or skills while restricting the use of others. Skill-based systems can achieve similar effects simply by restricting the maximum number of skills that can be known at one time or by degrading those which aren't used on a frequent basis.

The rationale behind all this skill and attribute tweaking is simply this: If characters possess highly individualistic advantages and limitations, this will affect not only the way they are characterized to the player but also the ways in which the player will want to use them. Avatars who are tough and dexterous can take the enemy head-on, and the player is going to call those characters in when physical confrontations are called for. If a computer network needs to be hacked, it's nice to have a computer whiz in the party who's spent most of their experience points on learning the ins and outs of computer systems rather than the fine points of swordplay. No matter how the player chooses to spend their character creation points or what combination of character types they choose to throw together for their party, the game that you provide for them needs to be defeatable with *any* combination of the types available to them. To make sure that this is possible, you're going to need to create an *opposition matrix*.

Understanding the opposition matrix is really as simple as understanding the childhood game of rock-paper-scissors. Although there are only three possible choices the player can make, every choice is either tied, beats, or is beaten by another choice (see Table 6.3).

Table 6.3 Rock & Scissors: An Opposition Matrix

	ROCK	PAPER	SCISSORS
ROCK	tie	loses	beats
PAPER	beats	tie	loses
SCISSORS	loses	beats	tie

Importing Trouble

Sometimes the job of balancing attributes isn't even restricted to factors immediately present in the game. In some role-playing series, players are allowed to *import* their built-up characters into sequels, but the advantage of doing so is almost always null. Imported characters usually start out without *any* of the levels, spells, or objects that they possessed at the end of the previous game. They may share a name, a collection of attributes, and possibly a basic look with a former incarnation, but for the purposes of gameplay, they might as well be an entirely new character.

The reasons that developers usually "neuter" these incoming avatars is because role-playing games are at their heart about growth. If at the end of *Dungeons of Despair V* a character has powers that make them nearly godlike, it's next to impossible to develop and balance a sequel that will give that godlike character room to grow and develop, *while at the same time* also making the game playable to someone who just rolled up a new character for *Dungeons of Despair VI*. When adapting Raymond E. Feist's universe for *Betrayal at Krondor*, I had to create a situation in the story so we could hobble Pug, an all-powerful sorcerer that appears in Ray's books. Had we allowed Pug to have all the powers he is implied to have in the Riftwar stories, we could never have allowed gamers to play his character because there would have been virtually no way in which he could grow, and there wouldn't have been a foe we could put in front of him that he couldn't just *sneeze* out of existence.

The beauty of this combination of three choices is that there is no clearly superior move. *None* of the choices can be universally applied to all situations to always arrive at a victory, and so all of the choices can be considered to be in perfect balance. You want to achieve exactly the same thing in a good RPG.

While you're in the process of developing your character system, you want to strive for something that allows for no *best* kind of skill, ability, or attribute to be possessed by a character. For every advantage you give, there should also be a corresponding disadvantage that comes with it. Maybe a thief doesn't have

Some people have suggested that the solution in long-term series is to gradually build up the power level throughout so that importing characters across titles is less troublesome. On the whole it's an interesting idea, but the problems posed by it are multifold.

It's impossible to know how long any given game series is going to run. You're never even going to be certain that the first game is going to sell, let alone whether there will be 1 or 20 sequels. As time goes by, the engines that drive these games are always changing, and it's impossible to make any kind of long-range plans that run longer than three or four years.

Of even greater concern is what the competition is doing. If by the end of your first game Herb the Sorcerer is casting his most powerful spell and all it does is make smoke come out of the bad guy's ears, you may be in trouble. Very likely your competitor is showing off spells that have the Earth cracking open, swallowing enemy opponents, and then belching up the half-digested skeletons. By comparison, your title is going to look like a joke. If you can't put the coolest thing you can think of in front of the player immediately, you may be running the risk of letting the other guy win the war for the consumer's game-buying dollar, and that's never a good thing.

many hit points to start with, but he's fast on his feet and able to get through tight spaces. A big burly warrior might be very strong and more impervious to injury, but at the same time she might make for a better target for distant enemy archers. Another trick is to implement paired resistances and weaknesses. Perhaps a dragon resists fire but takes extra damage from cold. A cybernetic hero may be able to jack into a computer system, but he may also end up being especially sensitive to electrical shock damage because of it.

At no time should the player be irretrievably stuck in the game because they didn't choose the right set of attributes or bring along the "right" kind of hireling. The player wasn't around when you were creating the scenario, so solving the problem shouldn't involve their trying to guess what you intended. Always design your scenarios in such a way that there are multiple opportunities for the player to creatively apply different combinations of skills to the solution of their problems. As long as the player is thinking about the resources that they have, there should be at least one way, if not more, to take down an enemy, penetrate a stronghold, or otherwise achieve a goal that the player wishes to achieve.

Objects, Spells, and Technologies

Most of the advice I have regarding the balance of objects, spells, and technologies ties back to my previous point. You don't want to put anything into your game that can't in some way be trumped by an opposing force. If you create an invisibility spell, there should be either a counterspell that should reveal invisible objects or characters or creatures who can naturally see things that have been rendered "invisible" by magical means. If there's any misery monsters can inflict on the avatar, there should be measures available so that they can either deflect or undo the harmful effects.

Beyond this very general advice, try and apply Neal's Top 7 Tips for creating good objects, spells, and technologies:

- **Be Generous Early.** Give players lots of goodies relatively early in the game, and let them figure out how to use the stuff *before* the point at which they really need to understand them. This gives players an early sense of mastery and will also instill in them a strong sense of confidence that they'll be provided with everything they need to win the game.

- **Give Charge Ups Instead of Swaps.** If you think about any great hero, there's more to their legend than just their physical person. Who can think of Indiana Jones and not think about his bullwhip? Michael Moorcock's haunting albino king Elric of Melnibone would be naked without his demon-possessed sword Stormbringer. The history of the blues legend B. B. King would be only half complete without his beloved guitar Lucille. People develop strong attachments to the artifacts in their lives, and it can come to mean a great deal to players if you allow them to hang on to their material "sidekicks." Don't force players to chuck away ol' trusty just because they've found another sword that is going to do more damage. In the first-person shooter *Unreal,* players could find "powerups" throughout the game that would enhance their weaponry without forcing them to give up their "original" weapon.

This also alleviates the annoying practice that often develops in many games when players are left sorting through their inventories, unsure halfway through the game if they still need to hold on to their Blade of Orc-Killing, the +1 Sword of Fireballs, the Enchanted Rapier of Togarth the Queasy, and so forth. If you're determined to have different, interchangeable powers that the player needs to choose between, you might want to implement a system similar to the one used in *Final Fantasy VII.* In that title, weapons and various pieces of clothing sometimes had a notch in them that could be used to hold *materia,* magically enchanted gems that granted extra powers to the wielder. Materia could be removed, sold, and traded throughout the game, allowing for players to continually upgrade their weapons and their abilities while holding on to their weapons themselves.

- **Limit One-Time Uses.** Avoid giving players any kind of skill, spell, or object that is designed to be used in only one situation in the game. The time to implement the art, code, and everything else tied to things of this nature rarely if ever ends up being worth the trouble.

- **Avoid Dead Squirrels.** There's nothing more irritating than being forced to lug around an object that's of absolutely no value to the gameplay. If you want players to ferry something back and forth for a quest, there's absolutely nothing wrong with that, but make sure that during the time the player has it in their possession, there's still some bonus they can get out of having it with them.

Don't load your game world up with books or e-messages going into a laborious history in which no real clues are being offered about some element of the gameplay itself. It's fine to sprinkle in back story to add to the realism of the game, but make it *relevant* history. Mounds and mounds of spurious exposition that don't serve the main story tend to turn players off, and they'll stop paying attention to this kind of exposition if you abuse their attention. Remember that players are playing to *play,* not to scroll through endless pages of text.

- **Don't Duplicate Uses.** During the creation phase of the project, comb very carefully through your object and spell lists and try to eliminate instances in which you've got multiple factors creating essentially the same effect. If you've got two spells that both paralyze a character for one round, try tweaking one of them so that maybe it affects more than one target, or it also does damage while holding the target in place, or give it some other spin that makes it a unique item or spell. Spell lists can sometimes be difficult enough to sort through without the design team adding any unnecessary duplications. If in doubt, throw one out.

- **Send Out the Clones.** Categorically, you don't *ever* want to create any kind of object or spell that can clone itself or another object. Never, never, never, never, never. Just take my word for it—it is never going to be worth the effort trying to make it work.

- **Encourage Use of Resources.** If players are finishing the game with a pack chock-full o' potions, the design team has done something drastically wrong. In most cases this usually means the player hasn't known when they should use them, or they've been reluctant to use their resources for fear that they're going to need them for some unknown event at some point in the gaming future.

    Both issues are tied to an information problem. It's easy for players to know when to use a restorative potion or spell. They've got damage they need to heal, so it's time to chugalug the potion. But when exactly is the right time to use a spell or protective body suit that protects the wearer against electrical shock damage? Traditionally the player learns when they need it about at the point at which they no longer do. They encounter a villain, he whips out a shockgun, and blam! The player has just died from an electric blast. Without a doubt, the player now knows that they need to use the electroshock suit, but this is forcing the player to learn by dying. Vedically, that may be a very profound message, but from a game design position, it utterly bites. You never want to force players to have to use the Save and Load buttons to get through the majority of the gameplay.

    In some cases, the player has a pretty good visual indicator that tells them when and why to use certain objects. If they see a big spider, there's at least a 50-50 chance it may be venomous, and so it might be a good idea to drink an antivenom potion. When players see a river, it won't require much brainpower for them to realize the scuba suit is going to come in handy to them. But what warning does a player get that they need to use an electroshock suit if all they see is some guy standing in a corner?

One very simple solution to this problem might be to add a small bit of functionality to potions, spells, or other pieces of technology. They might function a bit like detectors, so that when the player comes into contact with forces that may require their use, they begin to glow or give off some other visual indicator. A preventative antivenom potion might be able to detect whether or not an enemy has a venomed blade, and thus warn the player that drinking it might be a good idea right now.

Whatever kind of solution you choose to apply, try to find ways to encourage players to use their resources in such a way that they don't have to die beforehand. Let their resources help give the player clues about when they should be used.

Balancing Scenarios and the World

If you compare the level layouts of professional and amateur game designers, there's one quality that you'll immediately be able to pick out about the arrangement of the amateur's levels. Taking into consideration the toughness of all the monsters, the value of all the items that can be found, and the general complexity of the environments in which everything will be placed, you'll see that the amateurs have created experiences that get steadily harder and harder from the beginning up to the bitter end. This are known as games of *logarithmic difficulty.*

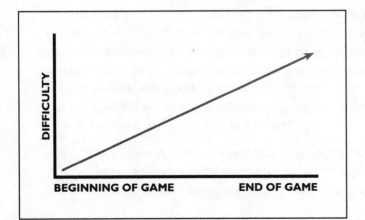

Figure 6.6

Logarithmic Difficulty Chart

It's a Dog-Got-Eaten World

All I wanted was a puppy.

Not long after I'd signed on to *Ultima Online* for the first time, I decided I wanted a dog. In the manual I'd seen that it was possible to have an online pet, so I instantly went off in search for a canine companion for my newly created mage-on-the-rise Fandercast.

After a frustratingly long period of bumbling around trying to learn how to acquire my new best friend, I at last learned the trick of Animal Training and soon had a wonderfully cute little pooch trailing after me whom I chose to name Argo (after my own mutt, a real-life golden retriever-cocker spaniel mix).

Within a matter of an hour, my virtual dog was dead. Not being aware that I had to feed him *extremely* frequently in order to maintain his loyalty, I became greatly dismayed as he wandered off toward the wilds. In a last-ditch effort I continued following him, frantically trying to reapply my Animal Training skills to regain his interest, but it was too late. An evil-looking creature decided Argo looked a whole lot like ogre food, and thus ended in tragedy the life of Argo Mark I.

The second time around, I got a few more of the details right. Before training another dog, I went and stocked up with enough chicken legs to feed a pet for a few weeks, then went off in search of a pooch who would fit the bill. Again I went through the heartbreakingly sweet process of recruiting a new best friend, and thus Argo Mark II came into the world a few hours later than his predecessor.

For a while I had a grand time wandering around, my virtual dog seemingly happy to be at my heels as long as I continued to chuck him chicken bones. Right before I was getting ready to sign off, I stopped for a moment to talk to another denizen who was sporting a feline companion as a pet. To my frustration I learned that before I signed off, I'd have to go find someplace to board the dog. Apparently if I didn't put Argo up somewhere safe in my offline absence, he'd suffer the same fate that Argo Mark I had suffered a few hours earlier.

Okay, so I couldn't log off yet. Fine. I'd just find the place in town, and that was that. Unfortunately, there *wasn't* a place in town where the dog could be boarded. The closest place was somewhere waaay out that direction, where I hadn't even been to yet. That meant more walking. I lobbed a few more dozen chicken legs at Argo and started off.

Suffice to say I spent a lot of time looking for the boarder, and at last, with relief, I managed to get the fellow running the place to talk to me. Only one small bad bit of news. Yes, this was the right place, but unfortunately the kennel was *full*. If I wanted to put Argo up for my offline time, I'd have to find someplace else. After a few more moments of soul searching, I decided that a virtual dog wasn't worth another three hours of denying myself sleep, and thus I logged off. I can only assume Argo Mark II eventually went to cyberpuppy heaven.

*   *   *

In terms of gameplay, it may *seem* that all this business with feeding and boarding the dog was meant to irritate gameplayers, but I can foresee a scenario where this may have been an attempt to keep the game in *balance*.

Think about it this way: Players wanted to be able to tame the wild dogs they met in the world and turn them into pets. In essence, this meant that anybody who wanted to could control at least one other creature that was combat-capable (pets always fight whoever has attacked their masters). Obviously this would be a complication, but alone this factor wouldn't vastly overturn the structure of the game. What *would* subvert the game, however, was the fact that new dogs were being "spawned" by the game on a regular basis, meaning the supply of dogs to any pet-desiring player was theoretically infinite.

Let's assume now that a single player does nothing but sit and train dogs all day, all the time. In a short period of time, they're not going to have one dog, but a full *pack* of dogs all at their command. If those dogs are all going to be in the same spot and under the control of the player the next time they sign on, the player could theoretically continue to build an army of hundreds or even *thousands* of servile dogs. Virtually no opponent in the game would be able to oppose such a Lord of the Canines unless they too got into the act. Once one player caught on to the practice, there would likely be dozens of other players who would be doing the same thing, controlling massive armies of ducks, horses, cats, or whatever they were skilled enough to train and control. Eventually *Ultima*'s servers would have collapsed under a thundering army of animal life, leaving very little room for the human inhabitants.

All of this just because players wanted a virtual Fido.

Confronted with this problem, the designers would have had only a handful of ways to solve the balancing problem. One would be to simply say that a player can't control more than one animal at a time and leave it at that. While it would be a solution, it would also smack of arbitrariness and wouldn't feel natural. Designers could also choose to crank down the rate at which animals spawned, but this would negatively affect the gameplay for players who like to go out hunting in the wilds. The easiest solution that also would have felt somewhat fair and realistic then would have been to do exactly what they've done:

The big problem with games that feature logarithmic difficulty is that they don't do a very good job of encouraging the player along. As the avatar gets better at whatever they're doing, the difficulty of the game is increasing at the same rate, so the player is effectively *standing still* from a gameplay standpoint. You never want players to be thinking to themselves, "Okay, so I got tougher. Big deal. I'm still getting my butt kicked on a pretty consistent basis, so gaining that extra level didn't really mean diddly squat to me."

If players begin to perceive that the game is getting steadily tougher from one level to the next, you're going to start losing players. Gamers stuck in Level 8 are going to be thinking about Level 9, and if you've convinced them from their past experiences in the game that everything is just going to get worse, you can be reasonably certain they're going to give up and walk away. The designer of situations like this may think they're providing a challenge, but in actuality they're punishing the player for making progress.

1. Mandate that if the player logs off without boarding their animals they'll lose control of all animals not in kennels.

2. Allow only a certain amount of space in kennels in which animals can be boarded, thus making it impossible for players to board whole armies of creatures.

The beauty of this solution—assuming there *was* a problem in the first place—is that it works within the context of the game, and it feels very realistic from a playing standpoint. When you're looking for ways to balance your own games, strive to find solutions that feel as internally consistent as this one does.

Sit, Argo, sit.

In order to avoid this problem, what you want to do is to break up your game world so that the player has absolutely *no* expectation of how easy or how hard the next level is going to be. When you chart it out on a difficulty graph, it should look a little something like Figure 6.7.

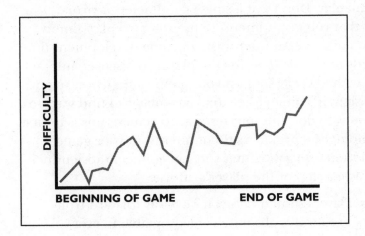

Figure 6.7

Modulating Difficulty Chart

DIFFICULTY

BEGINNING OF GAME   END OF GAME

The value of a game that uses a *modulating difficulty* scale is that players have no expectations either good or bad about what awaits them around the next corner. This will tend to make them more curious, driving them to explore further. If you follow up insanely difficult levels or encounters with very simplistic ones, players will revel in having something easy to do for a short period of time, and this will give them the confidence and spirit they'll need to scale whatever Mount Everest you choose to throw into their path next.

In order to maintain balance in your scenarios, only a few additional principles need to be added to those already discussed for characters, objects, spells, and technologies. Apply these ideas consistently, and you'll solve many of your scenario designing problems long before they have a chance to crop up.

- **Give Players Problems, Not Puzzles.** Don't put any obstacle in the player's way that can only be overcome with one specific method. If you plop down a dragon that they need to get past, don't have the only solution be to use the Rod of Gloom. Put a high ledge over the dragon's head that the player can use to sneak across if they've got a high enough Sneak skill. Have another adventurer parked near the lair who's willing to try and distract the dragon if the player plops down enough gold pieces. Your objective should be to create an environment that doesn't *feel* designed, but a natural place that allows for all the same kinds of choice making as the real world does. As I've said in previous comments, don't force the player to try and read your mind. Let them find their own ways.

- **Gamespace Is for Gameplay.** Don't put a single centimeter of virtual space into your game that you don't intend to use for gameplay. Empty rooms, caves, or forest paths are an utter waste of game development time and effort. There needs to be *something* for the player to discover, interact with, kill, or just goof with at every spot on your game map. If you've got dead space in your design, it's time either to make cuts or to find ways to introduce something new to do. The smartest way to achieve this is to first concentrate on developing the primary sites of interest in your game, then come up with all the *exciting* ways that you can connect those principal locations. Don't waste a step of the player's efforts.

- **Never Trap the Player.** Players should *always* have a way forward from whatever situation they are in. It is absolutely unacceptable to ever

force them into a situation where they've been stuck through no fault
of their own.

- **Warnings Are Mandatory.** If you're going to put some element in the environment that may have negative consequences to the player, you must always give them some kind of indication that there's something out of the ordinary. Make the bitmap for a dangerous button slightly different, have ominous sounds coming from down the corridor, put warning signs on the wall. Make sure players have at least a feeling of what they may be getting themselves into.

- **Build On What the Player Knows.** When designing a level, think about all the things the player has likely learned by this point. Build on the ideas you've used in previous levels, and try and find ways for players to apply old knowledge and abilities to do new things.

- **Make the Reward Equal to the Challenge.** Look at the amount of threat that all the monsters and other dangers in a level represent. Devise rewards that make the experience *worth* the player's effort. Never ever beat the player up and then give them nothing for having taken the damage. Fireball tossers that guard empty hallways or trapped chests that hold nothing in them are simply sadistic tools of bad game designers. Be better than that. Reward hard effort.

- **Reward Curiosity.** Build in elements of your game for the nonaverage gamer. If players really, really, really want to work hard and pay very close attention to the layout and design of areas, give them some bonuses for going the extra mile.

- **Let the Masses All Finish, Let the Few Get the Glory.** When you look at your entire game, construct it so that virtually any average person can get all the way from the beginning to the end with at least a modicum of concentration. Put everything they need to finish reasonably close to the main path of the game. Then, once you've laid out a good path that leads all the way through, go back and create some side quests that have been designed exclusively for the hard-core masochists who *want* a psychotically difficult experience. Put really rare items on these paths that will help them elsewhere and can be used as true "bragging rights" items.

Exercises

1. Play through a few of your favorite RPGs and take notice of all the times they give you choices. Ask yourself what impacts on the game those choices seem to make. Are they big or small impacts? Can you notably find any instances in the game when they denied you a choice that you wished to make? How would you fix it?

2. Come up with an idea for how you'd like some aspect of your future RPG to work and write an algorithm to deal with it. Make no assumptions about any step. If you have to develop subalgorithms, do so. How far down do you have to go to get a working system? Study the interdependence of your system. Are there any elements that might be more efficient if they were combined?

3. Think about games that you've played that you felt beat you up. What were they doing wrong? How do you think you could have addressed the balancing problems while staying internally consistent to the "reality" of the game?

CHAPTER 7

SOCKET WRENCHES OF THE GODS— BUILDING LIVING WORLDS

SHARP

"As midnight approached, the city was no less lively than during the daylight hours, but had merely taken on a different kind of life. In a virtual world full of thieves, murderers, and practitioners of black magic, and with many of them the alter egos of people who were up past their bedtimes, it was no surprise if Madrikhor changed as darkness fell from faux-Medieval heartiness to febrile mock-Gothic. It was hard to find a shadowy spot without someone hiding in it, a dark corner where someone was not conducting a transaction or a betrayal just beyond the glow of the streetlamp."

> — Tad Williams, *Otherland, Volume Three: Mountain of Black Glass*

"So many many worlds, so much to do
    So little done, such things to be."

> — Alfred Lord Tennyson, *In Memoriam,* lxxiii

The next time someone invites you over for a weekend role-playing session, ask them if they like the *dice*. After a moment of worried disorientation, your fellow players will probably comment on color, heft, or general reliability. You may even get a slightly more thoughtful sort who will expound on whether or not they actually like using dice during the course of a game. Before they have a chance to recover from your first question, flip open the rule book of the day and find a table or a chart of rules and ask them if they like *that*. Assuming your group doesn't decide to have you carted off to Arkham Asylum for observation, they will probably tell you that they like the layout, or they will complain that it's kind of hard to find in a pinch, or they may even relate a story about how that particular rule really, really screwed them over one time.

What will all the things they tell you have in common?

Think about the way in which gamers talk to other gamers about their playing experiences. You are not very likely to hear one player say to another, "There was this time playing *Bloodquest Online* that my health bar was only a tenth of the way filled with green liquid so I clicked on the inventory button, and the inventory window opened. I then clicked on the restoratives potion, drug it out of the window, and dropped it on the icon of my half-elf Vinnie and healed 6 points of damage, which gave him sufficient stamina to increase his speed. I was then able to pit my improved movement rate of 6 against that snorglerat's movement rate of 2 and therefore evade him." This may very well be an *accurate* description of the way in which somebody would go about healing their character in the fictional game of *Bloodquest,* but it's *not* the experience that players are going to sit around and discuss. Instead, they are more likely to say, "Hey, remember that time I was almost dead in *Bloodquest,* but I found that restorative you gave me in the Cathedral of the Damned right before those snorglerats could eat us up?" What's the difference? Although both stories describe exactly the same event, the first story is a technical description of what happened, while the second is a personal, *experiential-*based description.

Still puzzled? I'll stop being mysterious and get to the point. What the questions about the dice and the rule book and the stories about *Bloodquest* all have in common is that *players care about rules, mechanisms, and interfaces only inasmuch as they impact the player's overall experience.* No one would care one whit about DVD players if they didn't understand that they make movies look and sound better. When choosing a car to drive, who wouldn't prefer to have a Porsche than a Honda, even though functionally they both do exactly the same thing? Players do not play games for the elegance of the programming code. Players play games for the experiences that they can see, hear, and directly perceive.

The practical upshot to you is that role-playing games are *not* about rules. RPGs are about characters living in interesting lands with challenges to be overcome. Unless you do a very astonishingly bad job with your design, players are primarily going to talk about the things that happen in the gameworld. They'll talk about that time they broke up the Galactic Consortium, the time they took down a Silver Dragon with one lucky shot, the fun they had when they all got together in Haven for Lord Thornhead and Lady Dementia's wedding. Role-playing games are about worlds that people want to visit and explore, places where they will put the lives and skills of their electronic alter egos on the line to destroy or to defend. Your job will be to build a world about which the player will *care.*

Evicting the Elves: Honoring the Spirit of Worldbuilding

When I give talks at science-fiction conventions about evicting the elves from modern fantasy, some audience members become outraged. Many mistake my approach as hostile to the sacrosanct memory of J. R. R. Tolkien, undoubtedly one of the greatest worldbuilders of the 20th century and indirectly the father of both a literary and a gaming genre. Make no mistake. I don't have the slightest problem with Middle Earth or the elves, dwarves, and dragons who live there. I love and cherish all those things so dearly that I can't imagine having grown up without them. But for many, many years the fantasy gaming industry has survived by endlessly recycling thinly veiled rip-offs of *The Lord of the Rings.*

> **Worldbuilding.** The process of creating the history, culture, politics, technology, and general back story of an interactive world. This information will not only suggest the ultimate look and feel of the product but will help you make internally consistent game design decisions.

I have no doubt Tolkien would be appalled by the stultifying lack of originality reflected in many modern games. At the time he was writing *The Lord of the Rings,* he was troubled by a similar feeling about English mythology and later expressed his concerns in a letter written in 1951: ". . . I was from the early days aggrieved by the poverty of my own beloved country: it had no stories of its own (bound up with its tongue and soil), not of the quality that I sought . . . Of course there was and is all the Arthurian world, but powerful as it is, it is imperfectly naturalized, associated with the soil of England but not with English; and does not replace what I felt to be missing."

Tolkien took meticulous care to be innovative, and it is an exceedingly poor tribute to his accomplishments to continue recycling his material. The best way to honor his talent is to *do* as he did. Apply his methods—not his content—to the construction of new and exciting worlds that will live and breathe for the gamers.

So what did he do that was so all-fired *fabulous?*

If you're one of the seven people on the planet who haven't read Tolkien's works yet, I highly recommend that you do so. You can learn more about creating an immersive world by studying *The Lord of the Rings* than reading any 10 books written by me or any of my game designing colleagues. While literary critics discuss his hypnotic use of language or the archetypal power of the tale he weaves, Tolkien's works go far beyond just presenting an interesting *plot.* If you were to excise the heroic tale of Frodo Baggins entirely from *The Lord of the Rings* and were only given an encyclopedia detailing all the information about the *background* of Middle Earth, you'd still find that it's a very interesting world to visit. It has an ancient history. It has a detailed geography. It has unique traditions and folklore. It has a multitude of different languages and a unique alphabet known as Tengwar, which Tolkien especially created for use in his fantasy setting. The reason that Tolkien's world works is that he treated it as though it were a real and living place, and the professional game designer should always do the same. After all, if *you* don't treat your world like it's a real place, what makes you think the *player* will see it that way?

While working on the world I created for *Elysium,* I had to rethink the reality in which it would take place. I knew that I didn't want to do a rehash with a world full of elves, dwarves, and dragons, but I did want a world where magic existed and was common enough that the average individual knew something about it. I also wanted to get rid of the tired convention of a rustic medieval European setting, so I drew inspiration for its look and feel from classical civilizations like those that had arisen in Greece, Rome, China, and Meso-America. I chucked out thatched-roofed huts and replaced them with fabulous cities of marble, adamantine, and crystal, all sprawling across bizarre landscapes warped by ancient magical wars. Gods were not distant unknowable entities, but they ruled from capital cities of amazing beauty and terror. I turned to the Italian Renaissance to study espionage and the back-stabbing spy networks that I saw as ever-present in the treacherous Elysian reality. I sought mythological creatures from aboriginal dreamtime and Vedic traditions that had never made appearances in Western-themed games before. At every turn I sought to create a fantasy world that would be eternally surprising, exciting, and beautiful, one that also presented a vaguely familiar face that wouldn't be too alien for the audience to understand.

Thankfully, I have not been alone in the wilderness. In recent years I've been very gratified to see other designers striking out and creating new worlds of their own. Interplay's *Fallout* was a wonderfully postapocalyptic RPG that certainly defied most people's expectations. *Planescape: Torment* took players on a wild tour through one of the most bizarre landscapes yet attempted.

Possibly the best reimagining of fantasy in recent years has been thanks to the Fox television series *The X-Files.* Mainstream audiences often fail to connect with many traditional RPGs because they can't relate to fantasy settings. Medieval motivations and authentic-sounding dialog are too removed from modern sensibilities for ordinary people to understand them. But by bringing together a good old-fashioned monster show with the modern mythologies that surround UFOs, Bigfoot, spontaneous combustion, and the general distrust of the government, series creator Chris Carter managed to create a new American mythology that I'm sure will continue to be echoed for years to come. Already several computer games have made a stab at capturing the *X-Files* mystique, and *Deus Ex* creator Warren Spector has openly stated in interviews that his recent RPG was at least in part inspired by this modern-day myth.

Of course, not all the inspirations you use to reimagine your RPG need be all that far-out or necessarily even from American shores. *Shenmue,* an RPG for the Sega Dreamcast, featured a hero searching for answers to his father's mysterious death in mid-1980s Japan. Many of the role-playing titles in the *Final Fantasy* series have been decidedly un-Tolkien-esque, all the more alien because of the Japanese sensibilities for which they were originally produced.

The Other Side of the Coin

The people who will most stridently resist your efforts to create brave new worlds will *not* be gamers, but the managers who run your projects. The first time you start describing a fantasy role-playing game that doesn't trot out dwarves and dragons in the first ten seconds of the pitch, the people holding the purse strings of your project are going to start convulsing and foaming at the mouth. New things tend to frighten investors. New projects can't be as accurately predicted as safe sequels or rip-offs of other people's familiar game settings. The assumption is *always* that if you put things in front of the player they already know and understand, that's going to the safer course, the path less fraught with potential danger. Be aware of this mindset before you follow my advice. When you go in and plan to change the world, the first thing you're going to have to do is sell them on what the players *will* recognize and then slowly work up to your more radical elements. If you can make them see why this experience is going to touch players in a visceral and human way—whatever the setting—you can get them to come round to your way of seeing things. Be patient. There's always a way to find a reasonable middle ground between the familiar and the bizarre.

However you proceed when thinking about the world in which you will set your players loose, try and find a stereotype in the industry and set it on its ear. Break with time-honored conventions and slaughter the sacred cows. Even at the end of *The Lord of the Rings,* the elves knew when it was time to leave for the Grey Havens so that the new generations of men and hobbits could develop on their own. Have the courage to let them go so that new ideas can grow and flourish. The time has come for game designers to be as thoughtful, creative, and professional about worldbuilding as they are about laying down the laws of interaction. You can't very well expect to psychologically transport players to another world if the environment around them feels paper-thin. Yes, you may end up creating volumes of material that will never be directly experienced by the players, but the work you invest in building a solid world will pay off in look, feel, and gameplay.

"Describe the Universe, and Give Three Examples . . ."

In the late 1970s a professor of vocational studies at Oklahoma State University sometimes issued his outgoing class a prank finals question that few were prepared to answer: "Describe the universe, and give three examples."

While Dr. Knight's question is patently absurd on its face, it has a certain Zen koan wisdom when applied to the construction of an interactive role-playing environment. As a designer you have a responsibility to "describe" the universe of the game to the player in way that they will understand. If you wanted, you *could* stop players at the beginning of every game, give them a long and tedious explanation about the 3,000 years of ancient history of the game world, go through an exhaustive list of all the laws of physics that govern your universe, and then at some point eventually release the player to actually play. You *could* do all of this, but I'd advise you not to. This is a rather clumsy and inelegant way to handle the problem of getting critical information across to the player, and more to the point, it's a rather bad use of the gaming medium. In order to "explain" the universe to the player in the best way possible, you need to arrive at an *interactive* solution.

In books, and movies, and television, it isn't unusual to have some character randomly mention something that will eventually be crucial for the viewer or reader to know in order to understand a later development in the plot. This kind of information is often called *exposition*. Science fiction has traditionally carried a heavier burden of exposition than other genres, simply because laypeople may not get what the problem is if they don't understand the gadgetry or why flying near a black hole might cause a starship crew some concern. Old movies from the 1950s were deliciously awful at dealing with sci-fi exposition, and it wasn't unusual to hear gems of dialogue like:

```
                    SCIENTIST:
     As we both know, Dr. Mason, we've worked
     together for 13 years. In all that time we
     have been best friends, and our daughters
     attended college together. We shared the
     Nobel prize in 1946. The Blazitron Ray that
     we constructed together is capable of
```

generating 5 million gigawatts of neutron
power and is the most advanced weapon in the
United States arsenal against the mutant ant
invaders that we, in our arrogance and in
defiance of God, accidentally created in our
laboratories at Los Alamos where we both
live. . . .

No matter how you look at this dialogue, the above snippet of writing is an exceptionally bad piece of screenwriting. The first thing that's wrong is that it makes no sense for the scientist to be telling Dr. Mason how something works that they've presumably built together. This is as completely asinine as it would be for me to instruct my wife on how to make ice cubes, or for me to tell my neighbor Bob, "As you know, Bob, television allows an image of a person to be transmitted over long distances." Inhabitants of the world aren't going to stand about discussing things that everyone comprehends as common knowledge, unless of course something drastic and terrible has come along and *changed* the normal way of life, or unless someone has entered the picture who would not have cause to understand what's going on. (Role-playing games tend to have an overabundance of amnesiac and foreign-born heroes. Granted, this is a valid way to get around the fact that you're having to shove so much exposition toward the player, but make an effort to come up with more creative solutions if you can.)

The greatest sin in the above-described dialogue is *not* the discussion of the obvious between friends. The problem is that the story is being *told* to the audience instead of *shown* to them. In virtually *all* forms of entertainment, telling instead of showing is an absolute no-no.

When you go to see a movie, you don't expect to see two and a half hours of text scrolling up the screen while the audience reads along. Why not? There's no technical reason why you couldn't do such a thing, but it would be a horrendous waste of the capabilities of film. Film, television, and games all share the fact that they are primarily *visual* mediums. Having a character sit and tell the player that goblins are swarming into the lands isn't nearly as interesting as letting the player *see* the goblin invaders for themselves. Games alone, however, transcend the merely visual. Designers can allow players not only to find and see the firefight for themselves but also to participate in it and have an impact on its outcome. More critically, this allows a designer to show the player an expository truth about the world—in this case that goblins are the bad guys—without some old fogey standing around with no other purpose in the world than to tell the player what they should otherwise be able to find out on their own.

The need for exposition in games is far greater than in other mediums. Often it can be a tremendous challenge to get the player all the information they need in a way that doesn't feel heavy-handed and doesn't overload them. In movies, the audience can miss *all* the critical facts of what's going on, but no matter how much they get or don't get, the movie still reaches its ending. Unfortunately, the same cannot be said of a role-playing title. In order to get to the end of the game, the player will have to learn a great deal about the world in order to make informed decisions about what they can or should do to overcome the challenges with which they'll be faced. You will have to find fun and interesting ways to clue them in as to who the bad guys are, what places in the world are important, who they should trust, where they go to get supplies, even where home is supposed to be. But keep in mind the more alien you make your world from ours, the harder it is going to be for the player to understand what's going on. *Everything* you create will be a puzzle to the player until they have a chance to explore, and it takes very little effort to create a sense of mystery or complexity.

Exploit the fact that your world is both visual and interactive, and let players learn how the world works from everything they can see, hear, and do. If it's possible for players to walk up walls with the right kind of spell, let them see some other character using the spell so they'll know at some point that they can buy or acquire that kind of capability later on. Don't have Drew the Mysterious simply hanging around in his chateau, whispering to you that he's paranoid— *demonstrate* this to the player by filling up his home with traps or other devices that the player has to get past which *show* that he's paranoid. Everything the player experiences should provide examples of the world you mean for them to understand and should reinforce a cohesive, consistent picture in their mind about the "reality" of your game world.

Reality 101

Saturday nights in my childhood meant confinement to the family basement. I wasn't consigned there by cruel parents trying to hide my burgeoning were-wolfism, mind you, nor was I being forced to dispose of dead bodies like a member of the Butchering Bender family of Kansas fame. What drove my brother Gene and me to regularly hold vigils in the storm cellar was the fact that it was the location of the family's only "other" television set, and the programs we liked to watch on weekends often conflicted with the 10 o'clock airing of the local news. Originally we'd begun the habit to catch the British imported programs on PBS like *Doctor Who, Monty Python's Flying Circus,* and *Hitchhiker's Guide to the Galaxy.* Sometime during this period, however, programming got shuffled and we began to catch another series that not only contributed to the betterment of my education but forever impacted the way I would approach the construction of role-playing worlds.

Connections, written and hosted by the British science writer James Burke, was originally a 13-part series that explored the bizarre and sometimes unpredictable ways in which small, seemingly unrelated discoveries or events led to the creation of 13 different pieces of modern technology. Starting with the way that a group of French monks handled sheep rearing, he would then guide viewers through a series of developments that would end with the invention of the modern computer. In another episode he explained why something a doctor did in the court of Queen Elizabeth in the 16th century made it possible for television to exist today. What Burke did in *Connections,* and then later in several other related series and books, was demonstrate how a change in one aspect of society can domino out to affect other facets of people's lives. A scientific discovery might inspire a revolution in art, which in turn might incite an uprising of the disenfranchised and the overthrow of a government.

The insight that I gained from watching *Connections* was that the cavalier addition of even just *one* fantastic element to the world that we know would have profound long-range effects on its history, its politics, its social structure, its religion, and even its ultimate destiny. I realized that introducing a dragon into a world inhabited by men was problematical on several fronts. Mankind survived to achieve status at the top of the food chain on Earth because there was no other predator around that could outmatch him. How could he survive to evolve in a world that was occupied by a flying, intelligent, extremely tough competitor like a dragon? Are dragons herbivores, or do men just taste bad to them? Given the fact that birds have to eat roughly 10 times their body weight every day to survive, if dragons have a similar food intake requirement, how much territory do they have to lord over in order to survive, and how has this impacted human settlement patterns?

Of course there would be smaller, more practical considerations too. If you've got winged creatures like dragons or pegasi whipping through your game world skies all the time, broad-brimmed hats might be popular, and those charming thatched-roofed cottages might be less than complete proof against falling aerial

RAKINS
KEEP
LADY GREYSTONE
FALLEN REALMS   5-13-97

debris or fire breathed from above. Would people live in earth-sheltered homes or have steel-covered roofs? Is there a heavy trade in dragon dung disposal? How good is the fire department, and do they get kickbacks for their protection?

By following a chain of simple, practical questions like those above, you can begin to develop very interesting cultures and problems for your world. A procedurally thought-out environment will *always* have a greater ring of authenticity than one that's just been randomly "rolled up." If you're in a bind and just can't get the creative juices flowing otherwise, a random beginning can be useful, but don't let it take over the entire process. Yes, an element of randomness occasionally plays a part in the pageant of world histories, but aside from the very rare utterly cataclysmic events like asteroids slamming down from the heavens to exterminate entire species, very few events in history have totally random causes. The South lost the Civil War because the North was better equipped to deal with an extended war effort, not because General Lee lost a battle plan wrapped around a fistful of cigars. During the Middle Ages, Pope Urban II decided the best way to get minor unlanded French nobles to stop terrorizing the countryside was to send them off on a Crusade to Jerusalem, and unfortunately there hasn't been a lasting peace in the Middle East ever since.

To build your world, you can start just about anywhere you like. If you're a methodical sort, you can start with the planet on which the action will take place, then work forward to create the creatures, then cultures, and finally the characters who will play important roles in your universe. If you're a more organic designer, you can start in the middle and create several pieces simultaneously, then use what you know to build logical connections between them. I've often been in a situation where I knew the circumstances that I wanted to end up with, so I had to go back and think logically about what events, trends, and other factors would logically have had to occur in order for me to have reasonably arrived there. In many ways, the process can almost be like reconstructing the events leading up to the commission of a crime. Let's say you wanted to have dragons and men sharing the same world, as we discussed a bit before. To deal with the evolutionary problem, you might come to the realization that they evolved on entirely different continents and contact has only recently been made between the two species. Another possibility might be that they both had to fight a common foe at some point in the distant past and they've forged alliances that have allowed for their peaceful coexistence. The information you get from dealing with these problems will tell you a great deal about your world and in the long run will give you an internally consistent reality.

For your benefit, I'll try and touch on some of the big picture worldbuilding elements that usually tend to have the most pronounced "Burkeian" impacts. It would be nice if I could sit down and draw an illustration that would demonstrate exactly how Element A always affected Element Q and therefore Elements C and Z, but the nature of a well-developed universe is that everything ends up touching everything else. You are creating a whole milieu—not just a dungeon, or a genetic laboratory, or a galactic starport, but an entire culture with its own technology and traditions, affected by everything from weather to geopolitics.

Heavenly Orders

Building a world like Earth takes a little time . . . roughly about 4.5 billion years, give or take a billion or so. Although you can get the basic ingredients like helium and hydrogen just about anywhere in the cosmos, you'll have to get some of the heavier and more important elements from the heart of old, exploded stars. On your shopping list you'll need all the basics for life like carbon and oxygen (or silicon if you want to get radical) along with important metals like iron and nickel. Those metals will play an important role in the creation of a magnetosphere, the naturally generated magnetic "shield" that is generated through the rotation of the planet and that protects the life you're trying to grow from all those deadly cosmic rays zipping through the vacuum of space. . . .

Okay, so maybe you don't have to go all *that* far back into the history of your world. If you want, you can certainly piddle around with orbital mechanics and molecular formulas, but nobody is going to require you get a doctorate in astrophysics in order to build your game world. The only important things that you need to keep in mind about your planet are how its various resources and dangers affect the development, the communication, and the day-to-day lives of the people living on its surface.

It's easy to take for granted that life just arose on Earth without taking into consideration how really remarkable our situation is. Parked at roughly 93 million miles from the sun, we're in almost a perfect spot for life to have arisen. If we got much closer, we'd live on a hellish planet like Venus, which has an average daily surface temperature of 846 degrees Kelvin, featuring rainfall largely composed of sulfuric acid. Travel out past the orbit of Mars and the amount of radiant heat received from the sun is likely to be less than the heat generated by planetary cores. Life as we know it is possible on Earth because we've got a liquid ocean of water, oxygen to breathe, a magnetic field that helps protect us from cosmic radiation, and several other very special circumstances. If you change any of those factors, the ways in which we live would likely be very, very different. Here's an in-depth look at how just one planetary tweak drastically changes life on a world with many moons:

> Aside from the fact that they look very cool up in the sky, moons exert enormously important effects on the planets around which they revolve. On Earth, we can reliably predict when tides will be coming in and out because tides are created by the pull of our moon. If you add more than one moon, seafarers are going to have a much more difficult time at sea, and predictions of the tides will be much more difficult to calculate. This may result in sea travel being very rare or nonexistent in your world, which would mean all trade and contact with other peoples will happen overland or by air.

> Planets surrounded by numerous moons will likely also have increased stress on their tectonic plates, resulting in highly active volcanoes and increased earthquake activity all across the world. This in turn may influence natives to opt for flexible housing like yurts as opposed to permanent structures like an A-frame house. Local religions will probably talk *a lot* about angry gods.

> Traditionally on Earth, calendars have often been based on the phases and movements of the moon, but if you add more than one, calculation of time may fall utterly into the hands of priesthoods. Astrology practiced on such a world will likely be many, many times more complex to practice and understand.

Try and think of a few other transformative ideas that arise from changing single factors about the world in which we live. If you stopped Earth's spin so that one side always faces the sun and the other side always faces the darkness of space, how do you think that would affect where people lived? How do you think things like travel, trade, and other cultural factors would change if you made Earth's storms much more frequent and violent? Time spent learning a little more about astronomy will be well worth it and may help inspire new and creative ideas about the environments in which you want to start your new world.

Science, Magic, and Social Change

If you're thinking about dealing with a world in which powerful magic exists, or a far-flung future in which much more sophisticated technology will be available, you've got two paradigm problems you're going to need to resolve before you do anything else. The first issue will revolve around the technical aspects of how your magic or technology systems will function and is primarily a gameplay problem instead of a worldbuilding one. The second issue, however, concerns how the use of those systems is going to impact the peoples and cultures who use them.

Although there are numerous cases of technologies I've seen presented in games, or books, or movies that could have done with a tad more thought, one example I frequently pick on is the transporter technology presented in *Star Trek.* (Please know that I am a hard-core Trekkie of old, so I do this more out of love than spite.) Although the transporter was presented in the vein of a simple way for the crew to get between their starships and the surfaces of alien planets, I long ago came to the conclusion that transportation would be the *least* important way in which it would be used. It's exceedingly silly to watch the *Enterprise* trying to punch holes in the hulls of alien ships with photon torpedoes when it would be much more expedient to simply use the transporter to "beam" a section of the offending ship's hull into nothingness. Thanks to this realization, I introduced a transporter-like weapon into *Planet's Edge,* which was a supremely dangerous part of any starship's arsenal.

But beyond just simple tactical uses of the transporter, there would be much larger social and cultural issues to deal with as well. Because the nature of transporter technology is to annihilate something first and then reassemble it elsewhere, there's going to be a significant number of people who refuse to use them. Dr. McCoy's famed dislike of the device would be the mildest probable cultural reaction. Given the fact that the person who gets reassembled isn't really the same person, but effectively a molecular clone of the original individual, there would be people clamoring in the streets about its misuse. Abortion foes might get in on the act because of what would be done when pregnant women were transported, and suicide-prevention organizations would do whatever they could to sabotage the technology. There would be other concerns as well. Transporter technology would provide simplistic ways to clone huge armies in almost no time. Class considerations would be utterly erased between the wealthy and the poor because anyone on the planet could have whatever they wanted as long as they had enough raw matter available to make what they desired. Almost the very instant that this technology became available in a widespread way, almost any culture as we understand it would completely evaporate, and I have significant doubts that we would recognize what would come after it.

Regardless of whether you use magic or technology, the effects on the culture are largely going to be the same. The relevant questions are going to revolve around how easy the technology is to use, how much of the population has access to its benefits, and what kind of individuals are included or excluded from its use. Think about our world and how in the past two centuries, advances in technology contributed immeasurably to the social and political advancement of women. With mechanization in the workforce, brute strength became less important than fine motor skills, putting female workers on a more even footing with men. Meanwhile, medical innovations made it easier for women to decide if and when they wanted to have children. These two factors had amazingly enormous social impact, especially in the Western world. I'm certain the inventors that set the industrial revolution in motion weren't thinking about expanding the rights and roles of women, but regardless of their ultimate intentions, those were the effects with which society was left.

Ask yourself how important you want magic or technology to be in your world. Is it powerful or weak, rare or common? If it's powerful and rare, then the people who wield it are likely to be feared or distrusted, or revered. Either way, it will most definitely affect their cultural and social standings. If it's weak and common, then nobody is likely to treat it as anything special, and everybody will largely ignore its presence in the same way that we don't think much about the miracles of telephones, televisions, or the Internet. Establish for yourself how easy it is to access these tools of power, and be rigorous about applying that concept at every level of your world.

Growing Cultures

Astronomer Jill Tarter of the SETI Institute once said that her biggest fear *isn't* that we'll never receive a message from outer space. What she worries most about is that one day we may actually get that first message from an alien civilization but never be able to figure out what it *means*.

Anybody Out There?

Ready to create your latest sci-fi role-playing epic? Curious about how many different technologically advanced civilizations might reasonably exist out among the stars? Dr. Frank Drake, chairman of the board of the SETI Institute, was asking himself that very same question in 1961 when he finally decided that he'd whip up an equation that might someday be used to provide an answer. Called the Drake Equation, it has become one of the most widely accepted tools to study of the probability of life on other planets.

$$N = R_* \times f_p \times n_e \times f_l \times f_i \times f_c \times L$$

N = The number of civilizations whose radio signals might be detectable.

R_* = The rate at which stars (those that might have large enough "habitable zones" and that would have long enough stellar life spans to allow for the development of intelligent life) form.

f_p = The number of stars like our sun that are surrounded by planetary systems.

n_e = The number of planets that are in the habitable zones of the stars around which they orbit. (Such a planet would be within an adequate distance from its sun to maintain a body of liquid water.)

f_l = The fraction of planets that exist within a habitable zone in which life will arise.

Contact between different racial and ethnic groups on Earth has always been a difficult affair. That's even taking into consideration that we at least share a basic human biology and in countless cases come from closely related cultures. There are many, many instances in our history in which two well-meaning people have come into contact with one another, but barriers like languages, ethnic disrespect, and religious intolerance have turned races that should have been good neighbors into the bitterest of enemies. If you take this idea one step further, it isn't hard to imagine that contact with elves, trolls, or bug-eyed greys visiting from Cygnus X-1 would likely be even more troublesome and contentious than anything we've encountered before.

f_i = The fraction of planets on which life arises and has a high order of intelligence.

f_c = The fraction of planets where intelligent life-forms create technology capable of sending signals into space.

L = The length of time such civilizations release detectable signals into space.

Got all that?

Although the Drake Equation is expected to be a fairly good predictor of alien life, the difficulty with using it at the moment is that we don't have sufficient information to fill in most of the blanks. We have only begun to detect the *possibility* of planets orbiting around other stars, and since we only know of one planet for certain upon which life has arisen (don't get excited folks, I'm talking about us), several other factors in Drake's Equation are going to have to wait until time and technology can give us better data. Until then, we're going to have to settle for the guesstimates of the people most likely to be in the know. Several scientists have applied their own hypothetical figures to Drake's Equation with wildly different results, but an average "best guess" is that there are probably around a million different places in our galaxy that would be capable of broadcasting alien signals. (Art Bell's late-night AM radio talk show on UFOs and conspiracies certainly broadcasts some *very* alien signals, but I'm afraid he's not quite what SETI is looking for.)

But what is all that cultural stuff that mucks up communication between different peoples? Do you think the Native American tribes refused to passively move off their ancestral lands just because they knew it would irritate European settlers? Is it like what comedian Steve Martin jokes about when he says that he hates to visit small countries where the locals "don't have the *decency* to speak English"? It's a mistaken notion to believe that cultures are consciously developed by their adherents for the benefit, or the aggravation, of other social groups. True cultures provide a core set of values, traditions, myths, and beliefs that reflect the experiences and needs of a specific population of people. To give you an example of what I mean, let's look at how one aspect of geography had dramatic effects on the development of an American subculture.

If you know nothing else about the South, you've probably at least heard they grow good cooks down there. There's hardly a restaurant or coffee shop in the nation that doesn't feature Southern-styled exports like BBQ ribs, fried chicken, and country fried steak. For most people the phrase "Southern cooking" conjures images of high fat, lots of starch, and mounds and mounds of food just covered in creams and sauces, served in portions so large that some elephants would die if they were required to eat that much food. It's practically taken for granted that once you cross the Mason-Dixon Line, the rivers just naturally turn into gravy.

But what is it about living in that part of the United States that necessarily gave rise to eating those kinds of foods? Demographically speaking, the mix of folk who settled in the South weren't all *that* different than those who settled in other parts of the country. Should we blame it on something in the air or the water? Not quite, but that's getting very close to the culprit. The real agent of change here is the soil of the old Deep South.

Early settlers in the American colonies discovered that land in the South was very, very productive. It provided just the right combination of organic and environmental factors to do a good job of growing cotton and tobacco, both of which were turning into highly valuable cash crops for export. Unfortunately for everybody, working in such a steamingly hot region of the country meant that workers needed to eat heartier diets in order to survive. That meant more fat, bigger portions, and lots of salt to go around. In the short run it was an eminently practical solution to a problem, but as the plantations died out and more socially responsible institutions took their place, the eating habits stayed the same. Within a few generations, it became very common for Southern Americans to be running around with "spare tires" and having heart attacks in their 40s. Office workers, bus drivers, and other less physically active individuals continued to eat as though they were doing the jobs of their forebears, plowing five acres every day in 100+ degree temperatures in 80 percent humidity.

If you're wondering what this extended lesson in sociology and anthropology has to do with role-playing games, remember that no man or woman is an island. The characters they portray will have grown up in worlds where differing cultures or races will be competing for dominance. Individually they will define who their characters are by the kinds of decisions they will make, but they can also gravitate to one culture or another as a generalized way of expressing their identity.

If Sarah the Slayer likes to wander the countryside getting rid of menacing monsters, she may appreciate the opportunity to hang with a xenophobic tribe of warriors who reward her for her efforts. Another culture of order-loving monks may make Sarah's life increasingly difficult as she cooperates with the xenophobes, finding herself caught in the conflict between the ideals of two very different cultures.

There's no law anywhere that stipulates that an RPG must occur in a world inhabited by other intelligent creatures. You could set a player loose in a gigantic, interactive world full of monsters and traps and other devious devices where they'd never come across another soul like themselves. But unless a character has a world in which they can play a role, they have nothing to gauge their relative heroism (or villainy) against.

In isolation, the cultures of your world are likely to be relatively pure and unadulterated. The laws and mores of the locals are likely to be regularly adhered to and strictly enforced. Architectures and art forms are likely to be rather consistent, within the tolerance of the most liberal members of the societies who produce them. But in instances where cultures collide, almost anything should be able to happen. Wars may erupt as they compete for land, food, mates, or other important resources. One culture may attempt to leech technologies from a more sophisticated society, while another seeks refuge from the hostilities of a warlike neighbor. A handful of cultures might peacefully coexist on the surface but be broiling with spies, saboteurs, and assassins just below the surface of their polite public relations.

If you want, you can borrow examples of cultural conflicts from the world in which we live, but don't feel like you have to give your game world the same limitations as our own. Your situations will be more interesting if the problems faced go beyond thinly disguised replays of yesterday's headlines. What if racial differences weren't divisive, but something else was an issue? Suppose the conflicts involved the empaths versus the nonempathic? What if those with even somewhat higher than average intelligence were hated? (Okay, if you ever had a teacher that graded on the curve and you busted the bell, then you know that one's not much of a stretch, but you get the idea.)

The questions you must ask yourself when assembling the cultures of your world are really very similar to the questions you would ask if you were creating a character. Is it a somber culture or lively and celebratory? What part of the world did it start in? What does it value? Are there things they've experienced as a people which they fear or revile? Do they see themselves as a chosen people, or do they have an ethnic identification as a downtrodden or oppressed populace? What do they need but have difficulty getting? What do they have that somebody else might want?

Every question you put to yourself should help you feel out answers about how they build their buildings, the kinds of tools they're likely to use, the kinds of music they might like to play. As each culture begins to come alive, you should also begin to suspect what other groups might have the biggest problems with them, and which might be natural allies. In time, it should become almost instinctive to you to know how a specific culture would respond to a given problem it was faced with. One might fight, another might flee, another might try to broker a deal. Understanding your cultures will be to understand how the big pieces on your game board work and move.

Kilroy Was Here . . . Evoking a Mythic Past

Imagine you're in a store that sells old typewriters, and you're looking for a present to give to a sentimental writer friend. After looking around for a few moments, you spot a Smith Corona typewriter sitting in the corner. Assuming it is still in reasonable working order and has a good ribbon, what do you think you'd be willing to pay for it? $20? Maybe $30 if the salesman caught you on a really good day? Now imagine that while the salesman isn't looking, you lift it up and see there's a metal tag on the bottom that says "Property of Stephen King." If you had a way of verifying that the Stephen King mentioned on the plate was indeed THE Stephen King, and you were aware that *Carrie* or *The Stand* had been written on just such a typewriter, how much do you think you'd be willing to pay for that typewriter *now?* If you walk out of that shop and pay anything less than $1,000, you'll know you've gotten a steal, even though a few moments earlier it was just a cruddy $20 throwaway. What made the difference in the typewriter's value? Whether you're talking about people, places, or objects, what we tend to value the most are those things which have come into contact with the extraordinary.

Museums are full of mundane items made remarkable because they've been associated with a great person, a famous event, or an era long gone by. How much more important was this pen because it was Martin Luther King's, or how much better is that Apple II Computer because it was the one on which Andy Greenberg was writing the first *Wizardry* title? In my family, a saber has passed down through three generations of Hollands and Hallfords, connecting me to a war in which I had relatives spilling blood in the names of both the Union and the Confederacy. Because this was carried into battle by my great-grandfather Holland, it allows me to experience the Civil War as a matter of family history, not just an abstract thing that I was taught about in school. This sense of *connectedness* attached to places and objects can also be used to your advantage in the creation of a role-playing game. By evoking a sense that objects and places in your world have a real history, you will by extension create a sense of a living, breathing world.

If while playing under the guise of an avatar you wander into a shop and you have the choice of buying two equally priced blasters, but when looking at the descriptions of both of them you learn one had been the property of a bounty hunter known as The Angel of Death, which do you think you'd be inclined to buy? You'd at least *expect* Angel's gun to be a somewhat deadlier weapon, given the guy's reputation. But players like it if there's more than mere statistics associated with the objects they carry with them. They want the equivalent of a lucky rabbit's foot, something that rubs off a bit of its past onto its present owner. By choosing to carry Angel's gun, the player is identifying with Angel's reputation, using it as a foundation upon which they can further characterize their avatar. It's a declaration in the most classic, mythical sense: *I am he who can draw the sword from the stone, I am the rightful wielder of Excalibur.*

Of course not everything can *be* Excalibur. How cool is it to have Zhul's Ultimate Sword of Doom if every guy you meet is running around with virtually the same thing? Your world will need a selection of common, ordinary objects with which the player starts the game, but that doesn't mean those things have to be completely boring. When players examine their objects, in addition to the basic statistics (like weight, damage, base chance to hit, etc., etc.), give them a description that not only tells them something about how their inventory items work but also tells them a bit about the world. Here's an example:

> **FALCHARIN**   A short one-handed melee weapon commonly used by the nomadic tribes of the Kazarzi Mountains. Originally designed so that the user could trigger its deadly arm spikes at need to fend off whips and stinging tentacles, the Falcharin played a major role in helping the Kazarzi riders defeat the raiders from the Fire Sea.

In looking at this description, the player has not only learned a little something about their weapon's possible effectiveness against monsters using whips and tentacles, they've also learned a little something about the history of the world in which it was created. The weapon is more than just something they can carry around with them, it's an artifact of a culture.

This principle of using the material created by cultures to tell the world story can also be extended to the layout of your levels. Remember that the scary old mansion up on the hill wasn't built to be a place where good and evil could duke it out for world domination. It will be a place chockablock *full* of information that should tell players something about its occupants' personalities, their position in society, and maybe even something about their beliefs. If the player raids the place only to discover that it's a beautifully appointed, well-lit place without any secret dungeons or trapdoors, they're going to realize that maybe those zombies *didn't* come from the mansion after all. It's too clean, too nice, and not at all the kind of place where zombies get whipped up. Maybe the corporation CEO who lives there is telling the truth when he says he doesn't know anything about those genetic experiments he's accused of being behind.

You want to find symbolic ways to use your architecture to express things to the player that will help them buy into the reality you've created for them. I once had a disagreement with an art director on a fantasy project because he had innocently placed crosses on the graves of the dead, not thinking about the greater implications of his actions. It wasn't a question of whether or not the crosses were artistically valid—they looked just fine—but the problem was that the artist hadn't thought about what that symbolism *means*. In our world we bury people under crosses because that's a symbol of the life, execution, and resurrection story of Jesus of Nazareth. In our fantasy world we were dealing with a culture that had never known Christ or Christianity. Invoking a symbol that's so powerfully connected to a real-world religion will only serve to weaken your attempts to create a new world that has its own unique history, culture, and traditions. It's enough for the player to see a field full of headstones to get the point that a place is a graveyard. It's even better if the symbols that adorn those headstones are new and original reflections of the religious heritage of the world in which they exist.

To take this discussion of graveyard symbolism even one step further, think about what kinds of things you can imply about how you arrange those symbols. A cemetery where graves might be adorned with one of three different symbols—say moons, skulls, or swords—suggests a land where people of various faiths, heritages, or classes live and die side by side. Another kind of graveyard that has nothing but row after row of identical headstones would imply a unifying faith or an allegiance to something like a military order that only allows for one kind of burial. Think of other kinds of similar "statements" you can make about the cultures of the game world that will help inform the player at an instinctual level about how things work. Don't overrely on this to get everything across to the player, but do use it to help reinforce the rest of the reality that you're trying to project.

The history and culture that will be evoked through objects and place cannot be overstated. Subtract these elements from your role-playing game and there's really nothing left that will make your world worth exploring. A village square must be more than just a place to be. Maybe people gathered at that point in the past because it was on a crossroads of magical lines of power, it sat on the edge of a sea, it grew up from an encampment of soldiers who never left after the end of the last war. While you're creating swords, and blasters, and town halls, and wells, and dungeons deep, ask yourself where this thing or that place came from. Who was it important to? Did it ever have any purpose other than the one it now serves? What can the player learn about the world by owning or examining it? *Besides* the fact that the player can now use it in their quest to save the world or bathe themselves in glory, *why does it exist?*

Eating, Drinking, and Being Mary: The Inhabitants of Fantasyland

Gary Larson is a cartoonist who used to draw a wonderfully weird comic strip called "The Far Side," which ran in newspapers all over the United States. Although he created many, many memorable panels that regularly adorned university professors' doors and cubicle walls everywhere, there is one cartoon of his that I recall with great fondness. In the first panel, cows stand on their hind legs, casually talking about cow business until someone in the herd frantically yells "CAR!" In the next frame, the cows are passively cropping grass as a family station wagon trundles past them, the inhabitants of the car blissfully unaware that the cows lead far more interesting lives than mankind will ever imagine.

The nonplayer character inhabitants of role-playing game worlds are all too often presented like Larson's cows. In many cases they seem to be standing around doing nothing at all, just waiting for the player to show up and give their lives purpose. Without the intervention of the gamer, they would spend all eternity standing around, scratching their butts, staring at walls, or running around in terrified circles waiting for someone to come along and solve whatever problems are going on in their lives. Once someone does show up, most NPCs seem to exist only to deliver whatever line they've been assigned in the script, then conveniently walk a few paces away to evaporate into the same pixelated fog out of which they were born.

The reasons for the blandness of most NPCs are complex and not as easily resolved as newbie designers often want to believe. Creating a whole world full of living nonplayer characters who have their own lives and their own motivations can be an interesting experiment, but game designers are a long way off yet from creating game-controlled characters capable of passing the Turing Test just yet.

Even if you aren't up to the task yet of creating a wholly convincing intelligence for your role-playing games, there's no reason to despair. You don't have to believe the computer is thinking up all its responses on its own to enjoy the experience any more than you have to believe that James Bond could *really* drive a motorcycle out of an airplane and survive.

Games, like movies, suffer when you introduce *too* much realism. A real conversation between two human beings is usually laced with lots of repetition, awkward pauses, lots of repetition, irrelevant information, off-topic digressions, and most of all, lots of repetition. It's a great deal more fun to be playing a game and "questioning" the locals when you have a reasonable expectation that they're going to get to the point and have something reasonably lucid to say most of the time. If I had to hang out for an hour in a virtual tavern trying to get the truth out of some alien barfly while she went on about her idiot boyfriend, and how she liked Vodka tonics, and did I think Martian Blues were

Is It Live, or Is It Memorex?

In 1950 Alan Turing published a groundbreaking article entitled "Computing Machinery and Intelligence," which explored the question of whether or not computers were capable of "thinking" for themselves. Published in the scientific journal *Mind,* Turing's article proposed a test—now known as the Turing Test—which pitted a human investigator against the artificial intelligence of a computer. If the human experimenter asking questions was fooled enough by the computer's responses to believe that he or she had just carried on a conversation with another human being, the computer could be said to be a truly "thinking" machine.

Over the years, Turing's definition of intelligence has been derided by critics as behaviorist, examining only the output of the computer as opposed to the "thought" process that allowed it to create its output. Nonetheless, no computer has yet managed to pass the Turing Test when investigators have been given broad parameters for their conversations. If a true artificial intelligence is ever developed, role-playing games may well end up being one of the first real beneficiaries of the technology.

really any better than Altarian Jazz, I'd lose my mind. Characters in games are *meant* to serve the needs of the player, which sometimes means that you have to sacrifice the total autonomy of world inhabitants and cut to the chase. A good game character is a character who serves the needs of the player, even though on the surface it may appear they're acting in their own selfish interests.

Developing a nonplayer character is much like developing a good character in a more traditional kind of story. The more ways in which you can define them as their own person, the more interesting they will be to the player.

For example, let's say as you're guiding your avatar into a new town, you meet an NPC that's just standing around on a street corner railing against the evils of alcohol. He may draw your attention or annoy you slightly, but he's nothing all that memorable. If that same character railing against liquor is drunk, he's a tad more interesting because of the contradiction between what he's saying and the way in which he lives. If you can add an individual animation to him that has him flapping his arms about and knocking down trash barrels as he weaves through the street, you've added a visual component to his character, something that begins to really set him apart from the rest of the world around him. If this drunken fool then wanders around telling heavily armed soldiers that you've just called their mothers something unspeakable in the Low Speech, and thus getting you into unexpected trouble, he's crossed the threshold from a talking piece of scenery into something that affects events in the game. The last straw of course is when you learn he's the uncle you've been instructed to travel a hundred miles to see. When he's sober, he's an all-powerful magician, but when he gets a few drinks into him, he's a royal pain to have around. This is an example of a *true* game character, someone whose life or death is something the player is going to care about, and someone who will imprint themselves on the player's memory in a direct way. If you take a look at this example and break it down, you can see that this character has a number of important characterization traits like the following:

- **Unique message for the player.** His rail against drunkenness is something ironic and strange, given his condition.

- **Distinctive animation, visual style, or sound effect.** He has a drunken weave that sends him stumbling into objects in the world. He may even have a unique voice or sound effect associated with him.

- **Effect on the gameplay.** His actions or inactions can affect some aspect of the gameplay.

- **Reason for the player to care about their life or death.** He's an uncle of the player's avatar, and when he sobers up he's a good guy with the capacity of helping the player out. Getting him sober in itself may prove to be a fun miniquest for the player.

You're not always going to be able to do all of the above for all of your non-player characters. As cool as it would be to be able to give every character in your game an individual animation, mode of dress, or physical appearance, the restrictions of development time and budget make this a near impossibility. Let's just imagine that you've got 12 people in every town or level of your game. Now let's multiply that by the 35 levels you've planned. That makes you responsible for creating 420 unique animations, dress styles, or other modes of individually representing every character in your game. Even if you have the

Whatcha Talkin' 'bout, Wilhelm?

Few things in a game can be more distracting and counterproductive than to have the dialogue leaping up periodically and slapping the player in the face. If most of the characters are running around and talking in a pseudo-Elizabethan accent in your game, don't have some bozo stroll onto screen and start speaking like they've just walked out of East Jersey. It's jarring, it's unprofessional, and it's counterproductive to the ethos that you're trying to create. If your whole game is meant to be a comedy or is based on the idea that the characters are acknowledging the existence of the player, that's fine, but stuffing a line like "Don't click me! Don't click me!" into the mouth of a character in an epic-oriented game is tantamount to saying, "Hey you, loser! Remember that you're sitting in a chair and you aren't really in this nifty world we've created! You were starting to feel like you were here, but let's point out how fake all of this is! Wahoo! *Hey it's only a game, right?*" It's okay to be playful in the context of the events you've created, but don't disappoint the people who are trying to get into your world by breaking the narrative dream. The next time you think of doing it, be the anti-Nike. *Just don't do it.*

astonishing resources to create all those individuals, the big problem for the player is that if everything is unique, then nothing is likely to be all that memorable because nothing *really* stands out from the background. The trick is to reserve a certain number of looks or animations for "important" characters in the game so that they can be easily identified by the player.

Another trick to providing good characterization is to give every NPC in the game an *individual purpose.* Don't just randomly plop some talking billboard down on a street corner—populate your world with people who have a reason to be there. Ask yourself about the town in which you've placed them. Are they integral to a quest that the player needs to complete, or do they have something they need to get from the player? What's their social standing in the community? Are they armed and dangerous, or wise and helpful? Whatever your intent is with your characters, you should give them something to do. Better yet, try and give everyone a *job*.

Imagine for instance that you want to put an NPC in the game who will tell the player where there's a source for good iron ore. The most reasonable person in town to know that of course would be the town blacksmith. So let's just say that you introduce Ronnie the Blacksmith into your game, and you find him some nice place under a tree to stand. Instead of having him doing nothing, find him a hammer, give him an anvil, and let him *pound* on something. Now he's got an animation that lets him stand out from everyone else in town, and he looks like he's serving some purpose other than just waiting for the player. If you add a loud ringing sound of steel on steel to his actions that gets louder as the player gets closer, the player can even navigate toward his place of work by hearing him doing his job.

At this point, Ronnie the Blacksmith is doing a wonderful job of serving the purpose of the player. He's dutifully doing what he's supposed to be doing, and he's ready for the player's arrival. But in terms of serving the town in which he lives, he's just a very noisy occupant at the moment. A fun and potentially very exciting way to *really* give Ronnie a job as the town's blacksmith is to include him in a *dynamic* system of character interactions.

Let's say that you look at the local village in the context of a set of relationships between the characters. Every day Ronnie's job is to fix the swords that are brought down to him from the local castle by his daughter Missie. Providing that he gets what he needs to do his job, he'll finish repairing a sword every three game hours, and then at the end of the day Missie will run the repaired swords up to the guards. Every day this is what the characters do as part of their daily routines, much in the same way that you go about doing the things that you have to do. But now let's assume that because the player riled up the local orcs, Missie's been caught midway between the castle and the forge and she's been trapped by the orcs by the roadside. After she fails to show up for the first day's work, the blacksmith doesn't have anything to forge and he has to stop forging and goes out looking for his daughter. Until Missie gets recovered and Ronnie gets the next delivery of swords that he's expecting, the forge is closed up for business. When the forge closes, there may be other establishments in town that can't conduct business, and this in turn may affect other dependencies that occur in town.

Now the interesting thing about this web of relationships is that the designer hasn't directly had to create this little situation. All they've had to do is establish a set of conditional behaviors in the characters that establish their synthetic wants and needs. If you were to crack open Ronnie's skull and see what's driving him, you might see a list of behaviors that looks something like this:

```
Ronnie's Priorities:
1. Check for customers - Buy / Sell / Repair items, ELSE
2. Get a broken sword from barrel. If no sword go to step 9, ELSE go to step 3.
3. Go to Forge.
4. Pound on broken sword for 7 minutes.
5. Stick sword in fire.
6. Remove sword from fire.
7. Pound on sword for 7 minutes (repeat steps 4 - 7 for 20 minutes).
8. Take repaired sword to repaired sword barrel. Go to step 1.
9. Wander around shop, set "Daughter's late" dialogue to TRUE.
10. Go to step 9 for 12 game hours. If >= 12 hours, then SEARCH for Missie...
```

Ronnie deeply cares about his daughter, and he's going to do whatever he has to do to try and save her. If after a while the player hasn't shown up to help him out, Ronnie is going to try and tackle the problem on his own, which may either get him killed or locked up by the monsters.

What a dynamic character system gives you is a way for the game to respond in interesting but internally consistent ways to the player's actions. If Missie stays missing very long, eventually the whole town is going to shut down and go out looking for her, just as you'd expect to happen in a real-life small town. For the player this could be a minor inconvenience if they need to get their sword fixed, or it could be an utterly great thing if they have other objectives. What if someone the player needs to talk to has been locked up in the city jail? If everybody but a handful of guards has joined in the search, it might well be that the player will have an unexpected chance to break into the jail or to grab other resources they've seen elsewhere that were out of reach to them before.

The sudden eruption of bar brawls because a gambler NPC has lost too many hands of poker, the assembly of a mob in the town square because the mayor has been killed by brigands, and the reopening of a closed mining operation because the dragon in the depths has been killed are all examples of game events that could be driven by well-developed dynamic character systems. By taking the time to create contextually appropriate characters, assigning each their own jobs, and giving them individual hierarchies of need, you will give the player a much better sense that the game world is a living place that isn't just sitting around waiting for the avatar to ride in and save the day.

Exercises

1. Play through some of your favorite computer RPGs and try to identify the dumb and inconsistent ways in which a magical or scientific knowledge has been ignored. Be sure and think about how as a player you would like to have applied that technology. (A favorite of mine is the grenade launcher that's unable to blast holes through wooden doors a mere six inches thick.)

2. Come up with a simple idea of something you'd like to introduce into a fantasy title and try and think through all the weird effects that it's likely to have on everything around it. Think about the possibilities for gameplay just based on the connections you establish.

3. Think about how a dynamic character system would have changed some of your favorite games. Draw up a list of the things that you need on a daily basis to survive. Also draw up a list of the basic things you would like to have in life. Try and think what you'd do if any of those things were threatened. What actions would you take? What sort of actions might a different sort of person than you take? What are the consequences?

CHAPTER 8

The Architecture of Fantasy—Putting the Elements Together

Schikaneder: So let me see it. Where is it?

Mozart: Here. (points to his head) It's all right here in my noodle. The rest is just scribbling. Scribbling and bibbling, bibbling and scribbling. Would you like a drink?

—From Peter Shaffer's screenplay *Amadeus*

Imagine you're a humble bricklayer. Today you start work on what has been billed as the most ambitious building project ever designed by Monte Eidolon, one of the 10 most brilliant architects of all time. As you arrive on-site, you're anxious to see the blueprints, wondering if there's a special mortar you may need to mix for this job or a specific kind of brick that may take additional attention in the setting process. But as Mr. Eidolon begins to evangelize the crew about what the finished building is going to be like, you begin to realize *there are no plans*—at least not on paper. Eidolon has lofty and imaginative ideas that sound oh so amazingly cool when he talks about them, but he hasn't bothered to put them into a form anyone else can implement or, for that matter, *evaluate.* You are about to participate in the making of a disaster simply because the man behind the project could not be bothered to *write it down.*

As preposterous as the above scenario may sound, sometime in your game design career you *will* meet Mr. Eidolon. At times I have been guilty of being Mr. Eidolon myself, and the people on my teams have suffered for my laziness. Until such a time that you become psychic or develop a way to exactly transfer your thoughts from one person to another, the best way of making sure your team members are all on the same page is to *give* them a page to start with. Making the effort to communicate your ideas on paper as clearly and as completely as possible is the best way to avoid misunderstandings among your coworkers. Team meetings can be a great way to explore new ideas, but they are a notoriously rotten mechanism for letting people in on something they should have been *shown* in the first place.

Now it's completely possible you might be the most brilliant game designer in the world, but unless you're at least a passingly competent writer, chances are good your games will never get past the idea stage. Your ability to craft engaging proposals that excite designers and bean counters alike will affect whether or not your game actually gets funded. If you can't write a design document that communicates your vision in a way that everybody can understand and get behind, it won't matter what your original concept was to begin with. Everyone will simply head off in their own directions and the original idea will vanish almost as quickly as your company's confidence in the project. Being a good writer won't guarantee your success as a game designer, but being a bad writer will almost certainly prevent you from creating the game you dream about.

The key is not to look at the writing process as your enemy. Yes, it can be difficult. Yes, it can be labor-intensive. But once you get into the regular habit of condensing your game ideas onto paper, you're going to discover that the *process* of objectively explaining your concept can be very beneficial to your overall project. The same little gremlin who sits in your gray matter deciding whether you're going to use an adverb or an adjective is already highly skilled at *symbolic* logic. As he interprets your abstract idea into a workable plan of action, you'll be astonished at how good he is at evaluating your *procedural* logic. Writing down the steps a player needs to go through in order to perform a certain action may demonstrate an overcomplication in the design. Reading through the material you've created, you may spot opportunities for increased interactivity that never would have occurred to you without this written examination of the game logic. Absolutely great ideas have to be the foundation upon which your project rests, but they must be reflected in a clear blueprint that everyone can see, read, and understand.

Going behind the Cybernetic Curtain

Everyone knows that just below the surface of every computer game, there's a vast unseen body of programming code swimming in the computational depths, doing mysterious and wonderful things that give the game the semblance of life. People take it for granted whenever they see a play that there are dozens, maybe hundreds, of people working behind-the-scenes to create an experience that may only last for a few hours. In almost every form of mass entertainment available, what the viewer, player, or participant ultimately experiences represents only a small fragment of the total effort involved in the creative process.

Before your best-selling, insanely addictive role-playing game can ever hit the market, you're first going to be responsible for the creation of a fear-inspiring mountain of proposals, design documents, storyboards, flowcharts, scripts, e-mails, and product sales sheets. Here's just a sampling of a few of the documents you'll likely be called on to create during the production process:

- **The Proposal.** An exciting, simplified five- to ten-page explanation of what your game will be all about, focusing on the look, feel, and basic gameplay hooks that will make a title worth producing and playing.
- **The Design Document.** A massive, multisectioned document detailing all the technical requirements and content needed to produce a specific

The Designer's Communication Checklist

Writing helpful, user-friendly game documentation can be tough enough for people with a traditional writing background, but for some techno-manic designers the experience of trying to explain their ideas can be positively torturous. Here are a few basic writing principles you can apply to your own proposal, design document, or other materials that may help to clarify your message and arouse the enthusiasm of the allies you seek:

- ♦ **Grab Their Attention.** First impressions count. Developers are often very busy people, and if you haven't grabbed them within 50 words, you may not get them at all. Hit your audience with your strongest point, your best example, or the most outrageously creative opening that you can muster. The key is to give them a strong impression of what your idea is really about and generate the curiosity and excitement that will keep them reading.

- ♦ **Use the Present Tense.** Writing in the present tense bestows a greater sense of reality, immediacy, and importance on a game project. Saying that "*Betrayal at Krondor* is a terrific game" feels much more exciting than indicating it might be a terrific game at some point in the future, or that it was a terrific game in the past.

- ♦ **Keep It Simple, Stupid (The KISS Principle).** Writing a technical document doesn't absolve you of the responsibility of making yourself understood. Don't assume that your audience automatically understands what you're talking about. Avoid the use of jargon unless it's absolutely necessary. Don't make things more complicated than necessary.

game. It may include graphical documentation in the form of *flowcharts* and *storyboards* in addition to written explanatory materials.

- **The Game Script.** A close cousin of the Hollywood screenplay, the game script presents a game's FMV and dialogue sequences in a format ready for use by actors, animators, and sound engineers.

While only your team members and your financial backers will ever see all these materials, it's important you never lose sight of the fact that these documents

- ◆ **What's in It for Me? (The WIIFM Principle).** Explain what your innovative ideas are going to mean to a variety of end users in a way that's going to be meaningful to them. Just telling a reader that you'll be able to "shove 50 billion polygons per second down a telephone cable" may impress the hell out of a programmer, but that means absolutely nothing to your marketing director. With this example it would be better to say your game is "the fastest game ever conceived, capable of shoving 50 billion polys per second down a phone line! With our vastly increased polygon count we can present the most realistic-looking gaming environment that players have ever seen, and the player's character can run through the world with incredible speed!"

- ◆ **Be Professional.** Don't spend eternity kicking yourself in the head over dumb mistakes. While it's doubtful your ideas will be rejected on the basis of a single spelling error or a dropped word, a chronic lackadaisical attitude toward the design document can sometimes be misinterpreted as an unwillingness on the designer's part to pay attention to small details. Fix typos, check for missing sections, and number all your pages. If you're not good at these things, be honest with yourself and enlist the help of someone else who can proofread for you. A second pair of eyes is always valuable. Don't give a developer any reason at all to dismiss you or your idea.

define the architecture of your game reality. What you communicate through them—or what you *fail* to communicate through them—will have a very big impact on how well your ideas are expressed in the final product.

The Proposal

A proposal is like a very elaborate promise. In it you tell developers that you're going to make a game that looks a certain way, features a particular kind of action, and tells a specific kind of story. You're also promising that your idea is going to entertain a wide variety of different players and will turn a significant profit for the development house that agrees to help you make it. You're even making a promise to yourself that something is finally going to get done with all those ideas you've had floating around for so long. A proposal is a personal commitment to turn a dream into a virtual reality.

But no matter how satisfying it has been for you to finally get all your ideas down on paper, no matter how cool it feels to see all your ideas finally gelling into something you can see, you must never lose sight of the fact that game proposals exist for one purpose, and one purpose alone. They are the *bait* you will use to lure the developers who can fund, produce, and distribute your finished project. From your opening paragraph to your concluding period, everything in between must hammer home why your game will be fun, why everybody in the world will want to have it, and why the development house should risk millions of dollars producing and advertising your concept. First, last, and always, the primary job of the proposal is to *sell your idea*.

In most cases, what developers want to know first is what your game is going to be *about*. When you boil down all the narrative and interactive elements in your game, what is the one easy-to-understand principle that will guide the production team's vision and will be the concept with which players immediately connect? It may be that your idea is similar enough to other existing concepts that you can simply state it in terms that the developers already understand. It isn't at all unusual to see a designer pitching a concept by saying something like "It's *Resident Evil* meets *Gunsmoke*" or "*Quake*-style death-match fighting in a *Fatty Bear Goes to the Circus*-inspired arena." Other people prefer to avoid similes and come up with their own unique way of describing their gaming experience. Here's an example of an age-old idea serving as the foundation for what might be a very unusual space opera:

"You are Eric Fanfaron, dreamy boy stranded on a desert planet. Twenty years ago your father was one of the greatest knights of the Golden Republic. Slain by his one-time friend—the now all-powerful dark lord Olinbur—you have discovered your fallen father's sword of power. Compelled by the murder of your mother, driven by destiny, you must seek out Olinbur in order to join him in an unparalleled crusade of evil across the galaxy. . . ."

Okay, so Luke Skywalker your protagonist is *not*, but you have established a unique idea about what your game is going to be like. The player will be guiding the destiny of an antihero, which in itself suggests a universe of darkness and evil. He's embarking on an epic quest armed with a sword of power, indicating we're probably going to be doing lots of hand-to-hand fighting as opposed to ship-to-ship battles. While the protagonist's quest is corrupt, it is undeniably a story that will turn many of our expectations on their ear and may lead us into some very interesting gaming situations.

Once you've presented your general theme, you need to very simply describe what the actual gameplay will be like. Paint a sensory image that places the developers squarely in the action of the game. Will a player look down on the action from above, or will they be looking through the eyes of the protagonist? Will the hero be sharing resources with others in a party or conquering the world alone? Is there a multiplayer mode? How will the player be rewarded as he does well in the game? What unique technical innovations, if any, will your title be bringing to the genre?

By answering questions like these, you can begin to build up a list of *bullet points* that will uniquely characterize your game and define what it is the marketing team will have to sell. Try looking at the box backs of existing RPGs to see what features other titles are currently promoting. The bullet list on the packaging for Westwood Studio's *Nox* is very similar to what you might expect to find in a typical proposal:

Spells, Weapons & Abilities

With over 100 different spells, weapons and abilities you can:

- Crush an Ogre with the Fist of Vengeance!
- Summon a blood-thirsty wolf to track down a sneaky opponent!
- Conjure the Force of Nature to destroy a cavern full of ember demons!

Traps

Set traps filled with diabolical spell combinations to ambush unsuspecting victims, such as:

- Casting an opponent into a pit of lava or a room filled with venomous spiders and man-eating bears!
- Surprise them with an invisible trap that sheds their armor and weapons leaving them defenseless for your ultimate attack!

Interactive Environments

- Move rocks to block passages, break barrels of water to put out fires, or blow up powder kegs and watch the debris turn into deadly shrapnel.
- The innovative TrueSight™ system takes gameplay to an even higher level of suspense and excitement.

Multiplay

- Play FREE over the definitive Internet battleground, Westwood Online.
- Team up with your friends or dominate them in Arena, Capture the Flag, Elimination, Noxball, and King of the Realm.

Of course, the critical examination of your competition needs to extend far beyond box studies. The people holding the purse strings want a clear demonstration in your proposal that you understand the gaming market, and in particular, the current and near-future trends of the genre into which your game falls. If for instance dragon riding is a major feature of your game, point out the sales numbers of any currently best-selling RPGs that prominently feature dragons and explain why it is *your* dragons will out-fly, out-claw, and out-firebreathe everything players have ever seen before. If the developers are convinced that dragons equal dollar signs, and that your game will have the best dragons of all, you'll have a very good chance of selling your idea to them.

Another, slightly riskier, proposal tack is to show how your title fills an unexplored void in the market. Perhaps you have an opportunity to make the first game to feature a xenophobic lesbian metamorph, or you've come up with a whole game that can be presented from a knee-level perspective. Whatever your groundbreaking idea is, be aware that while designers adore new concepts, corporate executives tend to be positively allergic to anything they can't recognize. If you go too far off into la-la land and try to do too many new things at once, the developer is simply going to dissolve into a gelatinous, gibbering mound of terror and your proposal will languish in development limbo forever. Pick the most exciting innovations you've got, then try to frame them in relation to existing products or ideas that have been successful. Sometimes this may require you to stretch the boundaries of both your idea and the preexisting product, but you must do everything you can to convince investors that there will be a pot of gold—and not a bankruptcy court—waiting at the end of your rainbow.

The last thing you must do in your proposal is condense down all the most positive things your project has to offer and put them into a summary that the developer simply can't forget. Try closing up business with a phrase or a tag line, perhaps something you might like to see as a runner beneath the game's title. Who can forget the tags that went along with movies like *Dracula* ("Love Never Dies") and *Alien* ("In Space No One Can Hear You Scream")? It cements in the developer's mind a solid feeling about what your game was about and will later be used to describe your game to others.

Formatting the Proposal

By and large, developers really aren't too concerned with the formatting details of your proposal. It is an art that has developed organically over the past 20 years, and virtually every designer has their own template for creating one. Some are very elaborate affairs, complete with graphs, interface sketches, and screen captures. Other designers prefer to work fairly sparely, keeping the contents down to only three or four pages.

Generally I have my own rule of thumb that a proposal should be somewhere between five and ten pages long. Is there a games' Gestapo that will come along and shoot you if your proposal is longer or shorter than that? Not at all. That's just what has worked for me in the past. My only advice to you in this regard is to reiterate what I stated earlier: The people who run game development houses are *very* busy people. The longer you make your proposal, the greater the chances that the people who need to see it won't get the time to sit down and read it. If you're going to have a chance, you need to get in, do your business, then get out of their face. On the flip side of that coin, however, you don't want to make your proposal so short that they forget about it. A one-page idea can sometimes be very interesting, but it may not be all that memorable. You don't want the developer to forget the experience of having read your proposal, so you want to make sure they spend at least a few minutes fiddling around with it in their hands. Psychologically speaking, something five to ten pages long feels as though some thought has been given to it, and that will speak volumes to an investor about your capabilities and your seriousness about making a great game.

If you're absolutely someone who needs to have a template for putting documents together, here's the rough outline I use when putting a game idea together for the first time:

- **Introduction.** In a nutshell, communicates what your game is going to be about, and why the player should care about playing it. Provide a concept line that gets the idea across (e.g., "It's aliens but in ancient China").

- **Gameplay.** Put the reader into a moment of the game. Walk them through a bit of the gameplay, demonstrating very quickly what it is going to look and feel like and what kinds of things they can do.

- **Design Objectives.** Touch very quickly on some of the things your game is going to do that have never been done before, or point out the challenges your game is going to tackle. Be specific.

- **Sales Points.** Assemble a list of all the cool things you can say in one sentence that will make someone want to buy your game. What are its strong points?

- **Market Overview.** What games are likely to be competing against your title? How is your game going to be better or different from them? What are the sales figures for those games and can they be used as possible predictors for the sales of your title?

- **Summary.** Sum up everything you've stated and provide any additional information that might convince the developer that producing your title is absolutely a smart move. Reiterate your concept line and close with a tag line if it feels appropriate.

The only truly important things to keep in mind about the proposal's format are to maintain a professional attitude about its preparation (that isn't to say you shouldn't make it fun to look at), and include whatever it takes to get your idea across to the readers as clearly as possible. (If you're still fuzzy on what one should look like, check out the full proposal for Betrayal at Krondor, which appears in Appendix B of this book.)

The Design Document

Part I: The Introduction

Borrowing a page from modern pop culture, you might say that design documents are from Mars and proposals are from Venus. The proposal sits in an ivory tower, issuing vague, pretty sounding edicts to courtiers about everything it's going to do, its only concern in life to be beautiful enough to attract a mate that can pay for its expensive lifestyle. The design document, however, must toil down in the mud and the muck of reality, interpreting all of the proposal's glittering generalities into highly specific lists of tasks, budgets, schedules, and resources.

Proposals can get away with simply saying that a game will feature "an exciting 3-D environment." Design documents must explain every minute detail about how that 3-D environment will be created, who will work on it, what all its constituent parts will be, and how the player will be able to interact with it under a variety of very different circumstances. In the end, the design doc must be a clearly stated plan of action providing all the details that will be necessary for the team to turn the abstractions of the proposal into a fun-to-play gaming reality. Quite simply, the design document is where the rubber meets the road.

Vision Quest

The first thing your document must do is firmly establish the game's guiding *vision*. When team members sit down to write, or draw, or program, or design levels, they need to have a concrete source they can turn to that will tell them what the game should look like, sound like, and play like. They want to know what material and abstract qualities the game will have that will suck in players and make them never want to walk away. Because nobody wants to play on a losing team, they need to understand what it is about this game that will make it better than its competitors. More than anything else, a vision statement must make sure that everybody is seeing the same goal and approaching it on the same path.

The vision statement is not limited, however, to just providing raw data about a game's makeup. It must also feel a bit like a big pep rally that gets everybody revved up for what's coming, the atmospheric movie trailer that makes you impatient to see a summer blockbuster before its release. The introduction to your design doc must fire your team's imagination and get them so turned on with red hot passion for the *idea* of the product that they can hardly wait to get started on it. Get them behind your concepts, and the enthusiasm they have for the project will radiate from every detail of the finished game. Always remember this rule: *Excited developers will make exciting games.*

In many instances developers simply reuse or rework their proposals to function as the design document's introduction, and by and large you shouldn't feel as though you've cheated if you do the same. No one is going to take off points for creativity if you're able to reuse good material. The only rules here are that you be informative and exciting. Since you are no longer constrained by my five- to ten-page rule, feel free to throw in sketches, tables, and screen shots that will help you get your idea across in the most vivid way possible.

The Truth Is in Here: Story and Game Objectives

Once you've snagged everyone's attention with your razzle-dazzle routine, it's time to bring them inside the sacred circle, to initiate them into the cult of "they who know." Unlike Mulder's futile search in *The X-Files* to discover the truth that's out there, your team members need to know that *the Truth Is In Here*—in the design document, that is—laid out in an easy-to-follow outline that traces all the important action from the very beginning of the game to its climactic final resolutions.

The ways in which you outline the *critical path* of your game may take many different forms. If you have a strong central story, your outline may resemble a very terse short story, highlighting all the game events or obstacles that absolutely need to be present in the game. Here's a walkthrough drawn

Walkthrough. A narrative description of all the steps necessary to complete an action, a level, or an entire game. Typically a walkthrough represents only one of a multitude of possible paths or strategies that can be employed but will touch on the easiest or most interesting points of the experience. The focus is to explain how characters, objects, locations, monsters, and actions need to be combined to achieve a desired outcome.

from *The Riftwar Legacy II: Thief of Dreams* (the original sequel planned by Dynamix for *Betrayal at Krondor*):

88) Arriving in THESIUS, KAT, GRAVES and MALCOMA discover that none of the LOCALS seem to be very talkative when it comes to the subject of the old ASTALONIAN PRIORY (their ancestors were responsible for razing it to the ground). After coercing the locals to talk through a combination of good works and outright shows of force, they are eventually able to learn the location of the SECRET SURFACE ENTRANCE to the UNDERGROUND LIBRARY.

89) Using the secret entrance, they are above to navigate through the collapsing underground and eventually find the PRIOR'S CHAMBER of the lost library. Within is a treasure house of artifacts, jewels, and scrolls, the most important of which is AN ANCIENT BOOK describing the full potential and origins of the Veh Habbati. Reading it, Graves becomes deeply disturbed and says it's important they return to the Temple of Ishap in LiMeth, but AS THEY ATTEMPT TO EXIT THROUGH THE ARCH. . . .

(FMV: A SECTION OF THE ROOF COLLAPSES, STRANDING THEM IN THE UNDERGROUND COMPLEX.)

90) Awakening in the DARKNESS of the underground library, Graves feels around, eventually finding the still breathing bodies of both Kat and Malcoma. Finding a CANDLEGLOW SCROLL in one of the alcoves of the chamber, he casts a light spell, allowing him to take better stock of their surroundings. Glancing at the doorway, he is able to confirm what he already suspected, THE WAY THEY CAME IN HAS BEEN COMPLETELY BLOCKED BY RUBBLE (STRENGTH RESISTANCE: 40) and he sees no immediate way out. Waking Kat, Graves and Malcoma begin to survey the room for possible exits. Kat suggests that it's likely that such a library probably has secret doors. After investigating the room, they eventually find A HIDDEN LEVER, which was hidden before the roof collapse. WHEN THE LEVER IS PULLED, IT MOVES A STONE BASIN, REVEALING STEPS LEADING FARTHER DOWN. . . .

By stepping through the experience using this walkthrough format, people begin to get a real sense of how all the various parts of the game will be connected and dependent on one another. The numbered notations next to each section provide a quick way to refer to a specific area or level and later will be used to assign the reference numbers needed in the *game script*.

From the above example the reader knows that there's a secret entrance near the Astalonian Priory in Thesius that leads to an underground library. They understand that in the Prior's Chamber there's an ancient book in which is written a very old legend. All of these facts they know to be true because all of those factors are presented in ALL CAPS. This is a way of communicating that an element is absolutely necessary to the design and that all of the ancillary art, sound effects, and programming that will be required to make that object or event possible are tasks that are *critical* to the completion of the game.

What about the bits between the all-capped portions then? Events, or objects, or actions presented in a walkthrough that are described in lowercase are considered to be things that the player *may choose to do* to solve the current situation. It is possible that Graves might do as I suggested and use the Candleglow scroll to dismiss the darkness of the Prior's Chamber. It is also possible there might be braziers in the room that could be lit with a flamestaff. Maybe the player collects all the ancient and rare histories from the chamber, heaps them into a pile, and sets them ablaze using a twig and a pair of tweezers. In a nicely rounded game all those things should be *possible*, but it's unnecessary to describe them all in the walkthrough. All you must provide at this point is the most important solution path that will take the player all the way from the beginning to the ending of the game.

One Game, Many Endings

Creating a walkthrough for a multilinear game that has several possible endings is frankly a little more difficult. Without a very elaborate flowchart graphically showing how all the events are linked together, or a hyperlinked document that will allow the reader to freely navigate through the maze of possibilities, you may end up getting something that *reads* like a ransom note *looks*. Fortunately there's a narrative format you can use that may take a little more effort to get through than a standard walkthrough, but it does an excellent job at handling a complex story line with multiple forks.

The Loomis Ladder format takes a standard narrative and breaks it into a number of smaller, highly individualized *story cells* that can be arranged in almost any order. Each cell contains a description of a critical event in the development of the story line, and each points to at least one other cell depending on the actions of the player's character. Here's an example:

The Loomis Ladder. In 1976 Rick Loomis of Flying Buffalo Games created a fun little booklet called *Buffalo Castle*. Utilizing the popular role-playing rules that Ken St. Andre had drawn up for *Tunnels & Trolls* (D&D's biggest role-playing competitor through most of the '70s and early '80s), Loomis presented what was very likely the first solo adventure book in existence. Although many game and nongame publishing companies have liberally lifted his "choose your own adventure" format, very few of them have introduced any significant new conventions of note. In honor of his innovation, therefore, I like to call the format he pioneered the Loomis Ladder.

23) THORGATH stares at the DEATHSTONE, Anjikin's SILVER-HILTED SWORD protruding from its shimmering, mysterious depths. METANOONIAN smiles balefully at him, hand clutched on the hilt of the sword of power, ready to draw it out and unknowingly bring the end of all life on Leucadia.

-*If THORGATH:*

KNOCKS METANOONIAN BACKWARDS, go to 24.

SMASHES THE DEATHSTONE, go to 25.

GIVES METANOONIAN A BIG HAIRY KISS, go to 26.

24) THORGATH barrels into METANOONIAN's shaggy form, knocking him aside from the dreadful sword of power. As they both rise from the cold stone floor of the chamber, they both draw their respective weapons and prepare for a battle to the death.

-Initiate Combat- *If THORGATH:*

SURVIVES, then go to 27.

DIES, then go to 28.

25) THORGATH SMASHES THE DEATHSTONE INTO A BILLION SHINING BITS, its glistening shards exploding in all directions. A howl, a scream, a sound like all the breaking of the bonds of hell rushes out of the stone. The laughing voice of LEAFS-KRAGMONT, god of death, drifts over the room: "Welcome, children. At last you have returned to my net!"

-END GAME

26) THORGATH smooches METANOONIAN wetly on the cheek. Shaking his head, the terror of the north snarls ferociously, telling Thorgath, "Ah heck, honey. I didn't know you still cared. . . ."

-END GAME

27) THORGATH stands over the body of METANOONIAN, watching his nemesis of many years falling into the arms of the god of death. "Thus always to tyrants," Thorgath whispers. "The Wetlands shall again be free."

-END GAME

By virtue of the way the story threads through a series of actions and consequences, the Loomis Ladder does a good job of replicating the nonlinear *feel* of gameplay. Although the example I've given is a far more granular (and much sillier) approach than you're likely to need for your own walkthroughs, you can see how the structure provides a great deal of flexibility for telling a story with multiple endings. You can start at any point you like—such as Thorgath standing at the Deathstone—and weave through a series of choices to a theoretically infinite number of endings.

Other Uses for the Loomis Ladder

For both the linear and multilinear game, the point is to reach an *ending*. Eventually the player gets to the point where they've rescued the prince, destroyed the alien homeworld, banished Great Cthulhu back to his sleep in eternal R'leyh, and at last emerged victorious. Game over, roll credits. The formats I've given you so far work very well with both kinds of stories, but both assume the player *starts* in a particular place and that they *stop* somewhere else.

But if you're dealing with a nonterminal experience, such as you might encounter in a persistent universe like *Ultima Online* or *Everquest,* the process of putting together a walkthrough becomes a little more abstract.

Depending on what race a player has chosen for their character, or what shard they've logged in to for a particular game, there may be several possible *beginnings* to their experience. They might choose to talk to the NPC you've parked in one corner who relates a rumor about a shipment of Soylent Green. They might try instead to rescue another player from a vicious moss snake that's biting the cheese out of that player's character. They could also ignore everything immediately around them and try to find out what's causing that strange phosphorescent glow around the distant lighthouse.

All you can really do with the nonterminal walkthrough is describe the *environments* in which the player will find themselves and what monsters, objects, and NPCs might be permanently associated with a specific location. Once again, a variant on the Loomis Ladder can prove useful, but the emphasis must be shifted. Instead of discussing an important event that takes place in a room, you describe a room in which many possible events *might* take place:

> 36) THE LOBBY OF THE KOCHAB SPACEPORT, the primary port of call for the *ATAGI* starliner, the most esteemed cruiser in all the galaxy. Three WEAPONS-PROOF WINDOWS look down on the MAIN CONCOURSE where tickets for the *Atagi* can be bought and sold. (Due to an unfortunate trick of the spaceport's design, it is also a perfect place to spy on people as they enter their credit access codes.)
>
> A FOUNTAIN in the center of the room flows with Algiebian Mood Enhancers (+3 to health per 24 hr. period).
>
> In the corner, A VIOLENCE SENSOR glares ominously, an 8,000 terrawatt Cygnus ray ready to "adjust" the attitude of anyone who starts a fight inside the facility.
>
> On the opposite side of the lobby is a panoramic view of the LANDING PADS where starships drift down out of the sulfur clouds, landing on one of the 40 staging areas vanishing in the distance. A LIGHT RAIL runs between them, vanishing eventually into the FOETID SWAMP that lies beyond.

People frequently come here to talk, it being much quieter than other areas, and safer thanks to the protection of the Cygnus ray. The view of the landing ships is spectacular, and the occasional SPAWN OF SLIME DRAGON will wander out of the swamps and make trouble for the workers unloading the docks beneath the landing pads. (It's a cruel but common practice for a bookmaker to sometimes slouch about here, placing bets on how many dockworkers will get eaten before the security bots show up to save the day.)

-If the Player

GOES WEST, branch to #37.

GOES EAST, branch to #38.

GOES NORTH, branch to #39.

GOES SOUTH, branch to #40.

TALKS TO THE BOOKMAKER ROBOT, branch to #41. . . .

The point of the nonterminal walkthrough is not to lay out specific events that the player will *have* to take, but only to suggest certain activities in each area that *may* provoke interesting player interactions. In this instance you learn that the lobby of the Kochab Spaceport is a perfectly good spot to see a lot of the activity going on in the area. You can watch people buying tickets and try to steal credits from their imaginary accounts, chat with terrorists looking to hijack the *Atagi*, watch spaceships taking off and landing, maybe even make a few extra credits betting on the #4 slime dragon versus the kid mercenary who just rushed off to save the dockworkers. The emphasis here is to try to create a very interesting world that will make the players want to try various activities that will lead them inevitably to either conflict or cooperate with other players.

Flowchart It!

Once you've presented the in-depth walkthrough of the critical path events in your game, you should also provide a quick flowchart that demonstrates how various events and locations are related to one another. Figure 9.1 shows the map that designers used to keep track of events in Interplay's 1995 fantasy RPG, *Stonekeep*:

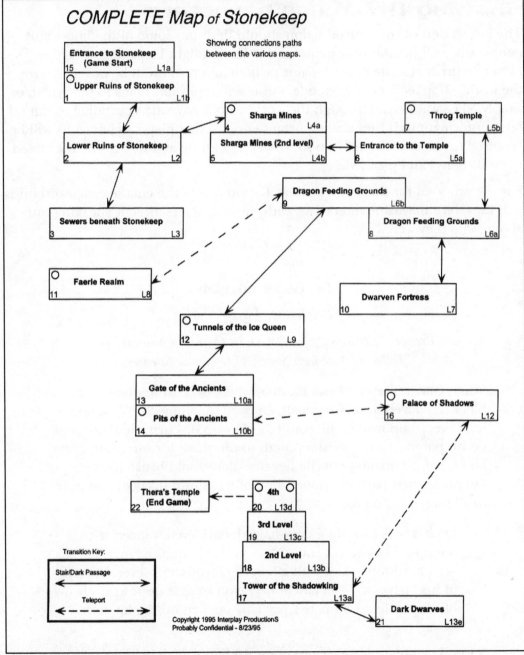

Figure 9.1 *Stonekeep flowchart. When preparing your story, be sure to provide your fellow designers with a clear map of how areas or plotlines are connected together. (Stonekeep copyright Interplay Productions 1995.)*

Showing Off Your Characters

The last section of your introduction should flesh out some of the important people who will inhabit your game world. These might be protagonists the player controls at some point, villains or henchmen who will be out to destroy the world, shopkeepers or bartenders who sell important items to the avatar, or simply NPCs wandering through the world who'll have the occasional useful tidbit of information. If they are important enough that player's characters will be required to speak to them, or in some way at least be aware of them, they need to be sketched and profiled.

For the proposal for the game *Elysium,* I approached the character backgrounds as if they were magazine interviews, with the characters directly speaking out about "who they were."

DR. GALEN SHEPPARD

(October 31, 1962 -   )

Director of Elysium Project, Ph.D. in Cognitive Neuroscience,
Fellow of American Society of Cognitive Sciences

When Galen Sheppard was 10, he was like every other boy on his block. He loved to play baseball, enjoyed watching *Star Trek,* and took every opportunity he could to blow up or burn whatever models his parents were foolish enough to purchase for him. And every night, before turning out the lights, Galen would brush his teeth, put on his best pajamas, pour a box of tacks into his bed, and pray to all merciful God to *die.*

> [*PHOTO:* A frowning, dark-haired, dark-eyed, nine-year old Sheppard before his counseling under Marcus Kezwig. He sits on a hardwood floor with a box of crayons and several sheets of his "artwork"—melancholy crayon images done entirely in black, rendered on paper partially burned on the kitchen stove.]

"Over a two-year period between my 10th and 12th birthdays, I sank deeper and deeper into inutterable depression," Sheppard says of the time, shaking his head. "My parents and I were living like nomads because of my problem. We moved from one specialist to another, each with their own version of what would take away the night terrors. I endured overmedication and endless batteries of conventional medical and psychometric tests, which would have driven most people over the edge. I'm not really sure how I held together."

Somehow Sheppard *did* hold on, having faith that science and Dr. Kezwig would find some way of treating the night terrors that had shattered his life. On May 13, 1974, that faith was rewarded by a poorly connected long-distance phone call in the middle of the night from San Francisco, California. Dr. Kezwig had just met a young woman at a conference who was working with a controversial new form of treatment called Lucid Therapy, and she wondered if Galen would be willing to try it out. She would understand if the Sheppards were reluctant, but Dr. Collins would be willing to pay for their travel expenses to Berkeley, *if* they were interested. . . .

*   *   *

"By the time he was 14, Sheppard had lost most of the gaunt, haunted look that had earned him the nickname "Ghost," but during his high school years, the nickname would take on a new propriety. A spectacular wide receiver for his home football team, he had a knack for appearing and disappearing at the right times, and upon his high school graduation, many people fully expected him to accept the football scholarships that were being offer from big eight universities like Oklahoma and Nebraska. To the surprise of everyone except his closest friends, Sheppard applied and was accepted to the University of Colorado as a psychology major. With the demons of his dreams banished, he hoped to follow in the footsteps of his very good friend and mentor, Dr. Lyssa Collins. . . ."

[*VIDEO CLIP:* Staged graduation day picture on the campus of the University of Colorado. Much more athletic looking than in his previous photo, Galen Sheppard stands with his parents, Don and Leslie, his girlfriend, Julie Howard, and his close friend and associate, Dr. Lyssa Collins. Sheppard is laughing as

Lyssa hands him his Doctorate in Cognitive Science, along with a tie-dyed T-shirt with the words "Dare to Dream" emblazoned on the front. She turns it to display the back of the shirt and the logo for the Colorado Institute of Cognitive Science.]

* * *

Early in his career as a psych researcher, Sheppard established the pattern he called "going wide," often stepping outside the main body of psychological research to embrace theories being advanced in fields like linguistics, anthropology, mathematics, and quantum theory.

"We can't behave as though the laws of the universe play to the categories we create," Sheppard said in a *Discover* article. "You can't say neuroscience ends here and biofeedback starts there. Over the past century, we've become such specialists that our scientists are becoming better and better at less and less. We need to study the connections that unify our knowledge, not isolate things into small boxes. Chaos has proved that small changes can cause big effects in complex systems. If anyone can point out something more complex than human consciousness, I'd be very interested in talking to them."

[*PHOTO:* An institutional photo for the Elysium Project. A hint of gray in his shoulder-length brown hair, Dr. Galen Sheppard holds a framed photo of Lyssa Collins as he stands in front of the Colorado Institute of Cognitive Science with his principal research team: Frank Castle, Marta and Carol McHarren, Li Tuong, Ravi Tagore, and Allen Wakefield. All of them wear a small, silver poppy emblem on their clothes, the emblem of the Elysium Project, designed by incoming lab assistant Tabitha Andrejkn (not pictured).]

* * *

Despite his ongoing research in the field, it took Sheppard a number of years to arrange the funding through NISMOG for the controversial program [The Elysium Project] to verify his mentor's early work. While many researchers had no doubt Collins' lucid therapy had been effective in reducing and even eliminating some instances of night terrors, few scientists gave any credence to her supposition that the landscape beyond her dream doors was anything more than interesting hallucination. Together they laid the groundwork for two studies to further their hypothesis, but Collins' apparent suicide in 1999 nearly brought the work to its knees. It would be four more years before Sheppard would finally be able to realize their common dream, the creation of the Elysium Project.

No matter how you approach the profiles of your protagonists, or who you inject into your cast, the important thing is to present a well-rounded picture that demonstrates who your heroes and villains really are. What do they look like? Why should the player love or hate them? What memorable physical traits do they have that lets the player quickly identify them? Do they have any habits that might be expressed in body language? By providing deep background details of the critical path characters, you will ensure that your team members *understand* the characters they are creating, and this in turn will ensure that dialogues, appearances, and motions present a consistent and compelling characterization.

Part II: Defining the Interface

So far, the introduction of the design document has concentrated on *content*, all that juicy gameplay and storytelling stuff you hope will hook players and have them babbling to all their friends to buy their own copies. But in the context of building a computer game, if you only provide your team with a written walk-through from point A to point Z, it's really going to be no more useful than giving them *Lawrence of Arabia* on DVD when no one has access to a DVD *player*. In order for anybody to experience all that content you've generated, you're going to have to specify the mechanisms by which a player will be able to interact with the environment. How will players make their on-screen avatar walk, talk, fight, or pick up objects? What will players have to do in order to save their games, change the difficulty settings, or initiate multiplayer contests? How will information be conveyed to the player about the health of their character, how much gold they have, or how many shots are left in their laser cannon? As you begin to put down the answers to basic questions like these, you'll begin to create the rudimentary shape of the *user interface* that will make the game playable.

Getting Around

Whether they're walking, leaping, traveling by spaceship, or driving an ox cart, the first thing players need to be able to do is guide their avatar through the game world. Isometric perspective games like *Baldur's Gate* often use a "click-and-follow" model, requiring the player to click the area on the screen where they want their avatar to be, and the on-screen character will then automatically navigate to the desired location. 3-D perspective titles à la the Mac version of *Deus Ex* use the mouse to control the direction in which the avatar is looking, so movement is accomplished by tapping the appropriate directional arrows on the keyboard. Console titles traditionally have neither keyboards nor mice, so they rely on directional input generated by their external game pads.

If the avatar has other special modes of movement, like running, jumping, swimming, flying, or riding, you'll also need to address what combination of mouse clicks or keystrokes will allow these tasks to be performed. No matter what form of navigation you ultimately decide to borrow or innovate, it should be something that requires the least amount of effort to accomplish and remain intuitively consistent throughout the entire game.

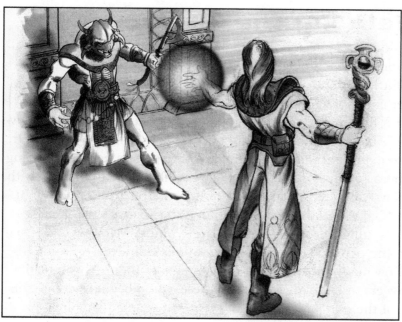

Figure 9.2   (© Shawn Sharp)

Fiddling with the Playground

Once you've set the player loose in your playground, the next thing you'll need to explain are the ways in which they will be able to interact with the environment. How will the player do simple things like use stairs or pick up objects? Will they click on them, hit a key, press a game pad button, or some combination of all three? Say you want to give the players the option of either calmly pulling open a door or savagely chopping it into firewood. Both are interesting ways to get into a room, but you'll need to specify what combination of actions the player will need to take to differentiate between a chop or a knock on the door.

In ye olden age of game development, it wasn't unusual to see a cluster of buttons at the bottom of the screen that said things like "use," "talk," "pick up," "attack," "open," and so on. These days buttons of this ilk are a waste of screen real estate. In most instances, you can save players the trouble of an overcomplicated interface by making the mouse cursor "smart." Instead of having to first click a button and then click on something in the world, your cursor should automatically be able to detect what it's pointing at and then present the viable option given your current circumstances. If my mouse pointer is hovering over a door, the game should *know* I'm looking at a door and present me with visual feedback indicating that I can enter here if I click my mouse button. If, however, I move my cursor and position it over the Golden Sword of Zhul, it should know that I'm looking at an inventory object now and that if I click on it I want to pick it up.

Many, many RPGs today use some form of the "smart cursor." Here's just a smattering of the different ways that they have been employed to give the player feedback about things they can do with characters, objects, and structures:

- **Grabbing Hand.** A flexing hand could indicate that a specific object can be picked up by the avatar.
- **Monsters.** A cursor may turn into a pair of crosshairs, showing green if the character is likely to be an ally, or red if they're likely to attack.
- **Characters.** A talking mask might indicate characters who have something to say to the player's avatar, or individuals who have things to sell.
- **Doors.** The pointer may turn into an icon for a door, showing it as open for an unlocked door, or a barred door for an unopenable or locked entrance.

- **Containers.** For objects that might contain treasure, the pointer might turn into an open container or a bag of gold coins to indicate a spot to search for treasure.
- **Stairs.** Sweeping a pointer over a rope, stairs, or ledges could indicate that something can be climbed by the player.
- **Gears.** Players searching for levers, platforms, or other devices can search for workable machinery by passing their smart cursor over various items in a room.

Of course, not all of the ways in which the player will interact with the environment will be restricted to a "one-click/one-interaction" relationship. If a player wants to move a barrel from one corner of a room to another, you might want to provide several different ways for this feat to be accomplished. On the one hand, they might be able to move the barrel across the room simply by walking into the box to "push" it, or they might be able to pick up the barrel and carry it across the room. In both instances, the rules that govern how these activities

Figure 9.3   (© Shawn Sharp)

will be carried out by the player must be clearly set down so that they can be implemented by your team and used by level designers in the creation of their domains.

Dealing with Game Maps and Journals

With game systems growing ever larger and more complex, it's generally a good idea to give players some form of on-screen game map or journal that allows them to track their progress. As straightforward as both of these options might sound, you're going to need to specify how players call them up and how content will be added or revealed in each as the game progresses.

Auto-mapping is probably one of the best features ever added to the electronic RPG, not only for the fact that it can help players remember where the treasure room or the dragon's lair was, but also because it serves as feedback to the player about the things they've accomplished. Some systems apply "fog of war" to their maps, leaving unexplored areas blacked out until the player has had a chance to explore them. Other games simply display a general map of an entire area and then add details as the player makes new discoveries.

However you decide to create your map, you'll need to address issues like whether there will be one large map that players zoom in or out of, or if there are to be dozens of smaller maps that players can page through to find what they're looking for. If you want to allow players to annotate, you'll need to specify whether they can click anywhere and start typing or whether they'll need to drop markers on the map with which text messages can be associated. You may also wish to discuss whether or not the map can be transparently overlaid over the main exploration window, or if individual objects, characters, or monsters will be detailed on the map.

A companion feature that is sometimes included is a form of online journal. If you've ever had to put away a game for six months and then come back to it later only to discover that you've lost the Post-it note you had your secret passwords written on, you can immediately see the advantage of having a note-taking system that's tied to the game itself. A journal that automatically saves a direct transcript or the general gist of all the in-game conversations the player has engaged in can be a very handy feature, but you'll need to document exactly how this auto-note-taking function works. Will the writer on the project have to write summaries of all the dialogues in the game, or will the game engine dynamically clip sections to be used in the journal? Allowing players to add their own notes to the automatic journal is an even better feature, but realize that it may mean implementing a mini-word processor whose features you'll need to specify along with primary functions of the journal itself.

Peeking In on the Inventory

Practically from their first step, a player's avatar is going to begin to accumulate an overwhelmingly complicated mountain of *stuff.* They'll have swords, and blasters, and credit chits, and holy orbs, and vibrating blue squirrels bulging out of virtually every pocket, satchel, and orifice they have available. If you let them, they'd be walking, talking department stores by the time they reached the finish line, but designers limit how much avatars can carry to maintain the balance of the game while also maintaining *some* semblance of realism. Unable to send the entire contents of the Mall of Middle Earth along with their avatar, therefore, the player is forced to make *choices* about how their characters will prepare for the adventures ahead. It will be up to you to create not only a handy place for them to stash all their cool booty but to give them an intuitive tool that will help them easily organize, evaluate, consolidate, and distribute all the items they'll come across in your world.

Moving things into or out of an avatar's inventory should be made as simple as possible, playing on the player's basic point-and-click instincts. If a player clicks on an object in their avatar's inventory and they drag it to the ground, the item is "dropped." If an object is clicked on in the world and dragged back to the character, it should be "picked up" by that character. Allow players to lasso and transfer several objects at one time, saving them the "I pick this up, and this up, and this up, and this up, and this up" routine that can make transfers of large numbers of objects tiresome. Here as elsewhere, you want to streamline the experience so that players don't feel like they're doing chores. The player's inventory usually does far more than simply provide a place for avatars to stash away their stuff. They'll want to be able to examine their objects more closely and find out more about them. It's going to be up to you to design the interface that will let them divine this information.

In an RPG, objects can often transcend simple functionality and become much-beloved personal mementos (especially if objects are shown to have long-term usefulness or if players discover ways to upgrade their existing weaponry). Prettier, larger images provide satisfying rewards for hard-earned artifacts, making the objects prized for their inherent beauty. Brief histories about a specific artifact, or general background on a whole *class* of objects, can sometimes lend an increased aura of authenticity to the world they inhabit.

All these niceties aside, however, players need to have some way of identifying how the objects can be used and what effect, if any, they may have on the objectives of the game. If an item is a weapon, how much and what kind of damage will it do? What's its effective range? Does it require ammunition? If an item is a key, there should be some kind of indication what kind of lock it will fit into, perhaps even a hint about the exact door it needs to be used on.

The last, most important job of the inventory interface is to help the player prep their avatar for the unexpected. Provide a way for players to designate certain objects that can be "hot-keyed" for quick use, like healing potions, magic scrolls, hand grenades, or other objects the player is likely to need at a second's notice. Players also need the ability to "suit up" their on-screen counterparts

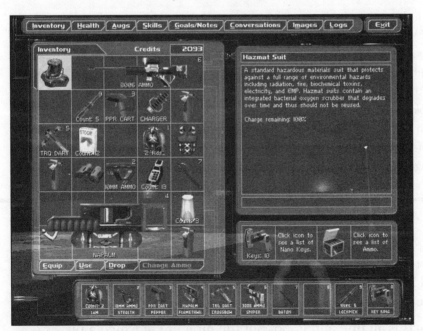

Figure 9.4 *Is that a flamethrower in your pocket?*

An inventory screen should not only give you a place to put your stuff, but it should also give you the capacity to find out more details about what you're carrying. (Deus Ex copyright 2000 Ion Storm LLP.)

Don't Feed the Goatmen!

As much fun as I've had playing *Diablo* and its sequel, there is one teensy flaw in the interface design of the Macintosh implementation that has repeatedly given me grief, and I've heard numerous other designers and players bemoan a related problem on the PC version as well.

Lined up along the bottom of the exploration screen is a row of four inventory slots, which the designers designated as the avatar's "belt." This is a very special inventory inasmuch as you can't use it to rearrange your objects, but only to have a selection of things to which the player would have very quick access— especially useful if you're facing down a Thorned Hulk and need to use a healing potion before he takes another swipe at you. Each of these four slots has a corresponding number between one and four, which the player is supposed to hit to quickly use whatever scroll or potion might be sitting in those slots.

The problem that arises is that those inventory slots on the avatar's belt *look* like buttons. When a player is in the heat of battle and they've been clicking on monsters to attack them, the natural *instinct* is to click on the potion in order to get healed. Intuitively this makes perfect sense—clicking anything *else* in the Main View "triggers" or "activates" whatever is being clicked on—but what happens in *Diablo* is that the player grabs the potion and then *hurls* it at whatever they click on next. Frequently this will be the monster, because the player is still trying to defend themselves. In the end, not only has the player not been healed of any damage, but their potion is now lying uselessly at the feet of the bad guy.

with the magical elven battle armor they found or put that steam-powered Gatling gun they found in Tarant into their hero's ready hands. With the avatar now boldly posed in new adventure gear, you can see the bold fashion statement they'll make as they reduce the forces of evil to a bloody pulp.

Discovering artifacts is all fine and good, but the moment at which a player is able to equip their character with something that makes them quicker, smarter, tougher, or more deadly is really at the heart of the role-playing experience. Objects can be cool by themselves, but the way in which they can extend the abilities and personality of the player's character is really what it's all about.

Granted, the designer-specified *proper* usage of the slots requires that the player punch a number on the keyboard or hold down the Control key while clicking, but this runs counter to what players need to be able to do quickly.

By way of contrast, *Baldur's Gate* also features a set of "quick use" buttons that run across the bottom of the screen, but they keep the usage consistent. Like everything else on the screen, clicking on whatever objects are in those quick slots will "activate" whatever function they've been assigned. Dropping or manipulating objects is handled in an entirely different way.

Part of this problem is not the fault of the poor guys who had to port this title. The Mac implementation is necessarily proceeding from the presumption that the player is using a one button mouse, and the designers had to prioritize what that one button mouse would do. The only flaw here is that more thought needed to be put into what kinds of things the player is going to need to be able to do *quickly*. The circumstances in which the player is going to need to rapidly drop something are not going to be nearly as frequent as the instances in which they are going to be in urgent need of a potion, scroll, or some other object.

Whenever possible, you need to think about the circumstances under which the interface will be used and try to make the experience as predictable as possible. Players need to be engaged in epic battles with the monsters, not with your interface.

It's All about Me: Getting into Character

After wandering around for a while in your world, players will begin to want detailed feedback about how well their characters are doing. They'll wish to know if that Radscorpion's attempt to gnaw off their avatar's face will have long-term effects beyond a temporary health loss. It might further occur to them they've been tossing off magic spells virtually nonstop at everything that moves, but they seem to be hitting their targets a little more frequently than when they first got started.

What the designer must do is address these kinds of questions about the character's development in an easy-to-understand status display. With one look the player should be able tell that their warrior is getting stronger or their sorceress is getting better at barbecuing the enemy with fireballs. For some games, this may mean throwing a numerical statistic up in a window showing by how many points the avatar's attributes or skills are increasing. More simplified systems might opt to present this information only as a simple graphic or a series of progress bars. Ultimately the format is unimportant. If a player can get the information they need about their avatar's current status, and it's presented in such a way that it will gratify their ego and give them something they can brag about to friends, they'll have half of the critical facts they need. Never forget the player's *best* source of information about their character should come from

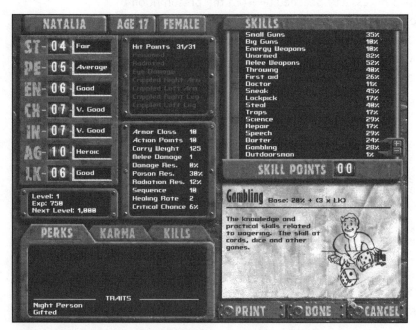

Figure 9.5   *All about the character.*

Fallout's fun and retro-grungy character status display not only did an excellent job of giving players the information they needed about their characters, but it also provided excellent in-game definitions of what all those skills, attributes, and numbers meant to the gameplay. (*Fallout* copyright Interplay Productions 1997.)

the gameplay itself. If they're constantly having to look at a scorecard to see if they're improving, you aren't providing enough ways in the game to test the avatar's abilities.

Aside from its ego-decorative facade, the character status display can have several very functional uses. First and foremost, it's the screen on which players should be able to take all experience points they've been accumulating and apply them toward the skills they wish to increase. When designing this feature you should make sure there are controls that will allow for unassigned points to be moved around freely between skills until the player commits to a specific distribution. Another important function of the character display should be to provide feedback on any unusual effects, like poisons, blessings, or diseases, which may have a long-term impact on the avatar's health or the performance of their abilities. Hard-core gaming enthusiasts will appreciate hyperdetailed data on things like the avatar's average target-to-hit ratio, the number of side quests completed, or even how much real-world time it took for the player to complete the game. The character profile window can even be used to lead players to background about a character's past or events in the game world related to significant goals or quests in the game.

Chatting Up the Locals: Interacting with Nonplayer Characters

Social interaction is a traditional staple of the role-playing genre. It's expected that the wise old woman can be consulted about the strange lights in the Haunted Wood or that it's possible to buy a medikit from the Xalnarxian Battle Droid of Schneezer VII. With their enemies defeated, players are going to need to buy supplies, get directions to the next town, or find out what the locals know about Princess Alucard's strange habit of vanishing in the middle of the day. Regardless of the final style of your game, you'll need to explain how players will be able to interact with the characters around them. As with everything else, the kind of dialogue interface you'll need will depend very much on the subvariety of RPG you want to produce.

On the bottom rung of the complexity ladder you'll find a relatively new form of dialogue delivery that has come into the genre via first-person shooters like Valve's highly successful *Half Life*. In this case, players rarely if ever have an actual *interface* with which to speak to other characters but can overhear conversations between NPCs or can be told things directly by in-game characters, providing the player's avatar is close enough to the speaker. The advantage of this system is that there's never a break in the gameplay. The player can continue to walk around the room, pick up objects, do whatever they like while they're hearing what game characters have to say. The downside obviously is that a player may accidentally walk off before hearing a critical piece of information, or they may not realize they need to stick close to the speaker in order to hear everything that will be said.

Next up the ladder you'll find intensely action-focused titles like *Diablo II*. Since this category of games emphasizes high-adrenaline combat action over rich character interaction, the kinds of dialogue interfaces typically required are usually fairly unsophisticated. In most cases, it will be sufficient to allow players to click on an NPC, get whatever canned message is needed, and then get back to the business of slaying the dishonorable opposition.

For a game that features stronger story lines and more well-rounded characters, you may need to climb up to the next rung of the complexity ladder, modeling your dialogue interface on titles like *Final Fantasy, Deus Ex,* or *Betrayal at Krondor*. All of these titles provide two-way forms of communication, which allow the player to speak to in-game characters using a list of keywords or predetermined response phrases. Over time, as quests are completed or as the player commits certain acts within the game, the responses available to them will change, as will the way in which characters react to them. (So if in *Vampire: The Masquerade—Redemption* the player goes and gets rid of the local head of the Brujah vampire clan, they might end up being very warmly received by the locals, but any NPCs with sympathies for the Brujah are likely to be less than civil with the player's avatar following the assassination.) If you choose for avatars in your game to have an intelligence attribute, you might have it determine the kinds of phrases or keywords the player has available, so a dumb character may only have a list of idiotic comments while an intelligent avatar may have a larger or more calculated selection of things to say.

The last and highest rung of the dialogue complexity ladder is occupied by titles that allow NPCs to be freely questioned using an *Adventure*-style text-parsing system. Interplay's *Fallout* not only presents its own version of the standard response-phrase paradigm but allows players to type in words and get brief, helpful feedback on anything NPCs should reasonably know about. In essence this

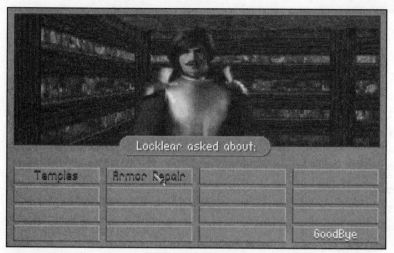

Figure 9.6 *Let's give 'em something to talk about.*

Before 1993 most RPGs had a very limited, back-and-forth system of character interaction, which made getting specific information very tiresome, especially on repeat visits. Betrayal at Krondor *innovated a dynamic, keyword-driven system of conversation, which allowed players to navigate very quickly to the information they desired. (*Betrayal at Krondor *copyright Dynamix, Inc. 1993.)*

provides a way for players to invent their own keywords and find out more about the world. A similar, slightly more elaborate text-driven system is utilized in *Ultima Online* to allow players not only to talk to NPCs but to chat with other players whose avatars are located nearby.

No matter how complex or simple a dialogue interface you believe is right for your game, you should keep in mind not everyone is enthusiastic about talking to characters in the world. Where possible, you need to provide mechanisms that will allow players to skip past dialogues—even those you consider to be important to the game story—and get on with doing other things. Preventing players from skipping the dialogue or the story should be a function of how well written, informative, and captivating you can make the content. Placing players into an inescapable cattle chute with a talking head will never be the right way to make sure players get all the information they need.

Text Parsing

Before the dawn of the graphical age of computer dungeoneering, all early computer-driven RPGs required players to type in sentences describing what they wanted to do. In games like *Adventure* and *Zork,* if the player wished to walk to the west, they typed in: GO WEST. If they wanted to get rid of the troublesome monster in front of them, they would enter: ATTACK THE TROLL WITH THE SWORD, and so forth. Unfortunately, computers don't natively understand English any more than they understand that you really didn't *mean* to delete eight months' work on your great American novel. Before a computer can do anything with an order like PUT THE BABEL FISH IN EAR, it needs to chop up the sentence into individual words in a process called *parsing*.

Once a sentence has been parsed into its component parts, each word, or group of words, is then compared to lists of commands, objects, monsters, or other categories the designer has prespecified. If a word like PUT matches a valid command, then the computer will check to see what procedure must be followed when that command word is encountered. In this case, the PUT command might require that the first valid object detected in the sentence (BABEL FISH) be placed into the second valid object detected in the sentence (EAR), scripted like so:

```
PUT <object 1>, <object 2>
```

Using this deceptively simple-seeming structure of commands and objects, text-parsing systems can still be used in games today to ask nonplayer characters questions, request training, view wares, and other actions for which a text-driven interface might be desirable.

This Means War! Dealing with Combat

When players set out on a quest to vanquish the ultimate evil, they expect at some point they are going to be called upon to put their virtual lives on the line. In some titles combat is light, an occasional nuisance that gets in the way of exploring the story or solving puzzles. In others it's a central gameplay feature, something which if subtracted out of the experience would simply leave the player with little or nothing to do. Light or heavy, easy or hard, the biggest trick of explaining and developing the interface for combat is finding a way to strike a good balance between control, simplicity, and excitement.

In several early CRPGs, combat was often treated as something strangely divorced from the rest of the in-game experiences. When monsters were encountered, the game would transition into a separate interface with special buttons and controls that *only* were available in the context of the fight. Over time some combat functions slowly began to migrate, allowing players to do things like hurl fireballs at distant targets or bash down doors. With the influential arrivals of FTL's *Dungeon Master* for the Atari in 1989 and then later SSI/Westwood Studios' *Eye of the Beholder* in 1991, combat not only became real-time but was fully integrated into the exploration experience. Today only some console-based RPGs have persisted in the use of separate exploration and combat interfaces, drawing a very clear distinction between times in which the player can safely do whatever they want and times when they need to be watching the enemy.

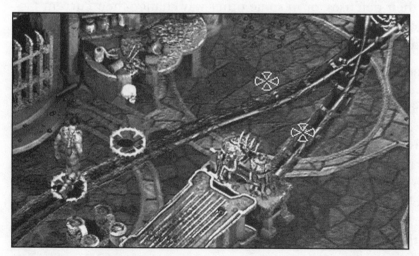

Figure 9.7   *Fighting on the console.*

Cloud and Barret slug it out with flunkies of the Shinra Corporation in Final Fantasy VII's *combat interface. Today some RPGs still use the age-old convention of separation between combat and exploration. (Final Fantasy VII copyright Square Co., Ltd. 1997.)*

With the exploration and combat modes now combined in most modern titles, and with smart cursors available to distinguish between targeting enemies and talking to friendly characters, combat is now a relative definition of the *way* in which the player uses what they've got available. In a fully integrated system, they should already have buttons that allow them to select and cast various kinds of spells or use hot-keyed objects while exploring the world. Whipping out a combat baton in *Deus Ex* and smashing a window is obviously a morally different act than beating up a bum in the subway, but as far as the way in which the game engine should physically treat those two events, they should be virtually identical. One is not an act of exploration while the other is an act of combat. They are both equal instances of damage being done with a baton. This follows a very important rule: *The use of an object should always be consistent, so that the result depends only on what the object is and what it is being used upon.*

If you're going to feature any kind of combat in your game, you need to make sure you provide an always-visible graphic indication of the health of the player's avatar. When they're taking lumps from the bad guys, they need quick visual confirmation that tells them how much damage they're taking and how fast. If it looks like they're taking too much too quickly, they need to very quickly grasp this fact so they can choose to either run away, use a health booster, recharge their defenses, or in some other way change their current tactics. Players also need feedback on any special diseases, poisons, or other conditions that may be affecting their avatar's general performance.

Beyond just the basic mechanical functions that allow the player to fight the forces of darkness (or the forces of light, depending on your bent of play style), there are several additional features you might choose to provide to further spruce up the player's combat options. Tactically minded players may want to form up their party into a specific formation, using menus or keys that will let them fan out into the configuration of their choice. A high-tech sci-fi thriller might want to give players a "radar" in which they can view the movements of off-screen approaching enemy units. If your game features real-time combat, you might provide a Pause button à la *Baldur's Gate,* which will allow players who like to make their moves in turns to stop the action and assign certain tasks to each member of the avatar's party.

Because the key idea behind combat is action, and because the very nature of the process is going to require the player to complete several repetitive tasks like firing guns, swinging swords, and casting spells, the most important interface consideration when dealing with combat is immediacy. For every submenu you make them navigate through just to take a simple shot at the enemy, you're stealing a quantum of the player's excitement about the combat, and you're making them think instead about how difficult your interface is to deal with. Provide the player with all the tools they'll need so they can get to their spells, to their weapons, to their critical inventory objects as quickly and efficiently as possible. Think about providing a way for gamers to script actions, create shortcuts, or elsewise tailor the combat tools to fit different playing styles. Everything you can do to speed up and streamline the combat process will pay back in player satisfaction many times over.

Have You Been Saved? Handling Loading, Saving, and Player Options

Although it isn't always the most glamorous or exciting aspect of interface design, you need to provide an explanation in your design document about how the player will manage their saved games and how they can change options affecting various aspects of the game's look or general performance.

Loading and saving games needs to be handled in the most straightforward process possible, letting players get in and out with a minimum of wait or confusion. Allow players to name their save games or even enter brief comments or descriptions for later reference. Most titles save a mini-screen capture along with the game data, giving players a visual way to search for the game they want to load. You might also consider including a save-game browser that would provide additional information on the health of the characters, makeup of the party, quests completed, and even objects currently in the avatar's

Save game. Players of RPGs and other kinds of games like to be able to save their progress so that if they have to turn off their computer for a while, they can later resume playing from the point at which they left off. When the game is saved, a whole multitude of things are being stored away *beyond* just the information about where the player's characters are standing in the virtual world. Typically information is going to be saved regarding what the avatars are carrying, what the status is of various quests they've accepted or completed, where monsters may be standing, the status of whether various objects have been destroyed or if doors have been left open. In essence the computer is taking a snapshot of *all* the factors in the game that are changeable and "remembering" all of it every time the game is saved. Each of these collections of information on the state of the gameworld is known as a *save game*.

possession. Not only will this kind of feedback help the player determine which game they want to restore, but it also provides a history of the player's progress through your world.

In the same way no two role-playing experiences will be exactly identical, no two gamers will like or enjoy the same things. More to the point, gamers are likely to have wildly different setups on which they will be playing your RPG, and many may wish to tailor your game's usage of sound or video cards to optimize the performance of your game on their machine. Here's a brief list of options you might extend to the player that will help them get more out of your title:

- **Difficulty.** This is an option only given to players in solo-player mode at the very beginning of a game. Although some titles have experimented with scaling monster difficulties or only providing certain areas to people playing games at the moderate or hard levels, the quickest and easiest way to change difficulties is to change the number, nature, and frequency with which players can find inventory resources.

- **Parental Settings.** If you've got a game that has content straddling the line between adult and teen-rated audiences, you can save yourself some undue harassment by providing *some* form of parental setting. This might mean giving parents a password-protected gore-level check box that makes all the blood in the game turn green, or it might prevent children from being able to lop off the heads, arms, and other body parts of enemies. Another thing that will win you a few points with the ratings boards will be a check box that filters out written and spoken obscenities. This aspect may be a little more difficult to arrange, but it will garner you the gratitude of many parents of younger children.

- **Subtitles.** Gamers playing on machines with subpar CD-ROM drives or marginal RAM may experience technical problems with garbled, inaudible, or skipping dialogue. Giving them the option of reading subtitles will help ensure they get everything that is being said in the game. An option for subtitles should also be present so that hearing-impaired gamers can get as much out of your RPG as everyone else.

- **Key Assignments.** Some players prefer to use the keyboard to call up interfaces or to perform certain actions. Give them a means to assign game functions or interface windows to whatever combination of mouse clicks and key commands that they wish.

- **Interface Configurations.** Different people have different likes about how they want to interface with a game. Some people want a very spare-looking screen, with most of the game's controls invisible, hidden, or "spring-loaded" in corners until such time they are needed. Another kind of gamer enjoys having the exploration area framed in by all the controls and gizmos they need to fiddle with every little detail. It's possible to satisfy *both* these kinds of players by giving them the power to select the interface configuration they like from a menu or allowing them to use an F-key to cycle through all the options. RPGs like *Nox* and *Planescape: Torment* both featured floating "tear-off" windows that could be relocated wherever the player wanted to put them on the screen. An additional fun thing to do is to allow the player to import different "skins" for the interface. (Part of the fun of playing the real-time strategy game *Starcraft* was that when you changed the race you were controlling, the general look of the interface changed as well.)

- **Video Options.** Give the player the option to toggle on or off certain video features, switch screen resolutions, or change the quality of texture maps being used within the game. Small changes like this may help buy speed and stability on systems that are running just above the minimum requirements of your game.

- **Audio Options.** Few things can be more annoying in a title when you're stuck running around in the world with a soundtrack you don't enjoy. Let players independently change the volumes of the music, sound effects, and dialogue present in the game. Also consider allowing players to choose alternative tracks that can be played under different circumstances.

Explaining Your Interface

Although there's no specific format you have to follow while explaining your game's player interface, it's generally a good idea to provide a rough schematic for what the finished product will look like and then break down how each individual button or element of that interface will work. Some variation on this basic approach has been used in design documents since the earliest days of the industry, and short of actually building a genuine working prototype, this will help designers and CEOs more clearly envision what it is you're trying to do.

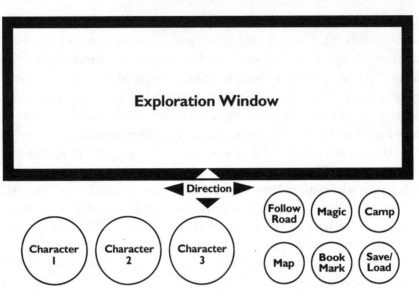

Figure 9.8 *Krondor's main exploration window.*

The following explanation of an exploration interface comes from the design document we used for *Betrayal at Krondor* (courtesy of Dynamix, Inc.):

- The MAIN EXPLORATION display is divided into two parts: the upper section, roughly one-third of the total screen area, will be the *exploration window*, while the lower fifth, or *interface window*, will have variable functionality, housing the six option buttons available to the player and containing a named portrait of each party member.

- **Directional Arrows.** In the center of the screen, between the two windows, is a series of movement icons, four "buttons" facing up, down, left, and right. The player can click on these buttons to step forward, backward, to the left, or to the right, respectively.

  Between the movement buttons, we may want to include a compass display to show the party's directional orientation.

- **Follow Road.** If the party is currently standing on one of the King's Highways, clicking the FOLLOW ROAD button will engage the road-following mode. In this mode, the player will "stick" to the road while moving forward, even if it bends or turns. This will be a fast and slightly safer way for players to travel through the Western Realm.

- **Magic.** Having chosen this option, the program should check how many magic users are in the party, and if there are more than one, a prompt should appear: SELECT A CHARACTER. Following this selection, a list of the spells available to that character will appear, and a message will prompt: SELECT A SPELL. (The spell list will appear in the main view window, beneath this display will be two rows of 10 buttons, labeled 1 through 20. These indicate the HEALTH point loss associated with each spell.) There should also be a button allowing the player to EXIT back to the main view window.

  Once a spell has been chosen, the message prompt (in appropriate situations, some spells don't require targeting) should change to: SELECT A TARGET. As the player moves their cursor over an acceptable target, the cursor should change to a "target" icon. Clicking the left (action) button will cause a spell to be aimed at the chosen target. If the spell is LOS (line of sight), a message should appear indicating the odds (based on how far away the target is) of actually hitting the target.

- **Camp.** When the player wants to rest for the night they select this option. This is an opportunity for characters to regain lost HEALTH points, and of course, moving in the dark will be next to impossible without torches or some sort of magic light spell. When this option is selected the player should be prompted SLEEP FOR HOW MANY HOURS? (The party can sleep for 1 to 24 hours.)

  (NOTE: The ENCAMP option should not be possible with a monster visible in the main view window!)

- **Map.** A map is available to the player at all times. This option brings up the MAP display.

- **Save/Load.** Here, the player may save their game or restore a previously saved game, quit to DOS, change their preferences, etc.

- **Bookmark.** The BOOKMARK button is the quickest way to save a game in progress. When this option is selected a file called BOOKMARK is automatically saved to disk, thus eliminating the need for a separate interface screen, file requester, etc. (This file will always be available in the directory and is simply replaced every time the option is selected.)

- **Character Globes.** The player can call up an "inventory" of any character by clicking on the desired portrait at the bottom of the screen with his left (action) button.

Final Thoughts on the Interface

Keep in mind the interface is the only connection between the player, the rules, and the world you're going to create. On the immediate level, it is the way in which the player will control the actions of their avatar. On a more abstract level, however, it is about subtly communicating the invisible rules that govern your game's reality. Players are not going to know what you've written up in the design document, nor will they be privy to the inner workings of the programming code. They won't have an awareness of any of the well-intentioned reasons *why* you've established the conventions that you have. The only thing they will know about your game is that when they do X, then Y happens in response.

A good interface should help the player learn things about the world. If people usually consider Kochab cola dealers dangerous, then when the player sweeps a cursor over them, the cursor should turn into a set of crosshairs indicating the creature is an enemy. When the player has a fireball spell prepped and ready to cast, they should get feedback indicating how large an area will be affected before they accidentally barbecue their lead warrior.

No matter what kind of elements you choose to use or not use on your project, you must never forget that the interface can make or break your idea. You can have the most fabulously well-thought-out rules system in the world, but if players don't *get* how they're supposed to do the basics, then all those rules will become moot when the player shuts off your game and never plays it again. Work on developing an intuitive, easy-to-use interface that gets them excited about exploring your reality and they'll stick around for all the other great things you'll have to offer them.

Part III: Inside the System

Okay! We've come pretty far along in our discussion of the design document. and there's not a great deal further we'll need to go, but maybe this is a good point to pause—just for a moment—and recap what it is we've talked about so far.

In "Part I: The Introduction," the importance of getting the team excited about the project as a whole was discussed and I laid out the guiding vision for the story and the primary game events. I also discussed several possible formats for your walkthrough, including the Loomis Ladder. I very quickly touched on flowcharts and how they can be useful for demonstrating the overall connection between events and locations within the game. Finally, I closed out our introductory section with a quick look at character sketches and the important role they play in helping the team connect with the characters they'll be creating.

With "Part II: Defining the Interface," I took you on a headfirst leap into a discussion of the many different kinds of interface issues you'll need to address while writing up the documentation of your RPG. I covered navigation and the prominent forms currently used in most modern titles. I also walked you through basic player interactions with the environment and the ways in which you might employ smart cursors to help players understand their environment. With maps and journals I demonstrated options that can help the player keep track of their progress and keep notes about things they'll need to remember in the future. My discussion of the inventory and the avatar's status display revealed not only the importance of feedback but also how these functional screens can be used to fill in details about the larger world. I also gave you a peek at the primary ways in which the player will interact with nonplayer characters—through talking and combat—and closed out with a few suggestions about how you can make your title more player-friendly through user-customizable options.

So far, everything I've discussed in the design document has touched on aspects of the game that the player can directly *perceive*. We started at the outermost level, discussing things like the story and the overall events that we hope the player will take away from the experience. At the next level down, we looked at all the elements of the interface that the player will use to get around and to manage various resources like inventory or character health. But once we prepare to descend to the next level of the design document, we come to the door through which only the designers of the game will be allowed. It is here that you will lay out the beating heart of your game, the spark that gives your world *life*. Here you will discuss the guiding rules of your game system.

In Chapter 6, we went pretty thoroughly over the basics of what gameplay entails and what kinds of things you should be incorporating into your rules and events to make your title live and breathe. Rather than cover again material we've already discussed in exhaustive detail elsewhere, let me instead touch *very* quickly on the points you need to communicate in the design document about your game system.

The World

The most important things you'll need to explain about your world are the ways in which the player will be permitted to interact with it. Can players set buildings on fire, break down doors, climb ladders, or fly over the treetops? All of these issues can have very wide-ranging implications for the art, programming, and level design teams, and they'll need to be aware of how these things will impact the way in which they approach their jobs. If you're using a sophisticated physics model, make sure you communicate the things you'd like to be able to do with it, as well as any concerns you might have with its implementation.

If players can freely use vehicles, portals, or spells to leap from one location to another, be sure the team members know this and that they understand all the rules and restrictions that may apply to all the instances.

Weather and environmental effects like ice, fire, and fog can be very fun, but you'll need to specify exactly how they'll affect the avatar's performance in the world, as well as if they have any effect on the way that monsters behave. If the sun will rise and set, how frequently will this occur in game time, and will these have any effect on the ebb or flow of activity around the protagonist? Will it affect their ability to hide in shadows?

Societal Issues

Unless the player is crawling through a dungeon during the whole adventure, they're likely to run in to a least a handful of other people. You'll need to establish if there are any general guidelines that will affect the behavior of NPCs in the world. Are there any factions, alliances, guilds, or other large-scale social forces that may change the player's status, depending on where he's been or who's he's done deals with? Will there be any automatic triggers that will turn certain groups of people against the protagonist?

Another important question you'll need to deal with is economics. Establish how much things are worth and whether the things the player's avatar finds can be sold back to vendors or individuals. If there are forces that may change the buying or selling price of various items, you'll need to create the mechanisms that govern your invisible stock market. On a somewhat related note, you'll need to determine whether shops open and close or if all the world's an all-night Wal-Mart. What are the basic rules for how objects will be distributed through the shops, and how will difficulty ratings that the player sets change which objects show up or vanish in the world?

The Character

At the very heart of your system should reside the rules that will govern the advancement and growth of the player's avatar. You'll need to describe whether your game is a class- and level-based RPG or whether it features free-form skill-based development. If you do feature classes, you'll need to specify what bonuses, advantages, and restrictions will be associated with all the classes you provide and the means at which each level is obtained. Skills will need to be very carefully explained in terms of what the player will be able to do with them, and you'll need to outline the activities and the frequency with which each of these skills will advance.

Central to the discussion of the character, you'll also need to define all the statistics or attributes that will affect the player's health, constitution, and ability to perform basic tasks. If the player can be afflicted with diseases or poisons, you'll need to address these issues as well, explaining what the precise effects will be on the avatar's performance. You'll also need to explain what special effects may be derived from eating, sleeping, or performing other in-game activities. If characters can die, can they be resurrected, or will you have some other mechanism for allowing the player to continue playing?

(For a particularly good look at professional design documentation on the development of the player's avatar, consult Appendix C, "The Design Document—Excerpts from Nox.")

Monster Intelligence

A critical part of game combat relies on the apparent intelligence of monsters to do things that seem logical. The trick is to develop routines for monsters that seem like reasonable courses of action while not being so intelligent that the player really has no chance against the enemy. In this section you'll provide the routines that monsters will follow when either attacking the player or going through their day-to-day business.

Magic and Technology

If your game has a system for some form of transordinary means of manipulating reality, you'll need to provide a description of how the system works. What kinds of effects can be generated by magic, and how will the player call up and use spells? If magic requires an external power source (à la mana), you'll need to specify how common it is, where it comes from, and if there are certain parts of the game where it might be more plentiful than others.

Combat

Last, but certainly not least, you're going to need to explain how characters will be able to attack and defend themselves in the context of the game. What kinds of weapons and attacks will the player be able to use? Will there be bonuses or deficits for hitting monsters that are hiding behind objects, firing down from above, or attacking in the darkness? You'll also need to specify the differences (if any) between ranged and melee weapons or if there other issues that may affect the outcome of battle. For a thoroughly modern RPG, you'll probably also want to address whether your game will feature multiplayer options and whether those sessions will be cooperative, competitive, or both.

Part IV: Miscellaneous Design Documentation

Where the first three sections of the design document focus on events, and rules, and procedures, the last section is really nothing more elaborate than a long collection of lists, and charts, and diagrams, and sketches, and virtually anything else that the production team generates as content for the interior of the game. It isn't at all unusual to see pages and pages of something like the following:

> Amulet of the Upright Man
>
> Icon #: INVICON.LBM #16
>
> Found:/Sewers of Krondor, Chapter 6
>
> Given To:
>
> Price: 293$s3r$
>
> Damage: -
>
> Protection: -
>
> Total Possible Charges: -
>
> Chapters:
>
> Repairable: No
>
> Function: This item has the effect of negating any *Nightfingers* spell cast on a PC who is carrying the item. A player who is carrying it would still be able to cast the spell on someone else, however.

Armorer's Hammer

Icon #: INVICON3.LBM #72

Found:

Given To:

Price: 65*s*4*r*

Damage: -

Protection: -

Total Possible Charges: -

Chapters:

Repairable: No

Function: This item allows a PC to utilize their Armorcraft skill to repair damaged pieces of armor. To use it, the Armorer's Hammer is picked up on the inventory screen and "dropped" on any piece of armor. The armor will then be repaired to the appropriate level as dictated by the PC's Armorcraft skill and the condition of the armor. See the *Skills* supplement, 6/25,92, pg. 3 for more information on how the Armorcraft skill functions.

. . . and so on, and so on. The last section of the design document becomes nothing more than a vast encyclopedia of monsters, objects, spells, sound effects, and music listings that will be required to construct the game.

Of all these endless appendices that appear at the end of a design document, probably none are more important than the individual *level layouts*. These very important documents take the general walkthroughs specified in the introduction and flesh them out into detailed maps indicating exactly where monsters, objects, traps, houses, and treasure artifacts can be found by the player. For those designers who have a familiarity with pen-and-paper role-playing games, the format will seem extremely familiar. For a better look at how a level layout is usually broken down, take a look at Appendix D, "The World Layout— Excerpt from *Fallout.*"

Formatting the Design Document

As with the proposal, there is no universally mandated format for the presentation of your design document. They come in all sizes, shapes, styles, and colors. I've seen some projects that did just fine with a 60-page record and others that

The Game Designer's Oath of Design Documentation

Hold up your mouse hand and repeat the following after me:

"My team members cannot read my mind. I must fully communicate my ideas in the design document so others will understand what I meant. A concept I fail to share with my team is just a disaster waiting to happen."

Excellent! Now walk around your house for an hour or so repeating this to yourself. Stop when your mom, or your sweetheart, or your dog threatens to call mental health services for you, but mutter it to yourself every time you prepare to fire up your word processor. Follow this basic principle while creating your design document and you'll avoid many of the pitfalls involved with the creation of this most important tool of your design team.

boasted 400-page encyclopedias that still needed to provide more explanatory information. (*Betrayal at Krondor*'s design doc represents a "career best" in documentary gluttony, tipping the scales at just a little over 10 pounds.) Long or short, thick or thin, the only thing your documentation must be is long enough to communicate what your team needs to know.

As before, even though there isn't a formal way that you're required to present your design document, here is the typical outline I use when preparing my own materials:

Introduction

Vision Statement

Story

Primary Game Objectives

Flowcharting Events

Important Characters

The Game Script

The format of the professional game script follows very closely on the heels of its most immediate forerunner, the traditional Hollywood screenplay. While some developers have struggled to create a new template for this still-evolving medium, I personally have yet to see any other format that gets the job done so easily or so well. More practically, this is a format with which most artists, writers, designers, and actors are *already* familiar. Don't give yourself the headache of trying to retrain a voice talent to read your innovative script format on a soundstage that's charging you $300 per hour. There are times and places to reinvent the wheel, but this is an area where sticking to tradition can only help you. Follow some of my suggested guidelines, and you'll be well on your way to having a game script that will serve your needs and save you headaches.

- Establish a habit of typesetting your text in a 12 point Courier font.

I know this sounds awfully pedantic. I realize Courier is the most boring font imaginable. But there are two very important reasons why this is the format of choice among entertainment professionals, and both reasons are rooted in the fact that scripts are ultimately read by actors.

The first point to remember is that one page of text set in 12 point Courier is roughly equivalent to one minute of screen time. So if you have a 60-page script, you've got about an hour's worth of audio you're going to have to record for your game. This gives you a handy way to track during the writing process whether you're writing too much, and it can also help you establish how much time you're going to need in the recording studio to get your game dialogue recorded.

The second benefit is that Courier is simply one of the most readable fonts around. Certainly Garamond is prettier, and Exocet is more artistic, but for actors sitting in a studio for long hours doing retake after retake, they want "easy-to-read" over "pretty-to-look-at." Nothing should distract them from the words themselves, and nothing should make the reading process any more difficult than it needs to be. The art of a script must always come from how well crafted the verbiage is, not from how it looks on the page.

- Set your left margin at 1.5 inches, your right margin at 0.5 inch, and both your top and bottom margins at 1 inch.

What do margins have to do with anything? These dimensions help hold your script to the "one page per one minute" rule, plus a wider left margin allows you to three-hole punch your script for ease of use. Bind your script using either a three-ring binder or brads so that you can very quickly pull out pages. This makes script updates easier to insert and allows you to very rapidly access the pages you need during a recording session.

- Page numbers should appear flush right in the upper-right corner of the script.

Will the world come to an end if you don't format page numbers this way? No, but this is the professional standard nonetheless. If you ever migrate into doing more traditional kinds of scripts for film or television, this is simply a good habit to adopt.

- Dialogues need to be indented 1 inch from the left margin (2.5 inches from the left edge of the page).

By indenting the dialogues, you're clearly setting apart what the actors need to say from other material presented in the script. This makes it much easier for actors, artists, and designers to identify the information they need without having to scan every line.

The Parts

Although I could fill an encyclopedia with all the possible "parts" that might make up a game script, the basic elements you need to understand aren't all that complex. Some of what follows you could find in textbooks on screenplay writing, but there are also twists here unique to the game industry, and in a few instances, unique to my own writing style. When I depart from conventional methods, I'll try to help you understand what purpose these new conventions serve.

Scene Headings

Before diving into the specifics on Scene Headings themselves, I should probably discuss what the word *scene* means in the context of an interactive game script. It isn't as if I'm going to discuss what the meaning of the word is, but there is a semantic difference.

The purpose of the Scene Heading is to give a very quick idea of where the action is taking place, whether it's in an interior or exterior location, and generally at what time of day it occurs (if relevant). If, for example, a scene is taking place inside the council chamber of Prince Arutha during the day, you would render it in the game script as:

```
INT. ARUTHA'S COUNCIL CHAMBER - DAY
```

To change the scene so that it's taking place outside of the council chamber, you would simply replace INT. with EXT. for *exterior*.

The language of the Scene Heading is terse, but it quickly gets the message across. Also note that headings are *always* typed in all caps. This helps people skimming the script immediately identify when a new location or situation has been established.

Sometimes you might need to provide additional information that might be special to the situation. Maybe there's a location frequently used in the game that the characters revisit after traveling through time or that they witness while hallucinating under the influence of a strange poison. This information would be added to the heading as:

```
INT. ARUTHA'S COUNCIL CHAMBER - ANITA'S SILVERTHORN
HALLUCINATION
```

or as:

```
INT. ARUTHA'S COUNCIL CHAMBER - TWENTY YEARS
EARLIER
```

The last important element that must be added to the Scene Heading is the *reference number,* as in the following:

```
11-B. INT. ARUTHA'S COUNCIL CHAMBER - TWENTY YEARS
EARLIER
```

The reference number provides a quick numerical way of indexing various scenes or locations in the game. This is *not* necessarily the order in which the scene will be encountered. Unless you're tying a rope around the necks of your players and dragging them through your game, they're going to encounter these scenes whenever it suits them to do so. All the reference number does is provide a shorthand way for developers to refer to scenes or locations and give them a tool to use when branching from one scene to another. I'll discuss this further in the section on Branches.

Note the presence of the dash B in the above example. This indicates that the scene about to be described is an alternative version of the primary scene it modifies, in this case, the second version of scene 11—the player is in Arutha's council chamber as it existed 20 years earlier.

Camera Directions

Camera Directions change the emphasis of what the player is currently viewing.
As they move from one area to the next, the position of the camera may be
scripted to move from one location to another, or the camera might zoom in
on a particular character while they're talking. If you're in Arutha's council
chamber and walking toward his throne, for example, you might script in a situation that changes the view to give a more dramatic angle. This could be rendered something like:

```
OVER ARUTHA'S THRONE
```

The most important thing to remember is that Camera Directions provide the
basic "frame" within which the action is taking place. When it comes to providing the details of what is occurring within that frame, the writer relies on the
script element known as the Description.

Description

Descriptions allow you to paint in information about settings or actions that are
not conveyed by the scene headings alone. They can provide additional information about objects that may be usable by the player or creatures that may be
confronted, or they may provide insight into characters that might not be otherwise apparent.

Let's look at the following Scene Heading and the associated Description for
the town of LaMut, one of the first that can be visited in the opening action of
Betrayal:

```
5. EXT. THE TOWN OF LAMUT - DAY

The town looks like something created on an
alcoholic binge. Rude dwarven shacks smash up
against delicate elven shops while weird Tsurani
taverns grow from a press of Kingdom-style
dwellings. A sign at the limits of the city seems
to sum it up well: All who visit LaMut are equal,
for in LaMut all is equally queer.
```

> A STONE BRIDGE arches over the dark and mysterious
> waters of the LaMutian River, a strand which can be
> searched for GOLD COINS tossed in by passersby.
> Nestled within the heart of town lies the Tsurani
> tavern, THE BLUE WHEEL INN, a place to grab
> something to eat before dozing off for the night in
> its safe, warm beds. THE FLETCHER'S POST is an
> elven establishment specializing in bowstrings,
> arrows, and other goods of use to archers. Looming
> over it all on its brooding granite cliff, THE
> GARRISON is a town unto itself, home to CAPTAIN
> BELFORD and his band of brave soldiers.

The first paragraph of this Description establishes the general mood for all the action the player should expect to find in LaMut. It's intended to be a strange place with odd things going on, and all the events designed for this area reinforced this central idea of the oddities created by the clash of cultures in LaMut.

In the second paragraph are a number of places, people, and things presented in ALL CAPS. These indicate critical elements that must be present in order to serve the needs of the story or the gameplay. Once these elements are introduced for the first time, in subsequent paragraphs they can be presented in lowercase to avoid confusion.

Another fundamentally important use of Description is to convey actions. Sometimes this covers big events that the player witnesses, like the collapse of a dungeon wall, or it may relate to actions taken by a particular monster or character. Here's an example of something you might expect to see in between clips of dialogue as the character Arutha considers his options:

> Arutha sighs, paces nervously back and forth
> between the door and the window, head down,
> studying the flagstones of the castle floor. He
> clutches A PARCHMENT SCROLL in his right hand,
> while he strokes his beard with his left hand.

Note that the actions given above are *very* specific. This is one aspect of the game writer's job that sets them apart from a more traditional screenwriter. If the above clip were interjected into a screenplay, the actors would have the writer lined up, shot, and run out of the country for being dictatorial. In a game script, there's very little room provided for physical "interpretation" by the actor simply because unless the scene is actually being shot on video, there won't *be* a physical aspect to their performance. Every action of the game characters will later have to be hand-animated or motion-captured by a team of artists who oftentimes will only be given a shopping list of the "moves" they need to complete. This means the writer must try and specify *all* the actions they want characters to make while delivering their lines so that all the critical nonverbal aspects of the performance can be appropriately rendered or captured. In a similar vein, all *sound effects* and *special visual effects* should be all capped so that they can be identified and added to production lists.

Dialogue

The Dialogue element of the game script covers essentially anything that is spoken, whether it's two characters talking to one another, a voice booming over an intercom, a computer reading back data, or a character thinking to themselves. If the gamer is supposed to hear voices, then you need to express it in your game script as Dialogue.

Unlike in other forms of prose, you don't need to use quotation marks or italics when dealing with spoken material. If you've properly formatted your script, it should be very clear to the performers which bits they will be reading aloud and which are only stage directions. Let's take a look at a properly formatted dialogue excerpt from *Betrayal,* when I introduced the world to Jimmy the Hand's previously unknown twin brother, Lysle Rigger:

```
                     LYSLE RIGGER:
                   (short of breath)
          Prandur's Teeth! We...we could be...


                         JAMES:
          ...Twins, yes, so it seems. Seeing you, a
          great number of things become crystal clear
          to me. What is your association with the
          Mockers of Krondor?
```

As you can see, the names of the characters are presented in all caps and centered. Also note that Dialogue is indented 1 inch from the left hand margin, or 2.5 inches from the left edge of the paper.

Just below Lysle's name you may have noticed the words *short of breath* in parentheses. This is an example of a *screen direction,* information to let the actor know if there are any special circumstances that should govern the way the line is delivered. Screen directions can also be used to indicate the use of special audio effects that might make the voice sound special in some way. James Earl Jones's voice in *Star Wars* was commonly run through an effects processor and "flanged" to give Darth Vader that distinctive, talking-in-a-bucket sound quality that we all came to know and love so well.

Sometimes you might want a character to be heard but not seen on the screen. To indicate this, you can place one of two abbreviations in parentheses next to the hidden character's name:

```
                  JAMES (O.S.):
      Of all the items we found on the dead
      company, both those items seemed conspicuously
      out of place and may be related in some way
      to our elusive murderers. . . .
```

or

```
                  JAMES (V.O.):
      We begin our hunt for the Nighthawks with a
      spider and a spyglass.
```

What's the difference between *O.S.* and *V.O.?* O.S., short for "out of shot," is used to indicate that the speaking character is present at the time and place of the event but simply cannot be seen from the current point of view of the camera. V.O., or "voice-over," means that the dialogue is being spoken from another time or another place, providing ironic commentary on the events currently before the player. (This kind of retrospective monologue was handled very effectively in the 1999 Eidos release, *Legacy of Kain: Soul Reaver.*)

Branches

Providing that you aren't going to be leading players through your game with a noose around their necks, you're going to need some kind of notation in your script that indicates the circumstances under which a particular piece of dialogue will be delivered and where it will branch to if a certain condition is met. Let's look at an instance of the players chatting up a fellow by the name of Navon:

```
[IF (hasMetNavon=yes) THEN (74-B)]
```

                              NAVON:
                So far from the Prince's court, I'm surprised
                any from your part of the world even knew
                Kenting Rush existed. Have you come for
                business or pleasure?

In the instance above, this bit of Navon's dialogue will *only* be delivered if the
player *hasn't* met him before. That's because of all that business going on
between the brackets. The game engine is checking to see if the condition
(hasMetNavon) is true, and if it is, then has Navon deliver the *alternate* dialogue
designated as scene reference number 74-B, as follows:

                              NAVON:
                I had not expected to see you three again for
                quite some time. How can Navon Du Sandau be
                of assistance to you?

Theoretically you could do multiple checks of several different factors so that
you would only deliver a piece of dialogue under very special conditions like:

```
[IF (hasMetNavon=yes) and (hasn'tMetDukeCorvalis)
and (hasKilledTheWyvern) THEN (74-B)]
```

. . . and so forth. The important thing to remember about the conditional tags
is that they follow a simple format of

     [IF (condition) THEN (play scene reference # X)]

Last Thoughts on the Game Script

When you look at the game script, it isn't far removed from its Hollywood roots.
It still serves essentially the same purpose but reflects a new, interactive medium
and continues to grow and change as game designers daily push the limits of
what interactive storytelling can do.

For a better idea about what a game script looks like, check out Appendix E,
"The Game Script—Excerpts from *Betrayal at Krondor*."

Conclusion

The proposal, the design document, and the game script—these three documents will mark the end of the design phase and the beginning of the production cycle. In them you will have condensed all your best design ideas, all your visions for the finished product, everything that you want for the player to remember and love about your game. Once you have all three of these in hand, you'll have virtually everything you need but time and money to begin the very rewarding process of turning your idea into a gaming reality. Over time, you'll find that you'll have to modify all three of these to meet the evolving face of your product, but this shouldn't be a source of sadness or dismay. Only something dead or inert remains changeless. You may have to tweak, and shift, and rewrite as your game continues to grow, but with each change you have to make, you'll learn even more about how games work and the steps that will be necessary to bring them to vibrant, interactive life. Good luck, adventurer. May the dragons be kind to you!

Exercises

1. Sit down at your favorite computer or console RPG with a pad of paper and sketch out the interface. Study the way the buttons work, how they are placed, what they do. Now, imagine that you have to very accurately explain this game to someone who doesn't have a copy of it. Write out an explanation of exactly what every button does and any effects they seem to have on the characters. Map an area of the game as precisely as possible down to the locations of trees, houses, and other objects. Try to figure out why the designers may have arranged the world in the way that they have.

2. Pick up copies of traditional pen-and-paper RPGs like *Dungeons & Dragons, Call of Cthulhu,* and *Vampire: The Masquerade.* Study the rules very carefully and try to see what things that they're doing are similar and what things are very different. Write out an explanation of why you believe each system has taken the approach that it has.

3. Run around in an RPG like *Baldur's Gate* and talk to as many different characters as you can. Save right before initiating a conversation, then try using different responses to the things they are saying to you. If they make reference to other events in the world, try and track down the exact way that your different responses may have changed the larger story of the game.

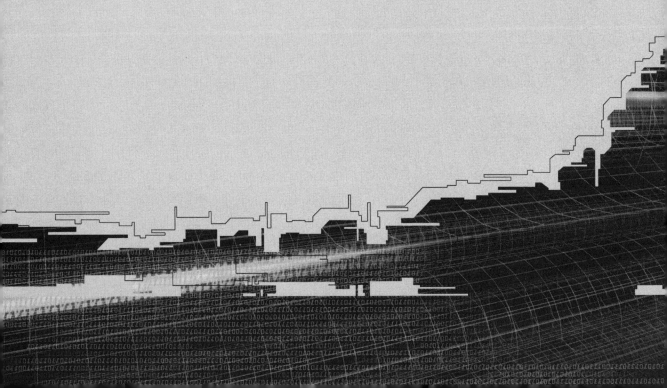

Part Four

The Games

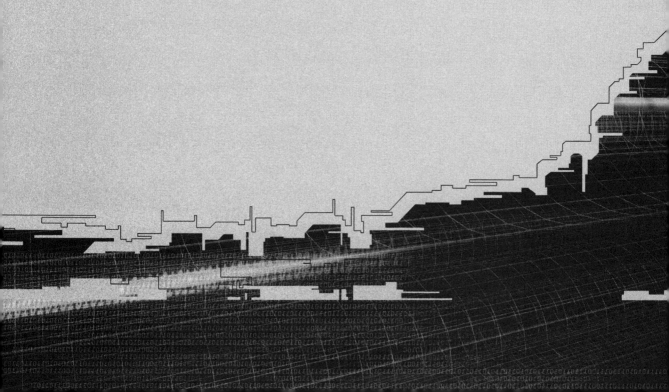

CHAPTER 9

JOHN CUTTER: BETRAYAL AT KRONDOR

John Cutter lives in Seattle, Washington, and has been working in the industry for 16 years. Best known for his work on the 1993 award-winning RPG *Betrayal at Krondor*, John has also produced and designed a number of diverse computer gaming hits like *Defender of the Crown*, *TV Sports Football*, *TV Sports Basketball*, *Wings*, and *Might & Magic III: Isles of Terra*.

Neal Hallford: What game are you currently working on?

John Cutter: I'm working for a company called Mass Media Inc. on a licensed X-Box title, but I can't say too much about it yet. I'm the lead designer on the project. I fly down to Moorpark, California, once, maybe twice a month for a week or so, but most of my design work is done at my office in the Seattle area.

Neal Hallford: How did you first get interested in game design? Do you remember the point at which you decided that this is what you wanted to do?

John Cutter: I'm not sure there was a specific moment when I realized that I wanted to be a game designer. As a child I was the weird creative one in the neighborhood. While everyone else set up lemonade stands, I created a monster museum and charged admission. I grew up in Wyoming, and my favorite memories are hot summer days when my friends and I would go down to the card table in my basement and play games. We'd just pull out an RPG or a card game or a war game or a chessboard and just play—mom would bring down cold pop and popsicles—it was really a great time. Sometimes we'd play *Dungeons & Dragons,* but I was a little put off by the complication of some of the rules. I thought "My god, the manual to play this is 400 pages long. I don't want to learn all that!" So I made up my own rules, and we had a great time.

One of the early computers, the Timex Sinclair 1000, came out when I was a sophomore in college. I wasn't very interested in it at first because I thought computers were all about math, which was never my best subject. But the box said, "it's easy to make your own games," so I decided to give it a try and I *loved* it! I couldn't get enough. I guess that's the moment I thought, "I could see myself doing this for a living. . . ."

Neal Hallford: Is there some moment from playing an early game that you remember that's stuck with you over the years?

John Cutter: My mother and father came out to visit once when I was still in college. We were at a restaurant waiting for our meal to arrive, and I got up to go check out a video game . . . I can't remember what it is now. When I got back to the table, my Dad had a long talk with me about how I needed to focus on my schoolwork and leave the blankety-blank games alone. He said that playing games wasn't going to help me get a job. Later, when my folks came out to visit that Christmas, Dad was probably less than thrilled by the Commodore 64 game my wife bought me. But Dad agreed to play the game anyway, and we spent *hours* playing it everyday. It was a game called *Mule* by the late Dani Bunten Berry—to this day, it's still my favorite computer title of all time. I think it convinced my father that a game career might not be so bad.

Neal Hallford: Is there anything else that contributed to your decision to make computer games for a living?

John Cutter: Actually, I have a story. It isn't *my* story, but I like to tell it anyway. One of the first people I worked for in the industry was a man named Bob Jacob. He and his wife started a company called Cinemaware, and they hired me to be the director of product development. Bob used to be a Hollywood agent, and one day I asked him why he left that industry to make games, since the software entertainment industry wasn't exactly big at the time. He said, "I'll tell you what it was."

Bob used to go down to the local library to use their new Apple computers—he suspected computers were going to be a big thing, and he wanted to know more about them. Anyway, every time he went in there he found a boy playing a computer FRP, which he later discovered was called *Wizardry*. It was very simple, stick-figure type graphics . . . not a lot of detail . . . pretty basic stuff—so Bob was amazed that this kid was spending so much time with the game. About the third or fourth time Bob went in, he was working away on his computer, and behind him he heard the kid yelling, "no, No, NO, NO!" and then the next thing he knows the kid is *sobbing*. Bob asked him what was wrong, and the kid finally manages to blurt out that his character had just died.

Now the real irony here is that Bob hated role-playing games, but at this point a lightbulb went on in Bob's head and he thought, "If people are this affected by a computer game, there's got to be something to this." And that's why he got into the industry. He wanted to help create characters and stories where people would have that much attachment—that they could be that moved by something they were playing.

Neal Hallford: So was Cinemaware your first gig in the industry?

John Cutter: No, that dates back to when I was first playing with and programming my Timex Sinclair. I was hooked on it, but I quickly ran out of room and processing power, so I decided I needed a *real* computer, which at the time meant a Commodore 64. I taught myself machine language and started working on a graphics program to help me make some cool games.

The Commodore used character graphics, so I created a program that allowed you to design characters using whatever colors you wanted, save the character sets, and then lay them down on the screen—it was one of the first editors to let you make scrolling games. I showed it to a company out in Santa Barbara, California, called Gamestar and said, "Hey, do you want to market this?" They said, "Maybe. Keep working on it." We kept going back and forth. They finally offered me a job because they didn't want to sell my tool but wanted to use it in-house instead.

Of course once I got inside, I realized there are a lot of people in the industry who are a helluva lot smarter than me. It was frustrating because I thought I was learning so much about programming, and then I realized I was never going to catch up to those guys who already knew more than me. Plus, I realized that if I decided to become a programmer I was going to spend most of my time learning how to program, and *not* thinking about how to make great games. So I transitioned from programming into more of a designer/manager role, and that's how I got started . . . and pretty much what I've done for the last 15 years or so.

> **Character Graphics.** On the Commodore 64 (C-64), there were essentially two different ways designers could get something onto the computer screen. When they wanted to create a robot that would walk or explode—essentially anything that needed to move—they relied on *sprite graphics* to get the job done. If, however, designers wanted to create motionless fortress walls, rocks, or trees, they used *character graphics*. This entailed modifying a "custom" set of letters onboard every C-64 known as a character set. By replacing individual letters of the character set with sections of a larger graphic element—say, by redrawing the letter *A* to look like the top of a tree, and making the letter *B* look like a tree trunk—designers could tile down the custom characters onto the screen as a background, essentially assembling a mosaic image.

Neal Hallford: What do you think is the biggest misperception about what a game designer does?

John Cutter: Well, I think there are a couple of misperceptions. One, people think game designers do nothing but play games all day. You hear that one *all* the time. The other misperception is that when I tell people I'm a game designer, they start talking to me about programming and code. I don't know about code. I'm a little bit of an oddity in the industry because a lot of designers are also programmers or artists or writers. I've done a little programming, and a little art, and a little writing—but I'm primarily just a designer. My job is to concentrate on the gameplay itself.

Neal Hallford: How do you personally define the job of designer?

John Cutter: Without getting into specifics, I think a game designer's job is to be the keeper of the vision—I hate to use the word *vision,* but I've never thought of a better word for it. The game designer has to have a clear idea of what he wants a game to eventually be and sort of guide the process. He writes design documents for the programmers and for the rest of the team, and he's the one other people come to with ideas. He helps focus people and he says, "Here's the direction that I think we need to go." When ideas come in, he helps sort through them all and decides which ones support the central idea of the design, and which ones don't fit in. He's also the one that adapts stuff and says, "We can't do that, but maybe if we change this it will work."

Neal Hallford: How do you meld all those different ideas into a unified product?

John Cutter: It's tricky sometimes. I've worked with designers who rule their projects with an iron fist—the guys who have the "my way or the highway" philosophy—but that usually doesn't work for more than one project. By the time the game ships, the team doesn't want to work with that designer anymore, even if it came out really great. Personally, I'm a firm, firm believer in getting the whole team involved with the design right from the beginning. That's not to say that I believe in design by committee; you've got to have one person who holds the vision and acts like a shepherd, helping guide the ideas and move them in the same direction.

Neal Hallford: What's the worst thing you've seen happen in a design-by-committee approach?

John Cutter: If you don't have a leader who has a clear idea of what they want to do, truly great creative ideas won't get through into the finished product. I've described innovative games as being like a spiky ball. First, you've got the core, which is the really solid gameplay that everyone agrees on—the fundamental basics which make the game a game and not a movie or a book or something else. But great games—ones that really break new ground—also have these little spikes going around the outside of the ball that are the little, cool, unique, even *edgy* ideas, that add a sense of fullness to the experience. Those little spiky left-field ideas are really important to a project, but committees never give them a chance to develop. It only takes one person in a room to say, "No, that's sort of stupid," and that spike gets chopped off and dies. So I think games that are designed by committee are these perfectly round ideas that are completely generic and "safe."

Neal Hallford: Whenever you're first putting together the idea for a game, what do you generally think gets you started? Do you start with a play mechanic, a story idea, a technical issue? What's the process that helps you get the ball rolling?

John Cutter: It varies a lot from project to project. When I've worked with you, a lot of the game design ideas I have come out of story or character concepts that you've worked up. But when I'm not working with a Neal Hallford and I'm just thinking more about game mechanics and gameplay, I like to start thinking about gameplay "hooks." I ask myself what little cool idea is going to sell this product to management, to the marketing department, and ultimately to the consumer. I suspect that there are a lot of great concepts out there that never get produced because there wasn't anything for the marketing department or management to get excited about. With great implementation, a game about "saving the earth from aliens" could be a big hit, but at the concept level, there's nothing there to make the idea sound better than the 10 thousand other ideas those guys have heard. So I like to start off thinking about hooks. "What about a game where the story is divided into episodes, like a TV series?" That's an interesting hook. Ultimately, though, the hook just helps get the game made . . . making it fun is a different matter.

Neal Hallford: So how do you make a *fun* game?

John Cutter: Over the years, I've isolated two main things that, I believe, make games fun to play. I've never shared these before because I didn't want my secrets to get out, but I've been in the industry long enough that I don't think they're secrets anymore. Number one, it's important to play to people's fantasies, particularly childhood fantasies: flying, cops and robbers, rescuing princesses, saving the world, and so forth. At Cinemaware, we did a knights-in-shining-armor fantasy called *Defender of the Crown*. We did a space shoot-'em-up called *S.D.I.*, which was kind of a *Star Wars*. *The King of Chicago* appealed to people who always wanted to be a "bad guy." I think a lot of designers sort of forget about all of that. In my games, I like to put players into positions or situations that people fantasize about, and to make them feel important. Power is another great fantasy. Haven't you ever wondered what it would be like to be a general commanding massive armies? They're all listening to what you say and doing exactly what you tell them to do. You say, "do it now!" and they say, "Yes sir!"

The second secret, and this one is the most important, is feedback. I have found that the quality of the feedback players receive from a game is directly proportional to the enjoyment they perceive from the experience.

A group in Salt Lake City programmed *S.D.I.,* one of the games I made at Cinemaware. Midway through the project I had our internal art team redo all the graphics, and a month or so later we got a new version of the game to check out. I called the producer in Utah and said, "Nice work guys! The new graphics look great, and I really like the way you tweaked the gameplay!" He said, "What are you talking about? It took a month to put in the new graphics . . . we haven't *touched* the code." Shooting down an enemy spaceship was more fun when the explosion looked better. That was when I realized the importance of feedback. Another game I worked on had a fistfighting sequence in it that wasn't fun until we added digitized sound effects from an old John Wayne movie! Suddenly the game was a blast because you almost felt like you were in the middle of a movie fight scene.

Providing good feedback is even a guideline that I've used in the design of interfaces. In *Betrayal at Krondor,* for example, you drop items on one of the character globes at the bottom of the screen to "give" something to that character. Early in the project, when you dropped an item, it would just disappear. But I thought it would provide better feedback—and also be more indicative of what was actually happening—if we could shrink that object so it almost looked like the item got "sucked" into the globe. It worked great. It was a pretty simple thing to do, and it made the game more fun.

Neal Hallford: Can you think of a particularly disastrous instance where you put something into a game that you later wished you hadn't?

John Cutter: There are a couple of instances, unfortunately. The first was a management issue. The lead programmer on my first game at Gamestar left the project near the end, and I was responsible for finishing the code. I mistakenly signed off on the code not realizing we had a third-party program on the disk. To make matters worse, when you tried to run the game normally it would run this other program instead, complete with a big copyright notice. Gamestar duplicated thousands of copies before we found the mistake.

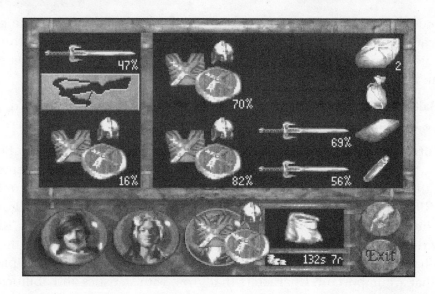

A big design decision I regretted was something I did in *The Three Stooges* for Cinemaware, but I didn't even realize what I'd done until it was 10 years too late to do anything about it. I was visiting my mom and dad one time, and they still had my old Commodore 64 down in the basement, so I hooked it up and decided I was going to play *Stooges* for nostalgia's sake. After I'd been playing it for a few minutes, I saw something which annoyed the hell out of me, and I wondered why I hadn't found this problem during development. *Stooges* was a board game, sort of like *The Game of Life*. Almost every square the player landed on would lead to one of about five or six minigames. And at the opening of all the minigames we had a canned animation sequence that lasted for 30 seconds or so. We *made* you sit through that animated opening every single time the minigame came up! We should have had it come up the first time, and then after that skip right to the game. That was a stupid decision.

Neal Hallford: What do you think is the most common mistake that designers make?

John Cutter: One thing that designers do that drives me crazy is rely too much on existing ideas. I don't know if they are just afraid to take chances, or if they lack time or imagination, but it almost makes me angry when game designers rehash the same ideas over and over again. There's no reason to assume that the staples of a genre are gospel. We need to approach things from a new perspective and spend more time outside the proverbial box. It's a balancing act, because you have to remember that gamers are expecting certain things and you don't want to disappoint them . . . or be so original and unique that they can't relate to what you are presenting.

Neal Hallford: Do you still think there are at least a few elements that a developer has to adhere to while making an RPG, or is the genre distinction irrelevant?

John Cutter: For me, someone else's definition of what the genre should be isn't that important. I get into disagreements with marketing departments over this all the time because I never set out to make a "good action game" or a "good RPG," I just want to make a "good game." I realize an RPG isn't going to be put into a "good game" category, though it's going to be put in the "RPG" category—and RPG fans are expecting certain things from the games they buy. So you have to be careful. There are obviously some staples of the role-playing genre that are important. Characters that grow, with statistics and abilities and skills, that's one thing that's very important. I think people expect a very large epic story of good versus evil. Certainly combat is another element that everybody expects. Resource management is another area—being able to find, and collect, and trade items is a big draw. One of the things I enjoy about *Ultima Online* is organizing my inventory. They have an interesting interface where you're not dealing with boxes and slots, it's just kind of free-form. You pick up an item, you drop it in your inventory, and it just floats there within the icon of the bag. People actually get dye and color their bags so that their magic items are in the green bag, and swords and other things are in the blue bag, potions are in another bag—believe it or not, that's actually kind of fun.

Neal Hallford: There are several people who argue that RPGs have strayed too far from their pen-and-paper roots, and that we aren't reproducing the feel of the original games. How do you feel about that?

John Cutter: I see them as two completely different styles of gameplay. They're both fun and interesting in their own way, but I think it's kind of silly that the argument even exists. It's like playing a football game on the computer and then saying, "Is this the same experience as playing NFL football?" Well no, they're thematically similar of course but in all other ways are completely different. I don't think you can really compare them.

Neal Hallford: What about the influx of the casual gamer? Should RPG designers be catering more to this growing segment of gaming?

John Cutter: I've gone back and forth on this issue a lot. Certainly on the video game consoles RPGs are extremely popular and can be extremely profitable. But on the PC platform, unless you're doing a *Diablo*-like RPG, I think it's become extremely difficult to make money on a hard-core RPG. It's not to say that there's not a large hard-core crowd out there. It's just that, by their nature, RPGs are very large epic games. And they are getting bigger and more complex all the time, which means more graphics, more programming, more writing, more audio, more actors, and more prerendered movies. It has become one of the most expensive game genres, and you can't spend that much money on a game and not appeal to a mass audience. You could a few years ago, but not today.

Neal Hallford: Mainstream gamers seem to demand greater control over who's holding the reins of the computer game. How much control do you think should be given over to players, and where do you tend to draw the line?

John Cutter: I used to think the designer needed to present the product in a way that he wanted people to play it. In other words, the designer was in control. In the last five or six years of my career, I've decided that you just can't do that. People are paying for the game to enjoy it, and you've really got to let them play it the way they want to play it. You have to provide a good challenge, but people don't like to pay $50 for a game and not see it all, so you have to let them save wherever they want, and get hints, and choose difficulty levels. . . .

Neal Hallford: Another relatively new segment of the RPG audience is the growing number of women gamers. You sometimes tell a story about the puzzle chests in *Krondor* and how women seemed to react to them. Do you think there's a clue there to how the industry might be able to attract more female gamers?

John Cutter: That was something that came up a lot when I talked to people about *Krondor*. At least a dozen different men told me that as soon as their wives heard the puzzle chest music they would rush in from the other room and help solve the riddle. We had lots of women who played *Krondor* on their own, mind you, but women really seemed to respond to the puzzle chests. As far as what that says about getting more women involved, I don't know. The chests were kind of a strange thing in the game. I really liked them, and it was something I always wanted to see in a game. I think maybe because it was a little more generic and wasn't really combat oriented it might have had more appeal to people who didn't want to just kill everything that moved. It wasn't really about

fantasy role-playing at all. We could just as easily have put those puzzles in a pure puzzle game, and I think they would have worked.

Neal Hallford: Do you think open-ended universes like *Everquest* and *Ultima Online* have affected the way stories are told?

John Cutter: I used to believe there was only one way of telling an interactive story. I thought the designer had to be in complete control of all elements, that the player needed to follow a linear progression from one plot point to the next, and that the climax had to happen at a specific place, with specific characters, at a specific time. I used to argue that anything else wasn't really storytelling. But I see now that there's room for another approach to storytelling, where you allow people to decide how they're going to play their way through the experience. Games like *Everquest* or *Ultima Online* do that well. I can play those games and sort of make up my own stories as I go, so there's this tremendous richness to the world because I've put it in there. In open-ended games the player doesn't have to rely on the writer to script every event in the game, and the designer doesn't have to be specific about exactly who's saying what and when and what camera angle we're watching from. Players can go in and make up their own little stories and their own little subquests. They can decide to try and get there and back before the dragon kills them. Sometimes that's not possible with the other style of game where the story doesn't want you to go see the dragon until later because you're not even supposed to know yet that he's there.

Neal Hallford: By contrast, you and I presented a very strong story line in *Betrayal at Krondor.* Did you feel that you were constrained by having a licensed, precreated world that couldn't change, or did you feel that it freed you up to concentrate on other areas of the game design?

John Cutter: I think the constraints were more on you. The fact that the world was already there and that I could read through Ray's books and read through your story summaries—I could base design decisions off all that ready-made material, all those known quantities. The disadvantage of a license is that you are locked into an existing world, and you can't change those rules to adapt to technical and other constraints. If the license says that dragons can fly, you'd better allow for flying in the game engine. We had a lot of those situations in *Krondor*—we wanted to make some compromises, but we couldn't do that and stay consistent to Feist's universe. That definitely added a level of complexity. In the long run, I think it was an advantage because it pushed us, and when we were done we knew the world made sense, and the game was fitted to the world as opposed to game universes that are a kind of a hodgepodge of random ideas.

Of course with any license, it's always a crapshoot. There are various levels of approval you have to go through, and sometimes that can be a real pain. I've worked on projects where the approval process was a nightmare. The licenser wants everything done in a particular way, and they don't always understand decisions that are made for gameplay reasons. They want something to be a particular way, and I'm thinking, "Oh my god, the game's gonna suck if we do this." And since these people don't play games, I can't even explain why this is important in a language they understand.

Neal Hallford: Can you think of any particular conventions of role-playing games you were trying to change in *Krondor*?

John Cutter: Well, I wanted to put more emphasis on storytelling. I really hoped to create a more *realistic,* more believable role-playing game with a truly immersive story that actually made you feel like you were in the middle of a great novel. Other games at that time—and I'm not going to mention any names—were a lot more abstract. You'd walk into a room and get a description that the room was full of merchants and other people, and yet there was nobody in there. Or you would be in a medieval setting and suddenly be fighting this weird monster that was part television set and part bunny rabbit. That kind of stuff really pulls me out of the fantasy. With *Krondor* I wanted to stay consistent to the fantasy, to the storytelling in the game itself.

We broke the story into nine chapters, each with a slightly different subset of the main characters. That was a real departure from other games where you always controlled the same character, or characters, through the entire game. I really thought we were going to get massacred in the reviews, but almost everyone loved it and I can't remember a single negative comment.

Neal Hallford: Were there elements of the design of *Krondor* that turned out better or worse than you expected?

John Cutter: I didn't believe we were going to be able to completely fill the entire world up in every chapter of the game. I figured that if we wanted players to go from point A to point B we should fill up that part of the world with puzzles, combats, and quests and block off the rest of the world. I figured no one would see it all anyway. For the record, that was something that you and I had a few arguments about. I'm glad I listened to you, because people *loved* the fact that the world was so full. I've talked to people who played *Krondor* for 100 hours and never even got out of chapter one!

This is one of the things that's really made me change my philosophy about acceptable forms of storytelling. I never used to like games that let players choose their own story line. I favored pushing them through the story in a particular way. But this is an interactive medium, and gamers don't always want to follow a particular story. They want the freedom to go out and explore, to do exactly the opposite of what they believe the designer wanted.

We put a lot of effort into balancing risks and rewards, but it wasn't until I watched my wife, Melanie, play the game that I realized how well we succeeded. There were at least three or four cases where she would get stuck somewhere and not know what to do, and then the very next puzzle chest, or the very next creature she killed, would have the exact item or spell she needed to get to the next chapter. Part of that was by design, obviously, but I think that worked out better than I had originally hoped.

The combat traps, on the other hand, didn't work out as well as I hoped. They looked good on paper, but they didn't work very well in the game. The idea was to come up with a simple trap editor, with properties and behaviors for a set number of items. Then we could come up with *hundreds* of trap puzzles just by strategically placing the objects in the world. And we did come up with some

Will the Real Krondor Sequel Please Stand Up?

Following the release of its best-selling game *Betrayal at Krondor*, management at Dynamix awarded the design team with an amazing surprise…they cancelled the sequel (*Thief of Dreams*) and broke up the role-playing department that had made *Krondor* possible in the first place. Although no one has ever explained why such an erratic decision was made, it was only the beginning of an even stranger tale of two sequels.

Realizing the error of what had happened and scrambling to capitalize on *Betrayal's* groundbreaking success, Dynamix's parent company, Sierra Online, decided that it would create an entirely new game using the increasingly dated-looking *Krondor* game engine. The new title would have a new development team, and they'd have the unenviable task of creating a new universe in which the sequel would take place. (They'd lost the rights to Raymond E. Feist's Midkemian universe in the aftermath of cancelling *Thief of Dreams*.) Thus, *Betrayal at Antara* became the first "sequel" to *Betrayal at Krondor*, although thematically wholly unrelated to the first one.

Meanwhile, Raymond E. Feist was cutting a deal with 7th Level to create *another* sequel to *Krondor* that would feature the same universe but that wouldn't feature any of the same technology. For a while both John Cutter and I were involved with the 7th Level sequel, but distance and previous obligations prevented either of us from being involved with the project past its earliest developmental stages. Eventually, 7th Level passed the project into the hands of Pyrotechnix, an exterior development house for—you guessed it—Sierra Online. Nearly five years after the release of the original, *Return to Krondor* became the second—though now "official"—sequel to be released by Sierra.

good ones—the problem was I did the original design work on graph paper, but the three-quarters perspective in the game made it hard to tell where things were lining up. It just didn't have the feel I wanted. The feedback wasn't there to the player.

Neal Hallford: What do you do in the instance when you're running out of time or money and have to cut something, but you've got two or more features you like equally? Do you have a procedure for deciding what you're going to leave in and what's going to get the axe?

John Cutter: You obviously have to take these situations case by case. I try to prioritize all the features I want in the game, and then I talk to the artists and programmers to find out how long it's going to take to implement each one. Then it's just sort of a balancing act. Sometimes it's better to give up one high-priority feature in favor of eight or nine lower-priority features that are simpler to implement. If I'm really excited about a feature, I'll definitely find a way to get it in, even if it means bending the rules a bit.

Back in the mid-'80s, sports titles consisted of only two teams. You played the game, and then it was over. When I worked on the design of *GBA Basketball,* I came up with the idea of creating a league and having seasons. The producer was never sold on the idea, and when we started running low on time he cut it. I argued with him for over an hour, but he wouldn't listen. So I bought the programmer a pizza and a bunch of beer and talked him into working all weekend to implement the feature. Monday morning rolled around, and we pretty much finished it. I showed the feature to my boss and he was not very happy, but he let us keep it in the game.

Neal Hallford: As hard as we all try while working on games, we all make mistakes. What's your spin on the best way to prevent bugs and fatal crashes from crawling into game development?

John Cutter: I think the most important thing is to have adequate testing. On *Krondor* we had an extended beta period. We started our beta testing three months before the game was supposed to ship, only it turned out it was more like nine months before we actually shipped. It was the best thing that could have happened to the project. Early in the project, we'd look at the tester reports and sometimes we'd say, "Okay, this is a silly one. Why are people complaining about that? There's nothing we can do about it." But some of those problems got reported over and over again, and we eventually realized that we needed to fix them. I think, in retrospect, we were all much too close to the project to recognize some of the problems. You really need that fresh set of eyes, and people that aren't hard-core gamers, to look for problems.

Neal Hallford: Do you think the fact that *Krondor* was one of the first RPGs to be put on CD-ROM may have played a role in its success?

John Cutter: Yes, I think the CD-ROM version contributed to the success of the game. But we never really took advantage of the CD-ROM's capabilities. We added some better music and a video interview with Ray Feist that probably wasn't a huge draw. No, what we gained from the CD-ROM version was a rerelease of the title that included a sticker listing all the awards we had won: Game of the Year, FRP of the Year, and so on. Of course, Sierra had the weird notion that it wasn't going to sell well, so they priced it pretty low to clear out their inventory, and then all of a sudden it started selling extremely well.

Neal Hallford: After *Krondor,* you and I reteamed in 1997 to design a role-playing title called *Elysium,* but we faced quite a bit of resistance to the episodic model we presented. Despite the fact that several companies now seem interested in the episodic model, there still seems to be a lingering worry about this approach. What do you think is behind the fears of managers and marketers when faced with this different approach?

John Cutter: I think there's partially a resistance to *any* new idea in the industry right now. As I said earlier, RPGs are very big and they're complex and they're very expensive to do. No company wants to take a chance on a large project with a brand new distribution and sales methodology.

I think marketing was worried about our episodic approach because the smaller games don't compete well against huge blockbusters like *Baldur's Gate* games. To get the attention of marketing people these days—and you have to grab them before everyone else—it's got to look like a blockbuster. It has to be the coolest thing that people have ever seen, and you want them to feel like they're going to die if they don't get it. Plus, it's got the greatest engine and the greatest special effects and the greatest story—the greatest everything. The episodic approach requires everyone to change their thinking. We were counting on the fact that *Elysium* would start small, but the quality would be there and it would be like *X-Files*. Each individual episode would be an enjoyable game offering 10 to 20 hours of gameplay. And there would be a story hook that grabbed hold of people and kept them coming back for more.

Neal Hallford: What do you think you learned as a designer from *Elysium's* later cancellation?

John Cutter: I think the most important thing I learned is to keep management and marketing informed and excited about the project. I was relying on the notion that they would be blown away by the game when they finally saw it. Unfortunately, we didn't get that far. The project was cancelled because management didn't understand it and because they had no vested interest in it. By that I mean that none of them had made any contributions to the design.

I didn't keep management well enough informed because the company president, Ron Gilbert, was giving me a great deal of autonomy. I was doing things my way, and frankly, I was worried that he would change some elements of the design that I was excited about. Ron's a great designer, but I've worked at some companies where upper management wants to help design your game, despite having absolutely no credentials or experience. In those cases you run the risk of the president saying, "I really like the idea that instead of the evil character being a wizard, he's really a giant toad that has magical powers." On the other hand, if you keep everyone informed, they may contribute ideas which actually help improve the game.

Ultimately, I've decided that you have to keep management and marketing informed and excited at every step of the process.

Neal Hallford: That's obviously the darker side of the industry. What trends in general do you see in the industry that you're glad to see, or are very encouraged by?

John Cutter: The biggest thing in the past few years has been the emergence of online gaming. It's going to take a while to really catch on with mainstream gamers, but that's one of the reasons that it's kind of exciting. *Everquest* and *Ultima Online* have been fairly successful already, and they're both targeted at hard-core gamers. It's still regarded as a sort of nerdy thing to do, you know, get online and play role-playing games, especially when you hear that people are taking days off of work to play the game. So I guess what I'm saying is that there's a small number of people who are incredibly enthusiastic, but there's a huge potential audience out there. It's big now, and it's going to get much, much bigger.

I think another arena where we may see expansion is in the episodic model. It's a little risky, but the start-up costs are pretty small. If done right, it could really take off and be big. There are probably some other ideas out there like that, that could start small.

Neal Hallford: What advice do you have in general for anyone who wants to go out and tackle the challenge of being a designer? Run for your lives, or come on in—the water's fine?

John Cutter: Challenge convention. Don't get locked into existing ideas. Think about what the audience wants, and try to give them even more.

I get a lot of letters from high school and college students who want to be game designers. My advice to all of them is to get a well-rounded education with lots of history, philosophy, psychology, literature, creative writing, political science, drama, sociology, and more. Next, I counsel prospective designers to play a lot of games and maybe find a job as a game tester. They'll learn a great deal about design as they watch a project go through the final stages of testing, and it's a good foot in the door.

CHAPTER 10

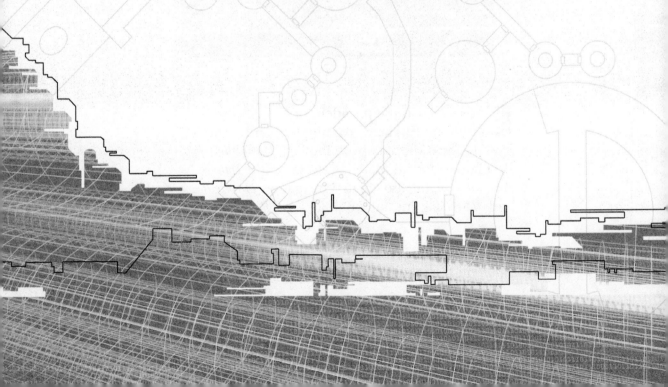

CHRIS
TAYLOR:
DUNGEON
SIEGE

Chris Taylor is the president of Gas Powered Games in Kirkland, Washington, and is the lead designer on the upcoming FRP *Dungeon Siege*. Best known for his real-time strategy title *Total Annihilation*, he also created the games *Hardball 2* and *4D Boxing* and the original *Triple Play Baseball*.

Neal Hallford: Can you remember what your first experience with a role-playing game on a computer was like?

Chris Taylor: I think the game was called *Kesmai* or something like that. This would have been back on my TRS-80 in about 1981 or '82. It was all done with top-down graphics, and you had an X or a C where your character was, and monsters were like Ms or something like that. You simply moved around with the arrow keys one increment at a time, and it's funny because *that was terribly exciting*. That's the thing I remember about it. It was also really difficult. I didn't have the brains to play it well. The next RPG I remember playing was *Wizardry* on a friend's Apple II. It was in a first-person perspective, incrementally turn based, going down hallways—pseudo-3-D hallways—and that's where it really took off in my mind. I thought, "This is exciting! We're here for real now." It was the first time emotionally where I really got scared, where I felt like even though it was all just green lines demarking hallways and horribly drawn monsters, that was *fright*. The fear wasn't so much that the monsters were scary, it was "That monster's going to kill my character." My character was going to be *dead*. There was real fear in that.

Neal Hallford: Did you play any pen-and-paper RPGs?

Chris Taylor: I played *Dungeons & Dragons* in high school. We spent half our time arguing and yelling and screaming about whether we were in the room or we weren't in the room, did you roll, did you not roll, did you use the wrong dice? Just hours and hours of that. The most fun we ever had was creating our characters. We all wanted to be the DM, so we'd all go off and create these dungeons, and that was half the fun. But when it really came down to playing, that's when the whole thing didn't work. It just fell apart at the play level. *Dungeons & Dragons* is inherently a difficult game to play when you're 15, and we were too young, and we didn't have enough savvy. We later started playing *Risk* on a ping pong table I had. I built an extended map of an imaginary countryside, and we ended up playing that more because that was easier.

Neal Hallford: How did you transition from that into becoming Chris Taylor, Game Designer?

Chris Taylor: If you teleported back in time to 1980 when I got my first computer and asked me, "Chris, what do you want to do?" I would have said that I wanted to make games. For me, that meant I wanted to design and to program them. I never wanted to just design. I had a disdain for people coming into the business who said, "I'm a designer." I was like, "Grrrrr. You rotten bastard. You don't know how to program. You can't be a designer." It's like Steven Spielberg saying I want to make a movie and *nobody* touch the camera. I was going to be the camera operator too, which was just ridiculous. If you want to take a camera and do a few shots, great, but you need to direct and let the cinematographer do his work.

The problem was I had no distinctions. I thought that programmer and designer were one and the same, and that the programmer sat down and made the stuff go. I guess I slowly realized in the last 13 years somewhere that I've transitioned from one extreme to another. I always wanted to be the guy who made all the decisions. I never wanted to be told what I had to do in terms of the game. I wanted all the creative control and all the freedom.

I finally got started in the business when I was 21. I got a job with a company called Distinctive Software in Burnaby, B.C., Canada. The first game I was told to make was called *Hardball 2,* and that launched my career in the video game business. I was the engineer. There was a sound designer that came on for a month or two at the end of the project, and an artist who probably worked half the time on the project, but otherwise that was it. I programmed the front end, the back end, the editors, the stats, the graphics, I connected the sound—whatever needed done. That's where it all began. I have to mention, however, that we did have an awesome set of low-level libraries to use, which really helped make my job easier.

After that I went on to do *4D Boxing,* which was cool because it was one of the first PC titles that used some kind of a motion capture system. I followed up by leading the programming and design on *Triple Play Baseball,* which was the first in EA's *Triple Play* franchise. That was when I really started to get my feet wet managing people and being a project leader. I later did a port of it to the 3DO console. That was icky because I was porting baseball—which I really didn't like a whole lot—to the 3DO console for the Japanese market. I used the old baseball saying "Three strikes and you're out." So that was basically it. I'd done three baseball games by that time and it was time for a change, so I left to pursue my RTS idea.

RTS (Real Time Strategy). A genre of strategy game in which all players make their moves simultaneously without waiting for other players to complete a turn. Each participant controls large numbers of *units* that can be dispatched to gather resources, build defenses, or attack the forces of other players.

From there I went to Cavedog—well, it wasn't Cavedog yet. It was Humongous Entertainment. At that point I was talking to Ron Gilbert, who was the creative director of Humongous, and I was telling him that I wanted to start my own company, but he convinced me to come down and join Humongous and build the game I wanted to build. What I had in mind was a *Command & Conquer* killer, so we came up with *Total Annihilation.* I ended up being the project leader, the lead designer, and lead programmer all rolled into one.

Finally, in May of 1998, I left Cavedog to found Gas Powered Games. I'm the president of the company as well as the project and design lead of *Dungeon Siege*—I say *lead* designer because we have many designers—including yourself now!

Neal Hallford: How would you define what the designer's job is?

Chris Taylor: That's a good question. I think a designer 10 years ago just said, "I think I'll just take this idea and lay it all out." Now I think the lead designer's role is more like a fusion between a designer and a project leader. You've got the fusion of the creative and the pragmatic. On *Dungeon Siege,* as lead designer I drove some stakes into the ground very early on. I said, "I want a gigantic, continuous 3-D world. I want a multicharacter party. I want a strategic element. I want to bring RTS into an action-fantasy RPG game. Let's go." That was my first lead designer decision, and that was heavily tied into what I thought the market was looking for.

But another part of the lead designer's job is handling hard decisions. A designer decides what can and cannot be put in a game based on a bunch of restrictions of time and money and guides it in a particular direction. I have an art director who looks after elements of art and style. We have someone on our team who looks after the lighting to make sure the lighting is consistent. We've got someone who makes sure the animation is consistent. We've got a world designer who makes sure that the world is consistent. We've got all these captains with their own ships, and it's my job as the lead designer to act like an admiral, making sure all the ships are sailing in the same direction. I don't tell them how to sail their individual ships . . . ermm, I try not to!

Neal Hallford: A lot of the designers I talk to seem to truly dread the managerial side of their jobs, but it seems at times the only way to advance a design career. Do you think that management is always the logical place for designers to go?

Chris Taylor: To get a little philosophical about it, it always means lopping off another part of what I love to go forward. I had to drop programming to be the president of this company. I've got to bang the drum and meet and greet and kiss all the babies. That takes a lot of time. If I want to set up a two-project company, I may have to give up design, which is really *painful.* It's difficult because you got to where you are because you're *good* at something. And then you stop doing it to go further? It's really like you're starting all over again. Nobody really ever tells you about that. Nobody ever wants to say, "Excuse me, you really don't have a clue about what you're doing in this role. Go back to what you were doing before." You earn the shot of doing some bigger job, going from project leader to, say, producer or executive producer, but if you screw up, you really do crash and burn hard. There's nobody there to catch you. That's what's really scary about the position.

Neal Hallford: Do you feel moving up the ladder leads to a loss of control over a product?

Chris Taylor: I think there's an illusion at all levels about what that control *is.* It's a common misconception that a designer just gets to sit back and whimsically dictate. It's fantasy to suggest that somehow artists and programmers are going to whip a bunch of stuff together and put it on the screen, and it will be the mirror image of what the designer had in their mind. The reality is that the designer wants a lot of things he or she can't have. The designer is given a ton of constraints. The designer is working with creative and eccentric people. The designer has to create reams of documents, diagrams, flowcharts, storyboards, sketches, and otherwise communicate their vision. That vision will be continually misunderstood and reinterpreted. It's everything from the teammates literally not hearing you, to they don't *want* to do what you're asking them to do. So the designer is no different than a salmon trying to spawn upstream, or that's what it seems like. The good news is, great people balance this difficult job marvelously, and the individual contributions they make, whether or not they agree with you, end up making the game better. So, sometimes the hardest part of game design is letting go and allowing creative people to do their job, even if you don't always agree with them.

In the end, it really matters what you're designing. If you're designing a baseball game, then you're probably looking at competitive product and you're looking at the next available step in technology, plus a feature set that's largely determined by the sport. But if you're a well-known designer who has to go out there into the wild unknown and craft something out of thin air, and if it vaguely resembles anything that has gone before, you may have failed for your own personal creative goals—that's the scariest other extreme of design. One is an industrial 9-to-5 designer, who has to crank something out, while the other is the kind of person who is trying to define new genres. Those are completely different jobs, or at least have completely different challenges under the "designer" title.

Neal Hallford: What are the most important considerations that either kind of designer needs to keep in mind?

Chris Taylor: Listen to the gamer inside you and trust that. Everyone has a different voice inside them that guides their decision making. If you stop listening to yourself and listen to everyone else instead, they're essentially designing the game. I think *Total Annihilation* was the first time I really had a clear vision and said, "Look, this is really the way I want this game to go together." And it's probably important to mention that this vision was not so much in the details but in the overall vision for what the game was going to become. What was beautiful was that we built the team in such a way that we didn't all start off with 20 people in a room at the very beginning. I didn't have to convince this group of people about what I was building. We built the team up slowly one person at a time. As each person came on to the project, they were brought in on that vision. But the important point here is that you need to build what you want. If what you want is to make a game that sells two million units, if you're saying to yourself that you're making a mass market game, then build *your* interpretation of what a mass market game is going to be, not Bob the Producer's version of a mass market game. Even if you're building it for a customer, and that customer is a million people, it's still *your* vision.

Another important lesson is to remember that games are for fun. Silly, whimsical things which are somewhat immature are probably going to be fun and really well received. A person isn't going to buy it because they want to suffer—they're going to buy it because they want to have fun and want to enjoy themselves. That's what the designer's ultimate job is.

Understand and respect that game design does not live on the other side of the fence from technology. They're all wrapped up in each other. If you don't understand technology, you won't create the next fantastic thing as easily as the next guy who *does*. Technology lives and breathes right in there with game design.

The most important thing to remember is that *people* make all the difference. You cannot get to point number two in this business in any way, shape, or form until you've addressed point number one, which is the people. Whether it's the makeup of your team, the talents of your team, the desires of your team, their goals, their wishes, their energy—it's all about *them*. That's why I say after the many years I've spent in this business that when you assemble your team, you're essentially constructing the DNA for your game. Your fate has been decided the day you've chosen your people, not the day the game is finished. I really pay more attention to people than to almost any other part of the project.

Neal Hallford: What's the next step for you after you assemble your team? Do you draw on any inspirations from outside the gaming industry when you're putting together ideas for your projects?

Chris Taylor: The only place I've ever tried to draw from visually was from movies. I try to make the visual components more interesting and more cinematic, but that's just so darned difficult to do. Cinema just has so many controls that we just don't have. It's a reminder to me that we have a long, long way to go.

Driving down the street I've come up with the oddest things. Just by looking around me I look at the basic relationship of *things* and I get ideas. I specifically remember driving down the 405 and thinking about *Total Annihilation*. We didn't have our economy model in place yet with the solar collectors and wind generators. I saw a miniature windmill spinning on someone's barn, and I started to think about that, and then all of a sudden the pieces came together.

To expand on this, I think one of the mistakes is that if you're a programmer, you find that you tend to design *symmetrically*. Programmers have a nasty tendency to design in threes, fives, tens, in increments, in integers. You say "a wind

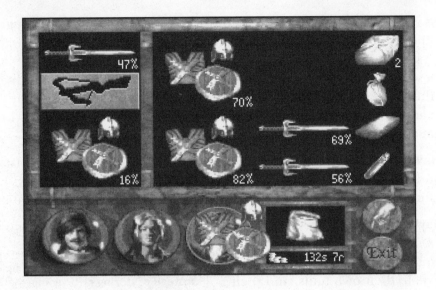

generator is a one, I need a two, I need a three, I need a four. I've got a thermal generator, it's a seven. I need an eight, I need a nine." That was something I had to break myself free of. I've realized that sometimes there aren't in-betweens, and you don't *need* in-betweens. You can just go from a power of one to a power of three and a half to a power of eight and the next one's 22. You don't need to hit these nice clean numbers. You can make it all work beautifully with this rough, randomness-of-life thing.

Neal Hallford: But you can get into trouble modeling from life. Typically you're not going to have the budget to make a real reflection of reality. You're going to have to make things vast and reusable, or small and detailed. Do you think you tend to lean one way or the other?

Chris Taylor: I'd like to say that I do neither, but it's almost impossible not to do one or the other. Sometimes if you begin with a highly detailed world, and you don't have the money or the resources to fill the world at that quality level, you have to start using tricks. You reuse art, reuse resources in any way you can, and then finish off with something at the end that makes people *think* that they were experiencing that level of detail all the way through. But if I had to say that I leaned one way or the other, I'd say it was towards a smaller and more detailed world. What we've done on *Dungeon Siege* is to compensate—because a smaller world means less playtime—by making the world somewhat more detailed. That way you've got a detailed world, but you're moving through it slowly, and you're enjoying every little thing in that world. You're really getting into it. I have to say I find it to be a big turn off when I get into a game and you have these massive stretches of land and you're walking for miles and then finally there's a bush and then there's a snake you can kill . . . okay, that's a gross exaggeration, but we designers tend to be a little over-dramatic—I don't find that as favorable as a smaller, more richly detailed world.

Neal Hallford: A larger world can also give you more room to make mistakes. Can you think of anything you've done in a past game that you really wish you'd done differently, or that you wish you'd thought more carefully about?

Chris Taylor: I can tell you that on *Total Annihilation* we had built the game to be data driven so that people could create their own units, and their own maps, and all this kind of thing. We didn't foresee that people would want to create their own weapons. We had one byte allocated, so we had 255 different weapon slots, and we might have used upwards of maybe 80, so we thought we had *all* this room. We made a whole game, and we only used a third of the weapon IDs. I might not be sure of the total number, but the point was that this was just horrible.

> **Data Driven.** *Data-driven* games are the godsend to the modern designer. Instead of storing critical information *within* the program—like how much damage a sword does, or how much a jewel is worth—a data-driven program stores the information in a separate data file. This allows level designers, artists, players, and other third-party developers to quickly and easily change the data file, and thus elements within the game, without being dependent on a programmer to recompile the main program.

What happened was that people wanted to take one of the weapons and slightly tune it or tweak it and give it a new ID, and there were *thousands* of people out there creating these things. They pretty much were screwed when they ran into this weapon ID problem. It's pretty much like saying, "Hey, we're going to build a car that can drive a long way," and we forget to put a comfortable seat in it. It was *that* dumb. Here we were going to build this game, and everybody's going to build all this stuff on it, and it was restricted.

Neal Hallford: That was something accidental that happened though. What's the worst thing a designer can intentionally build into a design?

Chris Taylor: Punishing a player for doing something, and then punishing them repeatedly. I think what I try to do in my design is to do the opposite. I try to design systems that do nothing but *forgive* the player. *TA* was a great example of forgiving the player at every opportunity. A player's not going to be upset with me if *they* sent in a unit and it got blown up, but they will be upset if they go to build a unit and they've invested resources in it and then they hit the Cancel button and they don't get those resources back. It's really foolish to punish people for changing their minds. That's the thing about people. We want to be able to change our mind. We want to be able to back out of something, to have a Cancel button.

What I did in *TA* is if you were building something and decided not to, you lost the energy you invested, but you got back the metal. That was a really nice compromise, a good example of not punishing people for changing their minds. They're going to get punished a lot of places where their strategic decisions are dictating that, and they don't have a Cancel button on sending a bunch of tanks into a heavily defended base. But allowing players an out when it makes sense is best.

I've got an analogy about punishing the player. What if movies had the same attitude towards moviegoers about screwing up as games often have towards game players? You'd be sitting there in the theater, watching the movie, and you'd miss a few lines of dialog because you were eating popcorn. Immediately, the usher would come over and see you out of the theater. And he'd say, "Hey, the movie's starting again across the hall. If you'd like you can go catch it again. But by god, this time put that damn popcorn down!" And you're just looking at them going, "You know, I'm just here to have fun." That's the problem with games when they cross the line and become too serious. Then they start to become grumpy old schoolteachers, and really bad ones at that. You've got to forgive the player. You have to remember that we're building entertainment, not some kind of sadistic torture device they've paid $50 for.

Neal Hallford: So you think we need to kick the ushers out of gaming?

Chris Taylor: I've had the philosophy that it's your sandbox. You can do whatever you want. I remember as a child my dad built a sandbox, he poured sand in it, and he said, "Go do whatever you want." If he'd stood over us and said, "Today, kids, you're going to build sandcastles, and tomorrow you're going to build roads," it would have taken pretty much all the fun out of the sandbox, even if my dad had really great intentions. So because we could go in the sandbox and we could dig a hole, fill it in, bury a truck, build a road, smash this, smoosh that— whatever we wanted to do—it was *our* sandbox. We could go in any direction we wanted and I really see video games like that. It's a place where you go in and you play. If you want to look at what the designer is doing, the designer is building the *sand,* he's creating the proportions of the sandbox, the designer's creating things you can play in the sandbox with, perhaps creating mechanisms whereby you and a friend can play in the sandbox together over the Internet. It's a whole lot of things. In a sandbox you've only got a few elements to work with, but in computer games we've got hundreds and thousands of elements, so I just definitely believe that you build a world, you build the toys, the goodies, the explosions, the characters—and you let the player have fun with them.

If you're really clever as a designer, you can build the game in a couple of different ways. You can build it for the player who wants to play by the rules or a player who just wants to do anything they want. If you can build the game so that it fulfills both those needs, then you've *got* it. You've really delivered to a high level of design which I can only hope to aspire to. It's the most difficult thing to design, one game for more than one type of gamer.

Neal Hallford: How do you feel about the fact that not even the RPG audience is really all that homogeneous anymore? *Diablo* and *Baldur's Gate* were both RPGs, but *Diablo* sold nearly twice the number of units. What do you think is behind the difference in sales?

Chris Taylor: Simplicity. The gaming experience was so simple that it became a no-brainer stocking stuffer. If you've got a friend who wants to get into video games because he's got that new PC, you say, "Here you go, here's *Diablo.*" Boom. He just knows it. You're not going to get a phone call in the middle of the night with him saying, " I just don't know what to do." It was like how could you *not* know what to do. You'd have to be from another planet. It's a beautiful game in that respect, and I struggle every day to keep the experience simple and yet engaging.

The importance about simplicity is that it's like driving a car. The car can be complex, or the road can be complex. If you make the car complex, it doesn't even matter what the road looks like. The minute someone gets into the car at the start of the journey, they're going to be overwhelmed. But if you make the road complex, or make it the means by which complexity can be delivered, now the road can start off simple and the car can start off simple. As the car rolls, the road can get more complex under the car. That's my design philosophy. You've got an educational element there, you have an acclimation element there, and you're getting some investment there from the player. When a player becomes invested and they've played for six or seven hours, they're much more likely to sit and read for a few minutes to learn an advanced thing than they were when they first sat down. So I've always felt that you need to put them in a simple car that takes them down a road that becomes gradually more complex. This is a way by which you can keep both audiences happy.

Neal Hallford: What's the single biggest hurdle that you have to clear when making an RPG?

Chris Taylor: Managing the massive amount of content effectively. You want to make sure you don't end up making half as much stuff because you couldn't get a grip on the pipeline. If you want to take the money you've got allocated to creating assets, and you want to produce the numbers of things that you think you can for the money you've set aside, you really need to understand that you're dealing with thousands of these and thousands of those—and they're going to get all mixed up along the way. You're going to lose a lot of work, just due to every reason you can think of. People losing stuff because they're not backing up their work, or they don't have a naming key that they've used, or a way of organizing it, or communicating about this massive amount of stuff to the rest of the team. Those are all things you need to have in place, and that's one of the big obstacles we overcame here.

Neal Hallford: One big reason that RPGs used to emphasize all that content was to ensure that games were replayable. How important do you think that distinction is today?

Chris Taylor: If you can deliver a good single-player experience of 30 to 50 hours, you've delivered some good value. If you can also add another 50 hours in multiplayer, you don't have to be too concerned that you've delivered something for the money. I don't think people really *want* to replay a single-player game over and over again. The single-player game is almost like a tutorial, a way to get your feet wet and get into it. You learn the game, and you move on to playing against *real* people. Sure, you can play through the single-player game multiple times, but what's better than that is to release your tools onto the Internet and have people build brand new single-player experiences, or multiplayer experiences, and to download brand new ones. We've invented the typewriter and the paper, but we're telling people to go out and write their own book. Don't keep reading the same novel over and over again. We hope our novel is great and you enjoy it once or maybe twice, but we don't really expect you to do that. We hope that people create new ones.

Neal Hallford: Do you have any worries that by throwing the doors open and inviting everyone else in that you're going to make yourself obsolete, or is this something that's been needing to happen for a long time?

Chris Taylor: I think there was a certain nervousness on the part of the industry. A lot of people thought, "Hey, if we give out our tools, what are they going to need us for?" We needed to realize that we are giving them the tools, not a 20- or 30-person art and engineering team. John Carmack has proven over and over again that he can give away all sorts of source code, editors, and whatever, and it just makes his products *stronger.* You don't see him sitting there going, "Darn it, I left money on the table because I gave all that stuff away." It's totally something we could have done from the very beginning, and if we had, it would have been a much more fun business to be in, to have all that interaction with the people on the Net and gamers and the fans. That's what makes this job really fun. It's to interact and be a part of a community. I just wish this level of interaction had gotten here sooner.

Neal Hallford: Can you think of anything else that developers can do to encourage that sense of community with their audience?

Chris Taylor: Well, we should do whatever we can to support them in such a way that it makes sense from a business perspective. The bottom line is that you have to pay the rent. If you sit around all day and talk to people on the Internet, and do nothing but fixing problems they have, you aren't going to generate revenue, and you go out of business. That's bad for you, and that's bad for them. But you do what you can, and you build your next game, and you try to find the balance there.

Neal Hallford: You were very well known for doing *Total Annihilation,* a real-time strategy game. Why did you decide to make the leap to doing a role-playing game as the first new title for your new company?

Chris Taylor: Basically my two favorite genres are RTS and RPG. Having done an RTS, I decided I wanted to take a break from it, and RPGs are the next, most interesting and exciting thing to do. It's funny, when I went around to find people to join the company here, they were absolutely all RPG fans. RPG fans are *everywhere!* It's a big target. There are a lot of people who like to play them, and there are a lot of people who want to make them. People love them.

I mean it's really building and it's never gone away. I got swept up in it and I really enjoy it because it's a nice break from modern life. It was just such an easy decision for us.

Neal Hallford: What specific things do you think you're bringing from your RTS experience into the role-playing genre with *Dungeon Siege?*

Chris Taylor: We're bringing the multicharacter party that we're managing using RTS-like elements. We're bringing a strategic element to the game in that you have your fighters in front, your archers and your magic users and your helpers and pack mules in the back. Prior to now, there wasn't much of that kind of an order to your adventuring. It was more like, well, you've got a bunch of guys and they kinda head on down and do their thing. *Dungeon Siege* is really bringing some order to it. It's only logical. If you're going down into these dark dungeons, the guy in front should be the biggest, baddest, toughest guy with a sword who's good at close quarter combat. We're really bringing that element to it. That's just a natural thing to steal from RTS games and to draw into an RPG.

Neal Hallford: What about environments and things like that?

Chris Taylor: The environments were entirely different, so we didn't do a lot there. *Total Annihilation* was technically a 3-D game, but it was from a fixed view, with prerendered terrain. It really didn't touch on anything like what we're doing now. Our environments now are just way over the top from what we could or would have done in *TA*.

Neal Hallford: Can you think of any specific features that you think are going to make *Dungeon Siege* stand out among its competitors in the genre?

Chris Taylor: We've got a few, that's for sure. We've got a pretty amazing feature in that our game allows the 3-D world to stream in from the hard drive continuously with no loading screens. We've got another big feature, which is our multicharacter parties and our strategic RTS-like elements. Then we've got our rule-breaking features where we say, "Let's go in and change a bunch of stuff in this genre that needs changing. Let's play with the way stores work, the way potions work, the way our skill-based class system works." So we have a bunch of different features, but it's not like there's any one alone that's so important that the game wouldn't work without it. It isn't like all the other cars out there have wooden wheels, and we'll have rubber ones. It's just all these elements rolled into one brand new experience. When people plug in *Dungeon Siege* and they play it, they're going to go, "Ooooh. This is modern. This is high tech. This is ooey gooey goodness—at every level."

Neal Hallford: Was there any particular design issue in this game that you had a really hard time tackling?

Chris Taylor: The hardest thing from a design standpoint is probably figuring out how far to take the story. We had to figure out where the line was between an action RPG and a more hard-core RPG with lots of dialog, and where we were going to fit our game in between the two. I'd say that was probably one of the biggest challenges.

Neal Hallford: You're creating *Dungeon Siege* in collaboration with Microsoft. How has that relationship been, and do you think there's a reason people have been afraid of them over the past few years? Do you think that's an unfounded fear?

Chris Taylor: I'll tell you, when we got to doing this—when we started the game and did the deal with Microsoft—we only went by what we knew from our conversations and our dealings with them. They were a great group of people and they were really determined to make triple-A titles and the best there is. I bought into that, and that's proven to be very, very true. It's funny, because I couldn't imagine a better company to be working with. It's almost like a match made in heaven. We've got a set of skills, and we do things a certain way, and it meshes right into the way they like to do things. And I really believe in a company that's one of the biggest in the world. They got there for a reason. They have systems and they have methods and they all *work*. You do not hear me curse Microsoft. You hear me praise them, if anything. You don't hear that typically from other developers about their publishers.

As far as what's happened over the past few years, I think that Ed Fries has a vision of how he wanted to grow the entertainment group, and he's seeing that vision through. It's working. He said that he wanted to go out there and create partnerships with the best talent in the business, and he's been doing that. That's what got Ensemble Studios onboard. He got Chris Robert's company, Digital Anvil. He has various other companies he's bought. He bought Bungie. He's doing deals constantly with top talent in the industry. Ed's *serious* about building a first-rate game publishing company within Microsoft. He's doing what he said he was going to do, and that's pretty impressive.

Neal Hallford: What do you have to say to the next generation of designers? What should they do about getting into the industry?

Chris Taylor: No matter how much they do on their own, they're going to need to start working with people who do it already. The best thing to do is go out and find a mentor and learn how you can get working with that person. Learn as much as you can from them by working in the business every day. Going to work for 10 or 12 hours every day and working on a project is much different than just sitting at home reading and studying about it for two or three hours. Really just jam yourself into a team and live it and love it and learn about it. Hopefully then you will have developed an opportunity for yourself. You can either go off and start your own company, or you can do it inside a company you started with.

The key is to be working side by side with the people who make this happen every day. I don't think I'd be able to do anything if I hadn't learned the tricky little details from people in the business. When I worked at Electronic Arts I learned a ton of stuff. And then when I went on to Cavedog Entertainment, I learned so much from Ron Gilbert that it's mind-boggling. I think gosh, it's amazing how much I *didn't* know. And how much I learned that I didn't want to know. The point is that you can't get it all from a book, even a great book like this one. You've got to get in there!

CHAPTER 11

TRENT OSTER: NEVERWINTER NIGHTS

Trent Oster is the producer of *Neverwinter Nights*, *Dungeons & Dragons* role-playing game based in the Wizards of the Coast's *Forgotten Realms*. He's also worked on other well-known RPGs like *Baldur's Gate* and *Shattered Steel* and a shareware title called *Blasteroids 3D*.

Neal Hallford: What was your first experience with a role-playing game?

Trent Oster: My first experience with a role-playing game was playing pen-and-paper *Dungeons & Dragons* when I was 12. My first computer RPG was a text-based RPG on the Apple II. I don't remember the name, but it was an amazing game.

Neal Hallford: Do you have any particularly vivid memory from playing a pen-and-paper or computer FRP that "stuck" with you? What do you think it was about the experience that made it so memorable?

Trent Oster: I remember playing one of the gold box games from the *Pool of Radiance* series by SSI, and I remember an epic battle in the temple of Bane. I fought what seemed like a thousand orcs and a Banite Cleric. The battle took hours to play through, and when I was finally victorious I couldn't wait for the next major battle.

Neal Hallford: Are there any RPG systems/games from your childhood that you feel had a long-term effect on the way you think about games today? Why did it affect you so much?

Trent Oster: *Dungeons & Dragons* had a huge effect on me as a child and encouraged me to develop my own game systems in my spare time. *D&D* was my introduction into role playing, and it showed me the potential RPGs have. It was like being the hero of a fantasy novel.

Neal Hallford: What kinds of nongaming sources do you tend to draw on for inspiration? How much would you say those things have affected the way you approach gaming? Do you have any unusual history that perhaps gives you a unique spin on gaming?

Trent Oster: I draw from every source I encounter: books, movies, even political events, both present and historical.

Neal Hallford: Can you remember when you decided that you'd become a game designer? What made it click for you?

Trent Oster: I never made a conscious decision to become a game designer, it just happened that way. I became a game designer by building experience in every area of development and adding my own creative twist wherever possible.

Neal Hallford: At what point did you "officially" get into the industry? Were you formally trained for it, or did you slide in through a "back door"?

Trent Oster: I would say I "officially" got into the industry when we signed our first development contract with Interplay Productions for *Shattered Steel*. I completed three years of my four-year degree in computer science at the University of Saskatchewan, and I started a game development company/computer consulting company with my brother and a childhood friend for the summer. We worked insane hours and learned as we went. After about a year of work, we managed to sign a deal with Interplay. So in short I got into the industry by working for a year with no salary.

Neal Hallford: What do you think is the biggest misperception that most people have about what a game designer does?

Trent Oster: I think the term *game designer* means different things to different people. At Bioware, our game designers are chiefly in charge of the story and rules implementation. The core game design is actually done by a variety of people involved on the project. Most people tend to think of a game designer as someone who simply plans out the entire game and hands it off to the team to implement. The real truth is that design is an ongoing process driven by the story; the programming and the art of the title, and as such, it requires input from each area.

Neal Hallford: What lessons did you learn on the way up about designing games that were the most valuable to you?

Trent Oster: I've learned a large number of lessons in development, and the most important is that nothing happens in a vacuum. Every single aspect of a game is created through a combination of programming, art, audio, and design. Failing to take any one of these areas into account is a major mistake.

Neal Hallford: When you're first throwing the idea for a game together, what usually gets you started? Do you tend to start with a play mechanic, a story idea, a technical issue? In general, what process helps you along most?

Trent Oster: To be honest, it usually starts out as a primordial soup, part technology and technical ideas, part gameplay mechanics, part visual style, and part story ideas. The game itself firms up from what technology we have or we feel we can develop, what art look we are trying for, what we think would be fun gameplay, and some story/user motivation ideas. The game idea quickly coalesces from these varied ideas and is quickly implemented in a game prototype. The instant you have a working mock-up, it becomes very obvious what works and what doesn't.

Neal Hallford: Every game designer is usually faced with a financial budget reality which necessitates the game world either be small and very detailed, or vast and reusable. Which direction do you think you typically lean towards? Why?

Trent Oster: While it is true all games are driven by an underlying financial budget, the elements should be woven together in a tight compromise which blends the detail level with the scope of the game. When I work on a game, I vary the level of detail based upon the player's interaction. If a player is to spend a great amount of time on one facet of the game, that area deserves great detail. A minor background event gets less detail and could be reused. In short, we spend the development effort where we get the most payoff. In the project I am leading right now, we are totally on the vast and reusable side, so we can support end user modification. In summary, I would say the bias of reusable versus detailed is dictated by the project goals.

Neal Hallford: What's your personal philosophy about working with a creative team? How do you balance the creative input of several people and yet blend them into a unified vision for the product?

Trent Oster: A creative team is mandatory in my opinion. While you could argue design-by-committee mutes down some of the brilliance of a one-person game idea, it also mutes out the really bad ideas in a one-person design. The key to balancing the creative vision of a team is to have a unified and common vision. Maintaining a common vision is best attained through extremely open and frequent communication and frequent prototyping or visualization. I also believe a strong leader must be present and have the authority to make decisions.

Neal Hallford: What's the smartest design trick you ever pulled? What's the dumbest? Is there anything in your design career that you would go back and redo if you had the chance?

Trent Oster: The smartest design trick I've pulled off was probably on *Shattered Steel.* We had a game engine which did outdoor terrain very well but couldn't roll the camera side to side. So we designed the game around large walking robots who could auto-compensate for the terrain rolling. In terms of the worst mistakes, I would also point to *Shattered Steel* and the enemy AI system. I designed and programmed the AI system in two weeks as a placeholder until I had more time to rework it. I never had enough time, and it shipped with the game.

Neal Hallford: What's the worst design sin that a designer can commit?

Trent Oster: Not paying attention to technical limitations is the worst design sin you can make. When you ignore what the engine can and cannot do, you are wasting time. Anything you create without paying attention to the engine will not work how you intend it to. A second major sin is adding complexity that is not perceived by the player. If the player doesn't notice the complexity, the project would be better served with a less complex system.

Neal Hallford: The past 10 years has seen a distinct shift in philosophy about who should be "holding the reins" of computer games. How much control should be given over to players? Where do you draw the line or strike a balance between the designers and the players?

Trent Oster: I personally feel you can give the users as much power to modify the game as possible. Allow the users to create new game content and invent new methods of playing your games. At the same time, you should shield them from unnecessary complexity. An end user may want to write his/her own story, but they don't need to know how to create a collision detection mesh. With the project I'm leading, *Neverwinter Nights,* we are allowing the users to create adventures, characters, items, and even their own stories. So I would have to say I'm all for giving more power to the people.

Neal Hallford: By the fact that everything that appears in a computer game must be drawn, recorded, or programmed prior to shipping, the number of possibilities within a gaming environment are necessarily finite. How do you make the player feel there are more possibilities to the world than actually exist?

Trent Oster: One excellent way of making the world seem larger is to engineer a number of simple systems and allow them to interact. If you set up the framework in a correct manner, a great number of possible paths can emerge from a single well-engineered system. Another method to make the world seem larger is to add a series of subplots, allowing the player to diverge from the main game path and explore further in an area. The subplots require implementation, but they make the world seem much larger than they actually make it.

Neal Hallford: Contrary to audience opinion, developers don't enjoy program bugs any more than players do. What's the best way to bullet-proof a title against hangs, crashes, and fatal glitches?

Trent Oster: A dedicated, motivated QA department and sufficient QA time. Quality assurance personnel are the most maligned people in the industry, but they are also some of the most important. A great QA team can help nail bugs down extremely quickly and make the game a better all-round experience for the end user.

Neal Hallford: As you approach the end of a project, and it becomes evident that not everything you planned is possible, how do you choose what's going in and what's left on the cutting room floor? Do you have a method you consistently follow, or is it a case-by-case scenario? Can you recall a specifically grueling time that you had to decide which of two equally fun things was going to be cut from a game? Which way did you go?

Trent Oster: It is the nature of any creative enterprise for desire to exceed reality. When the time comes to cut, the method is always the same. First, we lay out every feature in terms of user impact. If there is a feature which is not high in terms of the in-game experience, we look at the time required for implementation. We evaluate every feature in the game in terms of cost versus payoff and cut the low payoff, high cost features.

Neal Hallford: An amazing amount of time is spent arguing over what is and what isn't a role-playing game. In your personal opinion, what are the characteristics or qualities that every RPG *must* have in order to qualify in the category? How important do you feel the genre distinction is?

Trent Oster: I think the primary attribute of an RPG is the playing of a role. You adopt a persona and interact with that world through the adopted persona. Other criteria such as directing the character's development and managing character attributes are also valid, but secondary. I think genre categorization is similar to music in that it serves the "if you liked X, then you will like Y" sense for directing people to similar gameplay models.

Neal Hallford: Is there any one characteristic of RPGs that you feel is more important than others? Why?

Trent Oster: I think the development of the main character is important. When you play a character and the character evolves as you play, it increases your personal stake in the character.

Neal Hallford: It's become a classic argument between pen-and-paper gamers and the computer crowd that a computer RPG can never match the experience of spending a Saturday night with a group of friends and a handful of dice. What's your spin on this controversy? Do computer RPG developers need to worry about winning over "the old guard"?

Trent Oster: Pen-and-paper gaming is still infinitely more flexible than any computer game can ever be. The freedom and creativity of a live person directing a pen-and-paper session cannot be matched now or in the foreseeable future. Computer RPGs support a different type of play than pen-and-paper gaming, but CRPGs are still role-playing games.

Neal Hallford: Few things are more hotly contested these days than how much designers should cater to the casual gamer. Do you think more attention needs to be paid to the mainstream, or do you think that there's enough room in the market-share pie for RPGs to remain profitable as they are?

Trent Oster: Hard question. My personal goal is to offer the best RPG I can without creating any barriers for the casual gamer to play and enjoy the game. I feel making a game more accessible to the casual gamer is always a compromise. If you compromise too far the game becomes dull. If you don't compromise enough the game is a niche title. The key is to walk the line between an interesting concept and mainstream accessibility.

Neal Hallford: *Baldur's Gate* and *Diablo* are arguably the two biggest role-playing games of the past few years, but seem to represent entirely different approaches to the genre. *Diablo* has sold nearly double the number of units of *Baldur's Gate,* but *Baldur's* seems to enjoy more critical acclaim by reviewers and players. What lesson do you think lies in the difference in the sales and criticism of these two highly successful titles?

Trent Oster: *Diablo* is a study in accessibility and a tight user feedback loop. *Baldur's Gate* is more of a study in story-driven tactical fantasy combat. The two games play very differently and have different mechanisms for keeping the player in the game. *Diablo* has the perfect feedback loop. As a player journeys onward, his/her character is constantly progressing, gaining levels, attributes, and items. The balance of reward versus effort is very satisfying for the player.

Baldur's Gate offers less feedback but counts on the story to drive the character forward. Both games manage to lock players in and give a satisfying gameplay experience.

Neal Hallford: How much have you felt that technology has driven your designs? Do you think the RPG genre is more or less dependent, or any more susceptible, to changes in the machinery than other genres?

Trent Oster: Technology drives all designs. You cannot implement a game without the underlying technology. For instance, *Zork* wouldn't have been possible without the Infocom text parsing engine which drove the game. RPG fans as a whole have been more accepting of older technology than any other game genre. I feel this is currently changing and the demands for outstanding graphics and technology in RPGs is becoming just as strong as it is for more action-based games.

Neal Hallford: What do you think the biggest hurdle is in creating an RPG?

Trent Oster: RPGs require large amounts of content to create. The largest hurdle is undoubtedly getting a content creation team together and completing the game before the technology window slips shut.

Neal Hallford: Most RPGs rely on statistics, attributes, and other measures of development of the player's character. How much of this do you feel that players need to know? Is it better to just show them everything, or should designers stick to the basics? Do you think it's possible to show the player too much?

Trent Oster: RPG game developers use attributes to measure and convey progress to the end user. I think it is important to give the player feedback regarding the progress of his/her character as the game moves forward. Some fans would like every last detail you could make available to them, while others would hate the convoluted display required. It is always a balance between the various types of players and has to be carefully managed.

Neal Hallford: Magic and technology in a game are certainly fun to goof with, but once players are able to walk through walls, float across rivers, and set the forests afire, the best-laid plans of mice and game designers tend to fall apart. How have you managed to give players a feeling of power without upsetting the balance of the design? Do you believe it's possible to have both ultrapowerful spells and an experience that's balanced to be fun for players no matter what they're able to do?

Trent Oster: All games are a balance of risk versus reward. When the player has become so powerful that there is no risk, the game is broken. The only way to keep the game fun is to keep the element of risk, so ultrapowerful characters are fine as long as there is still a challenge in the game.

Neal Hallford: Character classes seem to be both a blessing and a hindrance in one bag. On the one hand, it's easy for a player to quickly pick the kind of character they want to play, but on the downside there always end up being restrictions about items that can't be used, spells that can't be learned, and the like. Are classes a great bane or boon to the experience? Why?

Trent Oster: Classes are a bane in single-player games where you control one character, as they don't allow the player to enjoy all of the content you create. In a cooperative multiplayer game, classes are a blessing as they provide a reason to journey together and share experiences. I personally like the concept of classes as it represents the idea of specialists. Each character is a specialist in what he/she does, forsaking all other abilities to favor his/her focus.

Neal Hallford: Most single-player RPGs today seem to focus almost exclusively on combat skills, while persistent universes like Ultima Online seem to have growing lists of abilities which have nothing to do with fighting. Do you think single-player RPGs are destined to become a death-match ghetto? Are massively multiplayer games just wasting player time with unimportant tasks? What is *up* with player skills today?

Trent Oster: There are a number of reasons for the differences in skills between single and massively multiplayer games. The primary difference is in the social interaction. In a single-player game, the player is the hero and as such is driven along the story line. In massively multiplayer games to date, the player is one of a thousand players and there is nothing driving him/her along so it becomes more of a social environment. Additionally, in a multiplayer environment, the developer has to provide a greater variety of skills to allow personalization of the characters. In a single-player game, the personalization is automatically provided as you, the gamer, face the provided challenges. You define the character through action. In a massively multiplayer RPG, combat doesn't really allow for a huge amount of personalization.

Neal Hallford: We've got more stuff in our role-playing packs today than ever: The Helm of Doom, the Sword of Zhul, the Flask of Less Than Adequate

Healing. . . . Unfortunately, it's also getting harder to find and use what we need when we need it. What advice do you have about designing player inventories?

Trent Oster: Inventories should be large enough to minimize player hassle while still giving the player a feeling of realism.

Neal Hallford: What's the secret to making a combat system rich without being cumbersome?

Trent Oster: There is no secret to making a rich and not cumbersome system. Some users will find the most basic system cumbersome, while others find the most complex system too basic. Combat systems are just like any other system, a compromise between detail and usability. For a more mainstream game it is usually better to err on the side of usability.

Neal Hallford: In the long term, how do you see multiplayer and Internet games affecting the role-playing genre? Do you think there will always be room for both the solo-play and multiplay games? Have these issues affected the way you approached your projects? In what way?

Trent Oster: I see multiplayer games offering us the freedom as designers to attempt to capture the essence of pen-and-paper gaming, social interaction.

Neal Hallford: Is there something that every role-playing designer you know does that drives you nuts, and you just wish you could tell the whole frickin' industry to stop doing?

Trent Oster: Not every designer does this, but if you are working with a license, use the license. I hate it when games are based on a licensed product and yet do something totally different. A license is valuable because the fans are familiar with the material. If you change the material, you lose the value of the license.

Neal Hallford: Assume that the future of the role-playing genre hinges on one piece of advice. What simple thing should every designer who's getting into an RPG understand from the get-go that they might not learn anywhere else?

Trent Oster: If the game isn't fun, people won't play it. Analyze the game for gameplay enjoyment. Just because a rule set is wild and complex doesn't mean it is fun to play.

Neal Hallford: What was the toughest design issue you had to tackle on your most recent FRP?

Trent Oster: The toughest design issue was how to create a system which allowed the end user to create his/her own terrain to adventure in while ensuring high quality visuals. We fought over automatic terrain generation, height map-based terrain systems, constructive solid geometry building blocks. In the end we came up with a tile-based system which fit all of our needs very well and still allowed us a large degree of control over the look of the terrain. We weighed the various issues and solutions and we came to the basic conclusion that the system had to be very easy to use and yet offer enough power to create visually different areas.

CHAPTER 12

SARAH STOCKER: POOL OF RADIANCE 11: RUINS OF MYTH DRANNOR

Sarah W. Stocker is a senior producer and the assistant director of new business at Stormfront Studios
and is currently the lead writer and co-designer of *Pool
of Radiance II: Ruins of Myth Drannor*. She's also currently
the senior producer on *Legend of Alon D'ar*, an RPG
under development for the Playstation 2. Sarah is best
known for her award-winning work on the adventure
games *Byzantine: The Betrayal* and *Star Trek—Deep Space
Nine: Harbinger*.

Neal Hallford: Let's first talk about your background as a gamer. Can you remember your first role-playing experience?

Sarah Stocker: I sure do. It was *Dungeons & Dragons*. I remember the first time I played it with my friend Margi Goldsmith. We were about 11 years old or something, and we were really too little to understand the rules, so we just made up our own until we figured out the way it was supposed to be played. I think the thing that touched me about *D&D* was that it tapped into what I was most interested in which was *story*. I've always been a writer, even as a little kid. My first request for a present was a book to write my poems and stories in. *D&D,* which is all about story and character, gave me a great way to share that with my friends.

I think the wonderful thing about *Dungeons & Dragons* is that it lets everyone that plays it come up with a character and a story, and live through it in a very visceral way. You get very attached to your characters. You know every little detail about them. You know who their parents were, who their grandparents were, what they're carrying in their pockets, what things in the past have broken their hearts, and the things that they wish for—everything that makes them tick. Those are the kind of things good writers know about the characters they work with.

It was great for me to see that the thing that excited me the most—writing stories and characters—excited everyone I played with in the game. In the end, I think that's what we're all reaching for in role-playing games: that excitement. We want to bring the sort of depth of engagement to the player that keeps them up until 3 a.m. to get their beloved character through one last scenario. If you're very lucky, if you're very good, you can help the player get that feeling that you had when you were 14 years old playing make-believe with your friends.

Neal Hallford: Can you think of any experiences that you had as that 14-year-old player that you've carried into your life as a game designer?

Sarah Stocker: I remember two that really stick with me. One is the good example, and the other is the bad example. I really try and remember them today as I'm working on games.

Another Sleepless Knight?—*The danger posed by combat means all the more to players when they've got cause to care whether their avatars live or die. Make sure that you keep the stakes high enough that there's always something that stands to be lost or destroyed without the intervention of the player. (From Legent of Alon D'ar)*

The bad example was a time I was on a little power trip as the neighborhood Dungeon Master, and the kids on my campaign weren't playing *my way.* They weren't doing the things I wanted them to do. It was an outrage! They started exploring all kinds of areas I hadn't developed and doing stuff I hadn't counted on, and generally not falling into line with *my plan.* So I said, "Okay, fine! There's a bolt from the blue and you're all *dead!*" Game over, start again. And to my absolute surprise, they wouldn't start again. Nobody wanted to play in my dungeons anymore. Nobody would play with me for months and months and months. What I had tried to do was punish them for not playing my way, when as a game designer what we all need to do is try to imagine what ways the player will *want* to play the game and support as many ways as you can. Really let your own ego be subsumed by their excitement. So that's something I keep on the negative side. I say to myself, "Don't do that. Don't try and tell the player what is the way to play."

The positive thing I remember is one particular day when I was out with my friend Susan Yuhas and our little gang. We had gotten so into our *D&D* characters that we were actually dressing up and had made these really elaborate costumes. Behind Susan's house there was this construction site that had been abandoned, so it was all just huge, soft hills of sand. We got out there with our little plastic swords—mine would glow in the dark, so I was the coolest of course—and we staged these battles that we had worked out from our campaign. Big huge orc battles and stuff. Eventually, we announced that we had slain everyone and decided to camp.

We celebrated our victory around this little campfire of twigs, which, to our parents' absolute horror I'm sure, we had built in this old construction site. And we sat around this fire and we pretended to eat our meal while we talked and told stories about our supposed valor. I was a bard in that campaign, and so I started singing some song I just made up on the fly, and some other guys started singing as well. We were just a bunch of kids in weird costumes clumped around a smoky bunch of twigs on a dirt mound, but we were so *there,* in that moment, that in my mind that construction site turned into a hill where I could feel the grass and could see the trees, and the song we were singing, which was undoubtedly a cacophonous *mess,* was instead this absolutely melodious bard song to me.

It never left me, that feeling of having created out of nothing an experience and a world that was so palpable to us that we could *go* there when we wanted to. I think that's something we reach for with our players, that we try and build into our games. We try to build worlds where you *want* to be there so badly that you'll imagine out all the parts we can't build for you. Just as we were on that hill that night, we were imagining out a whole countryside that really didn't exist.

Neal Hallford: How do you make that connection with a computer gamer though? It's different than playing in a pen-and-paper game.

Sarah Stocker: It's a sort of theater, isn't it? Just like any theater, you need to ask the audience to suspend their disbelief. And as part of your bargain with that audience, you need to uphold that belief that they're suspending. I think the key element to doing that lies in developing and nurturing the *trust* of the player. Your world needs to be consistent and rewarding enough that the player learns to sit back and trust the game. It's like how with a good movie or a good theater piece, the first minute that you're sitting there, you're thinking, "Eww I'm in my theater chair and it's hot in here . . . ," but the minute the players get on the scene they sweep you up into their world, grab your attention, and never let you go.

The games that gain and keep the trust of the player are the ones where you just forget that you're living someone else's dream and it becomes your dream. At that point, you're just in the world and following the story, exploring and discovering things for yourself. Those are the games that feel the most alive and the most coherent.

It's all about that trust we talked about. The game needs to communicate to you in a vocabulary you can understand and a logic you can follow. For example, in a game that incorporates environment exploration, you don't have situations where there's an obvious enticing door in a room and you can't open it. If there's a door in the room, you need to be able to open it somehow, or it needs to clearly communicate that it's locked and you need a key. If there's someplace you're not supposed to be able to go, it should be *obvious*. There should be a wall rather than a door or the game should build a clear visual or sound vocabulary for doors you can open versus doors you can't. The ways in which you can lose that player's trust is by forgetting that they're seeing the game for the first time, so they're looking to learn the vocabulary of the game and the logic in the game world. Let's say that I'm building a creepy castle that I want you to explore. If I have an up staircase and a down staircase, the player needs to look at that and say, "That's a staircase. I can go up, I can go down. If I go down, I'm going to find something new. If I go up, I'm going to find something new. If, once I go up, I go back down again, I'll be back here." If all that stuff is true, *consistently* true throughout the game, if the environment behaves like a real environment and the cues that we give you—the visual cues, and the text cues, and the audio cues—are all coherent, then you start to build that trust.

Over time you want the player to forget that they're actually playing a game. They're just exploring this environment. If you betray that trust, and you've got a staircase that goes nowhere, now you've got the player going, "Oh, damnit! I clicked on that and it didn't work. Am I going to find other things that I click on that are not going to work?" You've made them doubt the veracity of the world. You're risking their trust.

Neal Hallford: It's interesting though because we get ourselves into a metagame issue. If we put something in a game, there's always an automatic assumption by the player that obviously there must be something that must be done with it.

Sarah Stocker: I think metagame is a good phrase to use. To me it's always about making the world that you've created for the player really feel alive and dynamic. I don't mean necessarily a ton of animations happening. That's great if you can get it, but it's more about the world has its own rules and its own culture, and that culture is something I can make sense of.

For example, I know if I'm in a town, there will be people I can talk to, and people I shouldn't talk to because they may attack me. Those are all things that will make sense with me. If characters behave erratically, or behave repetitively, I start to lose trust. But even if a game has repetitive characters, as long as it's consistent throughout the game, the game is still communicating what the rule and culture of the world is. The closer you can get it to the rules and cultures of our world on a *vocabulary* level, all the better. The farther you get from the culture of our world on a fantasy level, again the better.

Neal Hallford: But you're not talking about vocabulary in the traditional sense.

Sarah Stocker: What I mean by vocabulary versus fantasy is this. In my world, where I live in Marin County, if I see a door and it has a handle on it, I know I can open that door. If it's locked, I'll hear a locked door sound. That vocabulary, that *visual* vocabulary, is something we want to create and maintain for our games. You want to make it clear to the player what the consequences of their actions are. You don't want them to be puzzling out basic navigation. You don't want them to be puzzling out your interface. You want those to be as clear and as coherent as possible. To continue with the door metaphor, a door always means "Open me!" That's now part of the *vocabulary* of the game world. But what is behind the door? If I open the door in my world in my Marin County game development office, I'm going to see a guy who's sitting in a cubicle with a bunch of graph paper in front of him. If you open the door in the computer games we're building, there's a wizard that's huddled over his potions. That's what I mean by the vocabulary being the same, but the content being as fantastic as possible, as heroic as possible.

I think another key part of what keeps game players engaged and interested in role-playing games particularly is a sense of heroism. There are a lot of people who enjoy cyberpunk games, or a sort of dark reality where you sort of play an antihero—those are a different slant on it, but I think the core of role-playing is all about doing heroic deeds, achieving things that we don't have the opportunity to do in our real lives. You want to be able to elevate the player's sense of self. Make them feel stronger, more noble, and more intelligent than their daily life allows them to feel. That heroism I think is key to keeping the player engaged in what you can have them do. That's what keeps them coming back to the game.

We can't give the player complete freedom to do anything they want in a game. But I don't think that's what players really want. We come to entertainment products looking for structure—a beginning, middle, and an end that make sense of the experience. As a player, I want to know what my goals are and surprise myself in the way that I achieve those goals. For example, I know that the story tells me there's an evil troll that lives in the basement of this castle, and that it's got the elf princess held prisoner. I know I have to save the elf princess. That's what everybody in the village is talking about. How am I going to *do* that? That needs to be surprising to me. So I think the challenges that we put in the way of the player have to intrigue the player to the point that they feel when they've overcome those obstacles, they feel incredibly brilliant and *very* heroic.

Neal Hallford: Do you think that surprise necessarily ever means violating the expectations of the player?

Sarah Stocker: I guess what I always look for in the work that I'm doing is am I *hosing* the player? That kind of goes back to that keeping your own ego out of the game. It's very tempting sometimes to go, "Oh, I've got so much trust from the player that I can have them walk down this path, and then *ha Ha!* They thought they were so smart, but no. That's the way to certain death!" That's not the right thing to do. I think surprises like that—unpleasant surprises—are the game designers letting their own egos get in the way of the player's enjoyment. At that point, you're just trying to say, "I'm cleverer than you."

The way that you want to surprise the player is not, when they've been expecting a logical chain of events, to throw a wrench in the logic. I think you always want to keep the logic understandable and accessible. What you want to surprise them with is in the results of performing that logic. Going back to the door example, it would be a terrible thing to have a series of doors in a dungeon where you opened every single door by walking up to it and hitting X on the controller, but one time you walk up to the door that looks exactly the same as every other door, but now when you hit X your guy gets an electric shock and he loses 60 hit points. To me, that's a hose. I had no way as a player to know or suspect that the game would do that. If I don't have a way to know or suspect that damage is coming, it shouldn't come to me. That's not *fun*. The game is defeating the player's expectations in that case. But if that door looked different, if blood was dripping down it or something, then I have a clue as a player. "Whoa, whoa, whoa. I'm not touching that door. I'm gonna see if I can throw this little bat at it or something and see if the bat explodes."

Surprising the player would be more along the lines of you've opened the seventh door in the chain and there's a pair of orcs at the table and instead of attacking you they run up and say, "Oh! Thank god you're here!" There the designer has set up a situation where the player says, "I know orcs. I know what orcs are. Orcs are something I need to kill." But now the orcs are surprising the player by saying, "Wait, wait, wait. We've got a really important reason for you not to kill us." That's a positive surprise: "Hmm. There's more here than I thought there would be," not "There's damage here that I couldn't avoid."

Neal Hallford: Where do you turn for your inspirations?

Sarah Stocker: The side of work I do in the game design process is really all about the story. The way we work here at Stormfront is that we have a team of people that build the design of the game. I'm just one part of that team. Of course, we've got one person that owns the design doc, and has the final call on the design elements, but we've got programmers, artists, writers, level designers, and audio designers that all help to define the design. The role that I have in that process, most recently on *Pool of Radiance II*, is lead writer. I work, usually with a writing partner, to come up with the story, characters, dialog, and overall game flow for the game. I'm always coming from the story perspective on the products that I work on, because that's my background. My degree is in creative writing.

With a fantasy game, *Pool* for example, my writing partner and I read every piece of literature on the *Forgotten Realms* that we could get our hands on, since the game was set there in the *Dungeons & Dragons* universe. Wizards of the Coast was wonderful about providing material for us. It was really terrific.

But aside from that, whenever I'm looking at a story that somebody can be engaged in, and it's in the fantasy genre, and it's heroic in nature, I go right back to Tolkien. *Lord of the Rings* is pretty much the definitive heroic *Dungeons & Dragons* starting point. There are other great fantasy series—Lloyd Alexander's *Chronicles of Prydain* and *The Narnia Chronicles* are skewed to a little bit younger audience than our games would be, but they all have one thing in common. They all built a set of characters that, while clearly communicating in *archetype*, do not become stereotypes. That's a fine balance that I think we walk in any kind of fantasy genre, whether it's games or books or stories or whatever. You want to have characters in the game that are archetypes so that they're recognizable. "Ahh, he's the wise old wizard. Ahh, she's the dynamic young girl searching for something. Ahh, he is the young male protagonist." You want to be able to immediately grasp what archetype the characters are in. But then, on top of that, you want to give them enough depth so that there's something unique and memorable about their personalities. It's not enough to have a stereotypical wise old wizard, you have to give them something that makes him *real.* What is his background, where did he come from, what does he *want?* That's a very big question you have to ask yourself. And what does he fear?

So I always start with the story. I look at Tolkien in particular because that's where it all comes from. It's still so wildly successful to this day because for most of us it was the first time any of us read a book and said to ourselves, "Oh my god, this is somewhere completely new, and I want to be there. I want to understand everything about that culture. I want to hear elves sing. I want to eat hobbit cooking!" It really created a world for us all that we could go to and feel comfortable in and feel attached to those characters. We feared for them and loved them and cried over them. I think we're all still reaching for that in computer games. We want to build a world for the player and engage them emotionally, not just take them for a quick spin around the mouse pad.

Neal Hallford: What's the most important things you've learned along the way about putting games together?

Somewhere, Inside the Rainbow: RPGs are always best when they can take the player to places they've never seen or to experience things impossible in day-to-day reality. (From Legend of Alon D'ar.)

Recapturing the Radiance

Pool of Radiance II: The Ruins of Myth Drannor is the follow-up to a highly acclaimed game first released by SSI in 1988. The first in a series of successful "gold box" games which utilized the *Dungeons & Dragons* ruleset, the first *Pool* is still regarded as a classic in the computer RPG genre.

Sarah Stocker: I think the most important thing is to get a lot of feedback early, and often. With the game story from when it's a concept that's only a page, to when it's a 40-page document, to when it's all the dialog in the game and it's hundreds and hundreds of pages—I try to give it to as many people as possible to get feedback on what they like and what they don't like and make changes. I think early on in people's careers it's difficult for them to do that. They're protective of their work, and they have to be the one person who knows what's right all the time. But you're going to get a much better story and a much better game if you get as many people's feedback as possible. It's sort of a first taste of what the player's reaction is going to be, and you should always tailor what you're doing to maximize the player's enjoyment.

The core thing is to focus on the player. Try to always put yourself in the player's shoes, try to always imagine it's the first time you've ever seen the game. The first time you ever encounter this scenario, or interface, or puzzle, what do you think your reaction is going to be? Never ever ever say to yourself, "Oh, this is just a game." Those are the words of death. You can never make a good game if you say that, because it's *not* just a game. It needs to be an experience, it needs to be something that the player remembers with joy afterwards.

With the fantasy genre, with role-playing in particular, its important to *embrace* the mythic. Don't be afraid to have a broadsword that's six feet long and 25 inches wide that no human could ever lift. Realism is not the point. We get enough reality in our everyday lives. Over the top is where the player wants to be, within the bounds of not making it campy—we don't want that. But mythic is what the fantasy genre is all about. We need to embrace that and not be afraid of it in the writing and in the game design.

Another important thing is to cherish the trust of the player. I know we talked a little bit about this before, but it's vital to game design and storytelling in games—you have to create and keep their trust. That's going to help them enjoy their experience. And don't forget that they have no clue what you *intended*. Don't confuse the effort with the results. They will never know what you meant to do. So if you're looking at a scenario that you think is crystal clear and somebody says to you, "Huh? What's supposed to be going on here?" there's a problem. If you have to write a paragraph to explain what's going on there, remember that the player is never going to *see* that paragraph.

Neal Hallford: A lot of lessons we learn by screwing up. Is there something in particular you've learned that you wish you could go back and fix?

Sarah Stocker: Oh, absolutely. One of them that is very, very obvious to me now is in *Star Trek: Deep Space Nine—Harbinger,* which was an adventure game, not a role-playing game. We had a three-dimensional maze in this alien fortress, and you had to make your way through it to get to a key power source. In theory I thought the maze was a great idea because it was in three dimensions. You had to get up, and then get down, and it was very difficult to navigate. In those days mazes were quite the rage. I remember having a conversation with one of the other game designers on the product and saying, "Make sure when you're laying it out that you have to go *back* through it to return to the other level. And anytime the player wants to go to the power source, they have to go all the way through the maze again." *What was I thinking?* Did I have a particularly bad day? Was I just letting my sadistic impulses run wild? It was just about the most evil design decision I've ever made. Unfortunately, by the time I realized it, the game was on the shelves. So yeah, if I could go back in time and change something, I would definitely make that a one-way maze. That was just way, way too difficult.

Neal Hallford: It's interesting that you mentioned the maze. It seems to me when I was getting started in the industry that all role-playing games had lots of puzzles and lots of mazes. That stuff seems to have almost completely vanished. What's your theory about what happened? Is it due to the influx of mainstream audiences that have less patience with that sort of thing?

Sarah Stocker: That's a good question. I think everyone in the industry has seen in the last few years a lot more mainstream growth, and we're really reaching out to the new players. We're thinking about those players who just bought their computers to get on the Internet, and we want them to be able to play and enjoy our games. So I think all of us have worked really hard at simplifying interfaces so that the learning curve for a game is much less steep than it used to be.

We used to have the hard-core gamers who were "geeks like us." They were willing to spend three days just figuring out the interface because they trusted that even though it's complex to get into, in the end, once you've mastered the game, it's going to be the quickest way to move around. But the new player, and increasingly the *core* gamer, is not willing to put up with complexity in interface anymore. In order to make sure that we're bringing those people, and then making the game accessible to more people, we have to simplify the interface, we have to get rid of *defeating* kinds of puzzles like mazes. Mazes are tough to make fun.

Frankly, I think the reason they used to be in there more often than not was because they were cheap. We used to have wall sets that we built games around. You could just blam in a maze and you've instantly got 30 hours of gameplay. I think now we'd rather sacrifice *hours* of gameplay for *better* gameplay, more enjoyable gameplay. Also I think audiences nowadays aren't necessarily looking for an *80-*hour game. They're looking for a game that they can finish in a few weeks. They're coming home from work, after a hard day, and looking to play for a few hours. On that schedule, they're looking for a few weeks of enjoyment for their $60. Then they're ready to go out and buy the next one. There's also a lot more good games on the market, so that next game is easy to find, which didn't use to be the case.

In any case, I think puzzles are still a part of most role-playing games, but they are often very expensive parts. So if you can find a good, really enjoyable core gameplay feature set, and build the game around that with reusable features at which the player can become more and more expert, I think that's a very attractive way to go.

Neal Hallford: What's been the toughest thing you've had to try and tackle on either *Pool of Radiance* or on *Legend of Alon D'ar*?

Sarah Stocker: It's hard for me to speak specifically about those two games because I'm very close to them right now. But I can be more general about the genre as a whole.

The toughest thing that I think we always, always have to deal with is balancing resources and scope with quality. You've got a set schedule and a set amount of money to make a game, and you want it to be the highest quality game that it can be, but you also want it to have a certain amount of scope. It's very difficult to rein yourself in on the scope and not make the game so *huge* that it's going to be too huge for the player to enjoy. You're going to be stretching your resources so much to make the game as it is. That battle is always a really tough one.

Technology is the other thing. We're always, always on the cutting edge of technology when we're making a computer game. We're always using the coolest new technology that we can develop, and there are risks inherent in that. There's also a big learning curve every single time for the designers to find out what is actually the coolest thing about this technology from the player's point of view. How can we best use the engine that we have so that the player will get the most enjoyment out of the game?

Neal Hallford: *Pool of Radiance II* will be the first computer game to utilize the new *Dungeons & Dragons 3rd Edition* rules, correct?

Sarah Stocker: Yes! We're very proud of that.

Neal Hallford: How much pressure have you felt about staying true to the world that was given to you? Were you given much leeway for your own interpretation of the rules?

Sarah Stocker: Wizards of the Coast have been the most amazing partner for us. They worked with us very closely when they were first developing the 3E rules, and they kept us in touch with where they were going. Whenever we would go to them with a problem and say, "Gosh, this is really difficult for us to do," they'd come back and say, "Okay, here's another way to approach it." So I felt like we had a wonderful resource at our elbow. Anytime we wanted to talk with them about it, the guys who were actually writing up the rules would meet with us and help brainstorm a solution to whatever problem we were running into.

But I think part of what's so *great* about the 3rd Edition rules is that they are simpler, and more logical. And they fit much more nicely into computer role-playing games than the previous edition did. So our job was actually in some ways easier using those rules than it would have been otherwise.

One of the tricky things, of course, was making sure that we kept up with the changes they had. At some point we had to freeze and say, "Okay, after this point we can't incorporate any new changes. We have to lock the design." But we're very happy with where that point was. We don't feel like there were any big gaps because they kept so clear with us all the time about what they were doing and what the rules were as they evolved.

So I guess I have to say that we didn't feel a lot of pressure. We felt very welcome into their world. They gave us a huge amount of resource material, which was just a geek dream. We got just boxes and boxes of *D&D* sets, and books, and other stuff. We were wallowing in it. "Woo hoo!" It was great. And when we came up with the story and pitched it to them, they really enjoyed it. We had worked in a lot of the background material, including lore from one of their most recent books, *The Cult of the Dragon*. The Cult of the Dragon is featured quite heavily in *Pool of Radiance*, so they were happy to see that we were digging deep into the background materials.

Occasionally they gave us gentle course corrections when we strayed from the heart of the material, but I really feel with any license it's my job as the writer to know the license and to communicate it well. The great thing about *Dungeons & Dragons* is that it is a very powerful license, but it's also very deep and very rich. It's *designed* for people to make up their own stories. So it was very easy for my writing partner and I to make up our own story within that world. It didn't feel oppressive in any way. It's also much easier to work with people who are gaming guys and who know that it's all about the player's enjoyment in the end. It's much more difficult to work with television and movie people who don't necessarily understand gaming and the needs of the player.

Neal Hallford: Let's talk about those needs of the player a bit. The faces of the people who are playing seem to be changing. When I got started, I was given the demographic of 18–25, male players. You still hear that a lot. But last year there was a study which seemed to indicate more women were playing online than men. How much difficulty have you had in addressing the "gender gap," both professionally and as a designer?

Sarah Stocker: There are stereotypes that people in the past have gone with that we have moved away from now. I don't know that it's necessarily because we're trying to appeal more to the female market, or whether we're just growing up as an industry. In a role-playing game now you wouldn't want to have a half-naked barbarian girl be your *reward* for some victory or whatever. We try to keep really blatant sexism out of it. I think that's come because we're more grown up as an industry, but it may be because Stormfront in particular is very sensitive to gender issues. We always have been, from when the company started.

Still, we always try to make the player characters in games, the protagonists, feel heroic and be of heroic proportions. In other words, if I'm playing a game and I as a woman decide to play a male character, I don't necessarily want to see a weedy, weak-looking guy. I want to play a big barbarian. And if I'm playing a female character, I want to play a very attractive, strong, dynamic-looking woman. I think no matter what gender a player character is, you want their representation on-screen to be heroic, to be superhuman. I don't mean like Superman, but more idealized than a real human would be.

In game stories these days, stereotypes are being broken down a lot more. There aren't just weak women and strong men. There are also strong women and weak men. There are evil women, there are evil men. It's a lot more even. There are a lot more women in gaming now, more women players. So it may just be an evolution of the culture that we're reflecting as well.

I've read some figures that seem to indicate women players tend to dislike complex interfaces, and so it may be part of the broader movement towards making simpler interfaces that's brought in a larger female audience. I've also read that women aren't very competitive, but *personally* I can tell you as a woman I'm very definitely competitive. Don't underestimate that if you ever play *Magic* with me! I guess it's hard for me to say there's a gender gap. I didn't feel any kind of tension between things that would appeal to the male audience and things that

The girl's got game: Women gamers want to see female protagonists who are more than eye candy for male players. There's nothing wrong with making them attractive, but make sure they've got an equal shot at being real heroes. (From Legend of Alon D'ar.)

would appeal to the female audience when I was working on any of these games. I did sometimes feel like I wanted to push for more equality in the roles of men and women in the story of the game. But I don't think that's necessarily just bending it towards the female player. I think it's just because we're moving towards that culturally.

Neal Hallford: What about women on design teams though? By and large, most of our designer colleagues I see working in the industry are still predominately male. What needs to change to make it more equitable for women designers?

Sarah Stocker: We've actually talked about this as a team, about how we can recruit more women. Part of it comes from the fact that a lot of designers come from the programming fields, and the writing field, and in some cases the art field. Those are all still very male-dominated. I think that's just because most industries *have* been male-dominated up into this century. We're just starting to see women in all kinds of different fields come to the top of the food chain because they started getting into the industry much, much later than men.

It's also only been recently that women as a huge demographic have been recognized as being *interested* in gaming. And this is so much a fan-driven industry. Most of us got into this business because we loved games. I answered the ad for Stormfront because it was a game company, and I just thought that would be the coolest thing in the world. So I think there'll be a kind of a cycle. The more female players, and especially the more younger female players we have, the more female game designers, artists, programmers, and writers we *will* have, because those players will start targeting games as a career choice.

There's a little bit of an insidious bent towards the 14–18-year-old gaming demographic being almost completely male. When you look at games made for that demographic, they tend to be very, very violent—and I don't mean to be perpetuating a stereotype—but I don't think women in general are that interested in *Quake,* or ultraviolent games. Until we get games that hit that female demographic, we're not going to have an overwhelming influx of women in the gaming industry. I think you do start young. You do get interested in games when you're a teenager. That's how the industry as a whole gets new players.

Neal Hallford: You're currently working on both a Playstation 2 RPG and a PC role-playing game. What do you see as being the biggest difference in how RPGs get implemented across the different platforms?

Sarah Stocker: I think what the console audience wants is very different from what the PC audience wants. The tools that we have to give the player what they want on both platforms are very different. On a PC, you have the mouse and the entire keyboard at your disposal for an input device. On the consoles, you only have the controller.

On a console game, the interface must by necessity be *extremely* streamlined so that you can give input through the interface, and complex things happen with a simple control. With the PC, you can have a lot more "pop-up" kind of interface items because you've got the mouse and the whole keyboard to work with.

The way that you interact with the environment is very different as well. On a PC, you're rolling over things with your mouse, and you can click on stuff. With a console environment you either use the *player character* as an input device, so that you walk your character up to something and hit X and something happens, or you get into a horrible situation where you have to tab through things using the game pad. So you really want to focus on the protagonist characters being the trigger for events. You're navigating your characters over towards objects and interacting with them that way.

I think the key thing is really about what the expectation is on the different platforms. I think PC gamers expect to have a very free-form, deep, and broad experience where they have a lot of control. There's a lot of exploration in PC RPGs where you're wandering around in a really wide world, and you expect to have a lot of freedom when you go back and forth. Whereas with a console game you expect to be guided much more clearly, and much more linearly, along a story line. You still want to have freedom in the environment, but you want to have a very clear sense of where the finish line is and you want the game to take care of more details for you.

Of course, a lot of what players expect comes from what games have been popular on those platforms. *Final Fantasy* has really defined for the console what an RPG should be on the console. And there are good and bad elements to that. For the PC gamers, all of the various role-playing games on the PC have defined that. There isn't such a clear-cut winner there.

Neal Hallford: Do you think there are any other content differences?

Sarah Stocker: There's a different layer of content on the PC than there is on the consoles. On the consoles, I think people expect a clear, almost operatic story line. On the PC, people expect a lot of depth of character, a lot of side quests, a lot of the world coming to life. There's almost a granularity difference. It's almost like a finer level of granularity on the PC. There's a lot of fiddly little bits. You can talk to every single person in town and interact with them. You expect everybody to be able to speak to you. On a console game you don't necessarily want that. You want to be *moving* through the game. You want action happening everywhere, movies rather than dialog. So again I think it does come down to expectation. And there's also an age difference in the key demographics for both of them. Consoles have historically tended to attract younger gamers than the PC market.

Neal Hallford: What developments have you seen in the industry which really excite you?

Sarah Stocker: Absolutely the most exciting thing I see now is the respect we're starting to give to excellent storytelling in games. RPGs are judged *very* heavily on the story. Players get attracted to the characters. They get engaged in the stories and move through them. And the industry has come to realize that that is a *very* valuable part of the package. Seeing people come to that realization over time has been fantastic. I mean, you and I both were there when game companies hardly even thought of hiring a professional, trained writer. They'd have the programmer put in something that says, "You pick up the short sword." But now that's simply not acceptable. We hire professional writers, and professional voice-over talent to create and bring to life the stories in games.

Neal Hallford: What's your advice to the future designers of tomorrow?

Sarah Stocker: What I would tell anyone who wants to become a writer is to write every single day. And when you're not writing, read. And only read excellent material. Don't fill your head with junk. And I'd give similar advice to game designers. Be thinking about a game that you would build, or a story you would want to tell, or a system that you want to refine all the time. Play everything you can get your hands on. Try to quickly identify if you like something or if you don't like it. If you don't like it, try to understand *why* you don't like it so you can learn things to avoid. If you're playing something and you're so sucked in that you absolutely love it, try and define for yourself why that is, in very concrete terms. And try to figure out what you would change to make it even better.

As far as getting into the industry, start from a position where you have a lot of contact with as many different disciplines as possible. Just showing up at a gaming firm and saying, "Hey, I'm a smart and dedicated person. I'm willing to do whatever it takes. Make copies. Put all the voice-over scripts into binders. Whatever it is you need, I will do it. Please, please bring me on as a production assistant." That's how a lot of people get into movies. You just go on set and do whatever is needed. Make yourself somebody who is indispensable because the way that you do your job is completely egoless. Just show up, help everybody else as much as you can, and *listen* to them. Ask as many questions as you can about what they do. Learn what it is everybody on the project is doing. The best designers are the ones that understand other disciplines enough to take the best advantage of what they're doing. So starting in that role I think is a good way. People can also break into the industry through the testing path, signing up to play-test and report bugs on games in development. These aren't necessarily big fun jobs, but the people you'll encounter and the experience you get will be well worth the work.

As far as general advice goes, I'd say don't lose sight of the player. Don't fall in love with some idea and forget that someone who sees it with fresh eyes may not love it as much as you do. You know, in writing, we have the phrase "kill your darlings," which means edit out the parts you're most attached to. It's true in game design. There may be some wonderful scenario that you've concocted which is super, super complex and you're just patting yourself on the back because it's so cool. You knew that it took so long to master the tool that you were using in order to get this to work, and you've just spent a ton of resources on it to get it to work. But if the players you try it run into it and say, "Well that sucked," cut it. Be ready to kill your darlings every time. It's a tough thing to do, but it's a vital step sometimes.

The best advice I've heard is "Keep it simple." Identify what is at the core of your game from the very beginning, always be able to tell yourself in a nutshell what's the theme of your game. What is the heart of the game? Check what you're doing against that theme, against the heart, against the core gameplay— every single time. If you can stick to it, you're going to help to build the player's sense of trust that is so vital.

CHAPTER 13

JON VAN
CANEGHEM:
MIGHT &
MAGIC 1-1X

Jon Van Caneghem is the president and founder of New World Computing in Agoura Hills, California. Creator of the long-running fantasy role-playing series *Might and Magic,* he is currently over-seeing the design of four separate titles: *Might & Magic IX, Heroes 4, Legends of Might & Magic,* and *Heroes Chronicles.*

Neal Hallford: Before we start getting into specifics, I'd like to talk about all the different *Might & Magic* titles that you're making right now. How are they all different from one another?

Jon Van Caneghem: *Heroes of Might & Magic* is our strategy line of games. They have their origins actually in a game I made eons ago called *King's Bounty*. We later decided to turn that into a strategy series using the *Might & Magic* name, background, characters, story, world—stuff like that. *Heroes 4* is a turn-based single or multiplayer strategy game where you control armies of creatures. The idea is to take out the other players or perform specific quests. It's an overhead type of a game with an adventure world and a separate combat screen.

Might & Magic IX is a continuation of the traditional *Might & Magic* series of 3-D role-playing games and is pretty much the same role-playing system that's been around forever. We'll keep making them as long as people still like them. We obviously try and keep up with all the newer technologies and graphics and sound, but the basic principles are the same as they've always been. You've got a party of characters in a 3-D environment following a preset story with a *lot* of freedom for the player to do whatever he wants.

Legends is pretty much a departure for us. It's a multiplayer Internet action title with a lot of role-playing and fantasy elements to it. It's a lot different from your regular RPG, but the *Might & Magic* name helps us get by the retailers. If you just tell them that something is Game X, they'll never have heard of it. They won't know what to do with it. So having the *Might & Magic* name on it helps. It's still wizards and dragons and stuff like that, but it's much more of a first-person action game based on team cooperation. You've got a good team and an evil team trying to accomplish exclusive or similar goals in a time-based scenario. It's played on the Internet with up to 20 different people playing at one time.

Chronicles is pretty much an extension of the *Heroes* line. We've taken the old *Heroes 3* game and made a simpler, you might say watered-down, version, with a lot less options. As we evolved from one, to two, to three, it got a lot more complicated like we gamers tend to get. But it made it harder and harder for new gamers to get into the series. So it was a call for a very simplified version of *Heroes 3*, and that's what *Chronicles* is all about.

Neal Hallford: What's your first memory of playing a role-playing game?

Jon Van Caneghem: That's easy. First edition, white box edition of *Dungeons & Dragons*. I think it was in the late '70s. It came from TSR and had three white booklets in it. I think I still have it here somewhere. We tried to sit down and figure out what the heck this thing meant. We got it all wrong of course, but the whole concept of it—a game with a game master with no really set rules, just some sort of system that everyone was clear on—that combined with the fantasy element of it was just totally intriguing.

Neal Hallford: What do you think your early role-playing experiences taught you?

Jon Van Caneghem: Probably the biggest thing that's stuck with me over time was that you can never predict what players are going to do. When I was a game master I learned that I had to keep my adventures open enough for any particular turn that players wanted to take. I've always tried to keep that in mind in *Might & Magic*. You don't want to make the story so rigid or make all the character interactions so tailored to the one grand story that people can't vary from it. That was probably the biggest thing I learned from the pen-and-paper experience. You just can't predict people, and the more you try and force them down an exact path, the more a lot of them fight back and absolutely refuse to do what you were expecting.

Neal Hallford: Given the fact that we're working with computers, and we don't have a dungeon master that can arbitrarily adapt to any given situation, how do you compensate for the desire of the role-player to go off into an unexpected direction?

Jon Van Caneghem: Well, I think it's been a misnomer over the years to call what we're doing role-playing games. We're actually making the farthest thing from it. There's really *not* much role-playing going on. What we're doing now is a cross between strategy and adventure games. We got mislabeled along the way, so we've been stuck with the comparison to the pen-and-paper games for years when it wasn't exactly a valid comparison.

But I think the key is that you have to understand that the computer does some things very well, and does horribly at other things. There's a lot of the person-to-person dynamic of the paper-and-pencil games that you just can't capture with a computer. But when it comes to rules, technical issues, figuring out the dynamics of a situation—the computer does phenomenally well at doing those tasks quickly. I've seen pen-and-paper games where people were sitting there with their calculators trying to figure out muzzle velocities, and it got pretty boring very fast. You'd have one combat that took seven hours to complete, and that's a problem.

The important thing about using the computer is that it allows you to handle all that stuff in the background. You can have a lot of combats, you can have a lot of dynamic things happening, and it all happens instantly. It's primarily an issue of focusing on the strengths of the medium you're working with.

Neal Hallford: What's your process when you're putting together a new game?

Jon Van Caneghem: I tend to start with something visual. If there's some cool effect or if there's some technical advance that will allow me to display a character in a new way—that's how I get rolling. If I can see a whiz-bang visual, I can imagine a whole game around it.

We're really reversed here from what most people think it takes to make these games. Story usually comes last with us. We're much more geared toward technology—not so much the mechanics, but the game system itself. Once that's much more solidified, we can make a story, an interface, and everything else that fits well with what the mechanics can do. A lot of other people have had trouble with designing a story and a concept for a game, and then handing it over to the programmers and saying, "Here, make this work." That can lead to disaster. Sometimes it can work for other people, but in our case it just doesn't fit with our approach. We get our system working first, and then we write our story and interactions around what that system does well. That's definitely the way to make a product in a reasonable amount of time on a normal budget.

Neal Hallford: Do you have many sources outside the traditional gaming industry that you draw on a lot?

Jon Van Caneghem: There's ideas everywhere. I try and keep up with popular culture—movies or big trends or whatever. The important idea is to keep an eye on the big picture. I also still play quite a few board games. One of the most *important* things is that myself—and many of the people on my team—play most all the other games that come out, and we're just as much a bunch of game *players* as we are game *makers*. That gives us some great ideas on what people have either tried to do, what they do well, or what went over well with the public. We think about what we could do better, or what we can take from someone else and move *forward*. The worst thing is reinventing the wheel every time you build a product. That's just crazy.

Neal Hallford: But reinventing the wheel is how many of us get started. Can you remember how you got started on your first "wheel"?

Jon Van Caneghem: It was the moment I questioned why the computer game I was playing didn't do what I wanted it to do. I was playing *Wizardry I* and *Ultima I* and was addicted to them both, but at some point I said, "Hey, why can't I do this? Why can't I do that?" I saw there were things that should be in the realm of what the computer could do that were perfectly logical, but the game wouldn't let me do them. That's when I knew I could add something new. Little did I know what I was getting into.

At that point in my life I'd played a lot of the pen-and-paper RPGs and other board games. I started looking into it games-programming-wise and didn't see any reason why I shouldn't give it a shot. So low and behold I said, "I'm going to make one of these. I think I can probably do it," and I went at it. I think it was my blind faith *knowing* that I could make a great game—just viewing the computer and the programming as obstacles I had to get over—that was what enabled me to go forward. I taught myself programming. I was already a math major, so I kind of understood the logics of it, but I still had to learn the coding side of it. So I banged away at it, and it took me a couple of years, but at last I came up with *Might & Magic I*.

At the time there wasn't a good publishing and distribution system in place. The industry was still young. I took out an ad in the game magazines—there were only two of them back then—and had an 800 number in my apartment. I put together the packaging, the advertising, and everything else that needed done. I learned a lot of different trades. It's amazing what you can learn when you're forced to. It then just became a chain of events. How am I going to make this? How am I going to do that? Okay, let's find out. So I went down that path and sold the game out of my apartment, and in the first month I sold 5,000 games. I was kicking butt. After that I got numerous offers for distribution and publishing. I eventually chose to go the distribution route, created New World as a publisher, then got some friends together and started growing from there. That was in 1984, 16 years ago now.

Neal Hallford: Now you're considered one of the founding fathers of the computer role-playing genre. What's that like for you?

Jon Van Caneghem: It's so funny, because when I first started, the industry really treated me as the newbie. And all the old, founding companies and forefathers were looking down on me: *How dare you break into our industry?* Now all these years later I'm one of the few ones left. There's been two generations since.

When you were at New World and we were doing *Planet's Edge* and *Might & Magic III* together, we were like the new kids. Now we're the old dogs. The weirdest thing of all is so many people have come, done a product, and moved on in the life of New World. So many of them, including yourself, have gone on to work on such great titles. I'm always proud when I see someone that's worked here that did great work for us, and that's gone on and done something really good on their own.

Neal Hallford: Obviously you and *Might & Magic* are still around for a reason. You don't survive for all these years in the industry unless you know what you're doing. What do you think the secret's been to *Might & Magic*'s longevity?

Jon Van Caneghem: Not to be selfish, but I think it's partially been because I've been working on them. I try and maintain my view on how the game should be. But the number one thing is that we want to make a game that's *fun* to play. We try not to succumb to the pressure of whatever the latest brouhaha is. As long as we can maintain the fun for the people working on it, it's going to come out good and we know that people will like it. That's the bottom line.

If the team working on it isn't totally into it, and they don't think it's cool, it's not going to work. It's my job to maintain that, to keep everyone happy. You've got to like what you're doing.

Neal Hallford: It's interesting though that you got started from a little company in your living room, and that it's survived the long haul. That seems like such a rarity anymore. We haven't seen a really successful garage game start-up since John Carmack did his thing. Do you think it's possible that the days of the one- and two-person companies have come to an end?

Jon Van Caneghem: Probably, but there's always exceptions. I think people thought it came to an end in the late '80s before Carmack did what he did, but he proved everyone wrong. But there hasn't been anyone since, not in any significant way. Nothing that's been as big of a hit. I think there will always be room for a brilliant, bright star to shine through, but in today's world of marketing and distribution it's *very* tough.

I think a lot of that comes from the pressure we get to only make absolute A titles. Sometimes there are things which I think *could* have been A titles that are lost because of lack of attention, marketing, and sales. They get overshadowed by other titles that happen to come out in the same quarter. The business side of it is much bigger and more complex.

Mighty Magical

As the *Might & Magic* series prepares to enter its second decade as a cornerstone of the computer RPG market, it's amazing to see how much ground has been covered in this long-running series. Chronicling the fallout from an epic cosmic battle between a mysterious race of *presumably* benevolent planet-seeders known as the Ancients, and a second race of creatures called the Kreegan, every title has built on the story premise first laid down in the original.

Semi-inspired by an episode of the first *Star Trek* series entitled "For the World Is Hollow and I Have Touched the Sky," the *Might & Magic* line has freely mixed technology with magic to create its own brand of science fantasy (though with a much heavier emphasis on the latter than on the former.)

Frequently laced with challenging puzzles, the series has featured many mind-bending posers which have forced players to "think outside the box." Players of the first title, *Might & Magic I: Secret of the Inner Sanctum,* had to pay very careful attention as they were mapping out the maddening "Soul Maze." The answer to a puzzle they had to solve in order to exit the maze was written out with the very walls of the maze itself. If the players were paying attention, and turned the map upside down, they'd find the answer they sought in form of a comical little message, "Help! My Name Is Sheltem!"

As well known for its sense of humor as for its clever conundrums, the *Might & Magic* epic frequently comments on popular culture and on itself. Puns and jokes frequently crop up in the games. Players are never too surprised to find themselves facing monsters with names like Quizinarts, or characters like Carrion who is looking for his "wayward son."

But for all the familiar qualities this historic role-playing series has developed over the years, it is also a series which has grown with the times. Originally players were only treated to a *Wizardry*-like *simulation* of a 3D world, but the latest editions of *Might & Magic* will be driven by the powerful Lithtec engine, opening up new possibilities for gameplay. Once stolidly single player, the series is now branching out with the *Legends of Might & Magic* line to embrace a multiplayer experience. Whatever its true source of magic, it has provided a "mighty" good playing experience for generations of role-playing enthusiasts.

In the old days, there was a lot more demand than there were games. So if you had something good, it didn't matter if it was well-marketed. It was going to sell. Today there's so many products. The production quality level is very high on almost all of them, and it's very easy to get lost in the crowd.

It used to be that play mattered 99.9 percent, and everything else was the rest. Now the actual play may even be less than half of the actual battle. In some cases it's not even *much* of the battle. It's a different game today, and it's not just about the game.

Neal Hallford: Given the fact that the competition for shelf space has become so vicious, how do you think that affects the overall place that RPGs have in today's market?

Jon Van Caneghem: There's always room for a great, well-made modern title that's well done, has modern production qualities, and is halfway decently presented to the public. It will still do well. The main problem is just that there's so many titles. You used to be able to count on a few hands all the great titles that would come out. Now it's literally in the thousands that come out every year. It's not even so much of what category it is. If there's a big title coming out in a particular month, it doesn't really matter *what* category of game it is. We're still in that fight for shelf space.

Neal Hallford: Was the diversification of the *Might & Magic* "brand" an effort to capture some of the *Diablo* market, or is it more of an attempt to bring the player in through a strategy title and then lead them into the main role-playing titles?

Jon Van Caneghem: The first thing to consider is that the shelf space of the world is so crowded, having the *Might & Magic* name on something—because it's recognized—gets us over the first hurdle to get the products to the consumers. You've got to get it to them first, and you have to give both the retail folks and the consumers the confidence that it's going to be a quality title, so having the name on it helps.

Right now with *Heroes 4* we don't even call it *Heroes of Might & Magic* anymore. It's going to be just *Heroes 4*. It's grown up, left the nest, and it's flying on its own. So that strategy worked. Now it's quite possible to *overdo* the strategy and dilute the whole brand, but it would be silly to have this great brand and not take some advantage of it. If you come out with a game called Game X, nobody even tries it. That's a disappointing fact of life in this industry.

Neal Hallford: When you first started telling people that you designed computer games for a living, what did they not get about what you do?

Jon Van Caneghem: Most people who aren't in the industry seem to think what I do is like a writing job. To me a true game designer is someone that's got to be in there all the way into the guts of the engine, into the code. They've got to understand how that works. They're managing every interface and piece of graphics. It's really the anchor to all the different pieces of the product. The designer has to be the one that understands how all the different parts come together, to be able to direct all the members of the team.

Many companies have split it up now where the game designer is just someone who lays out a technical document, and there may be other people above him who coordinate it, but I think the more successful ones are the ones where the lead game designer is in control of all the separate pieces.

Neal Hallford: Running all those separate elements, you've probably picked up a valuable lesson or two. What do you think has been the most valuable thing you've learned through the years?

Jon Van Caneghem: Probably the biggest thing is that for every person out there that buys your game, there's going to be *that* many different reasons—that many different little things—that someone will like or dislike about your title. When you build it, you're thinking about what you like and what you want to make. When people buy it and play with it, there's so many people out there who play it for so many different reasons. One person likes the graphics, one person likes the sound, one likes to just walk around, one likes to kill things. Every little combination of every variable in-between. So you can't be stubborn headed as the designer and say, "I don't like that stuff so I'm not going to put it in. I don't like that feature or that option, so I don't want it." You have to have an open mind. You may have to consider features that you personally might not even be that fond of, but your players enjoy it.

Neal Hallford: How do you make sure that you provide enough details to keep everyone happy?

Jon Van Caneghem: Most of our games rely on the game system to provide a lot of the details. We usually have a large world filled in largely by a system, and then we go back and add details *by hand* to places that feel bare, or we fix things that don't feel appropriate or just don't cut the mustard. That's the polish, and that's what takes most of our time. So we get the system in, take a shot at what we think is going to be the right size for the world—because once you commit you're stuck with it—and then as time permits, we fill in more hand work. When we run out of time, we're out of details.

From a business perspective, you always want to approach the design like you're laying down layers on a cake. If things go wrong, and if the game ends up being less detailed by your ship date than you had originally imagined it, you can still put it out the door. You'll protect yourself that way. You'll still have a good product that will stand on its own. If you don't do it that way, and you miss all the dates, and the things you thought were going to take a week each take a month instead, you're in trouble with your time. That's part of the challenge of being a designer. Not just putting together a great game, but putting it together in an allotted time period.

Neal Hallford: Do you think you're more in touch with the time demon because you've been on the administrative side as well as the creative end?

Jon Van Caneghem: Because I ran New World from when it was nothing all the way to the day I sold it, I had a real good handle on the implications of pushing a week or a month from the financial side of things. For me to make the call about whether a specific feature was cut or not was a lot easier when I knew both sides. I knew how important a feature was to make the game good, and I knew how much it was going to cost the company in terms of time and opportunity and money spent and windows and marketing. It's definitely a balancing call. If I know that a feature is absolutely critical, then there's no doubt I'm going to postpone the release. If I'm thinking like a game designer, I'm not as concerned by how many units it ultimately sells, but how good the product ultimately is. Of course from the business side you don't really, honestly care how good the game is as long as it *sells* well. But you have to give respect to both sides. A lot of people in the industry fight over this, but both sides are totally legit for what they want to accomplish and should be respected for it. It's when one side doesn't respect the other that I think the biggest problems arise.

Neal Hallford: What call do you think you've made as a designer that you're most proud of, something you made extra time for to put into a game?

Jon Van Caneghem: Something I did that I thought was really cool, but I never seem to get much credit for, was something I did in *Might & Magic IV: Clouds of Xeen* and *Might & Magic V: Darkside of Xeen*. If at any point you put them *both* on your hard drive they merged and became the *World of Xeen*. *World* had an additional endgame, and the two halves of the world allowed you to freely walk back and forth between them with the same characters, and items, and so forth. The whole story and endgame took that whole concept into account.

What happened was they were both sides of this big, flat world, and by uniting them through the additional quest that you could only complete if you had both games, the world expanded into a globe. So I thought that was pretty cool.

Neal Hallford: That was a pretty big challenge. It must have taken quite a bit of work before either was shipped to accommodate that kind of modularity.

Jon Van Caneghem: Yep, I thought it all out before I did the first one, and I didn't know I was *going* to do it, but I left the hooks in the code and the data in the first one that if we ever *wanted* to, we could do it. So we finished the first game and it worked fine, and as we started to work on the second game, we said, "You know, we've got those hooks—if we can do it, it will be great." But we focused on finishing the second game, and amazingly enough we had a little bit of time and it fell together really quickly. It wasn't as painful as we thought only because we'd thought of it before we'd started the first one.

Neal Hallford: Let's look at the flip side of that coin. What's the dumbest thing you've ever done and wish you could just go back and fix?

Jon Van Caneghem: On *Might & Magic II,* I let a writer who was working with me write a bunch of things at three in the morning, which after being up for several days seemed quite funny. And we put them all in the game. Later I kinda sobered up after a few weeks and looked at this stuff and said, "*Oh my god,* we shipped it with that stuff in there!" How embarrassing. Then it haunts you. These were clues and quest items that appeared in clue books and message boards and in reviews they got mentioned . . . I mean, they would not go away.

Not to humiliate myself, but we had an item called the +7 Loin Cloth. You had to deliver to a guy called the Long One. So I was at a game convention, and someone asked me, "Where do I take the +7 Loin Cloth?" And I had to with a straight face tell them that they had to find the Long One.

Neal Hallford: I remember when you and I were putting together the random item generator for *Might & Magic III: Isles of Terra.* I remember it spitting up something called the Vibrating Leather Buddy Rod of Aid. That was pretty silly too.

Jon Van Caneghem: Ah, days of games gone awry. That was quite funny.

Neal Hallford: Obviously those are all things that were quite unintentional to put into a game. What's the worst thing a designer can do on purpose?

Jon Van Caneghem: The worst thing is to design something that relies on a technology or code that hasn't been built yet. To have the entire game rely on that concept before it's been developed. That's the biggest problem. If you go down that path, and then you build the rest of your game design around that assumption, you've got a fifty-fifty chance of having a product that can't even be built.

Neal Hallford: Where do you weigh in on what does or does not constitute a role-playing game?

Jon Van Caneghem: In every hit game—choose whatever genre you like—if you look closely at the things that make them the best in their category, the things that tend to make them stand out are often actually elements borrowed from the RPG genre. That can mean allowing someone to build up a character, or a set of statistics, from one scenario to the next throughout the game. It can mean discovering more and more about the game world or story and continuing to use that information to go forward, and not just constantly starting over like in an old *Pac-Man* game or something. It can mean exploring, or conquering, or just finding and upgrading your equipment. I'm seeing *all* these elements now in flight simulators, in strategy games, in adventure games—you name it. I see products in almost every category that cross over now. It's hard to tell what they are anymore.

But that whole cycle—getting better stuff so you can kill the big bad monster, or finding the key so you can explore that next important area—that's what makes RPGs what they are. If you apply those ideas to any category, you're going to get better games.

The interesting thing, though, if you look at all the games out there that have become "mass-consumer," is that the people who created them built them for themselves, as something they really liked. It just happened to be a category that the mass consumer really liked. The key was giving easy enough access to the player that anybody could get into them and enjoy them.

Neal Hallford: What about in your own work? What makes one of your games a *Might & Magic* title, and not just someone else's RPG?

Jon Van Caneghem: The *Might & Magic* style is *free roam*. Whatever you can figure out that you can do, be my guest. Go for it. We try and be as least restrictive as possible. What I used to call it is *player tools*. We like to put as many player tools in as possible, and as many obstacles as possible, and not think about how the player is going to solve their way through the game. We're hoping that different players will use these tools many different ways to solve the same problem.

Neal Hallford: Access can take many forms though. That's interface, that's control over the environment, that can even be how you display vital statistics to the player. Is there such a thing as giving the player *too much* information?

Jon Van Caneghem: Everybody has their own preference. Some people don't like any information, and other people like so much of it that it can feel like you've got a spreadsheet in front of you instead of a game. It's tough finding a way to please everybody.

The big problem with statistics is that computers handle them so well that you *lose* a lot of the great pen-and-paper stuff. When you sit there with the dice in your hand and you say, "Okay, I've got a 12, and it's windy so it's +1 to hit, and I'm running so that's +2. 14! I've got to make 14 to make this roll!" On the computer, you just click on the monster and it does something. If you don't show any statistics, whether or not something's a success or a failure, the player can't tell if it's a random 1 to 6 or some 83,000-line piece of code that takes into account the weather and the barometer.

If you get too simplistic, you lose that *sense* of the wonderful complexity of your world. People don't even realize what the benefits or losses are for anything. It becomes rather nebulous. If you get too much of it, you have the bog-down effect of, well, what does all this junk mean? You have to find a way of balancing between those two sides of things, but it's necessary that the player have some clue about what's actually going on. Otherwise why put it in the game?

Neal Hallford: Staying on the topic of gamer *access,* let's talk about RPGs in the context of the worldwide audience. *Might & Magic* is among many games which has been translated into other languages. How does moving across the international borders affect how games get received?

Jon Van Caneghem: There's a big issue now with the language barrier. Products have to be worldwide friendly. The first thing you learn is the more graphical and less text reliant your title is, the better you do on an export basis. I think that's why we tend to see less of things like text puzzles in games anymore. So much of our market now is international, so it's definitely something you have to take into consideration while you're making your game.

There are some very interesting things that you see around the world. Take the Germans, for example. The harder the game is, the better. If the game is impossible to win, they'll give you five stars. If it's so difficult that you can barely get through the first combat without the party dying, they love it. They want it to be tough. The French seem to like prettier games. The better looking it is, the better it seems to go. I haven't quite figured out the British yet except to say that they tend to look at the sticker pretty intently. They want it as cheap as possible.

Neal Hallford: What about the Japanese market? They seems to be big fans of RPGs.

Jon Van Caneghem: They really seem to like love stories. They also like very abstract magical concepts. The more abstract, the better for them. Some things which don't even make sense to me they love. I mean, I look at things like *Final Fantasy,* and to this day I don't know what they're talking about.

I think the big thing is to understand that whatever country you're dealing with, they like to see references to their own mythological history. If you have a lot of shoguns or samurai, you'll do phenomenally better in the Far East than you will in Europe. I remember a couple of games—somebody else's, not mine—had some real serious eastern European mythology, and they did amazingly well in Poland and the Ukraine and some of those areas there that you'd think, "Those people are buying games?" They buy *a lot* of them. But those games focused on the folklore that the people in that part of the world really connected with. We tend to forget in the West how many other, ancient mythological folklores there are that we don't even know much about, but it's common in other places. It's always interesting to see the differences.

Neal Hallford: What happens when you cross a more abstract border and try to translate RPGs to other formats? What troubles do you run into there?

Jon Van Caneghem: The stuff I'm having to work on today is to keep in mind the next-generation video console versions of the game like Playstation 2. I don't want to call them ports because they're really not. You have to rebuild the game for the machine. But you can't design the original to be so unfriendly that it can't be put on a game machine. Hardware-wise, they're so different than a PC. You don't have a keyboard to play with or a hard drive or all sorts of things that you tend to rely on when you're developing PC titles. On the content side, you just have to understand that console RPGs tend to be geared to a younger gamer. The caricatures, the theme, the story—all that stuff has to be tailored to be more appropriate to that audience.

Neal Hallford: What's the biggest hurdle in putting together an RPG?

Jon Van Caneghem: For today's market, I think it's working in 3-D. It's created not just one, but two or three additional layers of people and technology in editors and a process that keeps the designer from just sitting at the computer and making the game.

I started out programming them, doing the art, doing *everything*. That was back when it didn't look like much, but I was *right there*. It was: design-to-code-to-consumer. But over the years, the more complicated the process became, and the better the machines got, more layers of people have come between the designer and the end product. That's because it's so very difficult to program, to do art, to implement data, and have everything interact like it had before. It changes everything from making maps, characters, objects, creatures—it's just a huge, giant step. It's actually slowed things down to the point where in the same amount of time it takes to make a reasonable 3-D game, you could build a 2-D game that's 10 times more detailed, like in the old-style titles. That's just the amount of work it takes.

Neal Hallford: When you take into consideration all the technical advantages that we have at our fingertips, do you think there's anything that designers today might perhaps *under*use?

Jon Van Caneghem: There's just no excuse today for any RPG designer not to include *some* kind of auto-mapping feature in their games. That just drives me so crazy I could shoot someone. Since 1985 we've had RPGs that had mapping systems, and if you can't do that by now, something's seriously wrong. But sure enough, so many games leave it out, and you drive yourself nuts just wandering around and around lost when you shouldn't have to. I should have something which tells me where I've been and where I am. It's just fundamental.

Neal Hallford: Well, where we are is at the end of our interview for today. Do you have any last-minute advice for the would-be designers of tomorrow?

Jon Van Caneghem: Do it because you absolutely *love* it and you have to do it. If you're really driven, you'll make games that will be fantastic to play.

CHAPTER 14

Carly Staehlin: Ultima Online

Carly Staehlin is the producer of *Ultima Online* for Origin Systems in Austin, Texas and is overseeing the integration of its newest expansion, *Third Dawn*. Prior to her duties as producer, she served as the online community coordinator and the online community services manager at Origin. She has also worked as a writer and designer in the first-person shooter genre, and provided voice talent on titles like *Quake II*.

Neal Hallford: What was the first role-playing game to catch your attention?

Carly Staehlin: My first experience with a role-playing game was when I was about thirteen years old and some friends of mine from theatre—I was in community theatre when I was younger—invited me to come over for a pen and paper session of *Dungeons & Dragons*. I'd read about it before and most of what I'd read hadn't been very positive. It was supposed to be all creepy and occult and only naughty people did that sort of thing, so of course I was interested. And I went and I sat down and had about a six hour session, and I played a warrior. I hacked on a bunch of ogres I recall, and I was actually very interested. I had a great time, but it was more about the special dynamic of the group even more than the game itself.

Neal Hallford: The social aspect of *Ultima* is obviously one of its major selling points. Would you say that was a lesson you took from your early experiences?

Carly Staehlin: Certainly. People have done a lot of research into the types of people who play games. You've got the achievers, the socializers, the killers and the explorers. Here at Origin we've even added a fifth category which is the nurturer category. I am definitely first an achiever, and secondly very closely a socializer. I recognize these qualities in myself. I love to achieve. I like to build a character. I like to build up my stats and skills. It has more to do with gaining stature in the game environment so I can socialize better, so I become more popular. People who are higher up in the game tend to be people who have more friends, who are more likely to be called on, more likely to be invited to things, and this is true with almost any online game I've ever played. Back when I played MUDs in college, that was absolutely a truth then as well. That was my approach to Ultima Online.

I started off as a community person in the RPG genre, and I was interested in how the communities responded and what they wanted to see in the game. As a producer, I'm always concentrating on the players and their needs and wants, whether they are capable and able to do the things they want to do in the game. It all largely revolves around the ability to talk to other people, to group with other people, to show off their things to other people, to invite other people to enjoy their environment. So that's definitely a major focus.

Neal Hallford: What social aspects of the old pen and paper RPGs have you found hardest to integrate? Are there things that are best left behind?

Carly Staehlin: When you're face to face with people, you can do a lot of very interesting things with body language, tone, and voice. You can trick people when you're face to face. People can realize they've been tricked, but they don't feel frustrated by that because they realize it's part of the game mechanic. In an online game, if you try to use misinformation as a game mechanic, people just think it's a bug. They think that's it's wrong. They don't recognize it as a game mechanic. So far I haven't seen it successfully implemented in any kind of a role-playing game that's got multiple players playing it.

The tone of voice and the body language and all that kind of thing…the technology hasn't evolved to the state yet where you can put enough that kind of thing into your online identity. It can't be seen. You have text and you have maybe a couple of animations, but that's about it. Without tone, without body language, you lose some of the crucial elements which exist in a pen and paper design.

Neal Hallford: In single player RPGs whenever you make a mistake you can stop, restart, and essentially go back and fix something you've done incorrectly. The online experience is very different. The player can't go back and un-talk to another player they've met in the game world and maybe made a bad impression on. It makes it a little more difficult to "learn" the rules of the world. How have you dealt with this issue?

Carly Staehlin: Without the ability to save and go back to a previous point in the play experience, there's always an issue of how you continue to introduce challenges that are exciting in a character arc, in a character's development. It's not only hard in a massively multiplayer RPG, but in single player games as well. Classic storytelling involves beating the hero up, and beating the hero up, and beating the hero up. As soon as he recovers, he saves the day and that's exciting. That's exciting in stories and in movies and in novels and in comic books. That's always been there. But if you keep beating up your player in a solo-play RPG, they're going to want to turn off the game. You've got to make sure the player feels like they are doing well, that they are getting better, that they can overcome the challenge that's in front of them.

The way that designers have tried to solve that challenge in the past has been to just make everything progressively harder. The player wanders around until they find someone in the game who can explain the problem, they go out and find the guy they're supposed to kill, they kill the bad guy, they get the prize, then they go and talk to the fellow who set them on this path in the first place. Once they talk to the quest dispenser again, he tells the player to go kill some *other* guy that's even harder to kill, and so off the player goes to kill another dude and to get a slightly better prize. And that's what keeps happening over and over again. That cycle of just pushing the player through these rings of concentrically more difficult monsters has been tried with massively multiplayer game in the past, but it hasn't been that successful. We made that same mistake here with *UO*. We built the veteran player shard Siege Perilous which is still up and running, and the whole concept was that it was going to be so much harder to build a character on Siege Perilous. What's our biggest complaint about Siege Perilous? It's too hard to build a character. It's just not fun enough. That's got a lot of us here thinking about that. It's not about making it harder, it about making a more engrossing and involving environment. That's where people really have fun.

In *Ultima* we try to find systems that rely on the *players* to present the tougher and tougher challenges. The idea isn't to just go kill the tougher monsters, it's to pit the creativity of each and every player against everyone else. You give them the tools to create scenarios. You can do that by giving them game systems that allow warfare, or capture the flag type stuff, or if you actually give them the power to generate quests and things of that nature on their own. At that point, you start to get back to that original D&D experience where you've got a game master in the room who is imagining up the scenario and using the feedback of the players to evolve a better game. That's where these online RPGs will be going in the future.

Neal Hallford: You're relying heavily on players to provide a great deal of the content of your games. That can be great if a subscriber runs into the right sort of players, but how do you ensure that people always will have a great experience, even if they *don't* run into the right sort?

Carly Staehlin: Massively multiplayer games get tackled from a number of different directions. There's firstly the player versus player direction, which means using the players to generate the content through competitions against one another. Then there's the player versus monster. That's where you try to populate your world with enough varied and interesting creature types so the player who wants a solo adventure or is just interested in exploring has lots of things to challenge them. That's driven by your AI, which is never going to be as interesting to play against as intelligence that comes from other players. You also have in your world things we call points of interest. Those can be a number of things. It can be an area where there's a puzzle that you have to solve to get something. It can be an area where it's just visually interesting to look at. Maybe butterflies flit around there, or it's the only place a unicorn will show up. It could be a place that drives social dynamics. It might be a secluded beach so that lovers can go there. It can be a dungeon that's a player versus monster environment, but it can also be a point of interest. You can also have non player characters in your game that are intelligent that can deliver pre-fabricated quests. The baker on the corner can say, "Help, help, my wife is gone! Help me find my wife!" You can then go off searching in the world for the baker's wife, then you find her and get her to follow you back to the baker. That's a sort of a role-playing interest. And it's really trying to find a good balance between all these things that makes the game engaging all the time.

Neal Hallford: There's a trick there though. Massively multiplayer games rely upon players repeatedly coming back to the game over a long term. How do you engage the interest of the player "all the time?" How do you keep them coming back not for day after day, but month after month or year after year?

Carly Staehlin: There are multiple folds. Part of it is that you have to have a good game mechanic. The act of simply building up your character has to be fun and rewarding and the payoff is worth the investment. But that's only good for a short amount of time. I don't think that would perpetuate it forever. I think that the long term comes from other people. It's the establishment of relationships and watching them evolve over time. Another key to that which I don't think has been explored yet—in this genre—is putting tools into the hands of the players so that they can *be* the content. If they have more tools which effectively allow them to establish any type of interest, whether it's putting on a play to hosting a wedding to being able to have a party to having a house warming. Any way that you can induce the players to generate content is actually what is going to drive this in the long run. For it to be a truly, truly fun environment all the time, the players need to be in charge of the world. As long as designers inside companies are the primary deliverers of content, games can be successful and have long lives, but they will never be as successful or as long lived as an environment which allows the player to be in charge of their own destinies.

Neal Hallford: What effect does that have on the way you test your product, though? The more tools you put into the hands of your players, the more difficult it becomes to test and fix all the bugs before your product hits the market.

Carly Staehlin: You have to make sure from the ground up that you're doing things in as bug-free a way as possible. Then, when you introduce a new tool or mechanic into the game, you make sure that it integrates with the other tools and mechanics in the game as well as they can be. That's why you continue to have live development teams continuing to work on these games. As you go into the game, we don't *ever* see the multiple combinations of things that can possibly happen. We don't have the bandwidth to do it. But I'll tell you what, two hours on a live shard or server, and *instantly* we find out what's wrong with the product. It doesn't take long. And then we also are able to take that knowledge and use it again the next time. So we hopefully won't make the same mistakes multiple times.

Neal Hallford: Generally speaking, there are going to be two different kinds of players. You're going to have casual gamers who play less than five hours a week, and you're going to have the power gamers who play forty hours a week or more. If you make the game too hard, the casual gamers are going to give up because they're frustrated. If you make it too easy, in a week the power gamers have done everything there is to do and have leveled up until they don't have anywhere they can go. How do you introduce content that going to keep both those kinds of players satisfied?

Carly Staehlin: I've been thinking *a lot* about that recently. I really think you need to have a very, very long arc for character builders—the power gamers that get that big thrill out of hitting that next level. You need to have a months and months long arc to be able to successfully hit all those levels. The problem with doing a really, really, really long arc like that is that your casual gamers won't catch up, so what I'm playing with now is that you need to have some way for the casual gamer to be able to experience short event style play where they are as powerful as the most powerful person who built up their character, but only give them access to that over a short period of time. It wouldn't become a permanent part of their identity where it has with the achiever type person that's been building their character for months and months.

For example, maybe you can set something up so someone drinks a potion or enters an arena and suddenly they are a level 18 knight and can wield the best weapons and wear the best armor. The instant they step out of that arena that's gone and they're still Joe Adventurer. But that's okay because they played for half an hour in the arena and that's very exciting and fun, and that doesn't take anything away from the guy who has spent three months developing the *true* knight who can run all around the world, and is always known as a level 18 knight. In my opinion the true knight won't mind that there are arenas where people can go in and enjoy that experience. It's not related to their identity. It's a short lived thing. A lot of it boils down to bragging rights. You don't want to ever give somebody a bragging right they haven't deserved. You do want to give them an experience to whet their appetite.

Neal Hallford: Between the casual and hardcore players, which audience do you think *Ultima* tends to lend more towards?

Carly Staehlin: To date, it definitely has leaned towards the hardcore gamer. That probably because the people who made the game in the first place were gamers. They came from MUD backgrounds, and *Dungeons & Dragons* backgrounds, and they came from a background where people understood the basics of what it meant to do an RPG. People have all these different definitions about what role-playing means. In the classic sense an RPG is a game where you build a character, and that is what *UO* was all about. That was what it was built to do. As it has evolved, what we have seen is that while there will always be a large contingency of hardcore players, they have a hard time helping a casual player enjoy the experience. They just don't understand how to make it worth the time of the casual who's playing the game for a short period of time. If you only had half an hour a week to play *Ultima Online*, you should be able to do that and enjoy the time you spend with it.

I've been the producer of *UO* for six months, and everything I've done to date has been to get us ready—without diminishing the experience of the hardcore player at all—to find a way to help the casual gamer enjoy that experience and feel involved in it. From the first instant they step in the door, to be able to feel this rich world welcoming them in. That's what *Ultima Online* is working towards right now, and we've been trying to do it for a little while. It's very tough because the game has been a hardcore game for a very long time. And, I have to say, I think it *needed* to be. If it hadn't been, when it first launched, I don't think people would have jumped on it. If you had tried to come up with a massively multiplayer casual game in 1997, it wouldn't have taken off. It's the sweat and the emotional commitment of the hardcore players that has made this such an interesting genre for people to play in. So I don't mean to speak badly of the fact that *UO* has been a hardcore game. It's due to that fact that we can even sit down and talk about how to make a casual gamer enjoy the same kind of experience.

Neal Hallford: Do you think that's necessarily part of the massively multiplayer production cycle now? Do all games have to start off as hardcore games, or do you think that it's possible with the changed market to start off with a casual game?

Carly Staehlin: I think it's very possible to start casual now. I don't think game companies would have bought into the idea, and they hardly did when UO was getting started. I don't think that gamers in general would have gone down that path, but now that there are 600,000 people playing in commercial massively multiplayer games, it's the word of mouth thing. Other people who don't have 12 hours a week to play want to get a taste of what this is. They're ready for it. Now we can create games that are more geared towards a casual experience. There's actually a market for it now.

Neal Hallford: There are countless websites and message boards floating around on the net that players rely on for information. Once anything in your world is discovered, it is immediately public knowledge to everybody, and that can really foul up certain kinds of quests. How do you factor extra-game communications into your process?

Carly Staehlin: That's definitely something that you have to factor in. Development resources to build those quests are not trivial. Why am I going to spend 80% of my development resources for a month developing quests that are going to be solved in two days and everybody's going to know how to do? That's simply not a good use of my time or resources. So the way we handle that situation now is that we don't do one solution quests because we don't get enough bang for the buck. We know people are interested in having a sense of discovery, a sense that the world is always evolving, that there are always new things to see and do.

The other part about Internet communications that factors in as well is that if you don't inform your audience about what is in the game, they will perceive new things that they haven't been told about as *bugs*. If it's new and they haven't heard about it, then it must be a problem. What we've done is we've started telling the player on a weekly basis that something new will be in the world. We're not going to tell you what it is, but there will be something new. And then we'll release a fictional story at the same time that describes whatever that new thing is, whether that's a new monster, or weapons, or whatever that new thing is, and we'll put it on the fictional part of our site. So we're training our audience to look for the clues about what this new thing is from our very own Internet communication. And that gets them very excited. Then they start talking about, "Oh, what is that new thing? What does this story mean? Let's go over here, it may be there." Then they finally find it, and they are very excited because they actually solved the quest to find the new thing, whatever it happened to be. Then everybody knows about it, but that's okay because they know in the next week or next interval that next thing will be there. That helps drive the discovery process.

Neal Hallford: Most of the massively multiplayer games out there have fallen into one of two different camps. *Everquest* is class based and *UO* is more skill based. How do you prevent the tank-mage problem from cropping up?

Carly Staehlin: Most of the time we don't know it's a problem until we find it, but that's changing. As the game matures we're able to recognize things before they get too far. But it's a constant rebalancing. Actually the term *nerf* comes from taking power away from something that's too powerful. Players don't like that. They like it when things may be too tough at first, and we make it easier. They feel like we listen to them and we made it better and they're very happy. They don't like it when we recognize something has been made too easy and we make it tougher, or if it's too powerful and we make it weaker. *That's* a nerf, even if it's better for the game. However, we have found that although a vocal minority of people will scream and yell about just about anything we do in the game, if we have made a smart choice, and been able to prove it with our own math and analysis before we make that decision, and if we allow the audience to discuss that decision before we actually implement it, the net out of the whole affair is that people like the game more. They are more satisfied with the game experience as a whole. There are people who feel slighted when that sort of thing happens, but after the initial sting has passed we have found that the audience generally reacts more favorably to the game.

Neal Hallford: *UO* by its very nature really seems to encourage the collaboration of the players. How do you make the determinations about what goes in and what doesn't?

Carly Staehlin: We've got two primary objectives. The first is to improve the game. The second is to provide the game that the players want. There are a couple of issues in here. One of them is the feedback loop. Early on in *UO*'s history, the feedback loop wasn't good anywhere. There weren't official ways or means by which the players could make their suggestions or comments heard. Player boards developed. The company eventually recognized the boards were out there and began using that feedback to help make choices and design decisions. But then again, the feedback loop was only one direction at that point, flowing from the players to Origin.

We've been working very hard over the last year to try to get that feedback loop to actually *be* a loop so that the player's questions and comments not only have a forum in which to be heard, but that there are also representatives of the company available to comment on and analyze those suggestions to stimulate more discussion. We want to find out what's not the knee-jerk reaction of the audience, but the real assessment of an issue, or concept, or feature by the playing community. We want to show that when we've accepted an idea that an idea is being worked on, and have on our website a development cycle section where something will go into the "in concept" phase. Players can then comment and give feedback on it, and then it actually goes into development and testing, and eventually becomes a part of the latest game published. Then players have a better way of seeing exactly how their comments and suggestions are being heard, and what's happening to them. It's key to keep that loop very solid, and open in both directions.

It's an interesting thing about the games community that that's the way it's turned out. I think that happened with the *Quake* phenomenon, and the plan files and all that stuff. That actually has given the players the expectation that they can speak with the developers if not in a one-on-one, at least in a hundred-on-one forum. That doesn't really exist in other forums of entertainment. You don't get to tell your favorite band face to face what you think about their songs. You don't get to tell Steven Spielberg what you think, or expect him to respond on a bulletin board about what you think about his latest film. But people *do* believe that they have that right or privilege to speak with developers in games. That's just something that game developers and companies have to acknowledge exists now. They must be able to respond to it and deal with it. It's actually a really cool thing because in the long run, what we're trying to do is create a game that will be the most satisfying for the people playing it. The only way we can truly do that is to understand what they have to say about it, so I consider that very positive.

I do say there is a collaboration, but it's important that you remember that a lot of time you'll find a single player or a group of players commenting on something when they don't really have all the information. They probably won't understand all the underlying game mechanic because you don't want your competitors to be able to use your thought process and your analysis to be able to build a game on their own. The players aren't dealing with as many factors as the developers are, so at times you have to make pretty tough calls when we know that the general consensus of the players that are commenting is leaning one way, but we know that the health of the game is going another. We may know that we can't go a certain direction because six months from now we're going to do something which will render that idea a very bad one. Our VP of online services, Gordon Walton, has the screenname TYRANT, and he's the first one to say that this is not a democracy, it's a tyranny. We have to make the decisions, but we also try to let people know that we are interested in their feedback and we want to actively use that feedback to improve the game. I think that the *Ultima Online* community in particular is beginning to have a lot more faith that that kind of thing is going on.

Neal Hallford: Can you think of a particularly outstanding example of something where the players came to you and suggested something which you just hopped up and down and said, "I can't wait until we can incorporate this into the game!"

Carly Staehlin: You know it's funny because I usually get asked the opposite question, about what kinds of features we've turned down, but it happens all the time.

Neal Hallford: Okay, well let's go ahead and reverse that. Is there a particular thing that you often get asked for, or a general class of things that are frequently requested that you just cannot put into the game?

Carly Staehlin: Players want to have the ability to create their own objects and name them whatever they want. While that is technically possible for us to allow players to create their own objects—and they do, there are craftspeople who make objects—we haven't come up with a way yet for players to have free rein over what they name an object. A hundred percent of the players aren't going to use that power appropriately. There's a tiny percentage of players who exploit the game in inappropriate ways to harass other people. The instant that we allow them to name their own weapons is the day we get the Jew Killer sword, or the Fag Basher. As it is, we're constantly having to monitor the names people are giving themselves. UO *is* a mature game, but we absolutely cannot tolerate that kind of harassment. We're a global game with a very diverse audience. Even though it is a tiny, tiny percentage of people who will do that sort of thing, we have to remove that ability from everyone because it's just not going to work.

People also want to have the ability to create their own housing structures. They don't want to be limited to the templates we provide them. That actually gets into a problem with just the landmass and space. If people are able to put add-ons to their house, you can't even begin to imagine the number of combinations of problems that are going to come up as a result of that.

Players also want the ability to teleport automatically to other people in the game. That can run into trouble too because if people can teleport to anybody else in the game at any time, then suddenly someone can turn sour and start killing other player characters because they can teleport to them instantly.

Player justice is another thing that's really tough to manage. I want the ability to kill people who are doing wrong, but the game isn't intelligent enough to judge intent. So if someone's being a jerk and running around and calling you names and you kill them, you're going to have to suffer the same repercussions of being a murderer in the game as someone who is killing innocent people. The game itself doesn't have the ability to understand the right in that situation.

All these kinds of suggestions and things we get from players, we can come up with ways to put controls on it to try to help it not be an issue. That's actually one of the very exciting things about *UO*. Pretty much anything you would want to see can probably be put into it. The game is so robust and so flexible that most anything can be done in the game, but for people who are anti-social, they can ruin the possibilities for everybody. So that's something we constantly have to balance.

Neal Hallford: Overall, what are some of the best and worst things that UO has put to use?

Carly Staehlin: One of the smartest things we put into *UO* was to introduce Guilds for the players. We didn't start with them. It comes back to giving players the opportunity to develop their own interests. If you put a mechanic in the game that allows one player to be in charge of a group of other players, you have *instant* interest.

Housing was a very smart. It works very well. We made it rare, which makes it very wonderful to have. It's a huge bragging right to say that you own your own place in UO. It's very desirable to have. People stay in the game for a long amount of time because they have this rare and wonderful item they can be proud of owning. They can decorate it. It's an extension of their own identity. That's a hugely smart thing, but at the same time it's dumb because if it's rare, then not everybody can have it, and some people are going to be very frustrated.

From Origin to Destination

If there's anything that you learn in the game industry, it's that things change rapidly. During the course of the writing of this book, a major shift in Electronic Arts' focus (Origin's parent corporation) led to the following announcement in early 2001.

> "After evaluating the futures and potential of both *Ultima Online* and ORI-GIN, Electronic Arts and Origin Systems have made the decision to increase their focus on *Ultima Online* by halting production of *UWO: ORIGIN (UO2)*. Rather than create ORIGIN as a parallel world competing with *Ultima Online*, many resources that would have been required to complete ORIGIN will instead be refocused into *Ultima Online*, making sure that we can expand and support it for some time to come."

Subsequent to EA and Origin's joint announcement, Destination Games opened its doors in Austin, Texas. Founded by Richard Garriott, creator of the original *Ultima* role-playing series, Destination is a company focused on the development of a massively multiplayer game code named "tabula rasa." Carly Staehlin decided to make the leap to Garriott's new online venture as a designer, and is apparently very happy to be working on Garriott's next-generation title.

> "Once you get a job in the games industry, it is critically important to never take that job for granted. I've always told my employees (and myself) to be very selfish with the work," Carly says. "I don't mean that you should be a jerk in the office, hoarding good assignments and credit. Rather, that you take the initiative to get as much out of your job as you put into it. Learn something everyday. If you don't learn something new everyday, you are slacking. Take advantage of every opportunity that arises. Tomorrow is not a guaran-

Another dumb thing we did—hugely dumb—was having no unique names. That's not a mistake I'm going to repeat. You must have unique names. You must have accountability. You will curb so much anti-social behavior if you have accountability. If you don't have a unique name, you don't know which Gandalf it was that whacked you yesterday. You don't know which one to go after.

tee. Anything could happen and you have to be prepared for that. By being selfish with your job and your work, you remain valuable to yourself as well as to your employer in this industry, or any other. And you can make informed decisions about the future strategy of your career with confidence.

"In April of 2001, I left Electronic Arts and joined Destination Games. What a lot of gamers, and even some developers, don't like to think about is that game companies are businesses. These businesses are required to generate profit in order to continue doing business. Electronic Arts determined that all the projects at Origin Systems, except for the original *Ultima Online*, were not good businesses. As a result, the studio focused all its resources on the development and support of the original *UO*. At that point I made the selfish choice to leave Electronic Arts in order to pursue a career with a studio that had a mission to create new products that were compatible with my goals as a developer and allowed me to stay in Austin.

"Richard and Robert Garriott, the founders of Origin Systems, partnered with Starr Long to form a cutting edge online game development group and online game support organization called Destination Games. The development group's goal is to provide the next generation of massively multiplayer RPGs for the online gamer. The focus of their products will be on fun, easily accessible, rich content. On May 17, 2001, Destination Games became a part of NCsoft, a Korean-based company that currently operates the largest subscription-based online game in the world, *Lineage: The Blood Pledge*, created by Jake Song. Having pioneered the online game industry, both in the U.S. and in Korea, this team is poised to revolutionize the marketplace. At Destination Games, I'm again knuckling down, learning everything I can, being selfish with my work, and preparing for whatever may come next."

Conversely, you don't know which one gave you the magical sword so you don't know who to thank the next day. Not having a unique name has actually put so many obstacles and roadblocks into the development of the game because we can't uniquely identify people by name.

Neal Hallford: What did you think the biggest hurdle is in making a massively multiplayer game?

Carly Staehlin: Today, I'd say it's balancing flash—technology and eye candy and that kind of thing—with emersive game mechanic. A lot of the things you can do to make emersive game mechanics is very expensive. It's expensive in terms of your CPU time. If you tried to do *Ultima Online* today and made it a fully flashy 3D technological wonder, the cost would be prohibitive. It would be prohibitively expensive to develop it, and prohibitively expensive in terms of the systems that would be required to run it. So for today, for the people who are trying to start, the hurdle is understanding that the polished and clean game mechanic is at least as important as the eye candy. Eye candy is good for about 2.2 seconds, and you better have a game to back it up.

Neal Hallford: With that last bit in mind, what's your parting advice to the game designers of the future?

Carly Staehlin: An RPG is really about understanding human beings and human interaction. For someone who wants to design an RPG, learn as much as you can about how you interact with other people, and how the people around you interact with one another. Understand what makes people tick. Understand what gets people excited. Understand why you pissed your friend off yesterday. Understand why your friend thinks you're the best person ever today. Try to really analyze the way people deal with other people. Then you can, just by filling your head up with all that knowledge, and all that information, all that analysis, you will start to actually see the world, see the planet as a massive RPG. All those things that happen in the real world are valuable, all fodder for your RPG that you're going to try and design.

It's good to learn, it's good to read. I would highly recommend reading all kinds of fiction and non-fiction. Understand the most charismatic evil leaders in history. History is a really wonderful place to draw inspiration from for RPGs. Understanding politics is good. A massively multiplayer game these days is just a society, and the game company is the government. Try and figure out how politicians do their jobs, how they evolve their countries and their ideologies. All that is going to factor in. It's also not a bad idea to be good at math, because you have to analyze your design theories by using math. You don't have to understand calculus and that sort of thing, but you have to have a good concept of math, and statistical analysis is really helpful as well.

Part Five

Appendixes

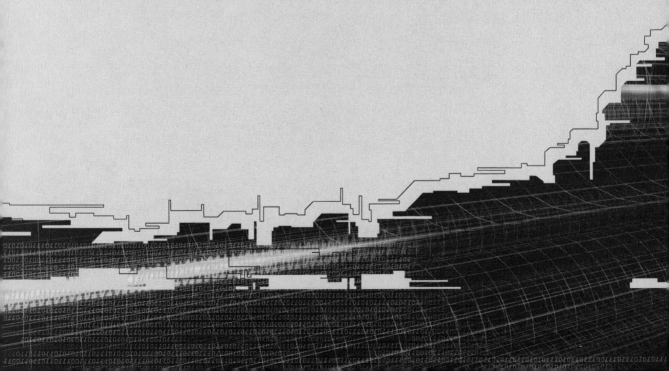

APPENDIX A

GLOSSARY

"A" Title. A game that is believed to have the best potential to become a best-selling title. Because of investor wariness in the gaming industry, it has also become the unofficial designation of the titles most likely to get produced.

Alpha Stage. The alpha stage is the point in a game's development at which most of the core features and primary content have been implemented and are ready for a first round of testing. Frequently this is the point beyond which no more major features will be introduced, and all remaining work will be concerned with completing content and fixing bugs.

Animation Cycle. A collection of animation frames that represent one specific cycle of movement and can be repeated over and over to create a larger effect. (*Example:* In a *walk cycle,* the motion of a character taking just one step forward is repeated several times to create the illusion of a continuous stride.)

Artificial Intelligence (also A.I.). A designer-defined set of actions, reactions, and priorities that can be assigned to nonplayer characters or monsters to give them the appearance of purposeful behavior. (*Example:* A monster might be assigned to walk sentry duty between two different points until the player's avatar comes close enough to be seen. At that point the monster then stops walking post and begins to attack the avatar. This assignment of conditional priorities forms the basis of this monster's A.I.)

Assets. The data upon which a game engine relies to create the "reality" of the game world. Bitmaps, tiles, sound effects, 3-D

models, backgrounds, recorded dialogs, A.I. routines, and motion curves are all examples of assets. Sometimes also called *resources.*

Attributes. An arbitrary set of numbers representing an avatar's "natural" mental and physical capabilities. Sometimes also called *stats, characteristics,* or *traits.*

Avatar. A computer-generated character controlled in the game world by a flesh-and-blood player. The primary means through which the game world is experienced and explored. Also known as the *player character,* or *PC.*

Back Story. A document detailing all the events that have led up to the current state of affairs in your game world.

Bandwidth. A measure of the amount of data that can be transmitted through a communications line.

Beta Stage. The beta stage of a product is reached when *all* features and *all* game content have been introduced and are ready for a final round of testing. At this point, the design team is solely concerned with play balancing and bug fixing.

Bit. Shortened from the words *binary digit,* a bit represents the result of a *binary decision* (i.e., a choice between only two possible options). The smallest subdivision of computer memory possible, a bit can only store a 1 or a 0.

Bitmap. Programmer speak for a picture or image, often stored in the .BMP image format. Pictures on computers are made up by *bits* grouped together into a larger data structure called a *map.* Thus *bitmap.*

Bug. Slang for a flaw in the design or programming of a game, which results in wildly unpredictable and undesirable results. *Crash, freeze,* or *lock-up bugs* that prevent the game from being played beyond a particular point are regarded as the most serious variety of bugs. (A common joke among designers is, "It's not a bug, it's a *feature.*")

Byte. A byte is a measurement of computer memory equivalent to 8 *bits* of information (see *Bit*). It is capable of storing a single letter, such as the letter A, or it can hold a number between 0 and 255. Multiples of the byte provide most of the terms with which you will typically be dealing, such as the *kilobyte* (1,024 bytes), *megabyte* (1,048,576 bytes), and *gigabyte* (1,073,741,824 bytes).

C. Originally developed in 1972 by Dennis Ritchie of Bell Laboratories, C and its offshoot C++ are the two most commonly used programming languages in the creation of today's best-known computer games.

Central Processing Unit (also CPU). The microchip at the heart of a computer, which interprets and executes the instructions of the game engine.

Class. The general "profession" to which an avatar or an NPC belongs. A character's class determines what special set of skills they are likely to possess and what kinds of objects they are likely to know how to use and affects how quickly they advance from one *level* to another. (*Example:* If Lothar of the Hill People belongs to the mage class, he is more likely to understand and learn from any magical scrolls he finds than would an ordinary warrior or an uneducated thief.)

Console (also Set Top Box). The generic term used to describe a class of small game machines that require attachment to an external television set. The Sony Playstation, Sega Dreamcast, Nintendo 64, and Microsoft X-Box are all examples of console machines.

D&D. The abbreviation for *Dungeons & Dragons,* the granddaddy of all modern role-playing games both on and off the computer.

Dead Squirrel. A wholly useless object that an avatar is forced to carry through a game in order to complete a quest. *See also Vibrating Blue Squirrel.*

Death March. Slang term referring to the sometimes grim final phase of game development. Often characterized by sagging team morale, managerial panic attacks, and frantic last-ditch cuts of content. A situation that you must strive to avoid at all costs.

Design Document. A document created by a design team that precisely outlines the look, feel, flow, and technical architecture of a game project.

DM. Short for Dungeon Master. In the pen-and-paper version of *Dungeons & Dragons,* the person who creates and controls scenarios for the benefit of other players.

E3. The Electronic Entertainment Expo, the largest (and arguably loudest) convention in the United States dedicated to showing off the latest electronic games and entertainment software. Most game companies use this event to preview and promote their upcoming products for the media.

Easter Egg. An easter egg is a feature, object, or event hidden in a game that can only be discovered under very special circumstances.

Emergence. The complex and sometimes surprising results of simple rules interacting within a system, giving rise to unexpected patterns, behaviors, or outcomes. (*Example:* The basic principles of chess are extraordinarily simple. There are only six different kinds of chess pieces, each of which has one particular rule governing how it can attack or move. There are only 64 places on the game board that a piece can occupy at any given time. Ultimately there is only one objective to be achieved in the game of chess—the capture of the enemy's king. Despite the seeming numerical simplicity of these factors, there are millions of possible strategies that can be developed by players to win the game, none of which are actually established by the rules that control how the pieces interact or by the stated ultimate goal of the game. The strategies are an *emergent* property of the conflicting goals and priorities of the players.)

Experience Points. A numerical measure representing the degree of physical and intellectual growth a character experiences over the course of an adventure. As avatars gain in experience, they become better at the skills they've attempted and, depending on the system, may gain additional *levels.*

Feature Set. Features are all the aspects of the interface, gameplay, and content that define a specific product and set it apart from its competitors. A feature can be a new way that an avatar can be controlled in the game world or a player-customizable menu bar that can be moved anywhere on the screen. Virtually *anything* that contributes either to the gameplay or to the overall experience can be considered a feature.

Feedback. A text message, visual or auditory effect, or observable shift in the gameplay that informs players about the results of their interaction with the game world. (*Example:* When a spell is cast in a game, both the sparkling ball of fire and the crackling sound effect accompanying it serve as feedback to the player to let him know the spell has been cast.)

"Feeping Creaturism." The insidious desire to continue to add "just one more feature" to a game's feature list, even after it is no longer practicable to implement. A common ailment among new designers.

First Person Shooter (also FPS). A genre of shoot 'em up game featuring a complex 3-D environment viewed through the eyes of a character in the game world. *Doom, Quake,* and *Unreal* are the most notable examples of this genre.

Flowchart. A graphic outline demonstrating how player choices affect gameplay, navigation, and interaction with the interface.

Fog of War. Primarily a feature of an *isometric perspective* game, the fog of war is a blob of darkness that obscures the player's view of regions his avatar has yet to explore or areas currently unoccupied by a character under the player's control.

Frag. Although popularized with the rise of games like *Doom* and its numerous offspring, this term meaning to kill or destroy something actually dates to the Vietnam War era. Individuals unfortunate enough to have met the business end of a fragmentation grenade were often said to have been fragged.

Frame Rate. The speed at which a game engine is capable of redrawing all the visible elements of the game world. Higher frame rates tend to allow for smoother, more realistic-looking animations.

FRP. Common short-hand for a fantasy role-playing game. This is exclusive to titles that definitely have fantasy (as opposed to sci-fi or horror) themed content.

Full Motion Video (also FMV). An animated or filmed noninteractive sequence that can establish a mood, assign a mission goal, or reward a player for having completed a game objective.

Gambit. Originally from the Italian word *gambetto,* meaning to trip someone up. A gambit is a strategic move made by a player that involves a small sacrifice of resources in exchange for a more favorable situation.

Game Engine. A collection of highly reusable programming code that assembles and arbitrates the reality of the game world based on data provided by a designer.

Game Script. A document generated by the design team's writer that lays out the basic story line and dialog for the game. Also known as the *screenplay.*

Game System. The core set of rules residing in the heart of every game that govern the way in which characters, monsters, objects, and environments can interact with one another.

Game World. The computer-generated reality through which a player guides his avatar.

GDC. Acronym for the Game Developer's Conference held annually in San Jose, California. Primarily a forum for designers to discuss the theory and practice of game design.

GenCon. The largest convention of game players in the United States, featuring everything from traditional card games to computer-driven RPGs. It annually draws more than 25,000 attendees.

Genre. The general category into which a game will fall, determined by its method of gameplay or feature set. (*Example:* Role-Playing Games, Real-Time Strategy, Simulations, and Adventure are all examples of genres that exist in the game market.)

Gold Stage. A game project that has reached the gold stage is deemed to be a finished, bug-free product and is ready to be released for the game-buying public.

Graphical User Interface (also GUI). Often pronounced "gooey," a GUI is a set of on-screen icons, buttons, menus, and dialog boxes that allow a player to guide the movements and interactions of avatars, review statistical information on characters, control aspects of the look or difficulty of an environment, and load or save the current state of a game.

Hit Points. A numeric measure of how much damage a player's avatar can take before it "dies."

Hotspot. An object or area in the game environment that will trigger a special interaction when clicked on. (*Example:* Doors are classic examples of hotspots in gaming environments. You click on the door and you get interaction—either the door opens, or you are informed the door is locked and a key will be required.)

Immersion. Using a combination of art, sound, and story to deeply engage the interest of a player in the game world.

Interface. See *Graphical User Interface*.

Isometric Perspective (also ¾ View). Games presented in the isometric perspective appear to be looking down on the action from a camera positioned above and to one side. *Diablo* is a classic example of an isometric game.

Kludge. Pronounced "klewj." Slang term for an inelegant way of solving a design or programming problem. Essentially like using a hammer to pound a square peg into a round hole.

Latency. The measure of time it takes a block of data to cross a network from a sender to a receiver. A critically important consideration in the development of games that require connection to the Internet. (If a user is playing on a network that suffers from high latency, they often will complain about *lag*. Lag is the delay that a user perceives between when they issue an instruction—like moving a character—and when that instruction is finally reflected in the gameplay.)

Level. There are two possible meanings, depending on context. *Game Design:* A small area of a larger game world in which a game objective must be achieved, characterized by a unified set of textures, tiles, objects, and monsters that convey a specific look or mood. *Character Status:* A measure of the degree to which a character has mastered their class. The more accomplished they are in their profession, the higher their level.

Level Editor. A special program used to construct the levels of a game. Level editors are often very powerful tools, and they can be used to assign monsters, terrain, spell effects, traps, and other effects to a certain part of the gameworld.

Linear Title. A game that requires the player to complete a set of predetermined tasks defined by the game designer in order to win the game.

Localization. The process of preparing a title for export into a different market or translation into another language.

Mapping. There are actually several different kinds of mapping frequently used during the game development process. *Texture Mapping:* When an object is texture mapped, a 2-D bitmap of a particular texture—say, concrete or steel or lizard scales—is wrapped around a 3-D polygonal model to give the illusion that it is made of that material. *Bump Mapping:* A special form of texture mapping that gives an object an illusion of depth. *Mip Mapping:* A process of swapping between differing sizes of an object's texture map as an avatar moves closer or further away from it. This is done to prevent distortions of color or texture that can otherwise occur.

Massively Multiplayer Online Game (also MMOG). A game that allows thousands of players to compete or cooperate with one another while exploring vast and persistent online environments usually rendered in 3-D. *Ultima Online, Everquest,* and *Asheron's Call* are the dominant examples of this specific genre.

Metagame. A larger, psychological game played between the player and designer, which recognizes that all the situations in the game world were designed with a purpose and a solution.

Milestone. During production, a game project is usually broken into dozens, even hundreds, of small tasks called *milestones.* These represent important stages in determining whether a project is on target, whether it needs to be readjusted, or if it deserves to continue to be funded. Milestones are the primary tangible means that management has for tracking the progress of a game's development.

Mod. A game that has been either partially or wholly re-constructed by altering the assets of a pre-existing game. For example, if a player uses a level editor on the first-person shooter *Unreal,* they can turn all the evil Skaarj in the game into Teletubbies, Santa Claus, or any other creature that they've got the will, time, and tools to build. Games that have been altered in this way are known as *mods.*

Monkey Problem. A derogatory term for any mindless, repetitive task that a designer puts in front of a player that could just as easily be solved by a monkey repeatedly slapping the spacebar for hours on end.

Monster. In the context of a role-playing game, a monster is anything that is ruled by artificial intelligence and has the capability to engage the player in combat. Monsters can be as exotic as a 12-toed Snortablog, as simple as a rabid squirrel, or as mundane as an Imperial tax collector. If it can kill you, it's a monster.

Morph. Short for *metamorphosis.* The transformation of an object or creature into something else. (*Example:* If your character is lurking around in a horror RPG on the night of a full moon, they shouldn't be surprised to see a man morph into a werewolf.)

Motion Capture. Motion capture involves the recording—or *capture*—of the motions of an object in the real world so that a precise mathematical description of that movement can be saved and later applied to a computer-generated model. This is often accomplished by putting a live actor into a special bodysuit that has markers placed at every major anatomical joint. As the actor goes through the motions assigned, a computer calculates the position and orientation of all the markers on the bodysuit and then creates a *motion curve,* a mathematical model of the motion that has just been performed by the actor. This motion curve can then later be used to puppet a computer-generated model in an extremely convincing and lifelike way.

Multiuser Dungeon (also MUD). A forerunner of the modern MMOG, MUDs allow multiple players to explore large persistent universes that are presented in a text-only format. Players navigate these environments using simple word commands like "GO WEST" or "TICKLE THE HERRING" and are given descriptions of the results of their actions.

Nerf. When designers of online games need to remove a rule, an object, a spell, or some other aspect of a game that has a serious, unbalancing effect on the gaming experience as a whole, this is frequently referred to by players as a nerf.

Nonplayer Character (also NPC). Any speaking or nonspeaking character in a game that isn't controlled by a human player. NPCs can buy or sell goods, dispense hints about the game, or provide dramatic conflicts or comic relief in support of a story line.

"On the Fly." Slang for an operation being performed "live" by the game engine. (*Example:* If a programmer tells you his game engine can *morph* "on the fly," that means it can spontaneously take one object and reshape it into a second object *without* requiring an artist to first create an animation of the transformation. In this instance, the game engine can take any two objects and morph from one to the other on an as-needed basis.)

Party. A group of avatars who share their money and material resources and may be under the control of one or more players.

PC. Depending on context, this can mean one of two things. If found in a discussion about computer hardware, PC is simply short for personal computer. In the context of a role-playing game, this usually refers to the player character (i.e., the avatar the player is guiding through the game world).

Persistent Universe. An online game world that continues to evolve whether or not there are players connected and playing. Persistent universes also entail a system that "remembers" where players were and what they were carrying the last time they signed off. Games of this variety sometimes also allow players to create their own imaginary homes, objects, and stories, which become a permanent part of the fabric of the game.

Platform. A game's platform is a reference to the specific hardware on which it is designed to be played. (*Example:* If a game is said to be a Playstation platform game, that means it can only be played on the Sony Playstation and *not* on a Sega Dreamcast machine.)

Play Balancing. The process of fine-tuning the rules or content of a game to ensure fairness, maximize player rewards, eliminate unwinnable scenarios, and simply make a game more fun to play.

Player. This is the real, physical human being who's sitting in front of the computer and playing your game. Not be confused with the *avatar*.

Polys. Short for *polygons*. The fundamental building blocks out of which all 3-D game worlds are built. The greater the number of polys your game engine can throw around, the smoother and less pixelated your world will look. (Keep in mind, however, that an increase in the number of polys also means the game engine has more to draw, which means you're likely to suffer a decrease in the frame rate.)

Port. A port is a translation of a game from one platform to another in which no significant changes are made to the rules, feel, or overall content of the game.

Real Estate. A slang term for the amount of space that will be taken up on a storage medium by the game's assets. (*Example:* "How much real estate will Level 6 occupy on the DVD?")

Real-Time Strategy (also RTS). A genre of strategy game in which all players make their moves simultaneously without waiting for other players to complete a turn. Each participant controls large numbers of *units* that can be dispatched to gather resources, build defenses, or attack the forces of other players.

RPG. Acronym for *Role-Playing Game.*

Scaling. There are two common definitions of scaling in a game design context. *Object Scaling:* The shrinking or enlargement of a map, object, or character. *Difficulty Scaling:* The on-the-fly modification of game situations or monster attributes in order to challenge the capabilities of the avatar. (*Example:* While exploring the wilderness, it's usual to meet Brown Wolves who sometimes will attack the player. Unfortunately, Bob the Adventurer is now a Level 8 warrior, and Brown Wolves are no longer much of a challenge. Taking this into account, the game engine scales the difficulty up so that now Bob isn't meeting Brown Wolves in the wilderness but Vorpal Bears.)

Scripting Language. A powerful, special language used by a designer and understood by the game engine that may be used to create a relationship between objects (such as specifying that monster A should be carrying object C), set a conditional behavior (like having a fireball fly down corridor Z when pressure plate Q is stepped on), or follow any of a number of other possible commands that have been built in to the game engine.

Side Scroller. A 2-D genre of game in which the avatar can only move up, down, left, or right. *Defender* and *Sonic the Hedgehog* are both classic examples of the side scroller.

Simulation. A genre of game that attempts to accurately reproduce a real-world experience in all of its details. Driving, flying, and most sports games often fall into this category.

Skills. Any of the tasks an avatar can successfully perform in the game world, such as picking locks, firing a blaster, or doing somersaults. Sometimes also called *abilities.*

SKU. Acronym for Stock Keeping Unit. Commonly pronounced "skew." A SKU refers to how many different ports of a game currently exist. (*Example:* If a game has been developed exclusively for the Windows operating system, it only has one SKU. If later ported to the Macintosh, then it would have two SKUs. If ported to the Playstation, it would have three SKUs, and so on, and so on.) Companies that only port games from one platform to another are sometimes called "SKU houses."

Sprite. A small animated bitmap.

Storyboard. A series of sketches prepared during the planning stage of a project illustrating what a finished FMV or special effect should look like.

Strategy and Tactics. Differing only in scope and scale, both strategy and tactics are plans of action executed to achieve a specific goal. Strategies tend to be concerned with the big picture, utilizing several different methods over long periods of time to arrive at the desired effect. Tactics, on the other hand, are essentially what happen in the trenches—small, short-term actions carried out by a small group of individuals that help support a larger strategy.

Subquest. A task given to an avatar by a nonplayer character, which when completed may result in a reward.

Texture Map. See *Mapping*.

Tile-Based Map. A tile-based map is like a quilt. By assembling the game world out of a pool of small but highly reusable bitmaps called *tiles,* designers can create the illusion of large and complex areas while using very few unique resources. Tile-based systems also make it very easy for programmers to do things like check for collisions or load new environments.

Turn-Based Game. A genre of game in which all action stops until each player has had a *turn*—the opportunity to move a playing piece or complete an action specified in the game's rules.

User-Friendly. Anything that has been developed with the needs and comprehension of a novice user in mind.

Vaporware. A term for any project currently under production that is unlikely ever to be completed or reach the marketplace.

Vibrating Blue Squirrel. Any random, mundane, or common object found in treasure chests or on the bodies of dead opponents. (Coined during the making of *Betrayal at Krondor.*)

World Editor. A powerful, visually based program wielded by designers to create game levels. Editors can be used to lay down tiles, rearrange 3-D walls, add monsters, assign A.I., set event hotspots, or generally modify almost any content within a level.

Zero-Sum Game. An interactive circumstance in which there will always be a winner and a loser.

Zhul. Anything that ends in "of Zhul" is an object of great power and is likely to be wholly unique in a game. This is the functional opposite of a Vibrating Blue Squirrel (coined during the making of *Betrayal at Krondor*).

APPENDIX B

THE PROPOSAL—BETRAYAL AT KRONDOR

In 1991 I teamed up with legendary game designer John Cutter to create the story, dialogue, and design for *Betrayal at Krondor,* a fantasy role-playing game that later went on to become one of the best-selling, award-winning FRPs of 1993. Based on the novels, characters, and universe of Raymond E. Feist and Midkemia Press, *Betrayal* featured a very powerful story line and gave me the very honored opportunity to contribute my own cast of new characters and situations to Midkemia, one of the most popular settings in modern fantasy literature.

The following excerpt from *Betrayal's* design document is a perfect example of how most games begin life. Taking the form of a five to ten page proposal, this is the document that excites the developer and gets your project funded.

Betrayal at Krondor

a game proposal

by

John Cutter & Neal Hallford

Based on the fantasy universe created by

Raymond E. Feist & Midkemia Press

Welcome to the Kingdom of the Isles . . .

*The hunting hounds of a dark elven race are snapping at your heels, prepared to kill any-
one in proximity to Gorath, a grim former moredhel leader and your accidentally acquired
traveling companion. Fleeing his own warring people, he bears a grievous warning for
Arutha, sovereign of the west and Prince of Krondor. Accompanied by Seigneur Locklear
of the Prince's court, you must weave your way south through a treacherous web of lies
and deceit to prevent a war of evil unlike anything ever seen on the continent of Midkemia.
Confronted at every turn by assassins, manipulated by gods and kings alike, it will be a
constant fight to stay alive as you seek to prevent a . . . Betrayal at Krondor!*

Ill-equipped at the outset of your adventure, you must scavenge, sell, and trade for the
goods you need as you wend your way south towards Krondor. Fighting off assassins, ban-
dits, and supernatural monsters, you'll hurl magical spells like *Mad God's Rage* against
your foes, and wield deadly weapons like the *Moredhel Lamprey*. When you're too badly
beaten up, you can wander into town and rest the night in an inn, encountering almost anything from a dangerous run-in with a surly dwarf to a friendly game of chess with the
local innkeeper. In the wilds of Midkemia you'll riddle over the mysterious moredhel
faerie chests, and be richly rewarded for your ingenuity at opening them. Using a wide
assortment of skills, you'll learn to pick locks, repair weapons, and sing for your supper.
Intercept the cryptic spynotes of your enemies, and you'll piece together where ambushes
lie ahead, or the locations of secret stashes of potions, spells, and gold which can help you
on your way. No matter which way you turn, there's always another path, another quest,
another wrong to be righted. Follow the road or wander off the beaten path. *Krondor* is
your world to explore.

The Krondorian Role-Playing Revolution

Ever since the release of Raymond E. Feist's best-selling novel *Magician,* fantasy fans all
over the world have enjoyed the ongoing adventures of Prince Arutha, Jimmy the Hand,
Tomas, and Pug as they have struggled to defend Midkemia and the Kingdom of the Isles
from all manner of medieval evil. Using Dynamix's pre-existing 3-Space engine to depict
beautiful and realistic looking worlds, we can bring together a very popular fantasy universe and a powerful gaming engine to create the most compelling role-playing game
which has ever been created for the personal home computer.

Betrayal at Krondor will be a revolutionary title in a multitude of ways. It will be a first-person perspective game set in a true 3D universe, a major departure from most of the other tile-based or pseudo-3D games currently on the market. Instead of being confined to dungeon-like hallways for most of the game, players explore a vast outdoor environment in which they can walk around houses, enter structures, follow terrain, or use trees and hills to block them from the attacks of enemies. *Krondor* will use 3D objects to create environmental puzzles which the player will learn how to defeat or evade.

Killer Combat

Krondor's combat will allow us to creatively "lap the field," as there are many improvements that can be made to the standard combat system employed by our competitors. These improvements cover virtually every area, including graphics, animation, gameplay, and interface. Combat will be turn-oriented, meaning PCs and monsters take "turns" making moves. Like a friendly game of chess, the player can take as long as he wants to think about each move, and how it figures into his overall strategy for the encounter. Even poorly equipped players will be able to outthink their opponents by using clever strategy, placing the burden of success on the player's participation in the game, not on an invisible, arbitrary dice roll.

Keeping the Best, Trashing the Rest

While retaining a feel that's familiar to most role-playing audiences through the use of resource management, exploration, combat, puzzle-solving, story, and character development, *Krondor* will shed tiresome RPG conventions like class and encumbrance which only impede player freedom and hinder creative exploration. Instead of the illogical sudden leaps in character development inherent in the level system, characters in *Krondor* will incrementally grow better at their skills each time they use them, and can focus how fast they "grow" the abilities they are most interested in.

A New Way of Puzzling

Krondor will introduce a new variety of puzzle, the *wordlock chest*. Rather than being forced to find the one character in the game who will tell the player the password they need, wordlock chests allow the player to solve a riddle through the use of on-screen briefcase-like tumblers instead of typing on the keyboard, making them both fast to solve and fun to play.

Sizzling Story and Character Interactions

Krondor will offer an improved mechanism for interacting with in-game NPCs. Characters encountered in the game will be able to dynamically respond to things they've seen and done through a *keyword* system, changing their responses to give the player meaningful information on the things they most need to understand. Best of all, *Krondor* will feature well-written dialogue and an epic storyline based on one of the most popular fantasy settings in modern literature. Instead of the typical pointless quests to gather the twelve jewels or a game in which the body count is the most important aspect, the player will be given charge of a band of complex and interesting heroes caught in a cosmic battle between good and evil. By dividing the story into chapters, the players can monitor how far along they've come in the game, and see how much further they have to go . . . a level of feedback which is unavailable in any other existing RPG.

Marketing Hooks

- The most realistic and detailed 3D computer-generated world ever created! Explore swamps, dark forests, snowy mountains, dungeons, caverns, and more! Advanced 3D technology is used to create the first Virtual "Fantasy" game!

- Simple "point and click" controls for movement, combat, dialogue, and puzzle solving. The sophistication is in the game, not the interface!

- Unbelievable combat graphics and incredible *rotoscoped* animation for super realistic look!

- Sophisticated AI (Artificial Intelligence). Finally, enemy opponents who actually think and act intelligently! No more random "wandering" monsters! Monsters have different personalities and combat strategies!

- Advanced, entertaining storytelling system! Follow the epic story through nine unique and exciting chapters, each a non-linear adventure full of story twists, engrossing subplots, and followed by a cinematic scene. It's like getting nine games for the price of one!

- Over 100 *unique* spells! (With intriguing names like: *Mad God's Rage, River Song, Eternal Silence, Eyes of Ishap,* and more!)

- Hundreds of objects to find: weapons, treasure maps, magic items, gold, valuable gemstones and treasure, and more!

- Each character in the game has a fully developed personality with likes and dislikes, strengths and weaknesses, even hidden motivations and ambitions.

- Simple, yet entertaining, Character Creation makes "getting into" the game fun and easy!

- Character faces change to show emotion: fear, anger, pain, and more!

- Exciting cinematic cutaways for spine tingling chills! Plus, dramatic close-ups!

- Hundreds of diverting and cleverly designed puzzles. (Solving them is helpful but not essential to finishing the game!)

- Buy or trade items at over 30 unique locations!

- Dramatic music score and sound effects bring the fantasy to life!

Target Requirements

- 386SX or better, 640K

- VGA

- 2MB of RAM and EMM

- 8–10MB of hard drive space

- Compatible with *all* major sound boards

- Release Date: Spring 1993

- Documentation: 65 page manual, map

- Suggested Retail: $69.95

- Completion Time: 70–100 hours

The RPG Market

The RPG market is unquestionably large, and apparently fairly broad, having proved its attraction across a variety of computer and non-computer formats. This makes it difficult to target an "average" RPGer. It *is* possible, however, to analyze key elements of the games themselves; and to look at the likes and dislikes of both players and non-players.

CompuServe Poll of Top CRPG Features

Several months ago CompuServe conducted a poll. Hercules, the assistant sysop in the Gamer's Forum, posted a list of RPG features and asked people to select the four that added most to their enjoyment of the genre. The following table shows the 12 features considered and how each fared in the voting:

Top RPG Features

I	Character or party composition and development.
2 (tie)	Story.
	Balance and feel.
4	Combat.
5	Game interface.
6 (tie)	Convenience features. (Auto-mapping, icons, etc.)
	Puzzles.
8 (tie)	NPC interaction. (Dialogue.)
	Replay value.
10	Non-linearity.
11	Graphics.
12	Sound.

(NOTE: It was quickly pointed out that had players listed their favorite games and the features of those games that made them the most attractive, graphics and sound would have ranked much higher on the list.)

Why Do People Buy and Play Computer RPGs?

1. It is great escapist entertainment. Players become totally immersed and can, at least for a little while, forget about the harsh realities of the real world. They can pretend to be a more exciting person, living in a more exciting time.

2. Fantasy games are set in a comfortable environment and recall childhood memories of imaginative games featuring Knights in shining armor, fire-breathing dragons, wondrous magic, and beautiful Princesses in need of rescue.

3. Many players appreciate the value. For the same amount of money they can buy an arcade game that will hold their interest for several days, or a role-playing game that will take months to finish. Good play balancing can produce a game where players are constantly being introduced to something new: an exciting monster to fight, a new spell or weapon to try out, a new dungeon to explore, etc.

What Don't People Like about RPGs?

1. **"The Games Are Too Difficult to Get Into."** The character creation process required by most products can take several minutes to complete. Also, new characters with low hit points are easy prey for hungry monsters, and it often takes several false starts before gamers are able to build up their character's ratings to a sufficient level to survive the early battles. And, somewhat ironically, the total freedom inherent to most games produces a helpless "lost" feeling. Players are thrust into the world and find themselves standing in the middle of a field somewhere wondering, "Now what am I supposed to do?"

2. **"The Games Are Too Complicated."** Even with the computer handling the "busy work" many games have a complicated interface for manipulating and controlling all the options.

3. **"Role-Playing Games Are Boring."** This complaint was registered by people who encountered products with improper play balancing. There may have been too little combat, or even too much combat, an oft-repeated criticism of *Phantasy Star 2* for the Sega Genesis. Or else perhaps there weren't enough new things to discover as the game progressed. Another offender is mapping, an imperative activity unless automapping is featured. A lot of people enjoy mapping, but most don't because it slows the pace of the game down to a crawl. Still another sleep inducer is the large number of meaningless quests which must be completed before finishing the game.

4. **"The Stories Are All the Same."** The stories are often similar, but even when there are differences they tend to get lost or go unnoticed because of weak storytelling. Non-linear designs are partially to blame, but the quality of the game script is equally significant.

5. **"The Games Take Too Long to Play."** The down side of the value argument above is that the games are *so* big very few people actually finish them. *Might & Magic II* was finished by less than five percent of the people who bought it (by New World's best estimates) and the gamers took between 150 to 300 hours to solve it.

The Competition

Several titles will be published during 1992, representing direct competition. These titles are:

Title	Announced Release Date
Ultima VII	June 1, 1992
Ultima Underworlds: The Stygian Abyss	March 1, 1992
New "Magic" Line from SSI	October 1, 1992
Darklands	October 1, 1992
Crusaders of the Dark Savant	June 1, 1992

Primary Design Objectives

Betrayal at Krondor is obviously not the only role-playing game which will be coming out over the next few years. Here are the ways in which we will respond to the player likes and dislikes which are currently prevalent in the market, and how *Krondor* will establish itself as a role-playing leader:

Increase Accessibility

The first and arguably biggest task is to make the game accessible to the mass market without alienating hard-core players. The hard-core audience expects certain role-playing staples: exploration, resource management, puzzle solving, and combat; so these items will be included in the design, but our game will also feature a simplified, more user friendly interface and more attractive, movie-like displays. In this way we will satisfy both groups: the mainstream player will be drawn to the "hot" graphics and sound, and hard-core RPGers will find a familiar and more visually exciting role-playing environment.

Lower the Cost of Admission

Krondor will be easier and more fun to "get into." The title/credits and especially the intro sequence will hook the player and make him anxious to play, character creation will be informative and entertaining rather than a necessary and somewhat artificial requirement before each game, and the learning curve at the beginning of play will be gently sloped to help acclimate player and interface.

Give Players Purpose and a Sense of Direction

This can be achieved several ways. First, an on-screen map will be available at ALL times, eliminating the confusion caused by the unfamiliar environment. Second, instead of forcing the player to travel great distances when there is nothing to see or do, our game will give players the option to make some movement automatic using 3Space and noninteractive sequences for cinematic transitions, and to show the passage of time.

Emphasize Story

The game takes place in an incredible, unbelievable world, that is, at the same time, amazingly credible and believable. Characters are multi-dimensional and capable of stirring the player's emotions. The story has been carefully plotted, with lots of surprises, a good mix of humor and pathos, and abundant amounts of mystery and foreshadowing to keep the player intrigued and guessing.

Encourage Strategic Thinking

This applies not only to combat and puzzle solving but in other areas as well. If the player is attempting to return to his home castle—having been warned it is about to be attacked by a large army—he might opt for a shortcut through the forest rather than risk encountering the enemy on a main road.

Improve the Production Values

The outstanding presentation is an essential part of *Krondor*'s storytelling experience, but it plays other, equally important roles: attracting consumer attention at retail, drawing critical attention in the media, and increasing long term replayability. Graphics and sound are critical factors in gameplay. It could be argued that long term replayability is a result of the size and quality of the gaming "waveform," which is comprised of an amplitude (height, or excitement level) and a wavelength (width, or amount of time the excitement is maintained). Most RPGs on the market have a broad wavelength with a low amplitude—long term playability is difficult because the games are never very exciting. By comparison, most arcade games have a much higher amplitude but a shorter wavelength—long term replayability is difficult because the gameplay, while relentlessly exciting, quickly becomes repetitive. The solution is to keep the wider RPG wavelengths, but increase the height of the amplitude with outstanding graphics, sound, and gameplay.

The Winning Combination

The market is ripe for a game like *Betrayal at Krondor*. By bringing role-playing games into the world of true 3D, we'll be presenting something unlike anything the players have ever seen before. More to the point, most of the RPGs in existence are using static systems with which most players are already beginning to grow bored (such as *Dungeons & Dragons*). Players are looking for a new look, a new feel, and a new way of playing. By coupling a new system with a well-established fantasy universe, we should be able to redefine the RPG by giving the players something with which they are already familiar while introducing a whole new idiom of gameplay.

Another consideration should be that Dynamix *already* possesses much of the technology required to bring this game to market. With only a few basic modifications, we should be able to put the *Aces of the Pacific* engine on the ground, and that will not only save us time on R&D, but will also give the company additional bang for its 3-Space buck.

APPENDIX C

THE DESIGN DOCUMENT— EXCERPTS FROM NOX

In 1997 while attending the Computer Game Developers Conference, *Nox* creator Michael Booth fulfilled the dream of every independent, garage-game designer in the world. Thanks to a fateful collision with John Hight, later an executive producer at Westwood Studios, Booth had the chance to show off the four-year project he'd lovingly created in his spare time, and *Nox* found a spot with one of the most respected game development houses in the country. With the addition of player classes and its fantastically addictive multiplayer mode, *Nox* became a critically acclaimed hit in February of 2000.

The following section from *Nox*'s design document focuses on one of the most essential elements of any role-playing game, the development of the player character.

Nox

Player Character

Final

Author: **John Hight**

Contributors: **Michael Booth,
Colin Day, Brett Sperry,
Eric Beaumont; Bryan Hansen,
and John Lee**

Modes of Play

Solo

This is the classic solo play game. You select a role for your character; this determines the type of character you will develop and the set of missions he will receive. You'll progress through a series of 11 chapters, each longer and richer, until you ultimately face Hecubah, the Queen of the Undead.

Multiplayer

Arena is for immediate multiplayer action. After setting your character's basic appearance, you jump into specifically designed maps to battle human opponents. Everyone is on a level playing field—characters don't gain experience (their attributes are all approximately the same as a Level 10 player—see below).

Character Classes

Warrior

Warriors defend the honor of the warlord Horrendous and serve as his military might. The elite wear plate armor, often imbued with magical enchantments, and carry heavy swords, axes, or war hammers. Warriors can equip all forms of armor except the bow. They are skilled at blocking blows with either a shield or Great Sword. They have a strict code of honor that eschews the practice of magic spells, although they aren't above using enchanted weaponry. Warriors tend to be very strong, sturdy, and quick.

Warriors start their adventures in the mountains near Dun Mir, the Fortress of Horrendous. They patrol the badlands preventing harmful creatures from coming into otherwise peaceful villages.

Wizard

Wizards are pure magic users. They rely on illusion and trickery to accomplish their goals. They tend to be physically weak, but very mentally adept. They can create magical traps that contain combinations of deadly spells. Their only weapon is the staff and they cannot wear armor for it interferes with their magical spells. Their magic is quite potent and they have an array of offensive and defensive spells.

Wizards start near the Castle of Galava, home to the wizards' academy.

Conjurer

Conjurers protect the people of the plains and forest. They are moderate magic users that can summon creatures of the land to do their bidding. They cannot set traps but they can create Bombers, special creatures that cast spell combos when they contact enemy creatures. Conjurers are heartier than wizards are, but not as skilled in magic. However, they can wield staff, bow, or crossbow and they can wear leather armor.

Conjurers start near the Village of Ix, home to the Conjurer's Temple.

Character Attributes

Attributes distinguish the basic characteristics of each class. Attributes (stats) increase with each experience level and some are capped.

Health (HP)

Health affects how much damage you can sustain before you die. A red meter represents the condition of your health. When this meter is full you are at your maximum level. Each hit point (HP) of damage that you sustain drops your health meter by one unit.

When you reach your maximum health you must go up another level of expertise to increase it further.

Physical energy will replenish itself over time. You can heal quickly by eating food (apples or steak), drinking a healing potion, or receiving a healing spell.

Mana (MP)

Mana determines how many spells a wizard or conjurer can cast. A blue meter next to the red health meter indicates mana level. As spells are cast their mana point (MP) cost is subtracted from your mana level.

Some spells use mana continuously as they are cast. "Lightning" will produce a lightning bolt from your fingertips and continue to electrocute targets until you run out of mana or move. "Greater Heal" will convert your mana into health for your target, at a ratio less than 1 to 1.

Your mana level will slowly replenish itself over time. You can regain it quickly by drinking a mana potion, casting a drain mana spell, or standing next to a mana obelisk.

Warriors do not use mana. No mana meter is present in their interface.

Strength (STR)

Strength affects the power of your physical attacks, the types of armor and weapons you can use, and how much you can carry.

Speed (SPD)

Speed affects the swiftness of your character. The greater your speed, the faster you run and strike.

Starting Attributes

All roles start with the same basic attributes. This represents you entering *Nox* as a regular mortal. Your role dramatically affects how these attributes change as you gain an experience level.

Experience Level (EXP)	Health (HP)	Mana (MP)	Strength (STR)	Speed (SPD)
0	20.00	78.00	20.00	17.25

Experience Levels

Experience and Attributes

Your experience level determines your basic attributes. Higher level warriors will strike more quickly with deadlier blows. Higher level wizards will be able to cast more spells. Conjurers get moderate gains in all attributes.

The following chart shows the progression of attributes for the 10 levels of solo play. When you play the solo game you should reach Level 10 by the end.

When you reach a new experience level, your health and mana reservoirs are automatically reset to the new maximum.

Multiplayer (arena) characters do not gain levels. All attributes are set at a reasonably high level.

10 Levels of Solo Play

PTS	EXP LEVEL	Warrior				Wizard				Conjurer			
		HP	MANA	STR	SPD	HP	MANA	STR	SPD	HP	MANA	STR	SPD
0	1	20.00	0.00	20.00	17.25	20.00	78.00	20.00	17.25	20.00	78.00	20.00	17.25
5,000	2	34.44	0.00	31.67	17.67	26.11	88.22	21.67	17.39	28.89	84.89	23.89	17.50
11,000	3	48.89	0.00	43.33	18.08	32.22	98.44	23.33	17.53	37.78	91.78	27.78	17.75
18,200	4	63.33	0.00	55.00	18.50	38.33	108.67	25.00	17.67	46.67	98.67	31.67	18.00
26,840	5	77.78	0.00	66.67	18.92	44.44	118.89	26.67	17.81	55.56	105.56	35.56	18.25
37,208	6	92.22	0.00	78.33	19.33	50.56	129.11	28.33	17.94	64.44	112.44	39.44	18.50
49,650	7	106.67	0.00	90.00	19.75	56.67	139.33	30.00	18.08	73.33	119.33	43.33	18.75
64,580	8	121.11	0.00	101.67	20.17	62.78	149.56	31.67	18.22	82.22	126.22	47.22	19.00
82,495	9	135.56	0.00	113.33	20.58	68.89	159.78	33.33	18.36	91.11	133.11	51.11	19.25
103,995	10	150.00	0.00	125.00	21.00	75.00	170.00	35.00	18.50	100.00	140.00	55.00	19.50

Multiplayer

PTS	EXP LEVEL	Warrior				Wizard				Conjurer			
		HP	MANA	STR	SPD	HP	MANA	STR	SPD	HP	MANA	STR	SPD
Arena	N/A	150.00	0.00	125.00	21.00	75.00	150.00	35.00	17.50	100.00	125.00	55.00	18.50

Ranking

As you reach a new experience level you get a new rank. This provides an easy way to boast your proficiency in *Nox*.

EXP	Rank Prefix
1	Initiate
2	Apprentice
3	Novice
4	Adept
5	Veteran
6	Expert
7	Master
8	Great
9	Arch-
10	Legendary

Examples: *Bryan the Expert Conjurer; Eric the Veteran Warrior; John the Legendary Wizard.*

Gaining Experience

(*Courtesy of Mike Booth*)

Player Characters in *Nox* have experience points that represent their overall world knowledge and increase over time. Higher experience level characters are more proficient with weapons, magic, and other skills than are "inexperienced" characters. The experience point total a player or character has is known as their experience level.

Experience can be gained in one of the following ways:

- Slaying a nonplayer character or monster in combat
- Completing a pre-scripted quest
- Solving a particular puzzle in a map

Experience points are monotonically increasing. In addition, experience can only be gained in the above situations if the player's experience level is less than the experience level of the opponent. In other words, a player with 3,512 experience points will gain zero experience from killing a creature with 1,200 experience points. A corollary to this is that each creature, puzzle, and quest must have an associated experience level. In addition, the simple rule of only gaining from a more experienced opponent results in a maximum experience level for the entire game. No matter how long a player plays *Nox,* his experience level will eventually "max out." This is a beneficial effect that prevents "god-like" super characters.

When an experience-generating event occurs, and the experience level requirement is met, the player will be awarded a certain amount of experience points to add to his experience level.

Awarding Experience Points

A character can only gain experience from an opponent of a greater experience level. The specific amount of experience awarded to the character by a specific event is determined by the difference in experience levels of the two:

Experience gained = $\min(F_x, ((F_x - C_x) * F + 1))$

F_x = Experience Point Level of foe or event.

C_x = Experience Point Level of character.

F = Gain rate between 0 and 1. Larger values cause experience to be earned faster.

(The "1" is added to avoid asymptotically approaching F_x but never reaching it.)

The following figure shows the effect "F" has on the rate at which experience is gained. A nice benefit of this function is the role of "F" in play balancing. In the event hordes of creatures are routinely battled and play testing shows players are gaining experience too rapidly, this global factor can be "turned down." If experience is gained too slowly, "F" can be "turned up."

NOTE

The release version of *Nox* uses a coefficient of 0.2.

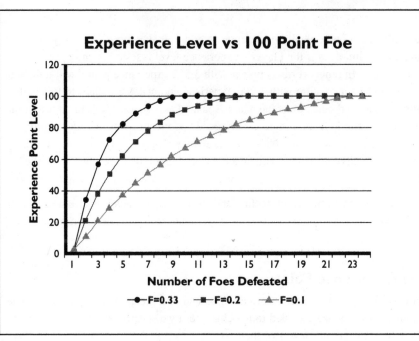

In the event that a player defeats a creature of much higher experience, they will gain a substantial number of experience points. However, this should be very difficult to achieve in practice, due to the other high level creatures which will inevitably accompany the creature, as well as the difference in hit points of the player and creature.

The Book of Knowledge

The Book of Knowledge contains three sections: Skills (Warriors only), Beast Scrolls, and Magic Spells (Conjurers and Wizards only).

Abilities

There are five (5) unique abilities that the warrior can acquire. Warriors get a new ability each level for Levels 2–6. When abilities are acquired their icons are added to the warrior's Skill Set at the lower center of the screen. The description of the skill is inscribed in the Skills section of your Book of Knowledge. Abilities require no mana to use. They are special, one-shot techniques that require activation with each use. Once a particular ability is used it will be unavailable for re-use during a period of time. The icon for the ability in the Skill Set will be darkened until the skill is available again.

Warrior Skill	Exp	Description
Berserker Charge	2	Select this skill then a target or direction. You will run at double speed toward the target and inflict 100 HP in damage (150 HP in multiplay). Target will be knocked back. Collateral damage will apply to your armor items. If you strike a wall or immovable object then you will be stunned for a moment.
War Cry	3	Select this skill and you emit a thunderous shout that can confuse and/or stun nearby low-level creatures. It will also disrupt any magic incantations in progress and prevent magic users from casting for a few seconds. It destroys or detonates all spells in a large area around the Warrior. Duration spells (lightning, obliteration, etc.) are cancelled. Creatures in the process of being summoned are also cancelled. It does not affect summoned creatures or wizard traps.
Tread Lightly	4	You will be able to walk past Traps and Bombers without setting them off. Crumbling floors will not cave in as you walk over them. Your footsteps will make no sound. This mode lasts until you release the mouse button.
Eye of the Wolf	5	When you select this you will see invisible wizards around you, for a short duration.
Harpoon	6	You sling a tethered dart from your sleeve towards the targeting cursor. Any enemies hit by the harpoon will suffer 1 HP and be reeled in towards you.

Beast Scrolls

Beast Scrolls acquaint you with the various monsters within *Nox*. Each scroll provides you with the knowledge of a particular creature. Once you have this knowledge you gain an attack bonus. This will add 20% to the damage you would ordinarily inflict via melee, ranged, or spell attacks.

Only one entry per creature will be added to your Book of Knowledge. Finding additional scrolls won't increase your knowledge.

Conjurers gain the ability to charm creatures in Chapter 3 and the ability to summon them in Chapter 8. You must have knowledge of a creature to charm or summon. A special icon appears above the creature's name in the Beast Scroll section of the Book of Knowledge when a Conjurer gets the summon ability. This beast icon is used like a spell icon to summon that creature.

Magic Spells

In the solo game, spells are acquired through adventuring. They are inscribed into the Spells section of your Book of Knowledge. All spells require mana to use.

To use a spell, you must drag the spell icon from the Book of Knowledge into your Spell Bar. Then select the icon. It will require mana (MP) to use so if you have insufficient MP the spell won't be cast.

Spellcasters get their first spell in Chapter 1. Conjurers get the Charm Creature spell in Chapter 3, the ability to summon Bombers in Chapter 4, and the ability to summon creatures in Chapter 8. Wizards get the ability to create Traps in Chapter 4.

As magic users acquire additional spell books for a given spell, the power of the spell increases. This may make the spell travel more quickly or inflict more damage. You cannot increase a given spell beyond Level 5.

In the multiplayer game, spellcasters have all spells and they are all at Power Level 3. There are no additional spell books in the multiplayer maps.

Spell	Class	Default Target	Mana Cost (MP)	Description	Effects of higher power levels	Effects in Traps & Bombers
Anchor	Wizard	Other	10	When cast, the nearest creature in front of the caster is unable to teleport for a period of time.	Anchor lasts longer.	Anchors victim.
Blink	Conjurer, Wizard	Self Only	10	When invoked, the target will instantaneously be teleported to a random location, unless they are anchored.	Teleport occurs faster.	Teleports victim.
Burn	Conjurer, Wizard	Other Only	10	Casting this spell creates a small flame directly under its victim.	Flame lasts longer, does more damage.	Creates a flame at the trap's location.
Channel Life	Wizard	Self Only	*	Once cast, this spell will convert the caster's health into mana. The player is not allowed to convert his last health point into mana.	More mana for each unit of health. The mana/health ratio may exceed 1/1.	N/A
Charm	Conjurer	Other only	10	This spell changes the loyalty of the nearest creature in front of the caster to that of the caster. The caster must have Lore knowledge of the target. If you banish a charmed creature it will be destroyed. Similar visual effect to Drain Mana with Green instead of Blue.	It takes less time to charm a creature.	N/A
Confuse	Wizard	Other Only	10	Casting this spell causes the target to become disoriented for a short duration. Small birdies appear over their heads. Monsters will attack randomly.	Confusion lasts longer and is more intense.	Confuses the trap's nearest victim.
Counterspell	Conjurer, Wizard	Self Only	20	This destroys or detonates all spells in a large area around the caster. Both friendly and hostile spells will be destroyed. Duration spells (lightning, obliteration, etc) are cancelled by this spell. Creatures in the process of being summoned are also cancelled. This does not affect summoned creatures or wizard traps.	Level 1 only.	Invokes Counterspell at the trap or bomber location.

Spell	Class	Default Target	Mana Cost (MP)	Description	Effects of higher power levels	Effects in Traps & Bombers
Cure Poison	Conjurer	Self	30	This spell removes some or all poison from the target player's system.	Cures more poison.	N/A
Death Ray (multiplayer only)	Wizard	Other Only	60	This spell does a large amount of damage to objects very near the end of the ray. No damage is dealt along the ray itself. Players killed by this spell vaporize into purple mist.		Casts a Death Ray from the trap location to the stored cursor location.
Detonate Seen Traps	Wizard	Self Only	10	When cast, all traps that are owned by the caster and visible will be detonated.	Level 1 only.	Casts the spell at the trap's location.
Dispel Undead	Wizard	Self Only	60	This spell destroys all undead creatures within range of the caster. The actual number destroyed depends on the power of the spell. Undead include ghosts, zombies, skeletons, necromancers, and liches. Effect is an expanding ring, first undead to touch gets as many 'kill points' as it takes to kill it, or until the ring is exhausted.	Increased kill points.	Casts Dispel Undead from the trap location.
Drain Mana	Wizard	Self Only	0	Once begun, the caster will drain mana from the nearest mana-source (obelisks, crystals, other players, some monsters). You can cast other spells while draining mana, such as Lightning and Fireball.	Drains faster.	Takes a fixed amount of mana from the nearest victim to the trap (no effect on warriors).
Earthquake	Wizard	Other Only	60	A bone-jarring tremor emits from the caster to the surrounding area. All enemies in the immediate vicinity experience a screen rattling and suffer damage. Line of sight is not taken into account (damage goes through walls).	Deals more damage.	Creates an earthquake at the trap location.
Energy Bolt	Wizard	Other Only	*	Single energy bolt comes from caster hand to victim. Damage is continuously dealt until the caster runs out of mana, moves, or is damaged. Unlike Lightning, it will not jump to other targets or chain. Warriors wearing metal armor take extra damage.	More damage.	Zaps the nearest victim with a fixed amount of electrical damage.

Spell	Class	Default Target	Mana Cost (MP)	Description	Effects of higher power levels	Effects in Traps & Bombers
Fear	Wizard	Other Only	30	Monsters enchanted with a fear will flee from their enemies for a time period. Undead are immune to fear.	Lasts longer.	Victim enchanted with fear (no effect on players or undead).
Fireball	Wizard	Other Only	30	This spell hurtles a ball of fire in the direction the caster is facing, which detonates into hot sparks upon impact. Caution is advised in close quarters.	Fireball travels faster, is larger, and does more damage.	Shoots fireball in the direction the caster was facing when the trap was created.
Fist of Vengeance	Conjurer	Other Only	60	Casting this spell conjures a giant stone fist that slams into the ground at the caster's cursor location. Only one Fist from each caster can be in the air at any one time.	Larger fist, more damage.	Fist is dropped at Bomber location.
Force Field	Wizard	Self	80	A spherical shield is placed around that caster that absorbs a portion of the incoming damage. The caster can never go below 1 HP while the shield is up. When the hit points of the shield are expended the shield goes away.	More HP on shield.	N/A
Force of Nature (multiplayer only)	Conjurer	Other Only	60	Create a glowing green ball of death that will destroy everything it touches, including the caster. The ball bounces off of walls. If the ball is counterspelled, it will break into 3 smaller, less damaging balls. Counterspelling these little balls will destroy them. If two Forces of Nature get too close, they will cancel each other out with a green lightning bolt. Only one Force of Nature from each caster is allowed in the air at any one time.	Does more damage.	Casts a Force of Nature in the direction the bomber was facing.
Fumble	Wizard	Other Only	60	When cast, this spell causes the nearest creature in front of the caster to drop all the items they are carrying.	Spell travels faster to target.	The nearest victim to the trap fumbles their items.

Spell	Class	Default Target	Mana Cost (MP)	Description	Effects of higher power levels	Effects in Traps & Bombers
Greater Heal	Conjurer	Self	*	Once cast, this spell will convert the caster's mana into health. To end the spell, press any mouse button. Cannot be used while moving. The spell stops if the caster is damaged. A stream of orange life essence flows to the recipient when cast on others.	You get more health for each unit of mana. The health/mana ratio can never be more than 1/1.	N/A
Haste	Wizard	Self	10	When cast, this spell causes the targeted player or monster to move at faster rate for a short time.	Lasts longer.	N/A
Infravision	Conjurer	Self	30	Eneables the recipient to see invisible objects (players and monsters such as ghosts) even if they are standing still.	Lasts longer.	N/A
Inversion	Conjurer, Wizard	Self Only	10	This spell causes all nearby incoming spells to be reversed, so they pursue their caster instead. Spells that are not currently targeting the caster are unaffected.	Level 1 only.	Casts inversion at the trap or bomber location.
Invisibility	Wizard	Self	30	Players and monsters enchanted with invisibility are more transparent the slower they move. They are completely invisible when standing still. They are faintly visible when running. The Conjurer's Infravision and Warrior's Eye of the Wolf can detect all invisible objects. This has no effect on any sounds made by the caster. The effect wears off immediately if another spell is cast or if the caster attacks something.	Level 1 only.	N/A
Invulnerability	Wizard	Self	60	Players and monsters enchanted with this spell become impervious to all forms of damage for a limited duration. The effect is cancelled if caster attacks anything.	Lasts longer.	N/A

Spell	Class	Default Target	Mana Cost (MP)	Description	Effects of higher power levels	Effects in Traps & Bombers
Lesser Heal	Conjurer, Wizard	Self	30	The caster gains a small amount of health each time this spell is cast. Can be used while moving.	More health for each unit of mana. The health/mana ratio is always less than the Greater Heal spell at a comparable level.	N/A
Light	Conjurer, Wizard	Self	10	When cast, this spell causes the caster to glow brightly for a duration.	Level 1 only.	Causes the victim to glow more brightly for a short duration.
Lightning	Wizard	Other Only	*	Lightning will jump to the closest target in front of the caster, and deal damage continuously. As it deals damage, it consumes the caster's mana. At high spell levels, it will also branch to other nearby enemies. The caster must remain still to cast this spell, and if he is hurt, the spell is interrupted. Warriors wearing metal armor take extra damage.	Higher levels let the lightning go between more targets.	Zaps the nearest victim with a fixed amount of electrical damage.
Lock	Wizard	Other Only	10	Lock the nearest door to the caster for a short duration. Only the caster can then open the door, but others can sneak through if the door is ajar.	Lock lasts longer.	Lock a nearby door (if it is in range of the trap).
Mark (1-4) (multiplayer only)	Wizard	Self Only	0	When cast, a marker is placed at the caster's current location, and is only visible to him/her. The first marker placed is numbered '1', the second '2', and so on, up to marker '4'. If more than four markers are placed, they are reused. Markers expire after 3 uses.	Level 1 allows one marker (marker 1). Subsequent spells give the ability to place more markers.	Place a marker at the trap location.
Meteor	Conjurer	Other Only	30	Casting this spell causes a burning meteor to plummet to the ground at the caster's cursor. Only one meteor from each caster can be in the air at once.	More damage.	Drops a meteor at the bomber's location.

Spell	Class	Default Target	Mana Cost (MP)	Description	Effects of higher power levels	Effects in Traps & Bombers
Missiles of Magic	Wizard	Other Only	15	Casting this spell produces homing missiles that track the nearest creature in front of the caster, and detonate upon impact. Each caster can have no more than 4 missiles in the air at a time.	More missiles. Level 1 = 1 Missile Level 2 = 2 Missiles Level 3 = 3 Missiles Multi = 4 Missiles	Cast missile spray in the trap's direction.
Moonglow	Conjurer, Wizard	Self	10	This spell causes the caster's cursor to glow with a bluish light, useful for illuminating dark areas.	Glow lasts longer and casts a slightly wider circle of light.	Gives Moonglow to the victim.
Obliteration	Wizard	Self only	all	A last ditch effort for the wizard. It takes all the mana that they have and channels it into a destructive blast. The blast damages everything within a radius of the caster and will kill the caster as well.	More boom for the mana.	Charges for a fixed amount of time and creates a large explosion. Fixed mana cost, does not hurt the caster unless he is nearby when the explosion occurs.
Pixie Swarm	Conjurer	Self Only	30	Casting the spell produces a cloud of protective pixies, which will swarm towards any visible enemies and detonate upon colliding with them. If there are no enemies about, the pixies will orbit the caster. Each caster can have no more than 4 pixies in the air at a time. Pixies are not monsters, and cannot be charmed. Pixies can be counter-spelled and inverted, though. To invert a pixie, make sure it has targeted you first.	More pixies. Level 1 = 2 Pixies Level 2 = 3 Pixies Level 3 = 4 Pixies Multi = 4 Pixies	Generates a pixie swarm at the bomber's location (unless the caster already has too many pixies in the air).
Poison	Conjurer	Other Only	10	Send out a poison spell that will inject the victim with some poison. More spells increase the poison up to a maximum level.	Increased potency.	Poison the bomber's victim.
Protection from Fire	Conjurer, Wizard	Self	30	The caster has a percentage of all fire damage absorbed by the protection enchantment.	Reduces fire damage by a percent proportional to the spell level.	N/A

Spell	Class	Default Target	Mana Cost (MP)	Description	Effects of higher power levels	Effects in Traps & Bombers
Protection from Poison	Conjurer, Wizard	Self	30	The caster is less likely to be poisoned by a single poison attack.	Reduces chance of being poisoned by a percent proportional to the spell level.	N/A
Protection from Shock	Conjurer, Wizard	Self	30	The caster has a percentage of all electrical damage absorbed by the protection enchantment.	Reduces electrical damage by a percent proportional to the spell level.	N/A
Pull	Wizard	Self Only	10	Casting this spell pulls all nearby loose objects toward the caster.	Move objects with greater force.	Pulls toward trap.
Push	Wizard	Self Only	10	Casting this spell pushes all nearby loose objects away from the caster.	Move objects with greater force.	Pushes away from trap.
Reflective Shield	Wizard	Self Only	30	This spell creates a magical oval shield to appear (and always remain) in front of the caster. The shield will bounce incoming missiles back at their source. The shield drops if the caster moves, but it remains in place as he rotates. The shield will remain until it is destroyed by physical or magical damage. The shield does not protect the caster from side or rear attacks.	Shield is stronger.	N/A
Ring of Fire (multiplayer only)	Wizard	Self Only	60	Casting this spell causes a lethal ring of flames to expand out from the caster's location. The caster can be damaged if he steps into the ring.	Size and number of flames.	Generate a ring of fire at the trap's location.
Run	Wizard	Other Only	10	Victim runs uncontrollably for a short duration. Enchanted players can still direct their PC's but they cannot slow them down.	Enchantment lasts longer.	Victim nearest the trap runs.
Shock	Wizard	Self	30	Invoking this spell causes the caster to become charged with a large dose of wild electricity. The shock is discharged when an object or creature is touched. Victims will receive a nasty jolt. The charge will dissipate after a short time if no victim is found.	Shock will last longer and do more damage.	Electrical damage to victim.

Spell	Class	Default Target	Mana Cost (MP)	Description	Effects of higher power levels	Effects in Traps & Bombers
Slow	Conjurer, Wizard	Other Only	10	This spell causes the nearest creature in front of the caster to become slowed, moving at half speed for a short duration.	Last longer.	Slows the victim.
Stun	Conjurer	Other Only	10	Weak victims of this spell become immobile for a short time. They can still rotate, attack and teleport. Stronger victims become slowed, instead of stunned. Stunned victims are shown with a circle of "birdies" over their head.	Last longer.	Stuns the victim.
Summon Creatures	Conjurer	Self Only	*	Calls into being a creature that will obey the commands of the caster. Casting cost depends on the type of creature summoned. Each creature has its own summon spell. You must have a Beast scroll on a monster before you can summon it. Summon spot gets a circle effect, and the monster fades in from translucent.	Time to summon is lessened.	N/A
Swap Location	Wizard	Other Only	10	This spell causes the nearest visible creature and the caster to swap positions.	Spell moves faster and on higher level creatures.	Teleport occurs faster.
Tag	Conjurer, Wizard	Other Only	10	Enemies with the tag enchantment will show up on the player's map.	Lasts longer.	Same.
Telekinesis	Wizard	Self Only	20	Allows caster to push objects with the cursor.	Lasts longer.	Tethers victim to glyph spot.
Teleport to Marker (multiplayer only)	Wizard	Self	10	Casting this spell causes the caster to teleport to the location of marker (1-4). A marker must exist to successfully cast this spell.	Teleports faster.	Same. Make sure the target location was the cursor location of the caster at trap cast time.

Spell	Class	Default Target	Mana Cost (MP)	Description	Effects of higher power levels	Effects in Traps & Bombers
Teleport to Target (multiplayer only)	Wizard	Self only	20	Casting this spell causes the caster to tele-port to the location of their mouse cursor. The cursor must point to a visible area of the screen for this spell to be successful.	Teleports faster.	Same.
Toxic Cloud	Conjurer	Other Only	60	Invoking this spell creates a cloud of noxious gases at the caster's cursor. These gases linger for a time, damaging and poisoning any breathing creature that comes into contact with them. Non-breathing monsters are unaffected, as are those monsters with natural immunity to poison (all poison-delivering monsters are immune to poison themselves).	More puffs, does more damage, larger radius.	Creates a Toxic Cloud at the bomber's location.
Trigger Trap	Wizard	Self Only	5	When cast, this spell causes the nearest trap under the caster's control to activate.	Can trigger from farther away.	Same.
Vampirism	Conjurer	Self	20	When invoked, the caster will gain life for a portion of the damage he or she directly deals for a short duration. This only occurs by damage done directly by the caster via melee, missile, or spells - this does not include owned creatures or bombers. The recipient of the vampirism health must have clear line of sight to the damage in order to receive it. This health transfer appears as a stream of red corpuscles from the victim to the attacker.	Vampirism lasts longer. You never gain as much life as you took from a player.	N/A
Wall	Wizard	Other Only	30	Places a magic wall section at the cursor, perpendicular to the caster. The wall will be removed when a subsequent wall is invoked. The wall can be broken by direct damage.	Wider wall section.	Creates a wall section perpendicular to the caster at the time the Trap was constructed.

Traps

Wizard Traps

Wizards can construct magical traps. Each trap can contain up to three spells that will cast sequentially when the trap is sprung. The mana cost for the spells is paid when the trap is constructed. The trap is placed at the wizard's feet. He can pick it up and carry it in his inventory. Once the trap is sprung it disappears.

The trap's owner, and his friends, can safely walk over the trap without fear of setting it off. The owner may retrieve the trap at any time by picking it up. Spells inside the trap that require a location will request it via a targeting cursor when the trap is constructed. Spells that require a direction will use the caster's facing when the trap was set.

A wizard is limited to eight traps in the world at any given time. Wizards can define three different spell combinations (Trap Sets).

Bombers

Conjurers can summon a Bomber containing up to three magic spells. A Bomber will track down any enemy within sight and release its spell effects on contact.

Like Wizards with their traps, Conjurers can predefine up to three different spell combinations (Trap Sets) from their Spell Bar.

A conjurer is limited to four bombers in the world at any given time. Since bombers are summoned beasts they appear in the conjurer's Creature Cage. They can be given commands like any summoned or charmed creature: Banish, Observe, Guard, Escort, and Hunt. Banish removes the Bomber from the world. Observe places the camera view on that creature (view returns to the player if he takes damage or the bomber is killed). Guard tells the bomber to guard his current position. Escort tells the Bomber to follow the player. Hunt tells the bomber to search for an enemy.

Weapons

Weapons are the principal means of attack for fighters. Conjurers may use magic staves and bows. Wizards may only use the staff. Some weapons require a good deal of strength to operate so they may not be useable to low-level players.

Weapon Usage

Weapon	Warrior	Conjurer	Wizard
Sword	*		
Long Sword	*		
Great Sword	*		
Axe	*		
Ogre Axe	*		
Mace	*		
War Hammer	*		
Quiver		*	
Bow		*	
Crossbow		*	
Shuriken	*		
Chackrum	*		
Wooden Staff	*	*	*
Sulphurous Flare Staff		*	*
Sulphurous Shower Staff		*	*
Fireball Staff		*	*
Triple Fireball Staff			*
Lightning Staff			*
Wand of Death			*
Force of Nature Staff		*	
Halberd of Horrendous	*	*	*
Halberd with the Heart of Nox	*	*	*
Halberd with the Heart of Nox and the Weirdling	*	*	*
Staff of Oblivion	*	*	*

Weapon Descriptions

The base damage of a weapon is the unmodified number of hit points (HP) it will inflict on a victim without armor. The effectiveness of the weapon and the strength of the attacker determine the actual damage dealt. Except for Flimsy weapons, the actual damage will always be greater than the base.

The base durability of a weapon determines how much damage it can sustain before it breaks. Durability is determined by the weapon's material, which is discussed in detail in the next section. Weapons sustain more damage from blocking than they do from attacking; this applies to the Great Sword and staves. You can repair weapons at a Shopkeeper.

Weapon	Base Dmg.	Base Durab.	Req'd Stren.	Weight	Description
Sword (1 handed)	5	160	20	40	The sword is the basic weapon of the warrior. It can be held in one hand leaving the other hand available for a shield.
Long Sword (1 handed)	9	180	30	50	The long sword requires more strength to wield than the sword.
Great Sword (2 handed)	50	400	70	125	The great sword requires more strength to wield than the long sword. It requires two hands so no shield may be equipped, but the great sword can block attacks.
Axe (1 handed)	21	220	40	125	The axe is devastating on victims without plate or chain armor. It requires a good deal of stamina. It requires more strength than the mace.
Ogre Axe (1 handed)	30	50	50	175	The Ogre Axe deals more damage than a standard axe, but it is crudely built and quite fragile.
Mace (1 handed)	6	200	20	90	The mace requires more strength to wield than the sword. It strikes faster than the sword and is particularly effective against things on the ground.
War Hammer (2 handed)	100	350	70	200	It is devastating on all victims, regardless of armor. It requires a good deal of stamina. The War Hammer requires more strength than any other weapon.

Weapon	Base Dmg.	Base Durab.	Req'd Stren.	Weight	Description
Quiver (default: 20 arrows)	10/100	500	–	20	A supply of arrows. Standard arrows rarely penetrate plate or chain armor unless fired from a crossbow. See details on different types of quivers.
Bow (2 handed)	–	500	20	20	The war bow fires any manner of arrows.
Crossbow (2 handed)	–	500	34	40	The crossbow fires arrows slower than a bow, but it inflicts more damage. The Crossbow uses the same arrows as the bow. It requires more strength than the bow.
Shuriken (default: 20 stars) (1 handed)	4	10	20	5	Shuriken are light, radial weapons that are thrown. They stick in their victims or break upon impact so only 1 per attack. They can be stacked in your inventory. They do less damage than chackra.
Chackrum (1 handed)	5	300	20	20	Chackra are thrown at victims out of reach. They do not break, they return to their owner (if possible). They bounce off of walls and victims.
Wooden Staff (2 handed)	4	120	20	30	The basic staff can be used to strike opponents and block incoming blows.
Sulphurous Flare Staff (2 handed)	2	100	20	30	A small pyrotechnic missile fires from this staff causing only minimal damage to the target. Unlimited charges.
Sulphurous Shower Flare Staff (2 handed)	6	100	20	30	Three small pyrotechnic missiles fire from this staff causing moderate damage to the target. Unlimited charges.
Fireball Staff (2 handed)	42	100	20	30	The Fireball staff hurtles a ball of fire at the target direction. The ball detonates on impact into hot sparks. The explosion can cause damage to the wielder if he or she is too close to the impact. Caution is advised in close quarters.

Weapon	Base Dmg.	Base Durab.	Req'd Stren.	Weight	Description
Triple Fireball Staff (2 handed) (multiplayer only)	148	100	20	30	Similar to the Fireball staff except three fireballs project per charge instead of one. (Spread firing pattern.)
Lightning Staff (2 handed)	36/sec	110	20	30	This staff causes a powerful bolt of lightning to leap forth and electrocute the nearest enemy in front of the wielder. Each charge powers the bolt for a finite duration. After a charge is spent the wielder may fire again to continue the assault.
Wand of Death (2 handed) (multiplayer only)	90	70	20	30	The Death Ray staff shoots a powerful ray at the target location, severely damaging any items situated there.
Force of Nature Staff (2 handed)	300	80	20	30	The Force of Nature staff calls into being a ball of ghastly green light that shoots toward the target direction. This force will do tremendous damage to anything foolish enough to cross its path, including the wielder. Inanimate objects can deflect it.
Halberd of Horrendous (2 handed) (solo only)	5	*	20	30	This is the first stage of the Staff of Oblivion. It is similar to a wooden staff, but it is indestructible.
Halberd with the Heart of Nox (2 handed) (solo only)	17	*	20	30	The second stage of the Staff of Oblivion adds the Heart of Nox, which causes 12 HP shock damage in addition to the base damage of the staff.
Halberd with the Heart of Nox and the Weirdling (2 handed) (solo only)	14	*	20	30	The third stage of the Staff of Oblivion adds the Weirdling, which will drain life from a victim and give it to the wielder. The Weirdling uses a portion of the Heart of Nox energy so the shock damage is reduced to 9 HP.
Staff of Oblivion (2 handed) (solo only)	300/sec	*	20	30	The final stage of the Staff of Oblivion adds the Orb. It emits a powerful plasma beam that removes the souls from enemies.

Weapon Enhancements

The effectiveness of a weapon is determined by three factors: *Effectiveness*, *Material*, and *Enchantments*. Each weapon is identified as:

[Effectiveness][Material]<weapon name>[of Primary Enchantment][and Secondary Enchantment]

Effectiveness

Effectiveness determines the amount of damage (HP) a weapon will inflict on the target with each blow. Bows, Quivers, and Shuriken have no Effectiveness. Note that "Standard" weapons bear no Effectiveness description.

Power (Applied to Standard Weapons)	Damage Multiplier
Flimsy	X 0.94 to base damage
(Standard)	X 1.00 to base damage
Sturdy	X 1.04 to base damage
Mighty	X 1.08 to base damage
Grand	X 1.12 to base damage
Titan	X 1.16 to base damage
Divine	X 1.20 to base damage

Material

Material is the type of metal the weapon is composed of. The material description is not present on staves, bows, or quivers. Material determines the Durability of a weapon. Each time a weapon strikes an object or blocks a blow it sustains some damage. Durability is the amount of damage a weapon or piece of armor can sustain before it breaks. When no Material description is present its durability is the same as Iron (base).

Material	Durability
Copper	X 0.94 to base HP
Iron	X 1.00 to base HP
Bronze	X 1.04 to base HP
Silver	X 1.08 to base HP
Gold	X 1.12 to base HP
Titanium	X 1.16 to base HP
Diamond	X 1.20 to base HP

Enchantments (Primary)

Primary enchantments give weapons additional powers beyond the initial damage they inflict. Parts of the weapon are colored to give a clue to the enchantment. The Level determines the power of the enchantment.

Enchantment	Level		Color	Effect
Blue Fire	1	Mana Singe	Cyan	Emits a blue fire that removes mana
	2	Mana Scorch		upon contact with a magic user. It does
	3	Mana Burn		not transfer this mana to the wielder.
	4	Mana Storm		
Confusion	1	Bewilderment	White	Confuses target. Contact between item
	2	Dazing		and target must occur.
	3	Stupor		
	4	Confusion		
Fire	1	Embers	Red	Inflicts additional fire damage.
	2	Flame		Hammers and axes striking the ground
	3	Fire		will produce a circle of flame radiating
	4	Inferno		from their impact. Wielder is unaffected.
Impact	1	Collision	White	Pushes target back after hit.
	2	Force		
	3	Impact		
	4	Concussion		

Enchantment	Level		Color	Effect
Stun	1	Numbness	Yellow	Stuns and anchors target.
	2	Stunning		Wielder is unaffected.
	3	Immobility		Contact between item and target
	4	Paralysis		must occur.
Shock	1	Spark	Navy Blue	Inflicts additional shock damage.
	2	Zap		Wielder is unaffected.
	3	Shock		
	4	Electrocution		
Mana Drain	1	Lesser Mana Drain	Sky Blue	Draws mana from the victim and
	2	Mana Drain		transfers it to the wielder.
	3	Greater Mana Drain		
	4	Mana Vampire		
Vampirism	1	The Mosquito	Purple	Transfers damage done to target to
	2	The Tick		health of wielder. The item must
	3	The Leech		actually land a physical hit for this
	4	The Vampire		to occur.
Poison	1	The Wasp	Green	Poisons target, in addition to regular
	2	The Spider		damage. Degree of poison depends
	3	The Polyp		on level.
	4	The Scorpion		Wielder is unaffected.

Enchantments (Secondary)

Secondary enchantments are the same as primary enchantments, but they never exceed Level 3.

Conjurer's Bow

There are two basic bow weapons that may only be used by the Conjurer: the Bow and the Crossbow. Each requires a quiver of arrows. Each quiver contains 20 arrows. Whenever a bow is equipped, the Equipped Weapon Indicator shows the bow with the associated quiver overlaying it. The number of arrows in the quiver appears in the charge counter.

You may find special quivers containing enchanted arrows: fire, poison, shock, etc. To use these arrows, select their quiver in your inventory. The basic quiver will be disassociated with the bow and the new quiver will be highlighted. Whenever the bow is equipped it will use the enchanted arrows. When all enchanted arrows are exhausted the enchanted quiver will disappear and the bow will switch to the next available quiver. The number of arrows in a quiver is displayed over the quiver image in the inventory.

Although Bows have durability, the only way they can take damage is if you drop them on a hazard like lava or fire.

Bow Primary Enchantments (No More Than One Per Bow)

The level determines the intensity of the enchantment.

Enchantment	Level		Color	Effect
Impact	1	Collision	White	Pushes target back after hit. Contact
	2	Force		between item and target must occur.
	3	Impact		
	4	Concussion		
Projectile Speed	1	Swift Bolt	Red	Arrows fly faster.
	2	Fast Bolt		
	3	Speeding Bolt		
	4	Charging Bolt		
Readiness	1	Readiness	Red	Loads and Fires more rapidly.
	2	Swiftness		
	3	Reaction		
	4	Quickening		

Quiver Enchantments (No More Than One Per Quiver)

Enchantment	Level		Color	Effect
Confusion	1	Bewilderment	White	Confuses target.
	2	Dazing		
	3	Stupor		
	4	Confusion		
Fire	1	Embers	Red	Inflicts additional fire damage. Wonderful pyrotechnics when arrow impacts.
	2	Flame		
	3	Fire		
	4	Inferno		
Stun	1	Numbness	Yellow	Stuns and anchors target.
	2	Stunning		
	3	Immobility		
	4	Paralysis		
Shock	1	Spark	Navy Blue	Inflicts additional shock damage.
	2	Zap		
	3	Shock		
	4	Electrocution		
Mana Drain	1	Lesser Mana Drain	Sky Blue	Drains mana from opponent.
	2	Mana Drain		
	3	Greater Mana Drain		
	4	Mana Vampire		
Vampirism	1	The Mosquito	Purple	Transfers damage done to target to health of wielder.
	2	The Tick		
	3	The Leech		
	4	The Vampire		
Poison	1	The Wasp	Green	Inflicts additional poison damage.
	2	The Spider		
	3	The Polyp		
	4	The Scorpion		

Bow Secondary Enchantments

There are no secondary enchantments on bows or quivers.

Magic Staves

Magic staves will fire their projectiles each time the action button is pressed. The Staff of Oblivion and the Staff of Lightning will fire continuously as long as the action button is held down. They will also block melee blows if you face the attacker without firing. Once the charges are exhausted these staves behave just like the Wooden Staff and can be used in hand-to-hand combat.

Staff	Charges
Wooden Staff	0
Sulphurous Flare Staff	200
Sulphurous Shower Flare Staff	100
Fireball Staff	20
Triple Fireball Staff	10
Lightning Staff	60
Wand of Death	5
Force of Nature Staff	3
Halberd of Horrendous	0
Halberd with the Heart of Nox	0
Halberd with the Heart of Nox and the Weirdling	0
Staff of Oblivion	250

Staves can have two special enchantments.

Enchantment	Color	Effect
Recharge	Red	Allows staves to be recharged at mana obelisks.
Replenishment	Red	Slowly replaces the charges in a staff over time.

Armor

Armor Usage

Armor Item	Warrior	Conjurer	Wizard
Shirt	*	*	*
Pants	*	*	*
Sneakers	*	*	*
Medieval Shirt	*	*	*
Medieval Pants	*	*	*
Cloak	*	*	*
Leather Helm	*	*	
Leather Armbands	*	*	
Leather Tunic	*	*	
Leather Leggings	*	*	
Leather Boots	*	*	*
Chain Coif	*		
Chainmail Tunic	*		
Chainmail Leggings	*		
Armored Boots	*	*	
Plate Helm	*		
Plate Arms	*		
Breastplate	*		
Plate Leggings	*		
Plate Boots	*		
Knight's Helm	*		
Conjurer's Helm		*	
Wizard's Helm			*
Wizard's Robe			*
Round Shield	*		
Kite Shield	*		

Armor Enchantments

The Armor Value determines the amount of damage a particular armor item will absorb. The higher the value, the more damage it will block. Your overall armor protection is the sum of the armor values for each item equipped. You will always sustain some damage since you can never reach 100% protection with body armor.

Warriors raise their shields whenever standing still. The shield will drop when the warrior moves or attacks. Shields block 100% of all damage directed at them. They offer no armor protection unless equipped and raised.

Armor items sustain damage as they absorb attacks. Durability determines how much damage an armor item can take before it breaks. You can repair armor items at a Shopkeeper.

Armor	Base Armor Value	Base Durab.	Req'd Stren.	Weight	Description
Shirt	10	*	20	5	
Pants	10	*	20	7	
Sneakers	10	*	20	5	
Medieval Shirt	20	*	20	5	
Medieval Pants	20	*	20	7	
Cloak	30	200	20	5	
Leather Helm	70	200	20	30	
Leather Armbands	20	200	20	5	
Leather Tunic	150	300	20	50	
Leather Leggings	80	200	20	20	
Leather Boots	50	200	20	10	
Chain Coif	100	325	30	50	Susceptible to shock damage.
Chainmail Tunic	200	400	30	100	Susceptible to shock damage.
Chainmail Leggings	100	325	30	75	Susceptible to shock damage.
Armored Boots	80	300	24	20	

Armor	Base Armor Value	Base Durab.	Req'd Stren.	Weight	Description
Plate Helm	120	675	40	50	Susceptible to shock damage. Extra protection from blades.
Plate Arms	50	600	40	75	Susceptible to shock damage. Extra protection from blades.
Breastplate	240	800	40	150	Susceptible to shock damage. Extra protection from blades.
Plate Leggings	130	700	40	100	Susceptible to shock damage. Extra protection from blades.
Plate Boots	100	700	40	50	Susceptible to shock damage. Extra protection from blades.
Knight's Helm	140	850	40	100	Susceptible to shock damage. Extra protection from blades.
Conjurer Helm	120	400	22	40	
Wizard Helm	120	350	20	20	
Wizard Robe	200	325	20	30	
Round Shield	*	200	20	50	
Kite Shield	*	300	40	75	

Armor Enchantments

The effectiveness of an armor item is determined by three factors: *Quality*, *Material*, and *Enchantments*. Each weapon is identified as:

[Quality][Material]<armor name>[of Primary Enchantment][and Secondary Enchantment]

Normal clothing has Standard quality and no enchantments. It remains on you after you are killed unless you have removed it. All other items are scattered near your fallen corpse. In a multiplayer game, when you restart you'll have your basic garb and your starting hand weapon (sword for warrior, staff for magic users).

Quality

Quality determines the armor value. This is the amount of damage (HP) a piece of armor will absorb with each blow.

Quality	Damage Multiplier
Flimsy	X 0.94 to base armor value
(Standard)	X 1.00 to base armor value
Sturdy	X 1.04 to base armor value
Mighty	X 1.08 to base armor value
Grand	X 1.12 to base armor value
Titan	X 1.16 to base armor value
Divine	X 1.20 to base armor value

Material

Material describes the composition of the armor. Material determines the Durability of the Armor. Cloth and Leather are included for comparison. Leather armor cannot be composed of anything but leather. Metal armor can be composed of Copper, Iron, Bronze, Silver, Gold, Titanium, or Diamond.

Durability

Durability is the amount of damage a piece of armor can sustain before it breaks.

Material	Durability
Cloth	X 1.00 to base HP
Leather	X 1.00 to base HP
Copper	X 0.94 to base HP
Iron	X 1.00 to base HP
Bronze	X 1.04 to base HP
Silver	X 1.08 to base HP
Gold	X 1.12 to base HP
Titanium	X 1.16 to base HP
Diamond	X 1.20 to base HP

Armor Enchantments

The level determines the intensity of the enchantment.

Enchantment	Level		Color	Effect
Fire Protection	1	Dragon's Scale	Red	Protects wearer from a
	2	Dragon's Claw		portion of fire damage.
	3	Dragon's Hide		
	4	Dragon's Heart		
Poison Protection	1	Wasp's Bane	Green	Reduces risk for poisoning.
	2	Spider's Bane		
	3	Polyp's Bane		
	4	Scorpion's Bane		
Shock Protection	1	Anti-Spark	Navy Blue	Protects wearer from a
	2	Anti-Zap		portion of shock damage.
	3	Anti-Shock		
	4	Anti-Lightning		
Light	1	The Stars	White	Helms only.
	2	N/A		Helm glows, increasing the
	3	N/A		light radius around the wearer.
	4	N/A		
Speed	1	Haste	Yellow	Boots only.
	2	Running		Increases speed of wearer.
	3	Leaping		
	4	The Wind		
Regeneration	1	Cure Wounds	Lime Green	Causes wearer to slowly heal.
	2	Healing		
	3	Greater Healing		
	4	Regeneration		

Armor Enchantments (Secondary)

Secondary enchantments are the same as primary enchantments, but they never exceed Level 3.

APPENDIX D

THE WORLD LAYOUT— EXCERPT FROM FALLOUT

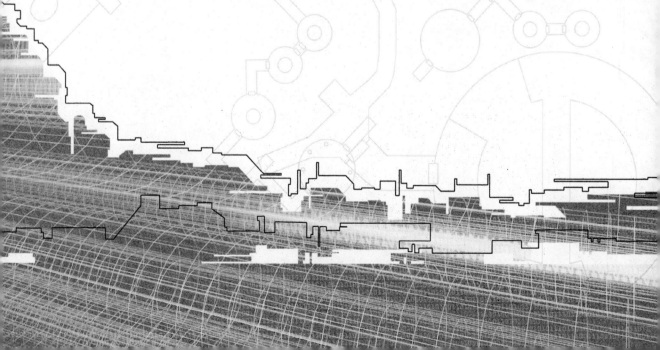

P*ostapocalyptic* isn't a description that usually pops into most people's minds when they think of an RPG, but this multiaward-winning title from 1997 breathed new life into the genre by breaking away from many long-held traditions. Inspired by a previous game from Interplay called *Wasteland* and utilizing Steve Jackson Games, GURPs role-playing system, the close-knit team of designers behind *Fallout* created a game loved by players, designers, and critics alike.

The following excerpt from their level design for "The Buried Vault" gives an excellent example of how designers break a game level into important areas, quests, and encounters. Not only are documents like this useful to the design team, but they are invaluable tools to testing teams and strategy guide writers who need to know where every important encounter in the game can be found.

Fallout

A GURPs Post-Nuclear Adventure

A Design By

Chris Taylor
Scott Campbell
Tim Cain
Jason Taylor
Dave Hendee
Scott Bennie
Leonard Boyarsky
Jason Anderson
Buried Vault Design

Version 1.0

12 December 1996

Timeline Effects

Invasion

The Buried Vault does not get invaded by the super mutant army.

Day and Night

Some locations will be different during day or night hours. This is marked in the document as DAY and NIGHT. Day in the Buried Vault Entrance is 0801 to 1800, twilight is 1801 to 2000, night is 2001 to 0600, and morning is 0601 to 0800. During twilight and morning, the light will gradually dim or lighten to the full day or night cycle. For purposes of the location documents, twilight and morning are both considered to be day time. Of course, all underground locations are considered dark.

Since there is not much difference between day and night once the player enters the Buried Vault, the locations just describe one setting (with the exception of the surface area).

Map Keys

First Entry

Buried Vault Entrance: E1 (on the surface, near the shack, about 15 hexes to the west of the shack)

Town Map Entrance Points

Buried Vault Entrance: E1 (on the surface, near the shack)

     & E2 (in the Buried Vault caverns, near the Airlock)

Buried Vault Living Quarters: E3 (near the elevators)

Buried Vault C&C Center: E4 (near the elevator)

Game Map Movement

Buried Vault Surface: Climbing down the hole in the shack will lead to the Buried Vault Entrance caverns.

For the rest of the Vault, climbing the ladders in the elevator shafts will move the player up and down the levels.

Captured!

If the player is knocked unconscious by the denizens of the Buried Vault, she will be eaten alive!

Miscellaneous

Critters in the Buried Vault have a chance of repopulating. Record the date of visit to the Buried Vault. There is a 10+5% chance (cumulative per day) that a particular critter will be regenerated (in the same location, with the normal HP). When the player returns to the Buried Vault, check for regeneration on all the dead critters in that map.

Map 1: Buried Vault Entrance

Surface (Day)

The shack is the only remaining entrance to the Buried Vault.

If the player is unlucky, or on a roll of 7- on 3d6, there is a hostile Radscorpion near the shack.

The shack contains nothing of interest. The first time the player enters the shack, display: "This is an old shack. It is barely standing, and seems to have been looted long ago."

Climbing the ladder will take the player to the caverns below. If the player uses the ladder, roll DX+4. If successful, they climb to the bottom of the ladder. If failure, display: "You fall off the ladder near the bottom." If critical failure, display: "You slip off the ladder, and plummet into the darkness below. You land with a crash and take [X] damage.", where X is 3d6-9. If X is 0, then print "no damage."

When the player stands next to the ladder the first time, and has the Phobia (darkness) disadvantage, display: "The ladder disappears into the inky darkness below. You do not feel well." The first time they attempt to use the ladder, roll against the character's Will attribute. If successful, "You manage to calm your fears and begin climbing the ladder down." If failure, "You cannot bring yourself to enter the darkness below."

If the player has the Quirk (Afraid of Heights), the first time she is next to the ladder, display: "That's an awful long way down. Your stomach is queasy."

Surface (Night)

The same, except:

If the player is unlucky, or on a roll of 11- on 3d6, there is a hostile Radscorpion near the shack.

Caverns

This area is dark.

If the player has Phobia (darkness), every 5 minutes the player is in darkness, check their Will attribute with a roll. If failed, the player will stop walking, display:

> "You feel the cold hand of darkness reaching for you."
>
> "The absence of light is starting to drive you mad."
>
> "Deep in the darkness you can feel movement."
>
> "It's really, really dark."

If the player enters a hex that is not pure darkness, reset the counter. If the Will attribute roll is successful, do not display anything, but reset the counter. If a critical success is rolled, then do not make any more rolls this time on the map.

There are a total of seven rats in the caverns.

Caved-In Tunnel

Roll Area Knowledge (Vault). If successful, display: "This is where the main entrance to the Vault should be." Roll IQ; if successful, display: "The collapse looks natural. You cannot find any evidence of foul play or explosives." This is a one-time only event.

Airlock

The airlock is open.

The first time the player walks through this area, roll Area Knowledge (Vault) +2. If successful, display: "If this is following the same layout of your home vault, there should be some flares in a compartment in the west wall."

There is a compartment in the west wall that contains six flares.

There is a single rat in the airlock.

Emergency Medical Lab

The lab is mostly destroyed. The first time the player enters this area, display: "This area has been previously looted. There is a large amount of damage to the delicate equipment."

There are four rats in the medlab.

A successful Area Knowledge (Vault) roll will display: "There is an emergency medical cache on the east wall. It may prove useful." This is a one-time only event.

There is a wall container on the west wall that contains two stimpatches. There is a another wall container that is empty.

Elevator

The elevator is not working. The player will have to use the ladder in the elevator shaft to climb to the next level of the Vault.

Climbing the ladder is difficult. It will require a DX+2 check to make a successful climb in the dark. If a flare is dropped at the base of the ladder, it will make it a DX+4 check. If the player failures the DX check, display: "You fall off the ladder about halfway up and take [X] damage.", where X is 3d6-9. If the player critically failsw, display: "You almost make it to the top before falling off the ladder. You land badly and take [X] damage.", where X is 5d6-10. If X is 0, then print "no damage."

A character with the Afraid of Heights Quirk gets a one-time only display message at the base of the ladder: "The ladder seems to travel forever upward." Those characters get a -2 to the DX roll to all ladder climbs in the Vault.

Characters with Intuition roll IQ when at the base of the ladder. If successful, display: "You get the feeling that some light would make the ladder climb easier." This is a one-time only event.

There are two rats near the base of the elevator. There is a mole-rat near the interior of the airlock.

Map 2: Buried Vault Living Quarters

Elevators

These elevator shafts lead from the Entrance level of the Vault to the C&C level. Using the ladders is similar to Map 1: Elevators.

Living Quarters

There is a total of eight rats in this area, and four mole-rats.

A successful Area Knowledge (Vault) roll will display: "This is the Vault Living Quarters. A standard design from the time before the War."

In one of the rooms, there is a pile of bones. The first time the player enters this room, roll Vision. If successful, display: "You see something in the darkness under the bed." If the player uses the bed, display: "You find a first aid kit that must have slid under the bed."

In another of the rooms, there is a wall container that is open. It is empty. On the floor underneath the wall container is an ammo box of 10mm JHP.

The room farthest south has a chair facing the wall with no computer on the wall. When the player enters this room, roll Vision-2. If successful, display: "Something catches your eye when you look at the chair." If critical success, display: "You see the tip of a key in a crack in the chair." First time only. If the player uses the chair in this room, they will get the Vault Key. This key will open the storage locker in the storage room on Map 3.

Map 3: Buried Vault Living Command and Control Center

Elevators

These elevator shafts lead down to the Vault Living Quarters. See Map 1: Elevators for the use of the ladders.

There is a mole-rat near the elevator.

Meeting Room

This room has been infested with mole-rats and other rodents. There are three mole-rats in this room, and five rats.

Much rubble fills this room.

Roll Area Knowledge (Vault) when the player first enters this room. On a successful roll, display: "You know this to be the meeting room for your Vault. Where the emergency supply cabinet would be is buried under tons of rock." First time only.

Roll Vision-2. Roll every time the player enters this room until they find the tunnel. On a successful roll, display: "In the corner of the room is a rat-sized tunnel. They must be burrowing their way into the Vault through here." A successful demolitions roll in this room, after knowledge of the tunnel via the Vision roll will display: "The explosion closes off the tunnel with a mighty blast!" No more critters will be regenerated. Award the player one Character Point.

Storage

This room has a locked storage cabinet. To open it, the lock will need to be picked, or the key from the Living Quarters used. The cabinet contains four 10mm AP and four 10mm JHP ammo boxes.

There is a mole-rat and a rat in this room.

In the back of the room is a pile of rubble. Hidden behind the rubble is an Uzi. The first time the player enters this room, and after they kill the mole-rat and rat, roll Area Knowledge (Vault)-1. If successful, display: "Unless it has been looted, there should be an Uzi in this room."

Rubble

Two large mole-rats guard this area.

The first time the player enters this area, roll IQ+3. If successful, display: "The large amount of rubble blocking this corridor looks impressive. You don't think that it can be moved, even with high yield explosives." A critical success also displays: "You are able to determine that the command and control center is definitely buried under even more rock. You will have to look elsewhere for the water chip."

As the player moves towards the south part of this corridor (towards the Central Core room), roll highest of IQ or Area Knowledge (Vault). On a successful roll, and/or if the player has Intuition, display: "The rest of the Vault in this direction had delicate equipment that has probably been destroyed and ruined. There is a very low chance of anything remaining of value."

Central Core

All the computers in this room are dead. If the player tries to use Electronics to fix one, display: "The internal hardware has melted due to extreme heat and pressure."

There are two mole-rats in this room, and four rats.

On a successful Area Knowledge (Vault), display: "This is the central core room of the Vault. It is here that the computing machines are located."

A holodisk is on the floor in the back of the central core. If used, it will add the following information to the PIPboy:

"Vault-15 Computer Log. 11 Dec 2067. The water-processing chip has failed. All backups have failed to correct the problem. The water reserves are at 2%. The Vault will have to be abandoned. Most everyone has already left. There are just a few people remaining to finish the Vault power down. We are preparing to shut down the power system to protect the equipment from surg#%^#. . . ."

Library

The library machines have been destroyed.

On a successful Area Knowledge (Vault), display: "This is the Vault library. Learning machines are connected to the central core. They teach the Vault inhabitants knowledge and skills."

A successful Vision roll will display: "There looks to be little of value left in this room."

There are five rats, and one mole-rat.

APPENDIX E

THE GAME SCRIPT—EXCERPTS FROM BETRAYAL AT KRONDOR

The following two excerpts from *Betrayal at Krondor*'s game script demonstrate how interactive and noninteractive sequences should be formatted for both the design team and the voice talents that will bring your game story to life.

This script excerpt from Betrayal at Krondor is used with permission of Neal Hallford, John Cutter, Raymond E. Feist, and Dynamix, Inc. Copyright 1993 Dynamix, Inc. Some portions copyright of Raymond E. Feist & Midkemia Press. All rights reserved. Dynamix, Inc. is a member of the Sierra On-Line family of companies.

The Noninteractive Sequence

Sometimes you may want to use a noninteractive sequence at the beginning or end of a level to give the player a new goal or to reward them for all the hard work they've done. Here is a scripted example of just such a sequence taken from the opening of *Betrayal at Krondor*'s second chapter, "Shadow of the Nighthawks."

OPEN HARD INTO:

A FIST

pounding hard onto a tabletop, overturning goblets of wine. As the CUPS ROLL TOWARDS THE CAMERA we CUT TO:

35. INT. ARUTHA'S COUNCIL CHAMBER - DAY

The room is claustrophobic, austere, a grey stone chamber meant to focus the attention of its occupants on the issues at hand rather than on the beauty of its appointments. Only an ancient pair of conDoin royal banners flutter against its otherwise spartan walls, unsubtle reminders of the family who have ruled Krondor for generations.

PRINCE ARUTHA stares coldly down the length of his table, unconcerned that he's just wasted a small fortune in fine Keshian ale. From his all-black wardrobe to the fiery look in his eye, it's clear this is a man who has ruled not with the cheerful love of his people, but a grudging respect for his intelligence and a fear of his wrath.

> Arutha:
> What I must or must not do will not be dictated by a renegade moredhel! If not for Locklear's good faith in you, I would have had your head staked on a pole and paraded up and down the low

quarters of Krondor once I saw you! I
have been tolerant while I listened to
your vague speculations based on half-
heard conversations, but how am I to
believe what you say? What evidence have
you laid before this council to *prove*
what Delekhan intends to do?

                  Gorath (O.S.):
What *evidence!*?

ON GORATH

dark eyes flashing with rage, lips curled
into a feral snarl. He trembles, attempting
to check his anger before his more savage
instincts as a moredhel compel him into fatal
action. But this is what these humans expect,
what they believe about their neighbors in
the frosty Northlands. To submit to his rage
is to fail in his mission, to forget what
must be done for the good of his people.

                  Gorath:
            (through gritted teeth)
However bitter a draught Delekhan may be
for your kith and kin to drink, his rule
is black poison in the gullets of me and
mine. He enslaves my cousins, and rapes
the land. . . .

WIDER

as Arutha's advisers lean in to listen more
carefully, studying Gorath's reactions. PUG,
the most powerful sorcerer in the known
world, sits silent and inscrutable, reserving
his private opinion for another time. Next to
him sits his equally enigmatic and beautiful
daughter GAMINA, and the strange aged visitor
from another world, MAKALA, a sorcerer from
the world of Kelewan.

                    Arutha:
    Where would you have me send my troops?
    If indeed he intends a strike against
    one of our northernmost possessions,
    which castle shall I garrison for the
    attack? Highcastle? Ironpass?
    Northwarden? If I am to fight a war,
    tell me where I shall fight it!

                    Gorath:
    Would that I could tell you! Delekhan
    holds in good confidence only a handful
    of cowering dogs. Among them, few are
    privy to his actual war plans, and only
    his advisers Narab and Nago, his
    mistress Liallan, his son Moraeulf and
    perhaps the leader of the Nighthawks
    know the truth of what he intends.

Arutha:
Nighthawks? He keeps foul company, that
leader of yours.

Gorath meets Arutha's burning gaze, but
shakes his shaggy head.

Gorath:
There may be those that follow him, but
I have never been among them.

Arutha sighs and turns away, unable to read
the truth in Gorath's face. It was easier
when the moredhel were simply enemies on the
other side of a war, not men sitting calmly
in his council chamber claiming to be allies.

Gorath:
(to Arutha's back)
Your highness, give me leave and I shall
uncover Delekhan's intent in this. Let
me be escorted to Romney and. . . .

Arutha jerks back, puzzled, arms crossed
across his chest.

Arutha:
Romney? It's a provincial river town in
the Eastern Kingdom. What could you hope
to learn there?

                    Gorath:
Of late Delekhan has emptied a
significant measure of his treasury to
revive the service of the Nighthawks. In
exchange he has demanded tactical
information about Kingdom holdings. . . .

                    Pug:
He's turned the Guild of Assassins into
a guild of spies?!

Arutha mirrors the concerned look on his
magical adviser's face. This doesn't sound
good at all.

                    Gorath:
Only for a time. Although the payments
have been left in various hidden
locales, the messengers were always sent
to a rendezvous in Romney. I may be able
to intercept information there
concerning a forthcoming attack. Would
such evidence suffice?

                    Arutha:
Perhaps.

(beat)

How can I trust you Gorath? How do I
know that this isn't a plot to move my
troops away from more sensitive

concerns? We can weigh the evidence to
our hearts' content and your cousins
could be slitting the throats of my
serfs as we sit dawdling.

                    Gorath:
That may already have come to pass. Wait
even longer and the decision will no longer
be yours to make, Prince of Krondor.

(a beat)

    Blunt Delekhan's swords and the unified
    tribes will cast him down in wrath. Let
    him cross your northern border, however,
    and ten other clans will join their
    strength to his and the legacy of
    Murmandamus will be but a *spark* next to
    his glory.

ON ARUTHA

soaking this pronouncement in, realizing it
can be nothing but the truth.

                    Arutha:
Very well. You will go to Romney, but you
will provide for yourself. If this is part
of some secret moredhel scheme, I'll not
look the fool before the world. Gamina and
Makala will show you around Krondor while
I make preparations. I have a few things I
need to consider on my own.

WIDER

as Arutha nods to Makala and Gamina to escort
Gorath out. Pug moves to join them but Arutha
grabs his sleeve, detaining him.

>   Arutha:
>   (for Pug's ears only)
>   If you don't mind, I would have your
>   council, cousin.

>   Pug:
>   Certainly. I am all attention.

Arutha unrolls a Midkemian map across the
council table, motioning for Pug to come to
his side. Arutha picks up a knife, points
with it.

>   Arutha:
>   As I see it, Delekhan could have only
>   two potential targets for attack into
>   the Kingdom: *Highcastle*. . . .

INSERT - MIDKEMIAN MAP

as Arutha's KNIFE points first to Highcastle,
then traces a line along the Kingdom's
northern border.

> Arutha (O.S.):
> . . . and *Northwarden*.

The knife point halts a moment, poised over Northwarden, then moves to a point north and west of Northwarden.

> Arutha (O.S.):
> His fortress at *Sar-Sargoth* is three hundred miles to the north and I doubt he has the resources to defend a line that long, so an attack at *Northwarden* seems unlikely.

The knife taps on Sar-Sargoth.

> Pug (O.S.):
> Leaving *Highcastle*. . . .

> Arutha (O.S.):
> But neither target seems to have an obvious goal.

The knife begins to move again, this time moving and circling around several points near a town marked *Sethanon*.

> Arutha (O.S.):
> I will call up the militia reserves from *Malac's Cross*, *Darkmoor*, and *Lyton* and join them to a detachment of the

Krondorian Lancers just outside of the
Dimwood. I'll have Seigneur James send
word to me there.

ON PUG & ARUTHA

both staring down skeptically at the map, as
if seeing the battle to come already forming
before their eyes.

>   Pug:
> What of the garrison?

>   Arutha:
> It will remain in place. I have
> considered the option of a full push
> south and it seems unlikely, but I will
> give Delekhan nothing. Our agreement
> remains. Now we can only wait, and see
> what this moredhel can show us in
> Romney, if anything at all.

(beat)

> Gods help him if he betrays us.

Branching and Conditional Dialogues

Character interaction is a traditional hallmark of the role-playing game. In *Betrayal,* any characters the player met would initially chat with party members and deliver information that related to the overall story of the game, then would halt to answer any questions the player might have utilizing a system of special buttons called *keywords.* These keywords were turned on or off based on things the player had already witnessed, heard, or done elsewhere in the game. If the same characters were encountered more than once, their opening dialogue branched to an alternative, shorter greeting, and then whatever keywords were logical for them to answer were presented.

Here's a quick key to help you translate some of *Betrayal's* technical commands embedded in the following script excerpt:

- %LEAD and %RAND. Both these commands were luxuries that we used heavily throughout *Betrayal.* Because all the dialogue in the game was handled exclusively through on-screen text and not through prerecorded audio, we had greater freedom to randomize dialogue content. The %LEAD command allowed the line to be delivered by whoever was currently the specified leader of the party. The %RAND command randomly selected a party member and had them deliver the line.

- BRANCH (*jumppoint*). This command redirects the dialogue to jump to the *jumppoint* specified between the parentheses. In the following example it is used to turn on the keyword buttons after the main dialogue is finished and to reactivate the keywords after a specific keyword has been explored to its logical conclusion.

- KEYWORDS (*sceneref, word, precon, closeact*). The Keywords command accesses a specific keyword, turns it on if all the preconditions are met, and executes any closing actions that are required after the dialogue is concluded. This command is broken into four different parameters. The first parameter, *sceneref,* indicates to what scene a specific keyword belongs. (In the upcoming example, the *sceneref* is set to 47, the scene reference number for Navon Du Sandau's dialogues.) The second parameter, *word,* determines what keyword is to be turned on. The third parameter, *precon*, checks for any preconditions that must be true before a specific keyword can be displayed to the player. If the precondition is true, then the keyword button is displayed. If the precondition is *not* true, then the keyword remains invisible. (For example, Navon's "Chess" keyword checks to see if the players have previously learned about the "En Passah" move from the character Ivan Skaald. If they have, Navon's "Chess" keyword is displayed.) The last parameter, *closeact*, allows a game event to be triggered or a variable to be set as a consequence of the keyword having been clicked on. (If a keyword doesn't require a certain parameter, that parameter can be ignored by setting it to *null*.)

- EXIT. This command quits the dialogue interface and returns the player to the main exploration window of the game.

- BUTTONSET (*sceneref, word*). Similar to the Keywords command, Buttonset accesses buttons from the scene defined by the sceneref parameter and displays whichever buttons are indicated by the subsequent word parameters.

- IF (*condition*) ELSE (*action*). This pair of commands is just a bit of straightforward programming lingo inherited from my BASIC programming days. If the *condition* stated after the *If* command is true, then display whatever text follows on the next line. If the *condition* is not true, then perform whatever *action* is listed after the Else command.

- START SCREENTEXT & END SCREENTEXT. Whatever text is sandwiched between these two commands is presented in a special text-only window.

- ADD (*item, quant, char*). The ADD command allows a specific number of a certain kind of item to be given to a specific character. The *item* parameter sets the item type, *quant* sets the number of the items to be given, and *char* indicates to which character the items are to be given.

The following example comes from an encounter with Navon Du Sandau, a minor villain of the Eastern Kingdom.

74-A. EXT. ROAD TO KENTING RUSH - ENCOUNTER
WITH NAVON DU SANDAU - DAY

The road is unremarkable, a meandering cow
path showing only vague signs of a more
recent, less bovine variety of traffic. Not
far off its course, NAVON DU SANDAU leans up
against a tree. Tall, attired in black with a
white scarf around his neck and a diamond in
his ear, he stands with a hand upon the hilt
of his very deadly looking rapier. Without a
doubt, more than one man has likely died on
the point of his blade.

[IF (hasMetNavon=yes) THEN (74-B)]

                    NAVON:
        So far from the Prince's court, I'm
        surprised any from your part of the
        world even knew Kenting Rush existed.
        Have you come for business or pleasure?

                    %LEAD:
        Chance has had a greater part in
        delivering us here than anything else,
        actually. We're travelling from LaMut
        for an appointment in Romney.

                    NAVON:
        Ah, the city of guilds. Some difficulty
        there, so I've heard. Something to do
        with a dispute between the Riverpullers

and the Glazer's Guilds. There are
rumors the Guild of Assassins has some
involvement, but I can hardly credit it.
Hopefully the affair will come to a
peaceful resolution soon enough . . .
You will excuse me for staring, but it
has been some time since I have seen an
elf in these parts. It is even more
passing uncommon I should meet one so
heavily armored.

                    %LEAD:
Our associate is working with us to
negotiate a new trading deal of elven
goods in the Eastern Kingdom. He trades
in armor, so this is simply the best way
to transport and show it. . . .

                    NAVON:
Ingenious, no doubt. You look familiar,
elf. Perhaps we have met before?

                    GORATH:
I have not been to this region of the
Kingdom before.

                    NAVON:
I must have only met someone who
resembled you then.

(a beat)

To other matters. As you are all
visitors to Kenting Rush, and visitors
are also good business, are there any
things I may be of assistance with?

[BRANCH (74-KEY)]

74-B. EXT. ROAD TO KENTING RUSH - COMEBACK
ENCOUNTER WITH NAVON DU SANDAU - DAY

                    NAVON:
    I had not expected to see you three
    again for quite some time. How can Navon
    Du Sandau be of assistance to you?

[BRANCH (74-KEY)]

74-KEY

[KEYWORDS (74,null,NO KEYWORDS AVAILABLE
YET,null)]

                    %RAND:
    Actually, I . . . well . . . no. When I
    first saw you, it occurred to me to ask
    you something, but whatever it was has
    utterly slipped my mind at the moment.
    Will it bother you if I come and ask you
    about it later? We have a few things we
    need to be attending to elsewhere.

                              NAVON:
          Go on then. I have a few things to do
          myself. . . .

                              %RAND:
          You are most gracious. Thanks and
          farewell.

     [EXIT DIALOGUE]

     [KEYWORDS (74,CHESS,HAS TRIGGERED IVAN
     SKAALD'S "EN PASSAH" KEYWORD,TURN ON
     IVAN SKAALD'S "CHESS" KEYWORD)]

                              %LEAD:
          Ivan Skaald in Malac's Cross tells us
          you are quite a chess player.

                              NAVON:
          High praise. He isn't too terrible at it
          himself.

                              %LEAD:
          He told us you had a move called
          Sandau's Retreat. I'd be intrigued to
          learn it from you.

> NAVON:
> I couldn't just give away a move like
> that. It's kept me undefeated for
> several years now.

> %LEAD:
> I'd be willing to pay you to learn how.

> NAVON:
> You're after Ivan, aren't you? He won't
> know what's hit him until you have him.
> As I recall he always bets an emerald,
> so I'll let you at least get something
> from the win . . . Say 100 gold
> sovereigns. Deal?

[BUTTONSET (47,YES,NO)]

[YES]

[IF (PARTY_GOLD >= 100) ELSE (YES-A)]

> %LEAD:
> It will be worth it just to see the look
> on his face. Proceed.

> NAVON:
> Give me a moment to find a few
> appropriate stones. If you would sketch
> out a board in the dirt, I will show you
> the architecture of a grand humiliation.

```
[START SCREENTEXT]

%LEAD grinned.

As Navon played out his moves using an odd
assortment of stones, it was apparent the
play would be devastating if used against an
aggressive opponent. "Think you can remember
all of that?" Navon asked, brushing the dirt
from his hands. "Not a problem," %LEAD
replied, dumping Navon's fee onto the hastily
created chessboard. "I think Ivan is in for
quite a surprise."

[END SCREENTEXT]

[ADD (GOLD,100, LEADCHAR)]

[BRANCH (74-KEY)]

[YES-A]


                    %LEAD:
          Well, it seems I am going to have to
          pass on it at the moment. I don't have
          enough money to cover the instruction.


                    NAVON:
          So the Sandau Retreat will be safe for
          yet another day. Try me again sometime.
          I'd like to see if it's successful in
          someone else's hands.
```

[BRANCH (74-KEY)]

[NO]

> ### %LEAD:
> Ouch, no . . . I would like to learn
> your move, but not at that cost.

> ### NAVON:
> It's best if I keep it to myself,
> anyway. Secrets like that shouldn't be
> unleashed on the unsuspecting public,
> particularly on Ivan Skaald. I don't
> think he'd know quite what to do.

[KEYWORDS (74,COUNT CORVALIS,HAS READ SPYNOTE
#14,TURN ON COUNT CORVALIS' "NIGHTHAWKS"
KEYWORD)]

> ### %LEAD:
> What reason would Count Corvalis have to
> dislike you, Navon?

> ### NAVON:
> Perhaps he is an overprotective father,
> who is to say? I'm frankly surprised he
> hasn't hired a band of Nighthawks to
> have me killed. I ask too many questions
> for his tastes.

%LEAD:
You think he has connections to the
Guild of Assassins?

NAVON:
It's a well-known fact he is surrounded
by Nighthawks. They guard his house, his
lands, Cavall Keep. When his daughter
Ugyne and I have time together, we are
always followed by assassins, though
they never wear their guild clothing
while working for the Count.

%LEAD:
Why don't any of the local people do
anything about it? Surely they object to
having the Nighthawks loose in the area.

NAVON:
They look the other way. As long as none
of them are being killed, it doesn't
concern them. I'm sure that's even true
in Krondor.

[BRANCH (74-KEY)]

[KEYWORDS (74,GOODBYE,null,null)]

LOCKLEAR:
As we have appointments elsewhere, we
should probably be on our way.

NAVON:
Good travelling to you then. And if you
ever have any need of anything and are
in Kenting Rush, be sure to come and see
me.

[EXIT DIALOGUE]

Index